TALES OF BYGONE
NEW
ENGLAND

Compiled by Frank Opel

CASTLE

Contents

On the Shore of Buzzards Bay (1892)

THE
New England Magazine.

NEW SERIES. SEPTEMBER, 1892. VOL. VII. No. 1.

Wing's Neck.

ON THE SHORES OF BUZZARDS BAY.

By Edwin Fiske Kimball.

BUZZARDS BAY has attracted special interest in these latest years from the selection of its shores as a summer home by ex-President Cleveland. But the charm of the bay has been perennial. To its peaceful waters, wooded points, sheltered coves, and sandy beaches have come, in their successive generations, the Indian, the discoverer, and the pioneer, the farmer, the scientist, the pleasure-seeker, and the health-seeker.

Buzzards Bay is one of the three noble bays of the Massachusetts coast. It opens into the ocean about twenty miles east of Newport, R. I., from which place many a yacht enters its inviting waters. Separating it on the south from Vineyard Sound is a chain of low islands known as the Elizabeth Islands, a name

which carries us back to the days of Bartholomew Gosnold and the Virgin Queen. The broad shoulder of the great right arm of Cape Cod forms the eastern shore, while on the northwestern side the mainland breaks into a series of irregular points, or necks, as they are locally termed, all with a southeasterly trend, forming many intermediate coves and harbors. Within its charming environment, the bay stretches for thirty miles to the northeast, varying in width from ten miles in the lower part to five in the upper, ending in a fine bit of water called Buttermilk Bay, which nearly touches the south boundary line of old Plymouth town. The entrance from the ocean lies between Gooseberry Neck, projecting in the town of Westport, and the rocks that make off from the end of Cuttyhunk, the western of the Elizabeth Islands, famous as the site of Gosnold's little colony of

1602. Vessels bound in look for one of the two coast light-ships, named euphoniously from the hidden boulders near by, *Hen and Chickens* at the north and *Sow and Pigs* at the south. Ten miles to the southeast of Cutty-hunk looms up the great clay promontory of Gay Head (the " Dover Cliffs " of Gosnold), the western termination of Martha's Vineyard.

Residence of Edward Atkinson, Mattapoisett.

Several small rivers, including the Acushnet, Mattapoisett, Sippican, and Wareham, flow from the lakes and slopes of the mainland into the harbors of the northern shore of the bay. Into the head of the bay, close by " Gray Gables," the home of the Clevelands, empties the Monument (a corrupted form of Mano-

met) River, whose source is up among the lakes of Plymouth, south of the Manomet Hills. It is but six or seven

miles across the isthmus of the cape along the line of this stream and that of the Scusset on the northern side ; and it is small wonder that, from 1776 to the present time, survey after survey has been made for a ship-canal to connect the two bays, Cape Cod and Buzzards, thus freeing coast navigation from the perils of the Nantucket shoals and those of the " back of the cape " with its wintry storms.

Inside the bay are many islands close to the shores, among them West Island, off Fairhaven, the largest in the bay, Bird Island, off Marion, with its pretty white lighthouse tower, and Mashnee, Cedar, Onset, and Wicket's Islands at the head of the bay, which in certain lights form a group of surpassing loveliness. I vividly recall a sunset seen over them from the roof of the hotel at Monument Beach. A gentle breeze stirred the blue waters of the bay ; vistas of distant shores appeared between the islands ; these, dark green to their edges, lay indistinct in the haze which had risen in the afternoon ; the sun sank, a ball of fire, below the misty horizon beyond Onset Bay ; high-peaked clouds formed towers of silver at the north ; long bands in the west made curtains of glorious color. Soon their golden hues faded to dull gray ; the sky above and the sea and land below grew dark ; and then, above the fading landscape, gleamed the red tints, holding long into the twilight.

The innumerable bowlders which strew the pastures and shores, making many a scattered pile on water-worn points, will not pass unnoticed by even the casual visitor. At the head of Aucoot Cove, between Marion and Mattapoisett, there is a huge accumulation of them, where the

Bowlder in Mr. Atkinson's Garden.

tides and a brook have washed them clean. Near by, all along toward Angelica Point, in the fields, in the woods, and on the shore, they are numberless and often very fantastic. Here, the native says, "The devil dropped his apron strings," remembering that he had loosened them at many other points. At Mattapoisett, on the estate owned as a summer home by Mr. Edward

Studios of R. Swain Gifford and Walton Ricketson, Nonquitt.

Interior of Mr. Ricketson's Studio.

Atkinson, the well-known statistician, lies one of the largest bowlders in New England. You see it where the grass land meets the woods, with its peak among the tree-tops. Its greatest height is forty-two feet, and its width thirty-six. It has split into unequal parts with a fissure of three and a half feet, through which runs a path, revealing its gigantic proportions. How came this fragment of the White Hills down by the sea two hundred miles away? The answer is a story from geology, essential to an understanding of the character of all southern New England. The immense glaciers of the Ice Age of North America were gigantic carriers of

broken and ground material from the mountains of the northern part of the continent toward the south. Where now the southeastern counties of Massachusetts are, the ocean in the previous cycle held full sway, and probably beat upon the Milton Blue Hills and upon irregular lines westward. Through the centuries of the glacial period, the drift of which their land is composed, consisting of sand, gravel, and bowlders, was scraped from northern New England and deposited in the sea or in visible moraines on a scale which the imagination fails to conceive. The ocean sorted and stratified much of this drift, though some crests are left in their original condition, like the "backbone" of Cape Cod, which has remained above sea-level. Three distinct terminal moraines appear in southern New England. The extreme outer margin is visible by its remaining portions, — Nantucket, Martha's Vineyard, No Man's Land, Block Island, and beyond in the southern hills of Long Island from Montauk Point to Brooklyn. The second line established by the melting and retreating glaciers is revealed by Cape Cod peninsula, from Provincetown to Woods Holl, the Elizabeth Islands, Point Judith, and Watch Hill in Rhode

A Bit of the Apponagansett River, South Dartmouth.

The First Colony in New England.

Cuttyhunk.

fields and shores of the bay, and one can make good use of it in observing the characteristic landscapes on every hand.

But human life and its romance is more interesting than ice and drift. Who have seen these shores, or lived upon them? There is considerable evidence that the Norsemen, under Thorfinn, following Leif Erikson, about the year 1007, explored this bay and named it "Straumfiord," or "Bay of Currents." For five hundred years after their visit, if the visit occurred, no European disturbed the savage life of the Indian tribes, Wampanoags on the west side, and Mashpees on the east, whose villages everywhere on the bay can still be traced by the accumulations of clam and oyster shells which mark their sites. For over thirty years, even after the discovery of America by Columbus, no bold navigator reached this portion of the New World until Verrazano, the fearless and enthusiastic French explorer, in 1524, made his famous voyage along our coast from Cape May to

Island, and westward by Fisher's Island and the northern hills of Long Island to Port Jefferson. Buzzards Bay, which has a maximum depth of sixty feet, lies between the second and the later vast moraines, and its form is no doubt due to the more rapid action of the warm currents which came from the south between Martha's Vineyard and Block Island. Its northwest shores belong to the third terminal moraines, which begin at the Manomet Hills of Plymouth and extend irregularly westward along a line of promiscuous elevations which give the character to much of the country to the Hudson River. Here, then, is the key to the hills, islands, and bowlder-covered

Cedars at Nonquitt.

Fort Phœnix, Fairhaven.

Nova Scotia. In his "Letter" is found a glowing account of a certain fine bay and port where he stayed fifteen days refitting his ship, and where he observed fertile shores and friendly natives. The latitude is given as 41 2-3°, and antiquarians believe he described the harbor of Newport, R. I. When Bartholomew Gosnold struck directly across the Atlantic from the Azores, after leaving Falmouth, England, he was in search of the wonderful haven of Verrazano, and believed he had found it in Buzzard's Bay, which he named Gosnold's Hope. This certainly was a better name than the present, given probably by the early settlers of Dartmouth, a half century later, from the great numbers of fish - hawks (called buzzardets, or little buzzards, in old works upon natural history) seen about the shores and islands of the bay.

Gosnold's attempted colony on Cuttyhunk Island was the first English settlement in New England, and has a ro-

mantic interest, however small its results on American history. This "active, intrepid, experienced seaman from the west of England" sailed for "North Virginia" on the 26th of March, 1602, with a company, all told, of thirty-two, twenty intending to remain as colonists. He made land, after forty-nine days, near York Beach, Maine ; then turning south for a day and a night, found in the morning his little ship, the *Concord*, encompassed by a "mighty headland." He anchored, and with others went ashore. On his return

Old Whalers, New Bedford.

he found that his crew had caught a great abundance of codfish. From this circumstance he called the headland Cape Cod, which was the first English name given to any part of New England.

an acre in extent, situated in a fresh water lake near the western end of "Elizabeth," he fixed the site of his house and its surrounding stockade, or "fort." A cellar-hole, with stones, evi-

A Club Race. — The Start

Doubling the cape and escaping the perils of the shoals below, he soon discovered and christened Martha's Vineyard. John Brereton, one of the chroniclers of the voyage, described the land as if it were some new Eden, so lovely was the scenery of this and the neighboring islands, with great oaks, stately pines, luxuriant shrubbery and flowers. How

Bird Island Light.

changed are the denuded islands now! Naushon alone attests the noble forests of the past.

The chain of islands lying north of Vineyard Sound was next explored, and the western one, Cuttyhunk, selected for the colony on account of its greater security from the Indians. In honor of his queen, Gosnold called it "Elizabeth," a name which afterwards spread to the entire group. On a rocky islet, less than

dently the foundation of the storehouse, was distinctly visible when, in 1797, Dr. Belknap, the historian, visited the islet, and this could be seen until recent cultivation of the land obliterated the remains. On this historic spot, Daniel Ricketson, the historian of Dartmouth and New Bedford, proposed to place "a small round and castellated form of tower, built of stone in a rude but substantial manner." It yet remains for some society or gentleman of wealth to mark with a suitable memorial the location of the first authentic habitation of Europeans in New England. Now all the land is barren of trees, but in 1602 the island and the little islet in the lake were finely wooded, as the chronicle says, "with oaks, ashes, beeches, walnut, witch-hazel, sassafras, and cedars, with divers others of unknown names." Game, including the red deer, abounded; the shores furnished great quantities of shellfish, while delicious wild berries grew luxuriantly.

The little settlement, however, was short-lived, for on June 18th, after a stay of twenty-five days, all the ship's company left for old England. Some writers have called them "fickle," but circumstances seem to have compelled their going. An ambushed party of Indians attacked the colonists, while Captain Gosnold was exploring across "the stately sound," as the chronicler, Gabriel Archer, "a gentleman in said voyage," calls our noble bay. With the remembrance of the fate of Roanoke fresh in their minds, with the fear of losing their shares of the profitable cargo of sassafras and cedar-wood with which they had helped to freight the vessel, and with the likelihood that their provisions would not hold out till the return of the ship from England, some of the colonists decided to go back with the *Concord* rather than remain in the mighty wilderness. Let it be recorded to the credit of Anglo-Saxon grit that there were twelve sturdy yeomen who were willing to take the risk with Gosnold. Reluctantly he abandoned his cherished settlement, and five years later found his unknown grave in Virginia, whither he had gone with Captain John Smith. Not by "adventurers" at "Elizabeth" was the soil of New England to be planted for its growth of civil and religious liberty, but, eighteen years later, at Plymouth, by the Pilgrim "seed-corn, winnowed by three siftings."

Old Dartmouth, at the southwest cor-

Richard Watson Gilder.

stately sound." As we approach the shore from the east, the red roofs of the pretty village of Nonquitt appear north of the Round Hills beyond Dumpling Rock Light. These are the hills which Gosnold called "Hap's Hill." Near them on the beach he was met by a company of natives, "men, women and children, who with all courteous kindness entertained him, giving him skins of wild beasts, tobacco, turtles, hemp, artificial strings colored, and such like as they had about them." A few days afterward fifty of these Indians went in eleven canoes over

A Corner of Mr. Gilder's House, Marion.

ner of the Bay, one of the early "plantations" of the Plymouth colony, shall be our starting point for a tour about "the

to Cuttyhunk and stayed three days, camping on the opposite end of the island and trading with the Englishmen.

Onset Bay.

Profile Rock.

Nonquitt is a quiet, restful resort, associated in the minds of most of us with the pathetic close of General Philip Sheridan's life. Here was his summer home during his last years; here, in July, 1888, the naval vessel, the *Swatara*, brought the dying general; and here, four weeks later, he passed away. The beauties of the wide expanse of the lower bay and of the undulating landscape, have attracted several artists to Nonquitt, notably R. Swain Gifford, who has a studio and a summer home overlooking the bay. Louisa M. Alcott spent several seasons during the latter part of her life in her pretty cottage there. Walton Ricketson, the sculptor, whose admirable busts of Miss Alcott and her father have brought well-deserved fame, makes an annual visit to Nonquitt, where he has a charming studio.

In 1650, thirty years after the Pilgrims had settled Plymouth, old Dartmouth received its first settlers, in the persons of Ralph Russell, his son John, and Anthony Slocum, who are said to have come from Taunton and established an iron forge at Russell's Mills. In 1639, the General Court at Plymouth had passed an order that the "old-comers," original *Mayflower* passengers, should make choice of two or three plantations for themselves in the territory of the colony before the December court. "The second place," so called, was the vicinity of Dartmouth; but not till 1652 was the right to the land acquired by purchase from the Indians. Massasoit, chief of the Wampanoags, and Wamsutta, his son (called by the English Alexander, as his younger brother, Metacom, was called Philip), sold to "William Bradford, Captain Standish, Thomas Southworth, John Winslow, John Cooke, and their associates, the purchasers, or old-comers," a great tract of land which was a considerable part of the old town. The purchase and its later additions stretched from Buzzards Bay to the colony of Rhode Island; out of the original township have been formed in later times, Westport, New Bedford, Fairhaven, and the greater part of Acushnet.

It is curious to note the compensation given old Massasoit and Wamsutta, viz: "thirty yards of cloth, eight moose skins, fifteen axes, fifteen hoes, fifteen pair of breeches, eight blankets, two kettles, one cloak, £2 in wampum, eight pair of stockings, eight pair of shoes, one iron pot, and ten shillings in another commoditie," — which, after all, was more in value than the famous twenty-four dollars which the Dutch paid in 1626 for Manhattan Island.

The original deed of West Island,

dated 1666, is in the hands of the island's present owner Horace S. Crowell. This curious old document, with its indented margin, was given by King Philip to John Cooke, bearing the signature and seal of the famous old royal savage.

John Russell and John Cooke were the leading men of the new plantation, which became a settlement mainly of Quakers and Baptists from the mother colony, seeking here more freedom of worship. Indeed, a study of their history reveals a remarkable contest for religious liberty, waged between them and the Plymouth General Court, and after the union of the colonies, in 1692, the Massachusetts authorities. They obeyed all laws except those of compulsory taxation for the support of ministers of whom they had no selection and with whom they had no harmony of religious belief. In addition to the Province tax there was annually laid upon them another for this purpose;

Joseph Jefferson.

and annually these inflexible "non-comformists" refused to collect it. The sufferings of these people in King Philip's war, in which many lost their lives, were met, after the burning of their homes, by an order of the Plymouth Court, saying that it took into "serious consideration the tremendous dispensation of God toward the people of Dartmouth in suffering the barbarous heathen to spoil and destroy most of their habitations," and expressing the fear that it was their carelessness about the ministry of the word of God among them which "may have been the provocation of God thus to chastise their contempt of his gospel, which we earnestly desire the people of that place may seriously consider and lay to heart and be humbled for, with solicitous endeavor after a reformation thereof, by a vigorous putting forth to obtain an able, faithful dispenser of the word of God amongst them and to encourage him

Joseph Jefferson's House, Buzzards Bay.

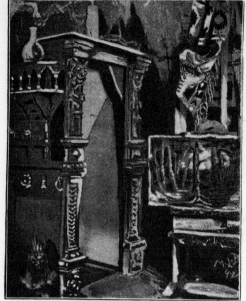

A Corner of Joseph Jefferson's Studio.

therein: the neglect whereof this court, as they must and, God willing, they will not permit in future." One in modern times may well deem this cold "comfort" for an afflicted people.

The struggle over the religious tax lasted more than fifty years, and was often bitter, yet the town never yielded a whit from its position. The crisis came in 1724 in an appeal to the King. Two years before, the legislature of Massachusetts had passed an act to raise one hundred pounds in the town of Dartmouth and a smaller amount in Tiverton (then a part of Massachusetts), for the support of ministers whose selection should be subject to the General Court. These towns were the only ones left in the state which had not been forced into "conformity," and this act was intended to accomplish that result. It was provided that the sum assessed should be included in the regular province tax and afterward withdrawn from the treasury. Mark the spirited action of the freemen of the town! In town-meeting assembled, they voted not to pay such assessment; and further to raise £700 (seven times the tax) to defray the expense of an appeal to the King (George I.) The selectmen

refused to assess the special tax ordered by the Court. They were imprisoned for a year and a half in Bristol jail, and released after the decision of the King to grant their appeal, with his order to have the obnoxious tax remitted. This conscientious and successful stand for freedom of worship, a century after the planting of Plymouth, can be counted one of the decisive victories by which the complete independence of the Church from the domination of the State was secured in New England. While the opposing Puritan party were doubtless sincere and patriotic in their motives, the descendants of the honest Quakers and Baptists of old Dartmouth may well take pride in the achievement of their forefathers.

Here and there in the villages of this region, and in the city of New Bedford, the visitor can see the simple "meeting-houses" of the societies of Quakers or Friends, as they like to be called, who still hold the faith and sit in the "silent assembly." In the territory which was once old Dartmouth

One of Mr. Jefferson's Windmills.

there were, thirty years ago, fourteen houses of worship, and there were others in adjacent towns. To the quarterly meetings came many from a distance, including, till infirmity prevented, John Greenleaf Whittier.

The harbor of New Bedford, the metropolis of the Bay, is the wide estuary of the Acushnet river. The appearance of the city, finely situated on the western hill-side, is at once imposing and beautiful. Great cotton mills occupy much of the lower ground both below and above the bridge to Fairhaven; and one can easily realize that the city ranks third in the country in the product of her new industry. The business and residential portions of the city stretch for over two miles along the harbor and river, up the slope toward the ridge behind. As the centennial orator well expressed it, " the city lies between the green pastures on the one hand and the still waters of the river on the other." The wharves are scenes of various activities, and some of them reminders of the old days of the whale-fishery. Many famous whaling vessels form picturesque groups in the docks, fastened there unused, superseded by the steam whaler, or not needed by the diminished demands of the present, decaying slowly, like old stage-coaches, relics of a former time. Still, New Bedford ranks to-day first in the world in whaling-products, having an annual catch from about seventy vessels of $1,000,000 to $1,500,000 — indeed a great reduction from the maximum of $6,178,728 thirty-

Mr. Cleveland's Boat " Ruth."

five years ago, when three hundred and twenty-nine vessels were engaged.

The interesting historical associations and local features of New Bedford are very tempting to one's pen; but a future article in this magazine will deal with this material, including the history and romance of her whaling industry. We will cross over to Fairhaven by the long bridge, and enjoy the fine views up the river and down the harbor. This bridge, the successor of three previous ones, which were washed away in the great gales of 1807, 1815, and 1869, crosses two islands on its way over, and has a draw-bridge close to the wharves of New Bedford, fishing projections or " pockets,"

Gray Gables. — Residence of Ex-President Cleveland.

and a long viaduct toward the Fairhaven side. Frequent horse-cars are crossing the bridge on their way back and forth from Fairhaven village, or from Fort Phœnix in its lower part on Fort Point at the entrance of the harbor. Thither let us follow the crowds of picnickers or sight-

Cove, south of New Bedford, to avoid this fort. After burning the village and whaling fleet of " Bedford," as it was then called, being a thriving village in old Dartmouth, they marched up and over to Acushnet, then down through Fairhaven, and re-embarked in their ves-

Grover Cleveland.

Mrs. Cleveland.

FROM PHOTOGRAPHS BY C. M. BELL.

seers who swarm about the little beach or the rocks around the fort. This picturesque spot makes a near resort for the factory hands and the poor people of the adjacent city; and here are the cheap amusements and restaurants that cater to them. The fort has an indefinite history. It was here in Revolutionary times, and was used in the war of 1812. In Sep-

sels at Sconticut Point, a long projection south-east of Fort Phœnix.

Fairhaven, as well as Acushnet to the north, was once a part of the town of New Bedford, but in 1812 was set off, because of the irreconcilable views of the Federalists of New Bedford and the Jeffersonian Democrats of Fairhaven about the "Embargo" and the War. Many years after, Acushnet was carved off from Fairhaven, owing to a bitter quarrel over the location of the common church. In such boundary stones of adjoining communities do we constantly find the monuments of old struggles.

"Gilnochie."—Home of John S. Bleakie.

Fairhaven does not belie its name. On water and land there are beautiful scenes. On both sides of the road to Fort Phœnix is situated the handsome estate of Henry H. Rogers, one of the millionnaires connected with the Standard Oil Company, and a munificent patron of his native town. His grounds are beautifully planted and kept, and stretch to the water's edge, offering a charming view of the harbor and the city of New Bedford. The house is large and substantial, but rumor says it is soon to be replaced by

tember, 1778, Maj.-Gen. Gray, with four or five thousand British troops, under orders from Sir Henry Clinton, raided this region, having landed at Clark's

an elegant modern structure more in keeping with the owner's wealth. Mr. Rogers has given Fairhaven a fine high-school building, also a library and a town hall, the two latter now in process of construction, — gifts aggregating, it is said, a half-million of dollars.

From the windows of the train which takes you from Fairhaven to Mattapoisett may be obtained views of coves and distant points with the intermediate marshes or farms which are characteristic of the low shores of this part of the bay. Mattapoisett harbor is a round land-locked sheet of water, beautiful from every side. On the north shore is the quiet, country-like village. Here live, in roomy houses, many retired sea-captains, who love their homes and their restful life after their years of peril on the ocean. The very meaning of the Indian word Mattapoisett is said to be rest; and it does not surprise one to find many summer visitors living at the small hotels of the place, or boarding with the inhabitants. A mile away from the village can be found the old Howes house, built by a Mr. Hammond in 1703, and used as a tavern to entertain travellers on their way from Rochester to Marion. Though not as old as some of the Dartmouth houses, four of which are coeval with its settlement, it is an excellent type of the colonial style, with long back roof, small windows, and pilastered door-way. Mattapoisett can boast of at least two modern improvements, — its miles of concrete sidewalk and its cosy Casino which one will find out in the fields near Mr. Edward Atkinson's estate. To this rendezvous come young and old to pass pleasantly the summer hours. Mr. Atkinson's place is noted for the huge bowlder referred to in a preceding page.

The house, situated in a recess of the woods, overlooking the fields and the harbor, is unpretentious. To it Mr. Atkinson has come for many seasons, being one of the pioneer summer residents on

The Vineyard, from Wood's Holl.

the Bay. Mattapoisett and Marion, whose postoffices are four miles apart, were once portions of the town of Rochester. Both are in Plymouth County, as is also Wareham on the north shore of the Bay.

No tourist should fail to take the ride between Mattapoisett and Marion, or on the way forget to ask to be taken round by the "shore loop" rather than go directly through the woods. We pass a white meeting-house, known to be one of the Friends' meeting-houses by it severe simplicity. We observe on the farms long lines of great stone walls, aptly called by Colonel Higginson the "Stonehenges"

Tower at Wood's Holl.

of New England. The pioneers and their descendants accomplished two results by their erection, — the clearing of the land for the plough or scythe, and the separation of field from field, — but with labor which no calculation can estimate.

There linger in this region traditions of the marvellous strength of a certain George Briggs, called "strong George," who alone, without weapons, captured a buck, and who at sea performed feats of strength and daring which thrill one's blood as they are told. He built alone, in his last years, a stone-wall with rocks so huge that visitors look upon them with wonder and a doubt whether mortal man could have done the lifting.

Notice how prosperous the farms appear, how tidy the buildings. Perhaps you will get a glimpse now and then of the interior of the tasteful front rooms.

These are the "plain people" of Lincoln's phrase, the reliance of good government, industrious, economical, conservative, and strong in all the Anglo-Saxon traits which in New England have won the battles of the Indian Wars and the battles for constitutional liberty.

Now we reach the woods. Tall white pines, with frequent oaks and walnuts, cast grateful shade over the narrow road.

Long Point, Red Brook.

One breathes the odor of the pines, and is soothed through every sense. We feel the force of Emerson's words, "the woods are medicinal to the soul." Why must we hurry? Is life not long enough to allow a few peaceful moments?

Again into open fields, bowlder-covered, yet returning well-earned crops! How the farmer would appreciate an acre of Illinois or Iowa! Now we are near Aucoot Cove, and can stop to see the rocky fragments strewed upon the shore. Here might the Titans have held their battles! The carriage winds through a wood road carpeted with soft needles from the pines, which, rising on either side, make an aisle like that of a cathedral. Too soon we reach the dusty road beyond, and are whirled into the village of Marion.

One remarks just outside the more thickly settled portion of Marion a group

Entrance to Hadley Harbor.

of buildings which the town has received from Mrs. Taber, a wealthy widow, formerly of New Bedford. Near her own residence are the Taber Academy and the Public Library and Museum, while nearer the village is the pretty stone chapel, also one of her gifts.

Marion is charmingly located on Sippican Harbor, which lies peacefully before you at every point. The soft Indian name "Sippican" meets you frequently. It is the name of the river forming the north boundary of the town, and flowing into the Weweantet about two miles above its mouth. The principal hotel at Marion, accommodating two hundred guests, is "The Sippican House," and near it are the "Sippican Boat and Bath Houses," used, perhaps, by the "Sippican Club." A short distance to the south along the shore is the house where Mr. and Mrs. Cleveland lived during the summers of 1889 and 1890, bringing Marion and Buzzard's Bay into prominence. The dwelling is a good-sized one, shingled, without paint or stain, with a piazza toward the harbor, and evidently much remodeled from its original condition. It lacks, however, the seclusion and admirable situation of "Gray Gables," Mr. Cleveland's present home across the bay.

Toward the head of the harbor one may find the old-fashioned house occupied in past seasons by Richard Watson Gilder, the editor of the *Century* magazine, one of the pioneers in Marion. It is a quaint, old house, shaded by great balm-of-Gilead trees. An odd flight of steps leads up to the front door and the recently built piazza which fronts the water. Inside, the rooms are little changed from their former character. In an ancient fireplace still stand the rude andirons, and from the crane above swings the water kettle as of yore, while near the brick recess are the well-worn shovels, tongs and bellows. In the parlor or sitting-room, one may read in "the visitor's album," these appropriate lines from Longfellow :

"For under that roof was no distinction of persons,
   But one family only, one heart, one hearth, and
   one household."

It does not take one long to learn that

Buzzards Bay is a paradise for the sail-boat. The popular boat, convenient for pleasure or for fishing, is the "cat-boat," having a small forward cabin, one strong mast, a long boom and a short upper one called a gaff, and a sail between these, which can be easily managed or "reefed" by one man. Pretentious yachts are sometimes seen, but hundreds of cat-boats flit about the bay in the day-time, and when seen "bunched" closely together it is quite certain that blue-fish have been found. There are possibly a thousand sail-boats owned at the different harbors. Races between the fastest of them is a regular feature of the season; and exciting and pretty the races are. A steady southwest breeze can generally be relied upon in the summer, often gentle under a lee shore, but "'alf-a-gale 'alf the time" out in the bay.

At Marion wharf we shall board a well-built boat and enjoy one of the pleasantest of recreations — a sail to Onset Bay. While waiting for the sail to be hoisted and things made snug about deck, we may observe the gay company on the Sippican float off the pretty boat-house. The young people of both sexes are in their jaunty bathing suits, and just now setting forth in several canoes to board a schooner, which is anchored in the channel. Strong brown arms wield the paddles. Hear the happy chatter and laughter ! Care has been thrown to the winds. This aboriginal life here, on the sparkling water, in the bright sunshine, with sweet air to breathe, reminding one of the life of the old Wampanoags, is the kind of life to restore the nerves exhausted in the crowded city ways.

The boat is ready and the start is made. The wind is light at first, but increases as we approach the mouth of the harbor. On Great Neck and Sippican Neck are several fine new residences, which add much to the landscape above the coves and cliffs. As we round Great Neck Point, Bird Island and its lighthouse are close to us, making, with the wide bay beyond, a scene which the artist of the party desires to obtain in permanent form. To the northwest is Great Hill, so called, though only one hundred and twenty-seven feet high, a coast survey mark in the triangulation of the region. On its point is the large house of Mr. A. W. Nickerson, of Dedham, Mass., who in 1881 bought a great tract of land there, on which stood a hotel, accommodating three hundred guests, called the Marion House. Mr. Nickerson admired the situation and transformed the hotel, at great expense, into a commodious dwelling ; and he has also spent a large amount in beautifying the grounds.

As we pass some one tells the story of Queen Awashank's treaty of peace, made near the beach of Great Hill. During King Philip's war, the gallant Captain Church met here the Queen and her tribe on their way to Sandwich to make peace with the Governor of Plymouth colony. The Queen entertained him cordially with "fried eels, bass, flat-fish and shell-fish," and then, around a great bonfire of pine knots, she and her warriors pledged her allegiance to the English, thus weakening Philip's power and probably sealing his fate.

What means this bustle? The magic word "blue fish" has been spoken, and the long lines are hurriedly drawn from the lockers under the seats. Are there fresh eel-skins aboard? Plenty of them ! Soon each has drawn one over his hook, and a quick throw sends the line far to the stern. Now the sail feels the stiff breeze of the wider bay, and the boat is running before it like a race-horse. Sixty feet behind the eel-skins show for a moment like flashes of silver as they drag along close to the surface. A sudden jerk — as if a shark had swallowed hook and lead and was away with them and perhaps with you ! You must stand the strain and pull steadily, no matter if the taut line does cut the forefingers. The fish is darting here and there like lightning. Now he leaps clear of a wave and strikes with an ugly splash. Will you master him? How long is the line? Will it never end? Take care ! Do not lose him at the last moment. Reach out and whirl him into the boat ! There ! — and, out of breath with excitement, you land your first blue-fish !

The preservation of the valuable fish of Buzzards Bay is the object of an asso-ciation of boatmen organized to protect the hook-and-line fishing of the bay, and, also, one of the objects of the "Old Colony Club," of which Joseph Jefferson is president and Mr. Cleveland a prominent member. The upper part of the bay is already protected by State law against the use of fish traps, pounds, or weirs, and no nets or seines can be used in any part, and strong efforts are being made to secure legislation relative to the remaining shores where licenses are still granted.

Near Tempe's Knob, where the bay grows narrow and the beautiful islands beyond break the surface into pictures all the way to Monument Beach, lines are wound, and attention is given to the scenery. On Indian Neck and along the shore eastward are the elegant summer residences of some of Boston's most exclusive set, among them being those of the Minots, Welds, Sargents, Stocktons, Lymans, and others. On Burgess' Point, at the south entrance of Onset Bay, the fine place of Lewis S. Dabney, the Boston lawyer, attracts our gaze. The house has a picturesque setting on the shore, and seems an ideal summer home, typical of many not far away. From our present point, we can see for several miles about the head of the bay. Nearly every estate has its tall windmill, which makes many a pleasing picture against the sky. Above the woods about "Crow's Nest," Joseph Jefferson's place on Buttermilk Bay, we see his two large windmills, whirling near the north horizon-line. On the points near Monument river are more of them, including that of "Gray Gables." Indeed we may say, as of the bowlders, that no landscape around Buzzards Bay is complete without windmills ; and while, as a rule, they are of modern construction, still, as in Holland, the eye never tires of them. The best farms of Buzzards Bay are under the waters of the upper portion of the bay and of the many little bays and estuaries, and are the "oyster beds." The products of these have the highest reputation and command the best prices. The beds are as carefully surveyed, staked, and cultivated as farmers' fields upon the land. The owners of these beds are licensees of the town in which they live, and the length of license is limited to a term of twenty years.

We are ascending Onset Bay, passing Onset island, and soon reach the romantic island called Wicket's. Before us, among the oaks which give the place its name, "Onset Bay Grove," lies the city of the Spiritualists, an over-grown seaside summer camp-meeting, with a population fluctuating from three to seven thousand people. The "camps" are five hundred cottages, costing all the way from fifty dollars to five thousand. Here this great company, possessed with its ideas of invisible things, has been coming annually for sixteen seasons, to hear their noted speakers, to confer under the trees, and to prepare, may be, for many existences beyond the grave. On the main street, not far from the wharf, are the head-quarters, in which are the offices of the corporation, and where the literature of the faith is displayed for sale. The rear of the building is built as an open rostrum facing the auditorium arranged in the grove like an amphitheatre. Here in good weather are held the public conferences, at which many rise to relate their experiences. On the hill beyond is the "Temple," a large structure with a high tower, furnishing an indoor audience room. There are several hotels at different points for the accommodation of the transient visitors, who number, on special days, as many as four thousand. The "regular" inhabitants, some three thousand, occupy their own cottages, and the owners pay taxes to the town of Wareham, as well as a corporation tax to the stock-company which originally bought the peninsula and erected the public buildings. Stores, and all the attendant features incident to feeding and amusing a vast concourse of human beings, are scattered about. Groups of earnest men sit or stand, discussing events in this world or the next; and, if you listen, you

may hear good science and philosophy, or the wildest imaginings of the "crank." You meet the healer, the medium, the "inspirational speaker," the genial editor, the seer, and the bore; and you go away, after a three hours' stay, with your brain swimming with novel thoughts

Old Mansion House, Naushon.

of the earth below and the heavens above.

At the wharf we shall find two steam-launches which go over hourly to Monument Beach on the east side of the upper bay. Seated in one of them we rapidly run down the glistening bay. In twenty minutes we are near Agawam Point, where Moses Williams of Boston has his residence. His neighbors, William W. Appleton of New York, John Parkinson, and Alpheus H. Hardy, both of Boston, all have excellent houses of the Queen Anne type. Mr. Parkinson's grounds are a revelation of what can be done by thorough cultivation of land which was formerly barren pasture. These are Mr. Cleveland's neighbors, as "Gray Gables" is just to the north, on Monument Point, where the Ex-President has bought a large tract of land between Cedar Pond Creek and Uncle Bill's Cove. Arriving at Mouument Beach, we land at the wharf of the Norcross House, which derives its name from its owner, James A. Norcross, one of the noted firm of builders, Norcross Brothers. The fine red granite sea-wall protecting the grounds is built of the stones rejected in the quarries when the material of the Alleghany Court House at Pittsburgh was selected. From the roof of this fine new hotel one may obtain unexcelled views in all directions. Southwest, beyond Mashnee and Tobey islands, the great bay stretches to the horizon. On Tobey island is the club-house of noted Boston yachtsmen, who have bought the whole island for its unequalled situation and its sheltered harbor. All the upper part of the bay is spread before you, and the shores with their cottages are beneath you. The people who come to Monument Beach to spend the summer months are largely from Worcester and Brockton. On the ridge to the south-east you see the handsome house of Fred Packard, and nearer the beach that of W. L. Douglass, both of the latter city, and of note in the shoe business.

As yet in our trip we have not been close to "Gray Gables" or to "Crow's

Penikese Island.

Nest." These we will now visit. Taking a carriage at Monument Beach, we drive north along the county road, passing the beautiful home of Charles F. Chamberlayne. an influential lawyer, the popular secretary of the "The Old Colony Club," then skirt the waters of Back River, where one end of the proposed Cape Cod canal is to be, and arrive at Mr. Cleveland's large estate by way of the Monument Neck road. Oak and pine woods screen the place on the eastern side, and a rolling pasture extends to the house, situated close by the rocky beach. Great bowlders are scattered about in the grass. Wide, shady piazzas nearly surround the house, which receives its appropriate new name from the six picturesque gables, three on the bay side and three on the land side. The unpainted shingles are turning to a quiet mossy color, which with the gables enables the passing thousands on the Old Colony Railroad, a mile

away, to recognize the house. Before the purchase of the property by Mr. Cleveland, it was called "Tudor Haven." It was selected by Mr. Cleveland for the sake of the retirement it afforded as well as for its attractive surroundings. The immediate and distant scenery is exceedingly pleasing and restful. Monument River, Cohasset Narrows, Onset, and the upper bay, each gives a charming vista. A cove furnishes anchorage and shelter for Mr. Cleveland's cat-boat, the *Ruth*, in which, with his skipper, he often goes out for a restful sail or a try at the fish. Fortunately for his privacy, the Buzzards Bay railroad station, a mile away as the crow flies, is four miles by the town roads.

We drive to Bourne village and cross the Monument River by the carriage-bridge, and are soon on our way to Joseph Jefferson's, over a white sandy road through pitch-pine woods, which are characteristic of the east side of the bay. "Crow's Nest" stands on a wooded bluff overlooking Buttermilk Bay, across which the prospect is beautiful, with sparkling water and the dark green forest beyond. The house is built of wood and stone, of pleasing modern architecture, and has a great piazza on the shore sides, supplied with all the appurtenances of comfort. The owner's taste is everywhere apparent in the surroundings and within the dwelling, where, among the handsome furnishings, are many rare and costly curios collected during his eventful career. The stable is worthy of a visit, and is apparently a favorite place for the children of the Jefferson family. Behind it are the windmills. The first one built is a novelty. The structure may be termed composite, a Dutch model with Yankee improvements; for the canopy is arranged on wheels and revolves as the four immense sails and vane are moved by the shifting wind, however slight. A long "traveller," supported by a wheel, runs around a circular overhanging piazza, half way up. The mill now serves for Mr. Jefferson's studio, which is on the second floor, on a level with the outside piazza. Its walls are adorned with some of the "settings" of the "Heir-at-Law," including a mantel and fire-place. Bric-a-brac and Indian and Turkish wearing apparel give a dash of color. A large easel, on which the actor has painted many a picture, stands in the centre, opposite a north window, from which and from four small stained glass ones, high upon the sides, the light comes in. There is to be no water-tank on the floor above, as leaks are always possible, and the treasures below are valuable. Therefore a tall ordinary mill was afterwards erected near by to supply the buildings with water. From the observatory of this mill you can obtain a comprehensive view of the region, well-repaying one for the climb — the woods stretching forty miles from Plymouth to Woods Holl being in sight.

Beyond Mr. Jefferson's residence, further along the shore, are the houses of his two sons, and to the south near the "Narrows," the estates of Mr. Ellerton L. Dorr and General Whittier of Boston. The present Whittier mansion is the largest private summer establishment on the bay. It was built by Eben Wright, on the grounds of the Tisdale Club, an organization of several gentlemen who were among the first to discover the advantages of Buzzards Bay for fishing and shooting. Mr. Wright bought out the interests of the other members and constructed this great rambling house, spending a hundred thousand dollars on the buildings and grounds. At his death, he gave the place to General Whittier's wife in recognition of her kindly services in his last illness. General Whittier's former house, north of the railroad track, on Buttermilk Bay has been occupied by Mr. Dorr, who has been at the bay since 1870.

But the landscape has a past as well as a present interest. We are pointed out the spot on the south bank of the Monument River, about half way from the branch railroad bridge to Gray Gables, where in 1627 the Pilgrims placed their trading post. Here they exchanged goods with the Dutch of New Amsterdam and the colonists of Virginia. We read the story in Bradford's Journal: "For our greater convenience of trade, to dis-

charge our engagements, and to maintain ourselves, we have built a small pinnace at Manomet, a place on the sea twenty miles to the south, to which by another creek on this side [the Scusset,] we transport our goods by water within four or five miles, and then carry them overland to the vessel; thereby avoiding the compassing of Cape Cod with those dangerous shoals, and make our voyage to the southward with far less time and hazard. For the safety of our vessel and goods, we there also built a house and keep some servants, who plant corn, raise swine, and are always ready to go out with the bark,—which takes good effect and turns to advantage." The post was continued only a few years, and is not considered the first permanent settlement of Sandwich. The roof of the house was blown away in the great storm of 1635, which ravaged the whole Cape below.

With pleasant memories of our ride we return to Monument Beach. Here, on a clear, cool morning, let us join an excursion party which is to descend the east shore of the bay in a steam-launch and explore the Elizabeth Islands. The charming, rounded character of Tobey Island, with its red-roofed club-house, is at once observed. Wenaumet Neck, which projects far into the bay, and has on its point "Wing's Neck Light," is at last passed. The principal owner of Wenaumet Neck is Rev. Cyrus A. Bartol, the noted Boston clergyman. Coming into sight, both at Wenaumet and Cataumet just below, are the summer homes of many cultivated people who particularly appreciate the climate and scenery of the east side of the bay. At Cataumet Neck, one of the most pleasurable places imaginable, is a little colony from Brookline, Mass., of whom Joshua Crane was the earliest settler, and who was followed by neighbors and friends, including the Unitarian clergyman, Rev. Howard N. Brown, and his family. Scraggy Neck to the west was originally owned by one of the first pastors of old Sandwich, and was given him as an inducement to spend his life in his parish. The agreement he fulfilled; and his heirs, about twenty years ago, sold it to Washington Allen, who still

...ed before the govr of new plimouth for the time being.
yts court of new plimouth aforsd Jn witnes wherof
th set to his hand and seale this eight day of march one
enders finds a whale within the above mentioned ginges
snes is to devide it equally) the marke & p phillip ye sachem

this Deed was acknowledged   and a ⊙ (seal)
and Read Jn open court as tss=
Hfield Thomas southworth
plimouth 28:th of august 1666

oe doe affirme that the Iland Markataw was myne unbill found
leave to phillip Saohem of mount Hope to sell it and J am well
id with the hands of others that know the same pepane his & mark
    The mark of Spamgitchanshount : The mark & Achawanannw
    The mark C of Mackesowe...   : the mark of Eye a nunin

witnis that the Indiens had any gaterprots: and undershood wha
the 6th day of July 1673) these above was acknowledged by the ed
selfe ye zamoo being an old man and likewise his Jorg to be them
    Before me James Browon assistant

    Jn testimony of the suete approbation of
    the sale aforsd made by allowanor of ye
    Cont and in confirmation therof this court
    and the publique good of this colony is be
    affecd to those presents: July 8:th 1656   Thos Hinckley gour
        Attost, Saml Sprague Secretary

now yee that J John Coofe of Dartmouth in the Conte of new plimo
Just Sum   th pounds currant money of ne   nd afores'd
there   diction of Rhard the
             J acknowledge:
             u, of them

Fac-Simile of a Portion of the Original Grant of West Island, bearing the Signatures of
King Philip and Governor Hinckley.

lives upon it, though he has sold it recently to Mr. Eustis of Milton. The prices, twenty years apart, furnish a good illustration of the rise of values along these shores. Mr. Allen paid fifteen hundred dollars for the place, and is reported to have received sixty thousand dollars, or forty times the cost. On the south shores of Cataumet Harbor, in the territory of North Falmouth, is a new and pretty summer settlement called Nonantum, after the Indian name of Newton, Mass. The word tells us that the people come from "the garden city" of the State; and they well represent its culture and refinement. To the west of Nonantum is the beautiful Downer estate at Nye's Point, with its cosey cottages.

During the long reach from Scraggy Neck to Chapoquoit Harbor, a well-informed companion talks of the Indians who once lived on these shores, and whose soft language is heard in the names of numberless localities. They belonged to the Mashpee tribe, whose few survivors still live in the town of that name, some ten miles to the east. To them went, in 1658, an earnest missionary, Richard Bourne, a companion of John Eliot, the apostle to the Indians. He had gathered at Mashpee by 1670 a church of Christian Indians, which has lasted to this day. The town of Bourne, along whose border we have just passed, is named for Jonathan Bourne, a descendant of Richard. The Cape Indians were kept at peace with the whites during King Philip's war by the labors of the Christian ministers among them,—Bourne at Mashpee, Treat at Eastham, Thornton at Yarmouth, Tupper at Sandwich, and the Mayhews, father and son, at Martha's Vineyard. Safe at home, the Cape colonists sent forces to the aid of their fellows. Had the numerous tribes of the Cape first massacred the few English there, and joined King Philip, who can say but the result would have been the extermination of the outnumbered Europeans? It was the missionaries as well as the soldiers who saved New England!

At Chapoquoit Harbor there is another village much like those above, — made up of red-roofed houses, with their windmills and boating wharves. A four mile run has brought us down to Quamquisset Harbor (shortened usually to Quisset), where we stop to take dinner at its large hotel. Not far away from this lovely sheet of water, we find several fine residences, notable among them "Gilnochie," owned by John S. Bleakie of Hyde Park, Mass. This fine house stands on the ridge between the bay and the sound, and commands views of both. Early in the afternoon, we reach Woods Holl village, a part of Falmouth, where one can take the cars for Boston, or the steamboat for New Bedford, or for the Vineyard and Nantucket. The southwestern part of Falmouth is a peninsula lying between Buzzards Bay and Vineyard Sound. Along the shores of the Sound are the princely estates of Daniel W. Butler, Ogden Jones, Francis E. Foster, John M. Glidden, Joseph S. Fay, Jr., and Henry H. Fay, the latter the sons of Joseph S. Fay, who owns the greater part of the upper peninsula. John M. Beebe has a handsome home with large grounds on the dividing ridge. On the bay side, where once the Pacific Guano works were situated — a nuisance in former days — there is a great change in progress. Long Neck has been bought by enterprising parties and rechristened "Penzance," from its striking resemblance in form to that peninsula of old Falmouth, England. Here, no doubt, in the near future, will be found some of the finest residences on the bay. But we cannot forego a hurried visit to the buildings of the Fish Commission, where the labors of the late Dr. Spencer Baird and his assistants have so greatly benefited the coast fisheries, by the millions of young fish and lobsters hatched at the place, nor can we miss a glimpse of those of the Marine Biological Laboratory, with the summer school of able professors and earnest students, who under the lead of Dr. C. O. Whitman, are carrying out lines of work that, were he alive, would make glad the great heart of Louis Agassiz.

The "earldom" of Naushon Island, as one may well call the noble possession of the Forbes family, is visible from Woods Holl; and, as we approach, a nearer view reveals the houses occupied by the father and the sons. A whole article might be written about Naushon, which has, by gift, transfer, or sale, been owned since 1641 by the Mayhew, Winthrop, Bowdoin and Forbes families. It was bought by John M. Forbes in 1843, for twenty thousand dollars, as a result of a compromise between the claims of Bowdoin College and the Bowdoin heirs. The suit expected was one for which the most eminent talent of New England

Naushon retains much of the old forest, and in the " stately groves " still roams the red deer, as in the time of Gosnold. The island has interesting associations connected with the British occupation of it in the Revolutionary War.

After a visit to Cuttyhunk, we make our home course by way of Penikese, a rocky isle, north of the Elizabeth chain. Here, in 1873, the summer before his death, Louis Agassiz conducted the An-

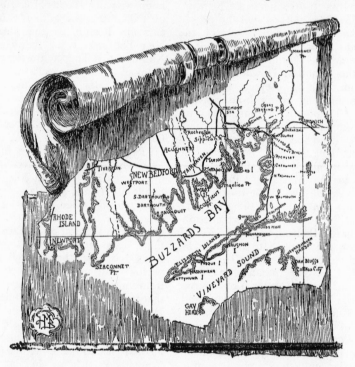

had been engaged, including Daniel Webster, Rufus Choate and Jeremiah Mason.

The old mansion on the hill at the eastern end of the island was built by Governor James Bowdoin, and is now used by Mr. John M. Forbes. The sons, Col. William H. Forbes and J. Malcolm Forbes, have large modern houses, the former one on a hill fronting Buzzards Bay, and the latter on the shore of Hadley's Harbor. The fast schooner yacht *Merlin* lies anchored a half mile out, while the masts of the famous *Puritan* are seen beyond a wooded point further up the harbor.

derson School of Natural History, with its fifty enthusiastic students and its distinguished professors. This school did not survive longer than through the next season of 1874, for the expense of maintenance was great, and the original endowment of fifty thousand dollars was spent mostly on the buildings and apparatus. However, many made there a beginning in scientific work whose results are felt to-day in school and university. The new and admirable school at Woods Holl is a natural successor of that at Penikese.

The climate of Buzzards Bay, in summer, is soft, equable, and comparatively cool, because of the southwest winds which blow almost steadily up from the ocean. There is usually a relaxing effect on the nervous system which soon refreshes the weary. This beautiful climate, with the dry, healthful soil, and the good drinking-water, make the bay an ideal summer resort. While gaining rest, and enjoying the sports, one may see nature face to face and experience peace of mind. With the wise old Autocrat at his breakfast table shall we not ask: "Who does not love to shuffle off time and its concerns at intervals, to forget who is president and who is governor, what race he belongs to, what language he speaks, and to listen to the great liquid metronome as it beats its solemn measure, steadily swinging when the solo or duet of human life began, and to swing just as steadily after the human chorus has died out, and man is a fossil on its shores?" And there are few places where the question is better asked or better answered than on the shores of Buzzards Bay.

The Harvard-Yale Races (1885)

OUTING.

VOL. VI.   JULY, 1885.   No. 4.

THE HARVARD–YALE RACES.

HE year 1885 closes a third of a century since Harvard and Yale first met as rivals. Their race in 1852 initiated a series of varied athletic contests, in which nearly all our better-known colleges have at one time or another taken part. Out of that race grew all American college boating. To it must be ascribed, at least indirectly, the credit of the physical development which thousands of graduates trace back to the boating of their college days. For Harvard and Yale, by inaugurating races and other contests between students from different institutions of learning, furnished the needed stimulus to care of the body as well as of the mind, and hastened the recognition of physical education as an essential part of the college curriculum. If the benefits of college boating were limited to the six or eight representative oarsmen, the value of boating might well be questioned. But such is not the case. The fact that a picked crew is to be sent out to do battle against a rival is the motive, the inspiration which draws hard-reading men, without claim to athletic distinction, from their sedentary life to the gymnasium and the river. Without these annual races boating at Harvard and Yale would languish, and perhaps utterly perish. The generation which has passed since these colleges were first pitted against each other on the water has brought a marked improvement in the physical welfare of the average college student, and in this, as I have indicated, the Harvard-Yale race has been no unimportant factor.

It may be, since this is the boasted age of progress, that some of us will see radical transformations in college boating as typified by the race between Harvard and Yale. But it is more than improbable that any changes which the future may bring will be as sweeping as those included in the records of the past thirty-three years. There will be no transition comparable to that from the clumsy barge, three and a half feet wide, rowed on the gunwale, to the slender paper shell of to-day. There will be no such series of changes as were presented by the early scratch-races on Lake Winnipiseogee, the turning races at Worcester, with their uproarious accompaniments, the intercollegiate regattas at Springfield and Saratoga, culminating in 1875 in the beautiful spectacle of thirteen six-oared crews ready at the starting-line, and finally, the more unpretending, but none the less effective eight-oared contests which began between Harvard and Yale in 1876, and in 1885 show no signs of interruption. The conditions of the race and the New London course have been well tried, and nothing better has been suggested. The race, as it will be rowed this year, promises to become as constant a quantity in our out-door sports as the race between Oxford and Cambridge. In short, the rowing of Harvard and Yale oarsmen

THE "ONEIDA," THE HARVARD RACING–BOAT OF 1846.

has been developed until it is placed to-day upon a reasonable and not unscientific basis. There may be further improvement in degree, but not in kind.

But the experience and general perfection of methods represented in the present Harvard-Yale race are derived from much vain groping in the dark, from beginnings and experiments which seem laughable enough in the light of our present wisdom, and from many costly blunders. Many an old oarsman feels even now a dull ache at his heart as he remembers how the result of some hard-fought-race betrayed his faith in a new " rig," a new stroke, or a new system of training. Many a graduate, recalling the fifty and sixty strokes to the minute, pulled by the men of other days, is still inclined to regard the sliding seats and slower stroke of to-day, as signs of degeneracy. *Consule Planco,* " when Wilbur Bacon pulled stroke of Yale," or, " when Harvard sent forth the Crowninshields, Watson, the McBurneys, and the Lorings," " then, indeed, there was a race of giants upon the earth." Well, the race endures, and the men who represent the two universities at New Lon-don, year by year sustain the traditions of their predecessors. Their contest may never be witnessed by as many thousands as assembled at Saratoga in 1874 and 1875, and the metropolitan journals may never again surrender whole pages to " special dispatches " concerning the oarsmen. But no Harvard nor Yale graduate will admit that his interest in the race has waned. He cares little for other victories which his college may win ; but he never fails to watch the wires when the decisive news is expected from New London. No one but a Harvard or a Yale man can fully understand the force of this feeling. Properly directed it is a stimulus to open and honorable emulation. Left uncontrolled it has led in the past to recriminations and ruptures which, I have faith to believe, have occurred for the last time. But there is a brighter side to this spirit of rivalry. It yearly recalls graduates to their college allegiance, and it is the most potent influence in keeping alive boating at the two universities.

Boating began at both Harvard and Yale about 1844, but received little attention from the majority of the students

THE START AT THE GREAT INTERCOLLEGIATE

THE MODERN SHELL.

until after the first Harvard-Yale race, in 1852. The challenge came from Yale and was accepted by the Oneida Club of Harvard. The date of the race was August 3, and upon August 10, according to the fashion of those leisurely times, the New York *Tribune* published a report sent by a correspondent at Centre Harbor, N.H. This account is as follows : —

The students of the Yale and Harvard boat-clubs met each other in the depot hall at Concord, where mutual introductions took place, and they proceeded together to Weirs. Here the " Lady of the Lake " was in waiting to convey them to Centre Harbor, where they arrived after a delightful trip of an hour and a half, just in time for a splendid dinner at the Centre House. Some idea of the immense capacity of these boats may be gained from the fact that the captain requested the passengers not to seat themselves all on one side of the boat. . . . The students have free passage in her to any part of the lake; and indeed their whole trip, as we understand, was free, the expenses being defrayed principally, we understand, by the Boston and Montreal Railroad Company. . . . The Yale boats arrived on Monday, which was mostly spent in fishing and practicing for the regatta on Tuesday. The boats are : From Harvard, the *Oneida*, 38 feet long, 8 oars; from Yale, the *Undine*, 30 feet long, 8 oars; the *Shawmut*, 38 feet long, 8 oars; the *Atlanta*, 20 feet long, 4 oars.

There is but one boat-club in existence at Harvard at present, which accounts for their sending but one. The crew have evidently had considerable practice,—somewhat more than the boats at Yale. The *Oneida* is quite a model for fleetness and beauty. The first regatta was run on Tuesday, at eleven in the morning. The shore was lined with a numerous and excited throng, and the betting ran quite high. At the third blast of the bugle, the boats shot forward almost with the speed of race-horses, while the band on shore struck up a lively tune. The sight was perfectly enchanting, scarce a breeze ruffled the water, and the whole crowd were anxiously bending their gaze upon the boats, which were flying over the water with all the speed which the vigorous and rapid strokes of the young oarsmen could produce. Meanwhile, the little parties who were out in skiffs were urging on the oarsmen with encouraging shouts as they rushed by them. The distance to be run was about a mile and a half, to a boat anchored off upon the lake. The *Oneida* ran the distance in seven minutes, the *Shawmut* being about two lengths behind, while the *Undine* and *Atlanta* pressed closely after.

This was what was denominated the scrub-race, being merely a trial of the strength of the respective crews and no prize being awarded.

The grand regatta came off this afternoon at four o'clock. The boats (with the exception of the *Atlanta*, which was not allowed to compete for the prize on account of its inequality in size and number of oarsmen) started at the distance of about two miles from shore and ran directly for the wharf. A large boat, with the band on board, was stationed midway upon the lake and [the boat?] played some very fine airs for the benefit of the lookers-on, for it evidently attracted no attention from the oarsmen, who were altogether too busily occupied.

RACE, SARATOGA LAKE, 1875.

The result of the race was the same with that of the first, the distance between the boats being almost exactly the same.

A fine pair of black-walnut oars, tastefully ornamented with silver, was presented to the *Oneida*, with an appropriate speech, by the Chairman of the Deciding Committee.

In the chapter on "Yale Boating," prepared by "Karl Kron" for the *History of Yale College*, there is a *résumé* of the Harvard-Yale races, republished by the author in the *Boat-race Bulletin*, of which he was the editor from 1878 to 1883. This record, with some slight changes and additions of my own, is as follows: —

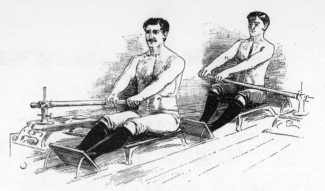

PRACTICING IN THE GYMNASIUM.

FIRST PERIOD — 1852–'60 — IRREGULAR RACES.

1. 1852, August 3. — Lake Winnepeseogee, Center Harbor, N.H., 2 miles straight pull to windward in eight-oared barges, class of '53. *Oneida*, of Harvard, defeated *Halcyon*, of Yale, by two lengths; time about 10m.

2. 1855, July 21. — Connecticut River, Springfield, $1\frac{1}{2}$ miles down stream and return, in barges. *Iris* (eight-oared) and *Y. Y.* (four-oared), of Harvard; *Nereid* and *Nautilus* (both six-oared), of Yale. Allowing eleven seconds handicap per oar for the smaller craft, the times of the boats in the order named were 22m.; 22m. 3s ; 23m. 38s.; 24m. 38s.

3. 1859, July 26. — Lake Quinsigamond, Worcester, Mass., $1\frac{1}{2}$ miles up the lake and return. Harvard shell, 19m. 18s.; Yale shell, 20m. 18s.; Harvard lapstreak *Avon*, 21m. 13s.; Brown lapstreak, *Atlanta*, 24m. 40s.

4. 1859, July 27. — Same course and same shell crews, in "Citizens' regatta." Yale, 19m. 14s.; Harvard, 19m. 16s.

5. 1860, July 24. — Same course. Harvard, 18m. 53s.; Yale, 19m. 5s.: Brown, 21m. 15s.

SECOND PERIOD — 1864–'70 — UNIVERSITY RACES. — SAME COURSE.

1864, July 29. — Yale, 19m. 1s., won by $42\frac{1}{2}$s.
1865, July 28. — Yale, 17m. $42\frac{1}{2}$s., won by $26\frac{1}{2}$s.
1866, July 27. — Harvard, 18m. 43s., won by 27s.
1867, July 19. — Harvard, 18m. 13s., won by $72\frac{1}{2}$s.
1868, July 24. — Harvard, 17m. $48\frac{1}{2}$s., won by 50s.
1869, July 23. — Harvard, 18m. 2s., won by 9s.
1870, July 22. — Harvard, 20m. 30s., won by foul.

THIRD PERIOD — 1871–'75 — UNIVERSITY RACES.

1. 1871, July 21. — Three colleges. Massachusetts Agricultural defeated Harvard 37s. (16m. $46\frac{1}{2}$s. to 17m. $23\frac{1}{2}$s.), and Brown 61s. (17m. $47\frac{1}{2}$s.) Harvards defeated Brown 24s.

2. 1872, July 24. — Six colleges. Amherst defeated Harvard 24s. (16m. 33s. to 16m. 57s.); Agricultural, 37s. (17m. 10s.); Bowdoin, 58s. (17m. 31s.); Williams, 86s. (17m. 50s.); Yale, 100s. (18m. 13s.); Harvard defeated Yale 76s.

3. 1873, July 17. — Eleven colleges. Yale defeated Wesleyan 10s. (16m. 59s. to 17m. 9s.); Harvard, $37\frac{1}{2}$s. (17m. $36\frac{1}{2}$s.); Amherst, 41s. (17m. 40s.); Dartmouth, 68s. (18m. 7s.); Columbia, 77s. (18m. 16s.); Massachusetts Agricultural, $87\frac{1}{2}$s. (18m. $26\frac{1}{2}$s.); Cornell, 93s. (18m. 32s.); Bowdoin, $110\frac{1}{2}$s. (18m. $49\frac{1}{2}$s.); Trinity, 154s. (19m. 33s.); Williams, 166s. (19m. 45s.)

THE OLD HARVARD BOAT-HOUSE, CAMBRIDGE, 1860.

4. 1874, July 18. — Nine colleges. Columbia defeated Wesleyan 8s. (16m. 42s. to 16m. 50s.); Harvard, 12s. (16m. 54s.); Williams, 26s. (17m. 8s.); Cornell, 49s. (17m. 31s.); Dartmouth, 78s. (18m.); Trinity, 101s. (18m. 23s.); Princeton, 116s. (18m. 38s.); Yale fouled, and withdrew.

5. 1875, July 14. — Thirteen colleges. Cornell defeated Columbia 11s. (16m. 53½s. to 17m. 4½s.); Harvard, 11½s. (17m. 5s.); Dartmouth, 17s. (17m. 10½s.); Wesleyan, 20s. (17m. 13½s.); Yale, 21s. (17m. 14½s.); Amherst, 36s. (17m. 29½s.); Brown, 40s. (17m. 33½s.); Williams, 50s. (17m. 43½s.); Bowdoin, 57s. (17m. 15½s.); Hamilton, time not taken; Union, time not taken; Princeton, withdrew; Harvard, defeated Yale 9½s.

6. 1876, July 19. — Six colleges. Cornell defeated Harvard 4s. (17m. 1½s. to 17m. 5½s.); Columbia, 7s. (17m. 8¼s.); Union, 26s. (17m. 27½s.); Wesleyan, 57s. (17m. 58½s.); Princeton, 69s. (18m. 10s.).

FOURTH PERIOD — EIGHT-OARED RACES — FOUR MILES.

1. 1876, June 20. — Yale, 22m. 2s.; Harvard, 22m. 31s.

2. 1877, June 30. — Harvard, 24m. 36s.; Yale, 24m. 43s.

3. 1878, June 28. — Harvard, 20m. 44s.; Yale, 21m. 29s.

4. 1879, June 27. — Harvard, 22m. 15s.; Yale, 23m. 48s.

5. 1880, July 1. — Yale, 24m. 27s.; Harvard, 25m. 9s.

6. 1881, July 1. — Yale, 22m. 13s.; Harvard, 22m. 19s.

7. 1882, June 30. — Harvard, 20m. 47s.; Yale, 20m. 50s.

8. 1883, June 30. — Harvard, 25m. 46½s.; Yale, 26m. 49s.

9. 1884, June 30. — Yale, 20m. 31s.; Harvard, 20m. 48s.

The first move toward an inter-collegiate regatta was made by Harvard in 1858. Yale, Brown, and Trinity responded to her call; but the drowning of the Yale stroke, Mr. George E. Dunham, at Springfield, July 17, 1858, caused the abandonment of the race. The first regatta, in which more than two colleges participated, was not rowed until the following year, and the second and last, for a period of ten years, was held in 1860. The experience of the Brown crew was not calculated to encourage other entries. Then the war, and certain restrictions imposed by the faculties of Harvard and Yale, made the boating record a blank until 1864. In 1865 Yale's time, first announced as 17m. 42½s., was afterward, according to the Harvard book "declared by both judges and referee to be a mistake." In this publication the Yale time is given as 18m. 42½s. The author of "Yale Boating," claims the faster time. In the Citizens' regatta, on the same course, a day later, the time of the Yale crew was 19m. 5½s. In 1869, Harvard, after sending her four best oarsmen to England, won an unexpected victory from Yale at Worcester. Two of the Worcester crew afterwards took the places of the men originally selected to

THE HARVARD HEAD-QUARTERS, NEW LONDON.

meet Oxford.   The unfortunate foul in 1870 caused an angry and protracted discussion, which was taken up by the daily press and put an end to racing at Worcester.   The advantage of the landlocked Quinsigamond course was its freedom from rough water.   Its disadvantages were the necessity of a turning race, with the chance of fouls at the stake, and comparative inaccessibility.   In the opinion of Yale the general sentiment of the good people of Worcester was strongly in favor of Harvard.   In the opinion of Worcester's

Yale neither participated nor consented to Harvard's acceptance of her challenge, which named Springfield and the intercollegiate regatta, as the place and time. Harvard's second acceptance came too late, and 1871 was the only year since 1863 when Harvard and Yale failed to meet. Harvard's unexpected defeat by the Amherst Agricultural crew, proved a text for much newspaper moralizing as to the superiority of "brawny country boys" over "pampered city youths," and others of the smaller colleges were encouraged to enter

THE YALE BOAT-HOUSE, DOBBS'S FERRY.

sedate citizens, the uproar which annually began at the Bay State House, and drove sleep from almost the entire city, finally became too dear a price to pay for the visits of either Harvard or Yale oarsmen and their friends.

So a new era was inaugurated. Yale positively refused to row at Worcester. The New London course was examined, and the report was favorable. But, in April, 1871, Harvard, Brown, Amherst, and Bowdoin organized the "Rowing Association of American Colleges," for the management of an annual regatta on a three miles straight-away course, and Springfield was selected for the first race.

the competition. When, in 1872, Harvard was defeated by Amherst, and Yale was the last of the six crews, the boating-fever broke out at almost every college which could possibly equip six oarsmen. Eleven crews entered in 1873, the year of the famous "diagonal line finish." The flags, first given to Harvard, were afterward recalled, and the race was awarded to Yale. The referee's decision is final. But those who care to review this curious controversy will find in the "Harvard Book" an explanatory diagram and various proofs and arguments which will appear convincing until the reader turns to the evidence and the special pleading set forth in "Yale Boating."

The crooked Springfield course presented peculiar difficulties to both judges and spectators, as is vividly suggested by the following account of the race in 1873, written for the New York *Tribune*, by Bret Harte : —

> The great race was coming. It came with a faint tumult, increasing along the opposite side into the roars of " Rah ! " and yells of " Yale " like the bore Hoogly river, — and then, after straining our eyes to the uttermost, a chip, a toothpick, drifted into sight on the broad surface of the river. At this remarkably and utterly novel sight we all went into convulsions. We were positive it was Harvard. We would wager our very existence it was Yale. If there was anything we were certain of it was Amherst; and then the toothpick changed into a shadow, and we held our breath, and then into a centipede, and our pulses beat violently, and then into a mechanical log, and we screamed of course it was Harvard. And then, suddenly, without warning on shore, and here at our very feet dashed a boat the very realization of the dream of to-day, — light, graceful, beautifully handled, rapidly, and palpably shooting ahead of its competition on the opposite side. There was no mistake about it this time. Here was the magenta color, and a " Rah ! " arose from our side that must have been heard at Cambridge, — and then Yale on the other side, Yale the indistinguishable, Yale the unsuspected, won !

The dispute of 1873 put a greater strain upon the relations of Harvard and Yale. A new race of oarsmen had come forward in 1872, headed on the Yale side by Robert J. Cook, and at Harvard by Richard H. Dana. The rivalry was intense, and when, at Saratoga, in 1874, Harvard was fouled by Yale, there was an outpouring of the spirit at the lake, and an outbreak of hostilities in the town, in the presence of which no one would have dared to predict such harmony as now attends the meeting of Harvard and Yale at New London. But the succeeding years brought satisfaction to both sides. In 1875 Harvard defeated Yale, and in the first of the eight-oared races at Springfield, in 1876, Yale was easily victorious over Harvard. In the four intercollegiate regattas engaged in by both Harvard and Yale, Harvard took second place once, and third place three times, while Yale was sixth in 1872, first in 1873, ninth after the foul of 1874, and sixth in 1875.

The race of 1875 was the first in which the plan of rowing in " lanes " marked out by flags was adopted, and in consequence there was a total absence of fouls. It may be because this race was the first which I had seen, that it appeared to me an extraordinarily beautiful spectacle ; but I still think that the sight of thirteen six-oared crews in line was sufficient warrant for certain descriptive extravagances. The newspapers that year, as at the two preceding regattas, devoted pages to detailed accounts of the training, stroke, boats, and even the personal peculiarities of the oarsmen. The moneyed aristocracy which assembles yearly at Saratoga gilded the grand stand and the shore of the lake, outshone in turn by the kaleidoscopic ribbons of the intent, excited, uproarious mob which represented thirteen colleges. What bitter memories could resist the wild celebration which followed the race ? Harvard and Yale joined in congratulating victorious Cornell, marched together in a

THE YALE HEAD-QUARTERS, DOBBS'S FERRY.

tumultuous procession, and mingled in a fraternal embrace. But this reconciliation really meant the end of the unwieldy Intercollegiate Rowing Association. Frequent postponements on account of rough water had shown the uncertainty of the Saratoga course, the only one available for a race with so many participants. Now that Harvard and Yale were able to arrive at a clear understanding, the advisability of returning to an independent contest was conceded on both sides. Yale withdrew from the association, and challenged Harvard to a four-mile eight-oared race. The challenge was accepted. Harvard alumni decided that a crew should be sent once more to an intercollegiate regatta, and, as a point of honor, Harvard was represented by a six-oared crew in the Saratoga race of 1876, as well as by an eight-oar in the contest with Yale at Springfield. The withdrawal of Harvard and Yale put an end to the association, and it may be predicted with reasonable certainty that neither college will ever again enter a similar organization. The eight-oared race has been rowed at New London since 1878, a period of seven years, without a single postponement over night on account of bad water. This equals the record of the Quinsigamond course, on which seven successive university races were rowed without postponement.

The improvement in the boats used in the Harvard-Yale races amounts to a revolution. The first boat owned at Harvard was the *Oneida*, built for a race between two clubs of Boston mechanics and purchased in 1844 by members of the class of 1846. She was a type of all the club-boats down to 1855. According to the "Harvard Book" the *Oneida* was "thirty-seven feet long, lap-streak built, heavy, quite low in the water, with no shear, and with a straight stem. Her width was about three feet and a half in the widest part, and tapered gradually towards bow and stern. She was floored half way up to the gunwale with wooden strips, and had a hard-wood grating in each end. These gratings were kept unpainted and oiled; and, although used by the bow-oar sometimes to walk on in using his boat-hook and in setting and striking colors, they were the principle vanity of the boat. Many a hard day's work have members of her crew done in sand-papering and polishing these gratings when things were to be made ship-shape for some special occasion! The boat had plain, flat, wooden

thole-pins fitted into the gunwale. Her oars were of white-ash, and ranged from thirteen feet six inches long in the waist to twelve feet at bow and stern. A plain bar of hard-wood served for stretcher, and each seat had a red-baize covered cushion. The tiller-ropes were stout, covered with canvas, and finished at the end with a knot known as a 'Turk's head.' The captain's gig of a man-of-war will give a very good idea of her general fittings."

Such was the first boat entered by Harvard in a race against Yale. The *Oneida* was used continuously for thirteen years by Harvard students, and tradition has it that she was never beaten in a race. The boats entered by Yale in the race of 1852, the *Halcyon*, or *Shawmut*, and the *Undine*, were of a similar pattern. In the race of 1855 the Harvard eight-oared barge was slightly outrigged with wooden pieces spiked to the gunwale, but the crack Harvard boat was supposed to be the *Y. Y.*, a four-oar from St. John, fairly outrigged, and furnished with oars of spruce instead of ash. The Yale boats, spoken of as much superior, had "bent wooden outriggers, braced like those of a wherry, running from the bottom of the boat across the gunwale."

This was the first appearance here of outriggers, although they were used in the Oxford-Cambridge races after 1846. Oddly enough the boat most deficient in these appointments won the race. Soon after, Harvard obtained from St. John an eight-oar, built especially for racing, fifty-one feet long, a lap-streak, fairly outrigged, without a rudder, and decked over with canvas fore-and-aft. This, the first university, as distinguished from club-boat owned by Harvard, was never used against Yale. Meantime, the use of outriggers and spoon-oars was becoming more general at both colleges, thanks to the influence of English boat-builders and the St. John oarsmen! In the fall of 1857 James Mackay, an Englishman resident in Brooklyn, built for Harvard the first six-oared shell ever constructed in this country. The *Harvard* was forty feet long, "made short in order to turn a stake easily," twenty-six inches wide amidships, and carrying iron outriggers, although the oars were not kept in place by wires. The material was white-pine, and the boat weighed one hundred and fifty pounds. The *Harvard* was shorter, wider, and higher out of water than the modern racing-shell, but the general plan of construction was similar to that now followed. The new shell was tested in local races. "The fight between the *Merrimac* and wooden frigates was not more decisive, and lap-streak boats were henceforth useless for racing." In 1859 Yale appeared at Worcester with a new shell, built by Mackay, and with spoon oars. The Yale shell, built of Spanish cedar, was forty-five feet long, twenty-four inches wide, eight inches deep. With her crew she drew four and a half inches of water. Each boat weighed one hundred and fifty pounds. The Yale shell, which was rigged for a coxswain, although said at the time to be the fastest racing-boat in America, was afterwards pronounced unsatisfactory by a member of the crew. "The stroke was on the port side, the outriggers were shaky and short, and the spoon-oars were but ten feet long, the length of single sculls." This boat was received only three days before the race by a crew which had practiced in a lap-streak without a coxswain, with oars thirteen and a half feet long, and the stroke on the starboard side. In consequence of the shortness of the oars the Yale crew was forced to increase their stroke from thirty-eight to forty-five, and, in a final spurt, to sixty. The Harvard crew rowed without coxswain or rudder. Under these conditions

the first race between the shells was pulled. As the record shows, Harvard won the regular university race on July 26, by sixty seconds, to be beaten by two seconds in the "Citizens' regatta" on the following day. This was Harvard's first defeat by Yale.

The result was significant. The two lap-streaks entered in the first race were easily left behind, and the time made indicated a remarkable advance, in so far as the records of those years may be trusted. Yale's time, 19m. 14s., was the best ever made, except that of the Harvard crew, 19m. 11s., in a Beacon cup regatta at Boston, — a comparison which may be accepted for what it is worth, since both courses and times were unreliable. Thus the superiority of the shell was clearly demonstrated. And another important outcome of these two races was Harvard's adoption of "a rudder connected with the bow-oarsman's feet by wires." In the "Citizens' regatta" Harvard drew the side most exposed to the high wind, which blew directly across the course, "some of the gusts being so strong that twice on one side the crew were obliged to hold water to get the boat's head around." Little importance is attached to the influence of the wind by Yale writers in view of Harvard's

THE HARVARD BOAT-HOUSE, DOBBS'S FERRY.

fast time; but the circumstance is mentioned here simply as the cause of a new departure in steering. Something had been done in this direction with the Harvard *Undine*, a four-oared boat, two years before; but the plan of a rudder worked by the bow oarsman was not adopted until the "Citizens' regatta" proved that a shell could not be satisfactorily steered by the oars. Although new boats were built for the Cambridge oarsmen the pine shell *Harvard* was used in 1860, winning three races, among them the race against Yale and Brown. In 1865 the *Harvard* was broken up and her pieces preserved as relics. The oarsmen of those days cherished a personal regard for their boats which, I think, no longer exists. The lap-streaks used in the "irregular" races, and the first shells, were named, a custom long since abandoned, and after a service, in some cases of several years, the parting from these old boats was like a parting from old friends.

Yale introduced the use of sliding-seats in 1870. A correspondent, writing from Worcester, naively described the Harvard men as having "seats some eighteen inches long, running fore-and-aft, polished smoothly, and coated with grease, upon which they slide. The Yale men have seats so mounted that they slide themselves." Notwithstanding Yale's new device Harvard reached the turning-stake first, but was disabled at that point by a foul. Yale's time was slow,—a fact due, probably, to delay at the stake. When sliding-seats were first used in the Oxford-Cambridge race, in 1873, faster time was made than has ever been known since. Harvard adopted the sliding-seat in 1872,

and was defeated by Amherst rowing with stationary seats; but Yale discarded the new invention in that year only to be the last of six crews. There was, therefore, some apparent reason for the earnest discussion, pro and con, which preceded the universal adoption of sliding-seats.

From 1873 on the changes in the rig of six-oared shells were only trifling modifications of tolerably well-determined standards. In 1876 "the Yale eight-oar was built by Keast & Collins, of New Haven, after the model of one built for Yale by Clasper, of Oxford (England), while the Harvard boat was the work of Fearon, of Yonkers. These were the first eight-oared shells that ever competed in America." Paper boats built by Waters, of Troy, appear to have been the favorites for subsequent races. The average length of these boats is fifty-eight feet. In 1882 Yale appeared with a boat sixty-seven feet long, so rigged that the men sat together in pairs. But I understand that the race of 1885 will be rowed in paper boats, of the regulation dimensions and rig. The substitution of paper for wood, as the material for racing-shells, which dates back to 1868, and the introduction of swivel row-locks

A HARVARD OARSMAN.

are changes by which the college oarsmen have profited. Wooden shells are so easily racked and twisted out of shape, that a material affording stiffness without undue weight was sought for, and apparently found in paper.

Closely connected with the changes in boats is the development of boating methods, understanding by this phrase, training and styles of rowing. When the Harvard-Yale races began, such a thing as systematic physical education was un-

TWILIGHT ON THE THAMES.

known at our colleges. Dr. Sargent's refinements in apparatus were not dreamed of. It was years afterward when Amherst became the pioneer in even and wholesome education of the body. In 1852 the Harvard crew only rowed a few times before the race, "for fear of blistering their hands." The Rev. James Whiton, of the Yale crew, wrote, in a subsequent account, "As to training, as now practiced, there had been none, — only that some care was taken of diet on the day of the race, such as to abstain from pastry and from summer fruit, and to eat meat in preference. One of the Yale clubs thought it was a smart thing when they turned out on Tuesday morning, an hour before sunrise, took their boat into a secluded cove, and rubbed her bottom with black-lead." In 1855 the Harvard men "had all rowed during the spring-time, and had the same general style." The Yale crews "rowed with short, jerky strokes, more than sixty [?] to the minute."

Up to 1864 the Harvard University crew had been beaten but twice, — by the Union Club crew in Boston, 1857, and at Worcester in 1859. The Harvard men had the advantages of studying the St. John oarsmen, and they were near the water. "Yale never saw good rowing except at Springfield and Worcester." Nevertheless, the Yale crew of 1859 was put through a severe course of training. Winter gymnasium work was taken up at both colleges after the second race. Among rowing men Yale's short choppy stroke and Harvard's longer swing soon became proverbial. Training then, and for many years afterwards, was largely guided by the empirical observances of retired

prize-fighters, — "physic first, sweat and work down, no liquid, plenty of raw meat, and work it into 'em." An intelligent knowledge of the subject on the part of medical men, or amateur athletes of experience, was almost entirely wanting.

The experiences of the Yale crews of 1864 and 1865 were forcible illustrations of old-school training. Mr. Edmund Coffin, a member of the Yale crew for three years, refers, in "Yale Boating," to the training of those years as "more severe than any other college crews have ever had in this country. I believe the old and time-worn stories of raw beef, and the other things accompanying it, were facts with us; that training lasted about two months in its severity before the race. On week days we rose about six, walked and ran before breakfast on an absolutely empty stomach, between three and five miles, running more than half the distance, and a part of that at full speed, often carrying small weights in our hands. Most of this running-exercise was taken in heavy flannels, for the purpose of melting off any possible fatty substance. After that we breakfasted, attended recitation for an hour, rowed about four miles, attended a second recitation, dined, rowed again the same distance, and had a third recitation in the afternoon. All the rowing was at full speed, much of it over the course on time. The bill-of-fare consisted of beef and mutton, with occasional chicken, toasted bread, boiled rice, and weak tea, no wine or beer, and very rarely vegetables." Such a system as this resulted in light crews, for one of its chief objects was "to get the men down."

In 1864 a professional trainer was first employed, — Mr. William Wood, — who was with the Yale oarsmen for four weeks before the race. In the same year "the Harvard men appeared with bare backs; and, as they had practiced all the season thus stripped, presented a rich mahogany color, while the Yale crews, who had rowed in shirts, were milk-white by contrast. The New York *Sun*, in its account of the race, attributed the hue of Harvard's oarsmen to the use of some artificial coloring matter." It was at this race that the magenta and crimson became popularly confounded as the Harvard colors. Magenta was the color of the class of 1866, which furnished the entire university crew in 1865. The crew of the preceding year, unable to find crimson handkerchiefs at Worcester, substituted magenta perforce, although the color was called "red" in the programs. Perhaps Worcester was the first town ever literally "painted red." In 1865 the shops contained nothing but magenta, and its use caused an erroneous impression, officially corrected some ten years later by a formal return to crimson. Yale's stroke in these two races was quick and jerky, the arms doing more than their share of the work. Harvard, pulling only thirty-six and thirty-seven to the minute, was severely criticised by the New York *Tribune*, which remarked editorially, in 1865, "No crew pulling less than forty to the minute has any right to expect to win a race."

But a change was at hand. Under Mr. Wilbur R. Bacon's splendid discipline Yale had been victorious for two years. Harvard was stimulated to new efforts, directed by Mr. William Blaikie and other veteran oarsmen. For the first time at Cambridge the rowing men entered upon regular work in the autumn. On alternate days they ran five or six miles. The old-school training was radically changed. "Instead of training off flesh the maxim was, keep all the flesh you can, and do the prescribed work." A far more liberal diet was adopted and continued up to the race; and, as the result, a heavy, "beefy" crew, well trained, won the race of 1866. A close study was made of English rowing, improved rowing weights were obtained, and on them the candidates for the crew pulled a thousand strokes daily throughout the winter, meantime applying the principles of the "English stroke." This meant more use of the back and legs, and a firm

catch at the beginning of the stroke. Yale although pulling a slower and longer stroke, still relied mainly on arm-work. In the race Harvard quickened up to forty-three; but Harvard's half-minute victory was considered due to her new style of rowing. Six years later Mr. Robert J. Cook imported an "English stroke," which won success for Yale.

In 1868, a year distinguished for the sign-stealing, howling, and other nocturnal disturbances at Worcester, the styles of the two crews were described as follows: "Yale is dropping the rigid-arm stroke. The men reach well over their toes and come back with a strong, steady pull, finishing up with something very like a jerk, then recovering more slowly than the Harvards. Their backs are much more bent, and they do not seem to get so firm a hold. They row with oars rather longer, thus making up for less strokes. Harvard's stroke makes the men reach even further forward, and row with perfectly straight backs, almost raising themselves off the seat at every stroke, giving the stretcher a most wicked kick at the beginning, and finishing up gracefully with their arms." Thus the successive stages of rowing may be traced from exclusive use of the arms, at first, to use of the back and arms, then of the back and legs, with as little employment of the arms as possible, and finally to the principle of assigning all the muscles of the body their fitting proportion of the work.

Of the slighter modifications introduced from year to year it is impossible and unnecessary to speak. The adoption of sliding-seats caused a slower stroke. The traditional "straight back" and "catch on the beginning" of Harvard date back to 1866 or 1867. After the time of Mr. Wilbur R. Bacon there was no radical new departure in rowing at Yale until Mr. Robert J. Cook spent the winter of 1872–73 in England studying English rowing, and gaining information of infinite value, which was practically applied in 1873. Newspaper ridicule of the "English stroke" was changed by the result of the race which was heralded as "a victory for Cook and for the slow stroke of thirty to thirty-two a minute with full use of the back and loins." Of this race "The Harvard Book" says: "Physically the Yale crew were not remarkably strong, but their captain had been able, by great perseverance and labor, to infuse into his crew the principles he had learned in England, and also his own energy and spirit. A great deal is seen in the newspapers about the English style, as if it were a peculiar and well-defined style. The fact is the English rowing-men have very different styles. When Harvard's four-oared crew were in England, in 1869, their style was preferred by the London watermen to Oxford's, as more like their own. The longer the race the slower should be the stroke, and what has been called the English stroke by the newspapers is simply the long stroke which is rather peculiar to Oxford and Cambridge, and to them only, when rowing over the Putney course of four and a quarter miles. Since the introduction here of

turned to the old stroke, and after their victory Mr. Cook remarked, "We are now back to where we were in 1873," and expressed a sincere hope that "the donkey-engine stroke" would not be seen again. At Harvard there was a new departure in 1877, which may be roughly termed a change from the "Loring stroke" to the stroke taught by Messrs. Watson and Bancroft. This stroke was begun with the body well forward, and the successive motions were, "first, the swing up, with a hard catch on the beginning; second, the slide with the legs, the arms still rigid; third, the arm pull, bringing the oar-handle to the chest; fourth, after the oar-blade

THE PRESENT HARVARD BOAT-HOUSE, CAMBRIDGE.

straight-away races, where there is no change or let-up like that allowed in turning a stake, the crew cannot live to row a quick stroke even in a three-mile race. This fact gives color to the statements that the present (1875) style of rowing has been adopted from England." It is rather the Cook stroke than the English stroke which Yale adopted in 1873, and, with a few exceptions, has adhered to since. In 1882 Yale changed to a short, jerky stroke, pulled principally with the arms, the bodies swinging very little from the perpendicular. I believe Mr. Cook promptly predicted defeat on first seeing this remarkable style of rowing, and his prediction proved correct both in 1882 and 1883. Last year the Yale crew re-

is lifted from the water, a quick, outward shoot of the hands; fifth, the slide back by doubling the legs, and, last, the downward swing of the body." This year there has been some change in the Harvard stroke, but I have found by a visit to the boat-house that the importance of the change had been exaggerated. Now the men swing and slide simultaneously, and the weight of the back is applied in the middle instead of at the beginning of the stroke, as the oar-blades are fully covered in the beginning of the stroke, which is pulled "hard through" until the hands reach the body. It does not appear that the stroke of 1885 is shorter than its predecessors, and I was told by Captain Storrow that it is no quicker. He informed me that, in practice pulls, the crews averaged thirty to thirty-one strokes a minute, running up to thirty-six in hard rowing. He defined the stroke as a combination of principles tested by three Harvard oarsmen, successful in recent years: Messrs. Bancroft, Curtis, and Perkins. Captain Storrow acknowledged his inability to understand the newspaper definition of the stroke as "an adaptation of professional arm-and-leg work to straight-back rowing." The Harvard crew of 1885 is composed of light men, seven of whom enter the university boat this year for the first time; but the crew will not experiment with a "quick professional arm-and-leg stroke" at New London. To the layman there will probably be few differences in the styles of rowing illustrated by the rival crews.

Training in these days is conducted more liberally and intelligently; but the prize-fighter school of training made its influence felt into the seventies. In 1871 the Brown oarsmen were limited to nine swallows of water daily, and in 1873 the Dartmouth giants were taken out directly after a hearty supper, for a six-mile pull at full speed, on the old principle of "working food into 'em." Very naturally, four of the six were made sick, much to the surprise of John Biglin, their trainer. Fortunately, such ignorant and dangerous "training" as this has passed away. The best resources of science and experience are applied to the physical care of college oarsmen. With a physician, a trained specialist, at hand to decide whether or not the candidate is fitted to compete for boating honors, the old argument of the dangerous over-exertion, and so on, of rowing, falls to the ground. It is acknowledged that there are men with tendencies to heart troubles, let us say, who should never enter a racing-boat, just as there are men forbidden by inherited appetites to touch a drop of wine. But the final answer to objections is, that, at Harvard, and, I believe, at Yale, no man is permitted to begin training until he has undergone a thorough physical examination, and has been declared competent by a recognized authority.

All this is of comparatively recent date, and yet, if we had such an American record as Dr. Morgan's "University Oars," I think it would be hard to find instances of permanent injury, even among our earlier and poorly cared-for oarsmen. Let us gather a few names from such records as there are at hand. In the race of 1852

Mr. Benjamin K. Phelps, afterwards District Attorney of New York, and Mr. George W. Smalley, London correspondent of the *Tribune*, were members of Yale's second crew, together with two future clergymen. Professor Alexander Agassiz was the bow-oar of Harvard's second crew, in 1855, and he continued to row "on the Varsity" in 1856, '57, and '58. In the last year Professor Agassiz occupied the bow, President Charles W. Eliot the waist, and the stroke was the veteran B. W. Crowninshield, — his fourth year in the Harvard crew. I regret to find in the records of that unsophisticated time that this crew rowed and won a race at Boston for a purse of $75, and another for a purse of $100. According to the fine distinctions of these suspicious latter days neither President Eliot nor Professor Agassiz can rank as amateur oarsmen. As the race of 1858 was abandoned President Eliot never enjoyed an opportunity of rowing against Yale. Mr. Caspar Crowninshield, who made his *début* in 1858, rowed for three years, and was followed by Mr. F. Crowninshield, in 1865,— the third Harvard stroke furnished by the family. He, like Mr. William Blaikie, Dr. C. H. McBurney, and R. S. Peabody, the architect of the Wall-street Bank building, in New York, and the Providence Railroad depot, in Boston, was a member of the famous boating-class of 1866. The names of Richard Waite, William P. Bacon, Charles H. Owen, Hamilton Wallis, and S. C. Pierson are distinguished in Yale's earlier boating annals, and "Wilbur Bacon's crew" has become a tradition.

On the battle-field, as well as on the river, college oarsmen have made a record of courage and endurance. A member of the Yale crew of 1859 writes: "Within five years after the race every one of the Yale seven, and all but one of the Harvard six, held their commands as United States army officers." Mr. Brayton Ives, Yale's bow-oar in 1860, won the rank of Colonel in the Union army, and, according to a class history, was "in command of the troops who escorted General Grant to the conference with General Lee, which resulted in the surrender of the rebel army." In after years Mr. Ives was elected President of the New York Stock Exchange, and President of the University Club in New York. Mr. A. P. Loring, a member of the Harvard crews of '66, '67, and '68, pulled stroke of the four beaten by Oxford in 1869. Mr. Robert C. Watson rowed on the Harvard crew in 1867 and 1868, and his valuable counsel to the Harvard oarsmen of the last few years shows that his enthusiastic interest in boating is still fresh and unabated.

Mr. William A. Copp entered the Yale crew of 1866, and rowed for four years only to be beaten every year. Yale had just won a race when he began to row, but she won no other until he was a graduate of four years' standing. I know nothing regarding Mr. Copp's personality, but I am filled with admiration at his courage in coming up, year after year, only to face defeat. So the roll might be prolonged, McCook, Bone, Day, Adee, Kennedy, Kellogg, Thompson, representing a few of Yale's more persistent oarsmen, and Lyman, Simmons, Goodwin, Dana, Otis, and Bacon serving the same end for Harvard. In the recent history of the Harvard-Yale race, there are two names deserving of conspicuous recognition, — Robert J. Cook, and William A. Bancroft. The author of the article on boating, in the " History of Yale College," alludes to the fact that the class of '76 furnished for four years a captain of the university crew, and says : " This was Robert Johnston Cook, whose five years' practice of rowing, at Yale, and quiet persistence in his determination to follow what seemed to him the best attainable methods of that art, — spite of ridicule, abuses, and slander, — resulted in a personal triumph and vindication quite unprecedented in the annals of American college-boating. It is simply a fact to say that no other collegian ever did so much to develop skill in rowing at Yale." Mr. Bancroft, in 1876, pulled stroke of the Harvard six at Saratoga, and of the eight-oared crew at Springfield. He continued as stroke of the Harvard crew for three years more, winning three out of the four eight-oared races with Yale. Very few men have worked more faithfully in the cause of Harvard boating, or studied styles of rowing more carefully, than Mr. Bancroft. He has done much to improve the Harvard stroke ; but, more than this, he has always taught his men the value and necessity of discipline. His services, both as captain and as coach, have left their mark upon Harvard boating, and no man who wears the crimson will hesitate to acknowledge their worth. There are other oarsmen, among them the members of Yale's splendid crew of 1876, and of Harvard's victorious crews of 1877, '78, and '79, whose work should be recognized, but

I can only single out a few, and I am confident that the memories of many of my readers will supply the deficiencies.

Since the Harvard-Yale University race forms my subject I have passed over the class and single-scull races and the intercollegiate and other contests, like those with outside clubs and professional crews. In the earlier years of college-rowing, races with professionals like the Ward and Biglin crews were of common occurrence, and judges or referees at regular college regattas were sometimes selected from the same class. Harvard never employed a professional trainer, although Yale crews, from 1864 to 1870, were under the care of " professionals." Their employment was forbidden subsequent to 1873 by a resolution adopted at an intercollegiate rowing convention. The disappearance of the professional element and the removal of subordinate contests left the way clear for the race between the university crews of Harvard and Yale, which is the chief reason for the existence of a substantial interest in boating at the two colleges. The difference in attendance at the Harvard-Columbia and Harvard-Yale races indicates the differing degrees of importance attached to each by Harvard men. Now that the Harvard-Yale race has become firmly established at New London, after efforts which date back nearly twenty years, the singular perfection of the course, its convenience for sight-seers and the accessibility of the town, — all indicate that the race has found a permanent home. The management of the New London races has been, I believe, almost entirely satisfactory. After the first race, in 1878, correspondents joined unanimously in praising the care and energy of New London's mayor, the exertions of Mr. G. W. Bentley, Superintendent of the New London and Northern R.R., and the active assistance of other citizens. That the good people of New London should do as much as they have done, in sharing the expenses of the race and contributing to Harvard's quarters, is more than creditable under the circumstances ; for the town profits little by the race, and there is no likelihood that it ever will. The pecuniary support of an affair of this kind must come either from the hotel or the transportation interests. New London hotels are unequal to the demands of a great crowd ; but, under proper management, there is no reason why visitors should remain over night. Such profit as the race may bring must be, for the most part, gained by railroads and steam-boats. Trains can be run from New York and Boston to New London, returning in good season, after allowing ample time for witnessing the race. If sufficient inducements are offered it is probable that a far larger number of spectators can be brought to New London than have ever witnessed the eight-oared races. This, according to those who have been interested in the management of the race, is the true way to make it a popular success. As to its local management, one point may be emphasized: the vital necessity of keeping the course perfectly clear before, during, and for a short time after, the race. With a crowd of boats following the shells, and a multitude of shipping and small boats poorly restrained near the finish line, the conditions are favorable for a disaster more terrible even than that of 1880. Thus far no serious accident for which the management can be held accountable has interrupted the enjoyment of race-day. But, the collision which occurred between the " Press-boat" and an intrusive steamer, in 1878, was a lesson which should be heeded.

The undergraduates themselves have an important, though very different part in forming the character of these races. Nothing has tended to lower college-boating in the eyes of outsiders so much as the disputes and recriminations which have accompanied some Harvard-Yale races in the past. Of these quarrels this article has taken little account, although in some boating-records to which I have referred this acrimonious spirit has been preserved in permanent form. Let the dead bury their dead. These issues are past, and it is the hope of all graduates that the newspapers will never again be filled with the squabbles of Harvard and Yale. The undergraduates of to-day have to sustain the dignity of their colleges and atone for some errors of their predecessors. This I think they are doing. Harvard and Yale oarsmen should meet in a fair and manly spirit on absolutely even terms. Attempts to secure an advantage by carefully guarded new devices, either in the rig of boats, or in oars, have a professional flavor which should be beneath the dignity of gentlemen. This race is, or should be, a test of the picked men from the two colleges, pitted against each other under conditions which each side should desire to make equal. In methods of training and styles of rowing each crew may well

endeavor to surpass the other. But anything which savors of a professional spirit must be discountenanced. This spirit is entering more and more into American sports, but the oarsmen of Harvard and Yale have it in their power to maintain a higher standard of amateur athletics than any to be fixed by conventional rules.

To visit New London for the race is a very different thing from a visit to New London for itself. The old order has not wholly passed away and contrasts of new and old face the lingering visitor on every side The old mill stands in its mossy, shaded ravine as it stood in colonial days, and beside it the Winthrop mansion rears a front still stately, although insulted by the changes upon which it looks. Up on the hill the crumbling stones of an ancient God's acre preserve, in quaint phrase and eccentric rhyme, the memories of departed worthies, some of whom worshipped in a rude meeting-house hard by, while sentinels watched for the approach of prowling Pequots. The meeting-house has vanished as entirely as the Pequot. The modern church has usurped its place. But, just as the name of the Mohegans is preserved by a few descendants to the northward, so the earlier life of this seaport town is embalmed in its buildings scattered here and there, the old side by side with the new. Legends of Indian stratagem, and Revolutionary warfare, and tales of the stirring days when New London's wharves were lined with whalers and merchant-vessels are represented by the odd old buildings which the passer-by scans askance. Outside the town the contrast continues. Ancient gambrel-roofed cottages look down from the hills upon the Newport-like villas and velvet lawns around the Pequot House, and a stone dwelling which might pass for the tower of the Master of Ravenswood, stands within rifle-shot of a beach artlessly called " the Coney Island of Connecticut." But it is not the old which lingers longest in the remembrance of one who has known New London. His is not a memory of ancient houses and traditions, but rather a memory of homes, with hearth-fires burning brightly in a welcome which never fails.

But this is not the New London of the boat-race excursionist. For him there waits the brilliant spectacle of a race which can be witnessed from start to finish. On the eventful day he finds himself four miles up the river, eagerly scanning the red-roofed cottage across the water, or the boat-house further up, below Yale's quarters on the point, until at last he sees stalwart student-oarsmen appearing on the floats, while the sunlight glistens on the polished shells raised in air for a moment, then tenderly lowered to the water. Now the two boats shoot across the river, welcomed lustily by the gayly-beribboned throng which fills the long line of platform-cars. Suddenly, the cheers die away. The crews are in line. Behind them is a generation of rivalry. Before them the silvery pathway of the Thames leads on past the navy-yard, past Mamacoke headland, to a wilderness of masts, and the grand stand on the point, while the Groton Monument on the one side, and the spires of New London on the other, seem to mark the finish line. And now, even while we are idly wondering at the beauty of the scene, a rifle cracks, and the roar of a thousand voices from the moving train breaks the silence of suspense. The crews are off, striving desperately for the vantage of the start, then settling down into their steady stroke. What can be better than this? Here before us are the best men of our two greatest colleges. For nearly a year they have led lives of ascetic self-denial. They have given up their pleasures; they have resigned their very wills to the control of others; they have exercised aching muscles in gymnasiums, on the running-path, in long, hard rows, for months, and for what? All for this, for the twenty thrilling minutes of a race, which shall either proclaim their year's work naught, or return them, crowned with laurels, to their college, to meet there such a triumph as awaited the victors in the Grecian games. Is it not magnificent, the sight of the splendid rivalry before us? Not one of these bronzed, sturdy giants needs the stimulus of the cheers wafted across from the shore. Each will put forth all that is in him, although his eyes grow blind and his heart break in the effort. And now we see the eight broad backs in one boat rising and falling more and more quickly. Keen eyes on shore detect the spurt, and there is a note of fierceness in the yells hurled at the lagging crew. Now the latter quickens, and so the race goes on. Likely enough we can tell its outcome by the time the two-mile flag is reached. Then for two miles more we shall hear an exultant, frenzied cheering, mingled with the sullen shouts of the defeated. Now the noise redoubles. The excited crowd at the grand stand have joined the chorus, and the yachts send back their cheers. Down close to the point, past the gayly-decorated yachts, flash the two boats, and the roar of cannon tells the end of the race. Both crews have rowed well. The vanquished congratulate the victors in open, manly fashion, while, on shore, frantic undergraduates leap high in air, embrace, and rush knee-deep in water. Up to the mast-head swings a signal-ball, and the Crimson, — or is it the Blue? — wins the race of 1885.

J. R. W. Hitchcock.

Rhode Island
(1892)

RHODE ISLAND.[1]

By E. Benjamin Andrews.

HETHER or not Rhode Island was the Norseman's "Vinland," it has many of the characteristics ascribed by them to that country. Though no one longer accounts the Old Stone Mill at Newport their handiwork, it is not at all impossible, many think it even probable, that these regions were visited by those hardy navigators from the North. Cabot sighted our shores in 1498, and twenty-six years later Verrazani anchored in the waters now called Newport Harbor. Adrian Block, too, ploughed our seas, as " Block Island " still reminds us. However, the proper history of " Rhode Island and Providence Plantations " begins with the advent of Roger Williams in 1636.

When, in 1631, Roger Williams landed in Massachusetts, he was welcomed as " a godly minister." The ship which brought him also brought provisions, which gave much needed relief to colonists hard pressed by famine. A day of thanksgiving followed, in which, no doubt, many a saint blessed God not only for the bread, but as well for the new defender religion had received in the sturdy young minister. But Williams did not long retain the favor with which he was at first hailed. As assistant pastor at Salem, he incurred the hostility of the Bay, and soon removed beyond its jurisdiction, accepting the office of assistant pastor in more liberal Plymouth. Here he remained two years. It was now that he became well acquainted with many chief sachems of the neighboring tribes, knowledge which subsequently served him in various negotiations. In 1633, he returned to Salem, where he presently asserted opinions which the rulers of the Bay could not tolerate. Cotton men-

1 In the preparation of this article the author has received valuable assistance from Professor Dr. Geo. G. Wilson, of Brown University, and also from that incomparable *connoisseur* of Rhode Island history, Mr. Sidney S. Rider, of Providence.

tions him as a " haberdasher of small questions against the power." Williams was several times brought before the court for his opinions, and finally, in 1635, sentenced to banishment on the following charges, as stated by the court :

1. That we have not our land by Pattent from the King, but that the natives are the true owners of it and that we ought to repent of such receiving it by Pattent.

2d. That it is not lawful to call a wicked person to swear, to pray, as being actions of God's worship.

3d. That it is not lawful to hear any of the ministers of the Parish assemblies in England.

4th. That the civil magistrate's power extends only to Bodies and Goods and outward state of man.

Williams was to depart out of the jurisdiction within six weeks, but as his health was at the time very poor the court permitted him to remain till spring. He did not cease to teach his " dangerous " opinions, and was therefore summoned to Boston that he might be sent to England. He refused to obey. The magistrates despatched Captain Underhill with a small sloop to bring him. When the officers arrived in Salem, " they found he had gone three days before, but whither they could not learn." Williams had started for the land of the Narragansetts. Of his travel thither he writes, " I was sorely tossed for one fourteen weeks in a bitter winter season, not knowing what bread or bed did mean." The Indians cared for him on his way. " These ravens fed me in the wilderness," he says. Williams first settled on the east side of the Seekonk river, but his " ancient friend the Governor of Plymouth lovingly advised " him " that he had fallen into the edge of their bounds," and as they were " loth to displease the Bay," if he would but remove to " the other side of the water " they " should be loving neighbors together." Williams obeyed in the early summer of 1636, and made a new settlement at the mouth of the " Mooshausick," not far from the present site of St. John's Church, on

North Main Street, in the city of Providence. The name " Providence," the
pilgrim gave to the spot in grateful remembrance of "God's merciful providence to him in his distress."

In banishing Roger Williams, Massachusetts Bay had but acted out the spirit
of the age. Williams suffered the fate
then usually meted out by all religionists
to obdurate nonconformists. Yet, whimsical as some of his contentions seem, his
central idea was massive and immortal.
" Toleration will," so men then thought,
" make the kingdom a chaos, is the grand
work of the devil, is a most transcen-
dental, catholic and fundamental evil."
The Simple Cobler of Aggawam exclaims :
" How all Religions should enjoy their
liberty, Justice its due regularity, civil
cohabitation, moral honesty, in one and
the same jurisdiction, is beyond the Artique of my comprehension." What the
Simple Cobbler and his wisest contemporaries found " beyond the Artique of their
comprehension " was to be made plain
in a colony begun and continued without their aid.

As Williams said, his " soul's desire
was to do the natives good." " It is not
true," he adds, " that I was employed by
any, or desired any to come with me into
these parts." He did not care " to be
troubled with English company." Yet
he soon found a considerable settlement
growing up around him, and in framing
its government he did not swerve from
the principles which he had so boldly
preached in Salem. For the first time
in human history, religion was sundered
from civil government, Church held apart
from State. Those who subscribed the
so-called original compact promised to
be subject to their rulers and laws " in
active and passive obedience," but " only
in civil things."

The settlement at Providence was soon
followed by others within the present
limits of the state. Williams had withdrawn from Massachusetts territory, but
his freedom of spirit had not. Not a
few people still remained there who were
" apt to raise doubtful disputations."
Mrs. Hutchinson's prophecy was even less
welcome than Williams's. " The church
with one consent cast her out." Those

of her belief were numerous, and many
of them with other exiles made their way
to Providence. John Clark and William
Coddington led a hegira of these. They
intended to settle near Delaware Bay,
but concluded to make the island of
Aquidneck their home. The island,
called from 1644 Rhode Island, " was
purchased by love, by love and favour."
The settlers, nineteen in number, before
arriving at their future home at the north
end of the island, resolved themselves
by a compact into a body politic, " agree-
ing to be guided and judged by the word
of the Bible." This was in 1638.

The little colony on Rhode Island
grew apace, yet soon developed grave
differences of view. A separation took
place. Coddington, with fifty-eight others,
withdrawing and founding Newport in
1639. Those who first went to prospect
at " Niew Port " reported " that the land
might reasonably accommodate fifty families." The town which they left was
now reorganized and named Portsmouth.
The government at Newport practically
reproduced that which had just been established. In 1640, the two island towns
united, and on August 6 of that year it
was determined " that each should have a
joynt and an equal supply of the money
in the Treasury for the necessary purposes of the same." They soon had
their seal and the other insignia of a
fully equipped government. In 1641,
" It was further ordered by the authority
of this present Courte, that none bee accounted a Delinquent for Doctrine : Provided it be not directly repugnant to
ye Government or Lawes Established."
From this time, therefore, religious and
state affairs were here, as in Providence,
separate, by law, and the principle of
" soul liberty" was fully established.
Yet the political organization was for a
long time much more complete on the
Island than in the Providence Plantations.

In November, 1642, a settlement was
made on the Shawamet purchase in Warwick, title being acquired from the Indians. Among the earliest settlers here
was Samuel Gorton. Gorton was a sort
of human porcupine. No one could get
on with him. His contemporaries called
him " a most prodigious minister of ex-

orbitant novelties," "beast," "miscreant," and "arch-heretic." Even the mild Williams mentions him as "having abused high and low at Aquidnek, bewitching and maddening poor Providence." As a recent writer puts it, "he might almost be said to have graduated as a disturber

ing between Portsmouth and Newport was for some years the sole bond of general union anywhere prevalent among the four towns. Their own feebleness, with threats from Indians, the Dutch, and the older English colonies, by whom Rhode Island had been refused

The Roger Williams's Monument, Providence.

of the peace in every colony of New England." But he and his Warwick allies had energy, and their plant grew.

The two sovereignties on the Island, with Providence and Warwick, formed the four centres of Rhode Island population during the early period. The partnership already described as exist-

admission to the New England Confederation in 1643, led to the conclusion that, to insure their hold upon the lands which they occupied, these towns must have a charter from the English crown. "This kind of government of their owne erection" no longer met the needs of the growing commonwealth. Providence and the Island accordingly joined in sending Roger Williams to England to obtain the needed parchment. Williams desired to sail from Boston, but the

The Old Mill at Newport.

authorities would not allow this, and he was compelled to make the long journey to New York. In the autumn of 1644, he returned, *via* Boston, bringing the charter of 1643–4, for "The incorporation of Providence Plantations in Narragansett Bay in New England." As had been requested, this charter limited to civil matters the authority to be exercised under it, while, "beyond this," in the language of Arnold, "a silence more significant than language proclaimed the triumph of soul-liberty."

While the charter of 1643–4 made provision for the union of the four little commonwealths, yet partly the discord within and between them, and, still more, threats from Massachusetts and Plymouth to oppose by force any action under this charter for four years prevented such union. In 1647, however,

they handed over a little power to a central government. It was agreed "that the form of government established in Providence plantations is Democraticall; that is to say, a Government held by the free and voluntarie consent of all or the greater part of the free inhabitants;" and it was further enacted that "all men may walk as their consciences persuade them, every one in the name of his God." At this early day there was here a custom like the Swiss *referendum*. The people in open town meeting had the power, by a majority vote, to annul or abrogate any and all acts of the General Assembly; and only so long as this was not done was the act of the General Assembly a valid and binding statue.

Even the limited harmony of action brought about by the code of 1647 did not long continue. In 1651, the towns fell apart again by twos, — the island towns remaining united and the mainland towns preserving a measure of common action. All were again brought back to a degree of harmony in 1654, largely through the intercession of Williams. Yet, whether between or in the towns, the alliance was more superficial than hearty. The statement of a contemporary writer that "at Providence the Devil was not idle," was equally true for the other communities. Boundary disputes, which were at no time wanting, were not more rancorous than the cease-

Birthplace of Commodore Perry, South Kingston.

less domestic dissensions, like that between William Harris and Roger Williams. Very apt was the phrase used in the prayer for the charter of 1663, wherein the Rhode Islanders sought permission to hold forth a "lively experiment" in free government. Many things conspired to make it lively. However, the colony in 1660 could fairly be said to be well established.

The Attack on the "Gaspee."

The charter of 1663, given by Charles II., was no less liberal than that of 1643-4. It acknowledged Williams's early contention concerning the rightfulness of Indian titles to the soil. Fortunately, it defined with some care the colony's boundaries: else Massachusetts and Connecticut would even now have left it no territory. It assured full enjoyment of liberty "in matters of religious concernments." Like its predecessor the new charter made the government "democraticall," although the laws must accord as near "as may be" with those of England. That this charter remained the ground law of the state until fifty years ago is a testimony to its enlightened character, as is also the fact that those primary Rhode Island principles later found expression far and wide, and are now part of our fundamental law, the Constitution of the United States. They were for a century the law of the colony before they thus became embedded in the nation's great charter.

Settlers had been moving into the Narragansett country ever since 1641, Westerly being the chief centre, situated in the disputed territory to which Connecticut laid claim. Tradition says that the first residents here — coming so early as

1648 — were John Babcock and his wife, Mary Lawton, a couple who had eloped from Newport. By 1660, the settlement was well established, and it was the first to be organized into a town under the charter of 1663. This occurred in 1669.

Most of the other Rhode Island towns have arisen by the division of towns existing at the end of the seventeenth century. Bristol, Warren, Barrington, Tiverton, Little Compton, and Cumberland claimed by Massachusetts till the settlement of

Scene of the great Swamp Fight.

the Rhode Island boundaries in 1746-7. Block Island, previously under Massachusetts's jurisdiction, was, in 1663-4, annexed to Rhode Island, and in 1672 it was made the sixth town of the colony under the name of New Shoreham.

In 1675, broke King Philip's War. Although it was provoked entirely by the Confederation to which Rhode Island had been refused admission, and although Rhode Island did not embark in the war as an active party on the English side but fought solely in self-defence, yet her territory became the field of many battles and her people suffered more bitterly than those of any other colony. Nearly all the towns sustained severe losses, from which they did not recover for years. Before the war ended, Providence had been nearly destroyed. For its own defence in this war, Rhode Island prepared the first naval

Sir Edmund broke the seal of the colony, but seals could be made more easily than charters. So soon as Andros was at a safe distance the charter reappeared, and its provisions were again put in effect on the downfall of his power in the English revolution of 1688.

It was natural that Rhode Island should become a leader in naval achievement. No other colony had so much sea-coast in proportion to its land. Harbors were many and good ; ship building

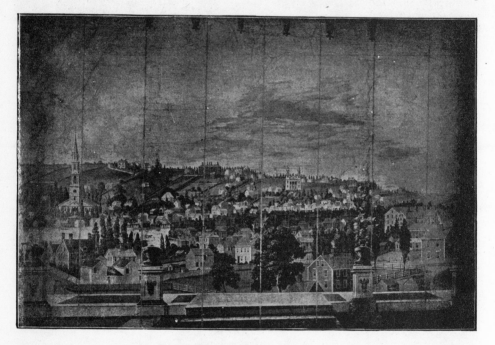

Old Drop Curtain, showing Providence in 1810.

armament in the history of the colonies — a prophecy of the influence the little colony was later to exercise in the naval history of our country.

During the years of Sir Edmund Andros's government over New England, the Rhode Island towns settled back into their earlier condition of separate self-government. Andros was reasonably well disposed toward Rhode Island. The fundamental principles of the state he could not change. When he visited Newport he, of course, demanded the charter. A vigorous search was made for it, but conveniently it could not be found.

was early a staple industry ; nautical knowledge plentiful and exact. French privateers harassed the Rhode Island coast in 1690, when our seamen gained a victory over their plundering crews. Narragansett Bay made the entire colony vulnerable, while Block Island was a specially convenient point of attack. The danger of such assaults developed a spirit of naval enterprise.

In 1706, Captain John Wanton captured a privateer and her prize. When the news of the declaration of war with Spain reached Rhode Island in 1740, a sloop of war and five privateers were

FROM AN OLD PAINTING.

Scene at the Bridge, Providence, during the great Gale, September, 1815.

straightway equipped. Again, in 1757, sloops of war and privateers were prepared to co-operate with the expedition against Canada. Of the privateers fitted out for this French and Indian War, some, after its close, gave themselves up to smuggling and virtual piracy, lucrative practices in which they found much sympathy even from the best citizens. For this the British government viewed Rhode Island with great disfavor, which, however, did not lead to the disuse of Rhode Island privateers.

The British vessels *Beaver* and *Gaspee* found it difficult to enforce the revenue laws in Narragansett Bay. In faithfully endeavoring to do this, Lieutenant Dudingston of the royal navy made the mistake of sending a sloop, which he had seized on the charge of smuggling, to Boston for trial, whereas the British statute requires that in such cases the nearest admiralty court should try. This mistake made Dudingston's act trover, and enabled General Greene, to whom the sloop belonged, to recover the value of sloop and cargo. The Rhode Island authorities did not show great respect to certain of the royal commands. In 1772,

Governor Wanton writes Admiral Montagu: "I do not receive instructions for the administration of my government from the King's Admiral stationed in America." The continued difficulties with the revenue vessels culminated on the night of June 9, 1772. The sloop *Hannah*, from New York for Providence, was pursued by the *Gaspee*, which, drawing more water than the *Hannah*, ran aground on a spur of land now known as Gaspee Point. This fact was at once made known in Providence. A meeting being called, it was determined to de-

The Coddington House, Newport.

stroy the troubler ere she floated again. Soon after ten o'clock, eight long and well-manned boats rowed quietly down the Bay. The hail of the *Gaspee's* watch was disregarded, that of Lieutenant Dudingston himself replied to with a bullet which wounded and disabled him. After the exchange of a few shots the colonists took possession of the vessel, and, re-

State Houses, Newport and Providence.

moving the crew, burned her to the water's edge. This may be regarded as America's first blow for freedom from Great Britain. A court of inquiry was instituted to bring to justice the perpetrators of this open attack on His Majesty's navy, but evidence sufficient to convict could not be obtained even by offers of large rewards.

The *Gaspee* expedition was headed by Captain Abraham Whipple, afterward so celebrated in the Revolutionary War. He was the first American commander to attack His Majesty's navy. After the *Gaspee* affair he received the following:

"You, Abraham Whipple, on the 10th of June, 1772, burned his Majesty's vessel, the *Gaspee*, and I will hang you at the yard-arm.
"JAMES WALLACE."

To this Whipple replied:

"To Sir James Wallace, Sir, Always catch a man before you hang him.
"ABRAHAM WHIPPLE."

In 1775, Nicholas Cooke, Deputy Governor, wrote to Captain Wallace, demanding the return of a packet which that officer had taken and was detaining as a tender to his vessel. In replying, Wallace inquired who Cooke was and whether the colony still recognized the royal authority. A few hours later Wallace's frigate was attacked by a war-sloop of the colony and after a sharp contest the tender was captured. Whipple commanded this expedition also. The war was now begun, and Rhode Island at once put two armed vessels into service under Whipple as commodore. This was the foundation of the American navy.

In August, 1775, the Rhode Island delegates in Congress were instructed to press for a united effort to obtain a fleet for the defence of the colonies. Rhode Island influence and initiative made the colony the leader in the undertaking. Esek Hopkins was confirmed by Congress as the first commander of the fleet. Under Commodore Hopkins the first American squadron sailed from Delaware Bay in February, 1776. Whipple commanded one of the largest vessels of the fleet, and Rhode Island men were among the other officers. The cruise was a success. In April, Hopkins brought back the rich fruit of his victories. During the Revolution, money from prizes greatly enriched Rhode Island ship owners. Though Hopkins was relieved of his command in 1777, Rhode Island seamen took active part in nearly all the naval engagements of this war. In the War of 1812, it was the same. In the Battle of Lake Erie, the story of which need not be recounted here, Commodore Oliver Hazard Perry made Rhode Island's naval renown veritably immortal.

In the military as in the naval portion

of American history, Rhode Island men have borne honorable part. Colonel Dudley, in command of the English expedition against Acadia in 1706, reported that "he had received very honorable assistance from Rhode Island." In 1710, the colony sent considerably more than her quota of men to Port Royal. In 1745, she sent troops to Louisburg, some of them arriving too

Thomas W. Dorr.

The Dorr House, Providence, on the Site of Roger Williams's House.

late to be of service, and again, in 1755, extra troops to steady the retreat of Braddock's men after his defeat.

On various occasions during the Revolution, Rhode Island soldiers were called to defend critical points, as the bridges at Springfield and Trenton, New Jersey. Their action in these cases evoked a letter of commendation from General Washington himself. The concluding clause of this is as follows:

"The ready and ample manner in which your State has complied with the requisitions of the Committee of co-operation, both as to men and supplies, entitles her to the thanks of the public and affords the highest satisfaction to Your Excellency's most obedient servant,

"GEORGE WASHINGTON."

The signal and splendid revolutionary services of General Nathaniel Greene are well known to all Americans. Lincoln, then Gates, having proved no match for Cornwallis in the Carolinas, Greene took command there December 4, 1780, and by his skilful and tireless activity, advancing, then twice retreating, and twice advancing again, victorious in lost battles

as well as in those gained, he conquered the Carolinas and Georgia, forcing Cornwallis to Virginia, where Washington soon had him in his power.

In July, 1777, by a clever plan, Lieutenant Colonel Barton, with forty militiamen, crossed over the mainland to Newport, and, passing through the English fleet, made his way unobserved to the headquarters of the British General Prescott. Securing the sentinel, they took the general from his bed, and quietly carried him and his aide, who was also captured, within the American lines. For this exploit, Congress voted Barton a sword.

Political activity has at all times

High School, Providence.

strongly marked Rhode Island life, sometimes rising to a morbid pitch of heat. In earlier days constables were often required at town meetings to keep the peace. To escape political conflicts Roger Williams was, it seems, once on the point of withdrawing permanently to his "little Patience" island. "Our peace," he says, "was like the peace of a man which hath a tertian ague." Political turmoil was not confined to the internal affairs of towns : colonial matters ran no more smoothly. Cast out from neighboring communities by the operation of narrow laws and social ideas, many early Rhode Islanders developed almost a hatred of social order, an ultra individualism, a hostility to united action even greater than that which characterized the average Englishman of the seventeenth century. This political disease became so fastened upon the body politic, that it has propagated itself even to the present time. Rhode Island has suffered bitterly in consequence. To establish

Samuel Slater.

FROM AN OLD PORTRAIT.

The old Slater Mill, Pawtucket.

schools, to reform the laws, to amend evil political and social customs, or to do aught else requiring the co-operation of many individuals, has probably been more difficult in Rhode Island than anywhere else in the northern states. Not understanding the causes of this, many outsiders wrongly blame for it Rhode Island itself, and think the principles on which the state was founded somehow at fault. The true explanation is to be

sought in the backward and unidealistic political thinking of early New England at large. But for this, Rhode Island might have filled up with a normal New England population instead of one composed so largely of people whom ostracism had rendered suspicious of all political power or social crystallization.

This spirit of aggravated non-conformity, bad as it usually was, at times worked well. Thus Rhode Island declared its independence of Great Britain two months earlier than the nation did so. This declaration is a most helpful gloss upon the political theory at the basis of the more famous one which followed.

"Whereas in all states existing by compact," so runs the Rhode Island manifesto, "protection and allegiance are reciprocal, the latter being only in consequence of the former; and whereas, George the Third, King of Great Britain, forgetting his dignity, regardless of the compact most solemnly entered into, ratified and confirmed to the inhabitants of this colony by his illustrious ancestors, and, till of late, fully recognized by him,—and entirely departing from the duties and character of a good King, instead of protecting, endeavoring to destroy the good people of this Colony, and of all the United Colonies," etc.

Then follow several enactments vesting the authority in "the Governor and Company of the English Colony of Rhode Island and Providence Plantations," instead of in the King. This paper was dated May 4, 1776. Money, troops and ships were promptly got ready to aid the continental cause, and the General Assembly's records for July 20, 1776, close with "God save the United States." This same assembly made the legal title of the government what it still remains, "The State of Rhode Island and Providence Plantations."

Soon, however, congressional measures calculated to touch the state's sense of sovereignty began to meet with the same hostile reception which had earlier greeted those proposed by the king. Thus, when peace seemed to be in sight, Rhode Island refused assent to a national customs duty. It was alleged that such a tax would bear unequally on Rhode Island as a maritime state, and infringe her sovereignty. Howell, one of her delegates in Congress, resolutely opposed the measure and was seconded by his colleague, Arnold. The delegates met with severe handling for the stand thus taken, but the state supported them.

The abuse heaped upon the little state for her free trade attitude made it no easier to win her to the new federal con-

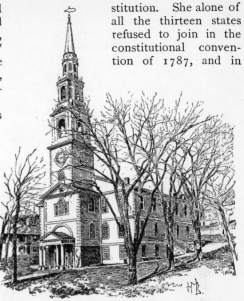

First Baptist Church, Providence.

stitution. She alone of all the thirteen states refused to join in the constitutional convention of 1787, and in 1788 she declined to call a convention to vote upon the instrument which that convention had framed. It is easy now to see the unwisdom of this course; yet, considering all the circumstances, it was far less senseless than most critics have represented.

Its feeblest and least noble occasion was the paper money delusion. In 1710, to meet her part of the expense of the second expedition against Port Royal, Rhode Island had resorted to the issue of credit bills. It was a most disastrous step, its unfortunate effects extending over a full century of the colony's history. The rural population was deeply in debt to the merchants of the towns, and wished the medium in which they were to pay to be at least no dearer than it was when they ran in debt. As a consequence, all extraordinary and even very ordinary demands were met by new issues of paper. If the state entered the Union, of course an end would be put to this system.

A far deeper and more honorable motive for Rhode Island's opposition to the

Old Ballou
Meeting House, Cumberland.

Old Quaker
Meeting House,
Lincoln.

Constitution was her determination to preserve her religious liberty. The great states of Massachusetts and Connecticut still had an established religion. So had Virginia, and so virtually, New York. Besides, it will be remembered that until its first amendment was adopted, the Constitution gave no guaranty whatever against religious tyranny. The people of Rhode Island would have been untrue to all that was most splendid in their history had they hastened into union

stitution, Rhode Island was left an independent nation. When, on the first Wednesday in March, 1789, government under the present Constitution began, John Gardner of Newport, the Rhode Island delegate in the Congress of the old Confederation, alone remained to constitute that body. North Carolina, alone recalcitrant at first, ratified in 1789, when Rhode Island had not a single companion in her precarious independence.

Whether or not Rhode Island's protest

Brown University.

with numerous powerful states not yet sufficiently educated to believe that religion could get on without support from law. Nor can it be doubted that Rhode Island's unwillingness to confederate before Amendment I. was added to the Constitution did much to make the separation of Church and State part of American public law. While, therefore, the Rhode Island Federalists of 1790 favored a policy which history was to justify, it is not so clear that on the whole they excelled their opponents in their patriotism or prudence.

After nine states had ratified the Con

would lead to the amendment of the new Constitution in favor of religious liberty, — a point which was still uncertain, — when the freshly formed union began to threaten the little nation it was madness for her to hold out longer. Accordingly, late on Saturday afternoon, May 29, 1790, the legislature, by a majority of two, viz., thirty-four to thirty-two, voted to adopt the Federal Constitution. Great was the rejoicing of the federal party. Next day, Sunday though it was, a national salute of thirteen guns rent the air of Providence.

A period of peaceful development fol-

President Manning.   Nicholas Brown.   President Wayland.

lowed, uninterrupted till the war of 1812. This war greatly disturbed commerce, yet the state on the whole bravely upheld the administration. The political complication brought on by the "anti-masonic excitement" which spread over the country and culminated in 1832 took strong hold in Rhode Island. In 1832, five attempts, all without success, were made to elect governor, lieutenant, governor, and senators. Three parties were in the field, each actuated by typical Rhode Island obstinacy. This imbroglio added intensity to the demand, which many had been urging for years, that the 1663 charter, up to this time the state's sole constitution, be revised. In 1834 and 1835, a constitutional convention met and adjourned several times, but did not complete a draft. In 1839, in a population of not far from 108,830 free white adult males, about 9,500 men composed the electorate, the freehold qualification being, at this time, $134. In 1841, the People's Constitution was framed and adopted by the people, 4,960 freemen and 8,984 non-freemen voting for it, while only 52 votes were cast against it. In 1842, the so-called "Landholders' Constitution" was framed. This also was submitted to the people but rejected. January 13, 1842, proclamation was made of the "People's Constitution," by order of the Convention which had drafted it.

Civil war was now imminent. Samuel W. King was the governor under the charter. Thomas W. Dorr was elected by the People's party. Dorr was determined to maintain the rights of the people even by arms. On the evening of May, 1842, bloodshed seemed unavoidable, but a fog came on, and in it many of Dorr's followers vanished. Attempts to maintain the Dorr power were subsequently made, notably that at Chepachet, June 28, but in vain. The "Dorr War" ended without serious disaster. In 1844, Dorr was tried and condemned to prison for life, but released next year.

The Friends' School, Providence.

" Better men," said he, " have been worse treated than I, though not often in a better cause." The end sought by Dorr and his party, viz., a widening of the franchise, has since been brought about by modifying the constitution, thus justifying the cause for which he staked all; but it has also been made clear that constitutional changes must be effected in a constitutional way. Dorr's idea that a new constitution may at any time be launched by the mere fiat of the people whether voters or not, without action of the General Assembly, has not prevailed.

Though never established here, religion has always flourished in Rhode Island. Roger Williams was the earliest and, on the whole, the most successful of all the missionaries to the Indians whom the country ever had. He was no mean preacher or theologian either, spite of Neal's statement in his "History of New England," that had Williams "never dabbled in Divinity he would have been esteemed a great and useful man." With eleven others Williams, in 1638, organized in **Providence** the First

Old Globe Bridge, Woonsocket.

been Pardon Tillinghast, James Manning, first president of Brown University, William Hague, and Samuel L. Caldwell. The Baptists of various names, among them, prominently, the Free and the Seventh Day Baptists, have formed a large element of the state's population.

Quakers were numerous in Rhode Island. As early as 1640, and on various occasions, George Fox attended meetings here. Many Quakers have held honorable places in Rhode Island life. Governor Easton was one of these. The influence of this body has been greatly promoted by the excellent Friends' School in Providence, founded in 1784 at Portsmouth, and transferred to its present seat in 1818.

The Congregationalists in Rhode Island, both Trinitarian and Unitarian, have at all times had many able clerical leaders and an extraordinarily intelligent and influential laity. The distinguished William Ellery Channing was born at Newport.

The Episcopal Church began its noble career in Rhode Island early in the eighteenth century. For the last fifty years its gains have been phenomenal. The state forms a diocese, of which Right Rev. Thomas M. Clark is bishop.

Trinity Church, Newport.

Channing Memorial, Newport.

Baptist Church in America. He was its first pastor. Among his successors have

Providence and Newport have naturally been, religiously as in other respects, the centres of the state. At the beginning of this century Providence had only six organized congregations, one of Baptists, one of Friends, one of Episcopalians, and three of Congregationalists. Since then churches have rapidly multiplied both in the city and throughout the state.

The Roman Catholics are now very numerous, Providence being the centre

Roger Williams was a pedagogue, teaching and practising Hebrew, Greek, Latin, and Dutch. "I taught two young gentlemen," he says, "a parliament man's sons, as we teach our children English, by words, phrases, and constant talk." Here are foreshadowed some of the most approved modern pedagogical methods. In Newport efforts to establish schools were made early. In 1640, Mr. Lenthall was called "to keep a public school there for the learning of the youth." In

Old Cabinet of the Rhode Island Historical Society.

of a large diocese reaching beyond the state limits. For fourteen years Right Rev. Thomas F. Hendricken was its bishop, succeeded at his death by the present bishop, Right Rev. Matthew Harkins. The Methodists, too, have grown strong, and the Presbyterians, the Adventists, and the New Church people all boast numerous adherents.

The progress of education in Rhode Island has been slow, hindered, among other causes, by the paucity of educated clergymen of the kind who did so much for the early schools of Massachusetts.

this southern capital culture has always flourished, even when in the other towns dissensions were engaging every one's thought. The aristocratic Narragansett planters followed English customs more extensively, it is believed, than occurred anywhere else in New England, and here we find private tutors living in the families as in England. The schools at Newport were seriously set back by the capture of the city during the Revolution as were the other schools of the colony, though in this as in other things Newport suffered most. Many school buildings were given up to the manufacture of ammunition. University Hall, in Brown University, then just erected, became a hospital and barracks for French and American soldiers. Providence and Rhode Island owe much to John Howland, and to James Manning, the first president of

in educational effort and achievement. In 1845, Henry Barnard was made Commissioner of Public Schools, being the first incumbent of this office which was created that year. For a time before this he had fulfilled the same duties as "agent." The office has year by year

"Purgatory," Newport.

Brown University, for the revival of interest in education after the Revolution. In 1800, the General Assembly passed an act for the establishment of a free school system. This was soon repealed, yet many of its provisions were carried into effect. It was not till 1828 that a permanent school fund was instituted for the entire state. Since this time, spite of utmost conservatism and too much apathy, there has been a steady progress

increased in importance, and been held by a succession of able men.

Brown University, incorporated in 1764, may claim to have exercised considerable influence in Rhode Island's educational advance. The university owed its origin to the happy convergence of two separate lines of events. So early as 1762 a "resolution to erect a college and institute a seminary for the education of youth somewhere in North America" had been formed by the Philadelphia Baptist Association. As Rhode Island had been settled on the principle of perfect toleration in religious belief, it was decided to apply to its legislature for a charter. Funds for the college came from South Carolina and Georgia, and even from England and Ireland.

Ever after the residence here, from 1729 to 1731, of the philosophical Dean Berkeley, subsequently bishop of Cloyne, Newport had been the centre of a pronounced intellectual interest, while the memory of Berkeley's scheme to found a college in America, with the actual erection of colleges in several of the other colonies, made it impossible that the suggestion of a college for Rhode Island should be strange or unwelcome to thoughtful people in that colony. The charter was granted, and was at the time far the most liberal instrument of the kind in America or in the world. Students of all faiths and of no faith were placed upon an absolute equality, while no immunity or special privilege whatever was provided for intending clergymen.

In September, 1765, Rev. James Manning, a recent graduate of the College of New Jersey, was appointed " President of the College, Professor of Languages, and other branches of learning." The first commencement was held at Warren, in September, 1769. The papers of the day remark it as proof of their patriotism, that " not only the candidates (for degrees) but even the president was dressed in American manufactures." In the spring of 1770, the college was moved to Providence. The corner-stone of the first building, still standing as the venerable University Hall, was laid on the fourteenth of May that year. During the Revolutionary War, college studies were suspended,

Roman Catholic Cathedral, Providence.

to be resumed again at once after its close. In 1804, in view of distinguished beneficence to the college on the part of Mr. Nicholas Brown, the corporation changed its name to Brown University.

Not only have a great majority of the men foremost in Rhode Island professional life been graduates of the university, but it has been largely through

Old Tavern, Kingston.

Pawtucket Falls.

the university that the state has exerted its influence upon the nation and the world. The works — not yet superseded — of its son, Henry Wheaton, made international law a new science. Its great president, Francis Wayland, shaped by his words, spoken and written, and still shapes by his writings, the intellectual and moral lives of multitudes who never saw him, while from his initiative have proceeded the great scope and freedom of election in study now characterizing higher education throughout the United States. Its graduates who have won national renown would form a catalogue far too long for this place. We can recall but two life-long residents of Rhode Island not graduates of the university, who have attained eminence in intellectual pursuits. They are Stephen Hopkins and Rowland Gibson Hazard. Both of these, however, were upon the Governing Board of the university and zealous promoters of its welfare.

For a hundred years judicial functions were, in Rhode Island, everywhere in the hands of men who also made or administered the laws. In Providence sentences were passed by the "major consent" of the freemen. Here Joshua Verin was tried,

found guilty, and deprived of the "libertie of voting, for restraining of the libertie of conscience." He had prevented his wife from attending religious meetings.

In 1640, a system of arbitration arose. At Portsmouth the town meeting judged alleged criminals, condemning some to the stocks. Newport early made provision for trial by jury. The judicial system developed far more rapidly on the island than on the main land. The code of 1647 introduced the "General Court of Trials for the whole Colony," the predecessor of the present Supreme Court. Between the towns it had a jurisdiction similar to that which the United States Supreme Court exercises in regard to the several states. It made the circuit of the towns. In each the head officers of the town had the privilege of sitting with the court, and in 1650 "equal authority to vote." Eight o'clock in the morning was "the farthest" time for opening court. Among the early judges were Roger Williams, Samuel Gorton, John Clarke, and William Coddington. The charter of 1663 also provided for a colonial court which was to sit at Newport. As the first judges served without pay, adjournments for lack of quorum were frequent.

To remedy this a fee of three shillings was appointed for any judge present at any sitting, and a penalty of twice that amount for unnecessary absence. Hitherto the governor, lieutenant-governor, and ten assistants had formed this upper court, but in 1747 a chief and four associate judges were constituted "The Superior Court of Judicature, Court of Assize, and General Gaol Delivery." The title was changed in 1798 to "The Supreme Judicial Court," and this in 1843 to "The Supreme Court." A law of 1780 made judicial and legislative offices incompatible.

Nature destined Rhode Island for a great commercial and industrial career. Numerous rivers furnish abundant water power; a long coast line, indented with harbors, offers wharfage facilities for innumerable water craft of all kinds. Many saw mills and grist mills had been established by the middle of the seventeenth century. As early as 1646, a ship of one hundred and fifty tons was built in the colony. Before this, Callender says, "About 1642–3, there were two trading houses set up in the Narragansett country; one by Mr. Wilcockes and Mr. R. Williams, the other by Mr. Richard Smith." Smith's was the first of these to be established, and Roger Williams's was the second. With which one Wilcockes was connected, and how, is not known, but it is thought that he was not Williams's partner, as Callender's state-

The Burnside Statue, Providence.

ment seems to imply. No seventeenth century business house remains in the state, but the firm of Brown & Ives runs back, with slight change of name, to 1731.

Already by 1658, Rhode Island commerce was a considerable affair. Wealthy Jewish families began to settle at Newport, aiding the infant trade by their

Casino, Narragansett Pier.

means and their shrewdness. Ship building multiplied, and with it naturally the related trades, such as the manufacture of tar, cordage, and general ship stores.

were offered to induce industries to settle in the state, though when it was found that any did not naturally flourish here the bounties were withdrawn. The slave trade was for years an extensive and profitable Rhode Island industry. In 1790, Providence had a larger ocean tonnage than New York, and more commerce than any other town of its size in America. Newport had reached the height of its prosperity twenty years before, when it had "17 manufactories of sperm oil and candles, 5 rope walks, 1 brewery and 22 rum distilleries." By the beginning of the nineteenth century, Rhode Island industry had passed through an agricultural, and was in a commercial stage. Manufactures were still in their infancy. In the year 1790, Samuel Slater brought into practical use some clumsy

City Hall, Providence.

During the Revolution a great number of vessels for the defence of the American cause were built and fitted out in Rhode Island. Narragansett Bay, at first a barrier keeping the colonists apart, gradually became the highway for easy intercourse among the colonists themselves and between them and the rest of the world.

Early in the eighteenth century foundries were established and axes nad scythes manufactured. Even so early, bounties

machines for spinning by water power, the first successful experiment of the kind in America. This innovation opened a new era in the growth of Rhode Island. Though the state still retained for many years great commercial importance, manufacturing was, by 1800, certain to lead.

The manufacture of woollens began at

Fort Dumpling.

Peace Dale in 1804. Looms were used here ten years later, and power looms at North Providence in 1817.

Newport Harbor.

In 1810, sheeting ranged in price from thirty-five to seventy-five cents per yard. Cotton and woollen mills arose with marvellous rapidity. In 1807, there were twelve cotton mills, in 1831, one hundred and sixteen. These industries begat others, as the manufacture of machinery, stationary, and locomotive engines, and nearly all sorts of heavy iron goods.

The jewelry business, for which Rhode Island is now so celebrated, rose at about the same time with the cotton industry.

are made at the Rhode Island Locomotive Works. In the manufacture of screws, files, and fine machinery, Providence is one of the foremost cities of the world. At Bristol, reside and work the Herreshoff brothers, whose yachts more and more surprise the public. Westerly granite has a national reputation; the lime burned in Lincoln is said to be the best made.

Rhode Island holds a unique place of honor in the development of the Ameri-

Truro Street, Newport.

A system of plating was introduced by Nehemiah Dodge early in this century. Jewelry shops multiplied rapidly, and the skilled workmen necessary in this business have become an important factor in the population. The artistic silver work of the Gorham Manufacturing Company is known to all. Heavy machinery of the highest quality is turned out in Rhode Island. The Corliss engine is widely known and its work has contributed immensely to the material prosperity of the country. The Harris-Corliss and the Armington-Sims engine are highly esteemed both at home and abroad. The Brown and Sharpe machinery and tools are standards in their kind the world over, having in exactness no rivalry. Locomotives of the greatest excellence

can fisheries. Till half a century ago, the old barbed hook and shore seine were in use here as elsewhere. Then a great stride forward was made by the invention of the trap and the purse seine. The trap is in the form of a sugar box with top off and one end out. It is anchored in the water, with a fence of twine from one side of it to the shore. The fish swim to the fence, then turn to swim around it, thus making their way into the trap. The original trap was a crude affair, for the fish could swim out as well as in, making constant attention necessary to capture them before their exit. In 1883, William R. Rose, of Tiverton, set for the first time the famous Rose trap, a marked improvement over the old instrument. It holds all the fish that enter it,

View in Roger Williams Park, Providence.

and it can be set in the open sea as well as near land. Another clever Rhode Island invention for catching fish is the fyke net, consisting of a series of tunnels set in line with each other, and held in position by stakes, with a twine fence to inveigle the fish just as in the case of the trap. But the greatest labor-saver ever invented for reaping the harvests of the sea is the purse seine, devised by the Tallmans, of Portsmouth. To James B. Church, of Tiverton, is due the credit of introducing steamers for menhaden fishing, which soon revolutionized the whole business. The first steamer for this use was built by the Herreshoffs, of Bristol, the first steam vessel which they ever constructed. She was called *The Seven Brothers* and was launched early in 1870.

It will be seen from all this that ingenuity and industry, not natural resources, have given the state its great wealth. The population, 345,506 according to the census of 1890, has an assessed per capita valuation of $931.28, a figure higher than that for any other state. In 1885, the entire population of the state was 304,284, of whom 201,138, or 66.3 per cent were engaged in gainful occupations. Of these last 71,695 persons, being 35.5 per cent., were employed in manufacturing and mechanical pursuits.

Of these 22,694 were making cotton goods; 8,774 woollen goods; 8,486 constructed buildings; 4,673 made clothing; 4,524 wrought metals; 4,520 manufactured machines and machinery, and 4,248 jewelry. The rest, viz., 18,327, were distributed among thirty-five other manufacturing or mechanical industries. Of capital, $21,154,255 was employed in the making of cottons, $8,568,450 in woollens. Messrs. B. B. & R. Knight, of Providence, are the greatest cotton manufacturers in the world, operating 404,911 spindles, and last year, turning 53,000 bales of cotton into about 100,-000,000 yards of cloth. Next (for Rhode Island) comes the Lonsdale Company, the Goddard Brothers, agents, with 183,-578 spindles, each revolving 9,600 times a minute during work hours.

Within recent years Rhode Island has found its Bay a new source of wealth. A novel industry has arisen, in which the famous Rhode Island clam nobly does his part, that of catering to the comfort of those who summer on our coasts. The state, with its numerous islands, has about three hundred and fifty miles of salt-water line, an average of about one mile for each four miles of area. All along the shore, from Watch Hill round to Seaconnet Point, and on Block

Island people find delightful opportunities for rest. For miles charming villas and cottages dot the sides of the Bay. Narragansett Pier, Block Island, and Watch Hill are sought by great companies each season; yet Newport still denies the existence of her rival as a watering place. The main business of this city is done during the warm months, when its population is swollen by guests from all parts of the world. With its wide beaches, beautiful walks and drives, elaborate summer homes, and unsurpassed natural beauties, it so attracts, that people who visit it once come again and again. The Old Stone Mill invests the place with an air of mystery, while Fort Adams opposite its wharves and the naval vessels frequently in its harbor give it much of the dignity of a national capital.

The Town of Brandon, Vermont (1897)

THE TOWN OF BRANDON, VERMONT.

By Augusta W. Kellogg.

URING the troublous times when New York, New Hampshire and Massachusetts were contending for possession of the New Hampshire Grants (now the State of Vermont), a settlement was begun there on the northern frontier of a chain of sixteen townships, to which was given the Indian name of Neshobe. There were five young men who, determined to hew homes for themselves out of the primeval forest, spent the summer of 1761 upon the ground; but, as winter approached, four of the pioneers returned to the more comfortable quarters whence they had come. Only one, Amos Cutler, a blacksmith, twenty-four years of age, remained, spending the winter — but for the companionship of his dog — entirely alone. One wonders whether he "stayed by the stuff" in a spirit of bravado or because he had no special ties elsewhere, or if perhaps the solitude were congenial to his temperament. However, with the summer his companions returned, and such progress was made in their work that it was never again necessary to flee from the rigors of the climate. It is said that Jedediah Winslow, a descendant of the Pilgrim, Edward Winslow, erected the first dwelling house.

Little is known of the settlers for the next quarter of a century. There are the usual traditions of incursions by savages, who, carrying off the robust, left the young and weak to perish. One tale, however, ends more happily. It is of Joseph Barker, who was led away captive, leaving a young wife and little child behind him. That night, alone and unfriended, Mrs. Barker gave birth to another baby. Fortunately assistance soon reached her from a neighboring settlement (now Pittsford), where later she was rejoined by her husband, who had feigned illness so successfully in the march northward as to be abandoned at Middlebury by his captors.

The name of Neshobe was changed in 1784 to Brandon, or Burntown, whereby an unusually disastrous fire seems hinted at. The situation that had been chosen for this settlement bespeaks both intelligence and foresight in its founders. There is no better land east of the Rocky Mountains than this watered by the Otter Creek, which runs from Dorset Pond through Addison and Rutland counties to pour itself over the pretty falls at Vergennes before starting on its eight mile course to Lake Champlain.

"Where from the dear incontinent caress
  Of mountains joying in so fair a child,
Slow Otter 'scaped through woody wil-
    derness,
  Illapsed into the lovelorn valley mild
  Of swaying vines, and weeping willows
    wild,
And many a bloomy grass and many a
    flower,

With fragrant kiss that the sweet way
beguiled;
Still in the rath, the late, the middle hour,
To stray through all its banks a bright,
continuous bower,
Neshobe was; a little lovely spot
You may have dreamed some drowsy
summer's noon,
But to have seen, has been above your
lot."

This "long line of intervale receives
annually the best of all top-dressings,
by the gentle overflow of the sluggish
stream, which subsides so quietly as
to leave its rich deposits, brought

mineral wealth." The State reports
describe "the town as situated on an
expanded terrace, or ancient sea-
beach, six hundred feet above the sea,
and, like everything in Brandon,"
they courteously add "this terrace is
well-formed and attractive to the eye."

In the southwest part of the town,
not far from the village, is a frozen
well, which, since 1858, the year of its
accidental discovery, has excited the
interest of such eminent scientists as
Sir Charles Lyell, Professors Agassiz,
Jackson and others who have visited

OTTER CREEK VALLEY.

down from the mountains, more
evenly distributed than could be
effected by any human skill."

Otter Creek receives as the Brandon contribution the Neshobe River,
which, rising at the foot of the Goshen
Mountains, is an outlet for Spring and
Burnell ponds, and in its serpentine
course through a light, sandy soil
drains a district ten miles in length.

According to geologists the town
of Brandon lies not only in "a portion
of one of the richest metalliferous districts of the world, but there is no
other town which furnishes a greater
variety or more extensive deposits of

it. This well lies between two nearly
parallel ridges of limestone, which are
about an eighth of a mile apart. It is
forty feet deep, the water very
clear, with pebbly bed. Ice forms in
the well no later than April, but if not
taken away remains usually through
the summer, while the stones are
coated with ice for four or five feet
above the water, the mercury marking
1° F. above freezing. The phenomenon of this frozen well is thus explained in the latest geological reports:
"The deposit is probably about the
age of moraine terraces, whose peculiarities we have supposed produced

by stranded icebergs, and that the gravel and sand among these were doubtless frozen (formed perhaps by successive layers of ice and gravel) tens of thousands of years ago, but marly clay and pebbles in interstratification is a poor conductor of heat. The conditions are like those of a huge sandstone refrigerator, whose increased and unusual effects beyond those of the ordinary refrigerator are due to the increased and unusual collection of poor conducting materials which form its sides. And more than the non-conducting power of the fragments is the evaporation, which would be large in large fragments. Coating of gravel and clay, twenty feet thick, protected from heat beneath by layer of impervious clay, stratum of pebbles, etc., etc., make, according to Prof. A. D. Hager, 'a perfect, improved refrigerator.'" This peculiar formation, called Hogback (see page 307), is solidly welded gravel in which are embedded larger stone and is a part of the above-mentioned ridges.

As early as 1810 an inexhaustible bed of decomposed brown hematite or bog iron ore was discovered, five or six feet below the surface of the ground, covered by strata of sand and ochre. The first attempt to convert this raw material into manufactured articles was made by Mr. Wait Broughton, who built a furnace with a stack chimney. This failed to "draw." In order to repeat his experiment he would be obliged to expend the remnant of his little fortune; but, encouraged by his wife, he ventured his all, with the result that in 1819-20 the furnace was in successful operation. This new industry, lasting for thirty years, built up a thriving town. The ore-bed teams brought their yellow loads to be weighed

on the village scales before being dumped in the "top-house" for smelting. The ore had been washed by putting it into the upper end of a long box perforated like a strainer and revolving in an inclined position while a stream of water passed through it. The ore rolled over and downwards, of course, falling from the lower extremity into a shallow vat. The blast furnace produced directly from this brown hematite a superior soft gray iron not liable to crack upon exposure to heat, and yielding thus treated fifty per cent pure iron.

Mr. Broughton's daughter married John Conant from Ashburnham, Mass., who, by the purchase of the Neshobe River water power did more than any other one person to advance the material interests of the town. He established grist and saw-mills, and succeeded to his father-in-law's iron business, to which was added in 1825 the manufacture of the first cooking-stoves made in the State of Vermont. It was a great invention for the time and revolutionized the culinary de-

THE PARK AND GROVE STREET.

partment of the New England kitchen. It superseded the old fire-place with its swinging crane of pots and kettles, the hearth-spiders on legs, and tin bakers for roasting before the blazing logs. "The Conant stove" had a fire-box, surmounted with a box-oven, an expanded pannier on each side for heating purposes, with large circular opening in the rear for griddle and wash-boiler, and doors at each end. These stoves went all over New England, and teams carrying them for shipment on Lake Champlain brought

Two hundred men, with machinery, were employed. The blasts, for some reason or other, were supposed to — and probably did — take place at midnight, thus greatly enhancing the mystery of a Dantean scene. It was most impressive to be admitted to the cave-like interior of the furnace, the floor of which was prepared with sand moulds branching on each side of one long, broad centre line. Here men whose children we knew and called by their baptismal names, even with whose own faces too we were more or

PARK STREET.

back the goods sent from New York or Troy via canal, river and lake. The introduction of cooking stoves was soon followed by that of box-stoves, and also of enormous potash kettles, much in use for the making of soft soap from the lye of wood ashes.

Meanwhile a new furnace was started three miles nearer the ore beds, where, in addition to iron, simple and pure, a variety of ornamental articles, like vases, statues and chairs, were manufactured. But the principal output at both furnaces was pig-iron. In 1845 twelve hundred tons were made, also eight hundred stove castings.

less familiar above ground, were, with bared breasts and brawny arms, ladling out from a boiling cauldron vast measures of molten liquid, which, slowly coursing across the black earth, sent out a blinding splendor of glowing flame. It was a weird scene, and those innocent men stand in memory as monsters of a nether-world.

A generation later the wheels for the Car Wheel Company were made in the village furnace. "At a blast lasting one hundred and eighteen days, 14,276 pounds of iron were averaged *per diem*." This was cast into wheels, and "by a process which hardened the

OLD BRANDON HOUSE.

of "variable quantities of protoxide and peroxide of iron and of deutoxide of manganese." As a similar paint could be produced in Pennsyl-

flange and surface of the rim covering the rail nearly an inch in depth, and the only part subject to wear, it polished like steel, while the tenacity of the body of the wheel, the part most liable to crack, was not at all diminished."

When the iron ore was washed as described above, there was released an ochre with a mass of decomposed feldspar, which at first went to waste, but later was filtered, fell into vats and, when settled, was shovelled off into drying houses. From this, mixed with oil, a coarsish sort of paint was made, by a company organized in 1864, under the name of the Brandon Paint Company,

with a capital of $300,000 and eighty acres of mineral fields. From five hundred to one thousand tons were made annually, consisting specifically

NEW BRANDON INN.

vania, nearer to the oil market, this industry was necessarily abandoned.

Another valuable mineral, the existence of which has been known here for upwards of half a century, is kaolin, or paper clay, sometimes called porcelain clay. It is among the best and largest deposits associated with the ochres and ores of iron and manganese. It is described technically thus: "When unadulterated it is snowy white, quite unctuous to the touch, slightly coherent, does not change color by being burned, and is extensively used in the manufacture of stone and earthen ware, porcelain, firebrick, paper and vulcanized India rubber. It is carefully elutriated, and when dried is packed and ready for market. It is applied to paper pulp in an impalpable powder, rendering it opaque and of good body at a much less expense than if white rags alone were used. Firebrick consist largely of kaolin and

THE SEMINARY.

arenaceous quartz, and as repeated burnings render the former more serviceable in resisting intense heat, the modus is to mould and burn bricks of it, then pulverize, mix with quartz sand, mould and burn again." The Brandon bed is eighty feet in depth and the bottom not in sight. Sir Charles Lyell thought this clay might eventually be more valuable than the iron.

Lignite exists only in small quantities, but preserves organic remains containing seeds and fruits varying in size from that of a fig to less than that of a barley-corn, and as these fossil seeds and fruit are unlike any vegetation now growing in this country, it is supposed that they have been transferred by water, and that the accumulation took place in an ancient estuary. The form is more or less obliterated, while the parts preserved (of course the hardest) are often botanically of slight value. The species are probably of the same age as the lignites and fruits of Oeningen, Switzerland.

It remains to speak of the marble quarries. The marble from those of the Brandon Italian Marble Company is clouded, and similar in appearance to the imported Italian, but having more character to its clouding. It is

beautiful when finished, and has a degree of hardness and strength of texture which makes it far more durable than the imported Italian for out-door exposure. There is also a pure white marble of great solidity and exquisite firmness but the quarry producing it is not now worked.

Other minerals not found in large quantities are black lead, a variety of psilomelane with implanted crystals of ore of manganese, scarcely differing from the sesqui-oxide of manganese, pyrolusite, copper and iron pyrites, galena, braunite, etc. There is a whole ledge of flux, while jail cell walls have been furnished from solid blocks of limestone from six to eight inches thick. There are two caves in limestone ledges which have been points of interest since their discovery in 1842. One of these contains a room from sixteen to eighteen feet square.

Vermont is full of pretty villages; and while Brandon may not be the prettiest among them, he would be a

ST. THOMAS CHURCH.

CONGREGATIONAL CHURCH.

bold man who tried to maintain that there is a prettier. From southwest to northeast, its longest diameter, is one mile, cut into nearly equal halves by the Neshobe River. Each half has its pretty park with fountain and trees, whence radiate the broad shaded streets.

"Two undulating lines of hill-top green
  Did hide the rising and the setting sun,
Yet that against the East, excelled, I ween."

This "excelling hill-top green" bars on the east the beautiful Park Street with its octuple row of trees embowering the entire length. At its junction with Franklin Street stands the handsome granite Soldiers' Monument, testifying by its long roll of honor that the town bore its full proportion of the loss of the State, which according to its population suffered more than any other in the North. On the one hand is the new Methodist church, on the other the old Congregational church with its mossed steps worn by many feet, now lying under the sod in the graveyard behind it. A charming new hotel built of marble and terra cotta stands on the site so occupied for over a hundred years. Passing a row of shops one comes by an easy descending grade to the bridge, near which are the bank, postoffice and town hall. Turning abruptly to the right is the steep street leading to the building of the old seminary, founded in 1806, and now occupied by a good graded school. The building itself, quite bare of ornament, is by actual measurement almost identical in size with the main building of Solomon's Temple — i. e., about 100 by 30 feet; and while the results attained there may have borne no comparison to the wisdom of the Oriental king, the fact has furnished a standard of interest and reality for Bible classes.

DR. C. A. THOMAS.

REV. W. G. T. SHEDD.

But this apart. Returning to the river and proceeding to a farther ridge, the lovely, gray-towered St. Thomas church is seen, fairly leaning against the green hillside; and just here begins the complement to the star-like arrangement on the other side of the river. The ancient militia ground is included in the breadth of two of the streets. Years ago it was the "chief resort of the trainers at their annual June drill, with their blue coats and white trousers and bell-crowned leather helmets with tall white and red plumes." General Burgoyne had said of the inhabitants of this region in 1777: "They are the most rebellious and warlike race on the continent and hang like a warcloud on my left." This spirit found expression in the "trainings" up to a date not so very far removed from the opening of our Civil War.

The old Baptist church faces this second park, and it is out from its doorway that the road leads to the Pine Hill Cemetery, two miles away. It is to an energetic ladies' association that this cemetery owes its charming rural beauty. An exquisite proportion between nature and art has been maintained, and it would not be easy to find a more attractive spot. From the number of lots belonging to whilom residents it would seem a common enough ambition among such to come back to the shadows of their native hills for their final sleep.

From the top of the Pine Hill itself is a grand panorama of the Lake Champlain valley, with the blue Adirondacks lying away on the horizon. One stone marks the grave of Richard Welch, who served under Wellington in the Peninsular War, receiving his death wound at the battle of Vittoria, June 22, 1813. The bullet lodged in the left leg. When the body was removed from the old to the new cemetery, there was found lying on the bottom of the coffin the fatal bullet flattened to the size and thickness of a large copper cent. The granite receiving tomb, a gift from Mrs. R. V. Marsh, stands near the entrance to the cemetery.

In this part of the town is the good old farm horse which, after drawing hay for twenty summers, was finally taken to Boston "to do depot work." No locomotive astonished him, no whistle affrighted; but one day, seeing a load of hay, he kicked up his heels and ran down Columbus Avenue like a wild creature. It was no part of his policy to betray his rural origin.

Mr. Charles M. Winslow has exerted an intelligent and practical influence upon the breeding of stock not only in the town, but in the state. He has held the position of secretary of the Ayrshire Breeders' Association most successfully for many years. At one time merino sheep raising was a profitable industry. Australian breeders valued this special breed for its extra weight of wool, which sometimes reached thirty-five or forty pounds. They readily brought $500 per head, and not infrequently $1,000

CONANT SQUARE.

blooded stock farm of Mr. H. C. Watson, who is doing much to raise the standard of both race and road horses. Since the days of the exceeding popularity of the Morgan horse, nothing will stir the blood of a Vermonter like the sight of a fine animal. A story is told of a was paid, while now half that sum could not be obtained.

The early rose potato craze too struck Brandon early in its career, and $5 per eye was not considered — by the seller — as exorbitant. Much attention has always been paid to floriculture, and several gardens, notably

THE MAIN STREET.

those of Messrs. John A. and C. W. Conant, Mrs. Button, Mr. Marsh and Mrs. Royal Blake were conspicuous. Drs. Woodward and Dyer continue to cultivate fine wall-fruit as well as flowers. From 1849 to 1856 Colonel David Warren conducted the manufacture of railroad cars in Brandon. Later the manufactory was used by the Howe Scale Company. All kinds of weighing machines were made under a patent issued in 1856 to the young inventors, Messrs. F. M. Strong and Thomas Ross. These scales took — and still bear, for they are now manufactured successfully in Rutland — the name of the purchaser from the patentees, John Howe.

By a coincidence at once singular and common, two young blacksmiths, *employés* at the New Furnace, received a stimulus or inspiration at the same moment, 1834, — the one, Thomas Davenport, thirty years of age, the other, Orange A. Smalley, ten years his junior, — the for-

mer from the fragments of a scientific book, the latter from a lecture given in an adjoining town. By these seemingly accidental means a simultaneous interest in magnetism was excited in these fellow laborers. Davenport heard that there was an

THE NESHOBE.

electro-magnet to be seen at the Penfield Iron Works in Crown Point, N. Y. Thither he betook himself, and found it to consist of a piece of steel bent in the shape of a horse-shoe wound about with copper wire and connected with a galvanic battery. Its weight was but three pounds, and by it 150 pounds of iron could be lifted. It had been used for charging or magnetizing pieces of steel, which were set in a cylinder for "separating" iron ore. Davenport was so happy as to secure this for $18. He carried it home, and experiments were immediately begun, which resulted in obtaining rotary motion by electro-magnetism. There was much excitement over the marvel, and Davenport prophesied that "in a few years steamboats would be propelled by this invisible and mysterious power." Let it be remembered that this was uttered more than a dozen years before the first steam railroad was built in Vermont.

The "Electrical Engineer" of January 7, 1891, thus described the machine. "A permanently magnetized bar was supported at its centre of gravity like a magnetic needle. By placing the pole of an electro-magnet in proximity to the imaginary circle described by the horizontal swing of the bar, and then breaking the circuit by hand at properly-timed intervals, it was found that the bar could be kept in continuous rotation. This proved

STEPHEN A. DOUGLAS.

to be the key to the solution of the problem of the electric motor." The little machine was taken to Middlebury College, and exhibited to Prof. Turner, who declared: "Gentlemen, what you have invented is not a perpetual motion; it is nothing less than a new motive power." Another member of the learned body, Professor Fowler, expressed his belief that the dozen curious bystanders "were then witnessing the first exhibition of what would prove to be one of the greatest inventions of the 19th century." It was not until the invention had reached this stage that Davenport learned —from Stillman's Chemistry — the names of the instruments he had made or of the materials he had used. His wife cut her one silk gown, a wedding gift from her father, into narrow strips, to be used in insulating the helices of the new machine. Davenport and Smalley connected their houses by a wire, on which they transmitted messages by means of electricity, using a battery. This battery they called "cups."

Davenport removed to New York and began the publication of *The Electro-Magnet*, which was printed, as the paper claimed upon its title-page, "by a machine propelled by electro-magnetic force."

Prof. Samuel F. B. Morse, of the New York University, was much interested in electricity, and had often spoken of his intention to experiment.

THE BIRTHPLACE OF STEPHEN A. DOUGLAS.

He was struck with Davenport's machine, and began at once to improve upon it. Davenport's telegraph for the sending of communications over long distance, had twenty-four wires, one for each letter of the alphabet. Professor Morse kept but one, abolishing the other twenty-three. There is but little doubt that Morse borrowed the basis of his invention from Davenport, just as Davenport was indebted to Henry for his initial steps. Morse applied his alphabet to Davenport's discovery. Among his other inventions was a model, two and a half feet in diameter, of a circular railway, embodying every essential element of the modern electric road. He also experimented in driving machines and an electric piano, since so successfully developed. A German baron purchased secretly, from a workman, drawings of some of Davenport's best models, for which the German Diet voted him a reward of $40,000. Thomas Davenport was born in Williamstown in 1802, and died at the age of 49 years. His eldest son, George Davenport, was killed at the Battle of the Wilderness, and his name leads all the rest on the Soldiers' Monument in the town.

Another native inventor was Patrick Welch, a printer by trade. He produced a type-distributing machine of such merit as to procure him a gold medal from the French Exposition of 1867.

Brandon has given birth to at least one man who has achieved a national reputation in political affairs, viz., Stephen A. Douglas. He was born in 1813, and apprenticed in boyhood to the cabinet-maker's trade. It is said that he originated the saying: "Vermont is a good State to be born in, provided you emigrate early." In accordance with this theory he went West and began, when about twenty years old, the study of law. When in middle life he was elected to the Senate, his power in debate was so marked as to earn him the title of the "Little Giant." Once when abusive language was used towards him, he rose with dignity and said: "What no gentleman should say, no gentleman need answer." In 1858, when Kansas was

AT FOREST PARK FARM.

secede from this Union without further cause, I am in favor of their having just so many slaves and just so much slave territory as they can hold at the point of the bayonet and no more."

"Every man must be for the United States or against it; there can be no neutrals in this war —only patriots and traitors."

asking for admission into the Union, the burning question whether she should come in as a slave or a free state was the subject of the famous debate between Douglas and Abraham Lincoln. Douglas insisted that the people of Kansas should be allowed to vote upon their own Constitution and not compelled to accept the fraudulent adoption of the Lecompton Constitution, which fastened slavery upon them. But when the cloud of civil war broke over the land, even before Lincoln had time to issue the proclamation calling for troops, Douglas's offer of support and co-operation was in the President's hands. Peril to the country blinded him to sectionalism, and he exclaimed: "Give me a country where my children can live in peace; then we can have room to settle our political differences." Of secession he said: "There is no justification, nor any pretence of any. If they will remain in the Union I will go as far as the Constitution will permit to maintain their just rights, and I do not doubt but a majority in Congress would do the same. But if the Southern States attempt to

The birthplace of Douglas remains almost unchanged as it has been in the eighty-seven years and more of its existence. The huge chimney, quaint door and high roof make it an excellent example of early New England architecture.

Brandon can lay claim also to one of the foremost of American Biblical scholars, Thomas Jefferson Conant, born in 1802. He occupied the chair of Hebrew and Biblical criticism in Hamilton University in 1838, and was in the faculty when that institution was removed to Rochester, N. Y. He was prominent among the revisers of the Bible, Genesis, Job and the Psalms coming especially under his hand.

The first newspaper to be printed in the town was *The Vermont Telegraph*, established in 1829, by Orson S. Murray, but was afterwards made an anti-slavery organ by Jedediah Holcomb under the name of *The Voice of Freedom*. Later changes were to the *Vermont Union Whig*, *The Brandon Post*, and *The Brandon Union*, which is at present a very live and attractive sheet. The Rev. Nathan Brown, one of the earliest mission-

JUDGE EZRA JUNE.

aries to India, was for a short time an editor of the *Telegraph*. His experiences abroad were terrible, among them the repeated exhumations of his dead child by the native Indians, for the purpose of despoiling the grave. At last, after vain attempts to secure a permanent resting-place for his little one, the poor father brought the few bones remaining from a feast of jackals to this country for burial. Mr. Brown went later to Japan, where when over sixty years old he learned the Japanese language, into which he translated the New Testament. His poem "The Missionary Call" first printed in Brandon, was sung by Japanese before enthusiastic thousands on the occasion of the National Missionary Meeting at Minneapolis in 1896.

The Congregational Church was

Ex-Gov. E. J. ORMSBEE.

recently remodelled with good taste. It contains a unique pulpit of flawless white marble, a gift to the society from Mr. Edward D. Selden, now of Saratoga Springs. With no special dissensions, this church has had a large number of pastors, some of them of exceptional ministerial capacity — Rev. Ira Ingraham, Rev. Harvey Curtis, dear to the hearts of children; Rev. Francis B. Wheeler, and the present incumbent, Rev. William Smart. For one short year, 1844-5, this church enjoyed the ministrations of Dr. William G. T. Shedd. Naturally he was called almost immediately to a wider sphere of usefulness, and accepted first a professorship in the Vermont University, and then in the Union Theological Seminary of New York city. He is well known in the literary world as editor of the works of Samuel T. Coleridge.

It is a sad pleasure to recall the men and women who labored here to build up the kingdom of God. Of the former, one of the most eccentric was David M. June, a descendant of one of the first settlers. He was an honest man and shrewd, much opposed to a specially educated ministry. In some of the many interregnums of regular

BRANDON ITALIAN MARBLE COMPANY'S QUARRY.

organized in 1785 by five men and five women. The first meetings were held in a log cabin. The present house of worship is the fourth, and has been

pastorates, he had opportunities to apply his theories, with appalling results of startling personalities and vain repetitions in prayer such as would have convinced a less opinionated man of the error of his ways. He had an inconvenient habit of riding up to his neighbors' doors, and, summoning the busy housewife from her morning duties by a brisk knock with the butt of his whip, calling out: "Do you believe in the Lord Jesus Christ this morning?" A man of very different temperament was one who never dared, when repeating the Lord's Prayer, to leave the phrase, "Thy will be done," without conditions, but immediately added, "measurably, at least, O Lord."

The Baptist church had for its devoted pastors, for forty years, the Rev. C. A. Thomas. He did not belong so much to his society and de-

ENTRANCE TO PINE HILL CEMETERY.

nomination as to the whole town. Both he and his excellent wife were the valued friends of all, young and old. For many years the baptisms took place in the Neshobe River, whose waters, even on Sunday, were heavily tinged with the ochery sediment deposited by the washings of the iron ore. It was not uncommon when women descended into the stream to see their light skirts belly out on the surface of the water as if "making cheeses," and when, as often happened, the gown was familiar under more everyday aspects, the impression upon a childish imagination was peculiar.

The story of Brandon would lose an impressive feature if Judge Ezra June were omitted. He was a factor

in the education of successive sets of young girls as they advanced into the ranks of womanhood, especially perhaps, in his Sunday school teaching, but in divers other ways also. His enthusiastic teaching of the Psalms, who that heard him can ever forget? As a bachelor his opinion on the verse, "A good woman is a crown to her husband," had special weight. He appreciated the book of Job, and loved certain Psalms so much that his very intonations in reading them ring in the ears yet, after forty years have passed. Sunday was always a field-day for him, and the inspiration caught from the pulpit or from his own meditations bore fruit in many ways all through the week. On Monday mornings, especially, it was his delight, armed with a favorite book or a new essay, to exact the attention of the young friend selected for instruction. Gradually books of reference were collected, a dictionary here, a pile of cyclopædias there, a history or two were added, and the subject under consideration was thoroughly sifted. Who shall say what help and stimulation lay therein? Judge June cared for nature. An unusual cloud, a wonderful effect of light, would arouse him to a high pitch of enthusiasm. Walking with him once through the little park, when the tree-stems were sharply defined on the snow, he brought his stick down emphatically, and exclaimed: "You never had a collar embroidered like that!" It was an exciting day for the whole village when he went to Boston to hear Jenny Lind's first concert in America. His own excitement was intense, yet subdued by a sense of privilege. Nothing in his experience quite equalled that, though the first coming of the

GRAVEL FORMATION ON HOGBACK.

steam railway train through the still country meadows might almost be compared to it.

That was in 1848. "Brandon had subscribed for more capital stock than any other three towns in the state outside of bids made by contractors," and the interest in the undertaking was enormous. Every town along the route had prepared a collation, and the directors, beginning early in the day, had been feasted from Massachusetts to Vermont. It was no wonder if the stoutest trencher-man began to flag at last, as Bellows Falls, Rutland, Pittsford, and Brandon hospitality was proffered. All this junketing had consumed the day, and it was in the splendid light of the cool autumnal evening that we finally saw the sight for which we had longed. A little group stood reverently on an overlooking ledge where the tangle of bitter-sweet and wild grape-vine sheltered them from the chill night air, while Judge June recited Job's words about the leviathan.

E. J. Ormsbee, who served his State as governor in 1886, resides in Brandon. His honorable war record beginning as second lieutenant in Company G, First Vermont Volunteers, ended as Major in the Third Division of the First Army Corps of the Army of the Potomac. He was Chairman of the Commission to treat with the Pi-Ute Indians in Nevada, and in 1893 went to Samoa as Land Commissioner. The products and curiosities brought by Ex-Governor and Mrs. Ormsbee from Samoa would worthily stock a small museum.

Mr. Frank Knowlton, a scientist connected with the Smithsonian Institute in Washington, D. C., is another citizen of whom Brandon may well be proud. His work in scientific terminology appears in the Century Dictionary.

As to the scenery of Brandon, the views in all directions are fine, in some directions superb. It is always a question whether the creek or the hill road shall be taken to Pittsford, "the best all-round farming town in the United States," but by neither road must the quaint, foreign hamlet of Proctor, three miles beyond, be missed. It is perched on a marble hillside as steep as an Alp. The picturesque Sutherland Falls glint in and out of the wooded country, hanging like a foamy veil before a rugged face. In an opposite direction one sees where Lake Dunmore lies in the lap of solemn Moo-sa-la-moo. Hidden away in the forest are the beautiful Llana Falls, so often painted by their loving friend, Mr. C. W. Sanderson, the Bos-

LLANA FALLS.

LAKE DUNMORE.

ton water-colorist. The Sierra-like outline of the Adirondacks jagging the horizon across the blue Champlain is as noble a prospect as there is in all New England.

One can hardly go amiss; if he auger his way up through the woods, criss-crossing the spiral stream to Silver Lake, minted with Nature's superscription; if he climb to the top of a Green mountain, following an excellent road along "the Branch," which leaps almost into his eyes, so straight and narrow is the way, till he must pitch over into Rochester; everywhere are solemn mountains, dancing streams and little hills. Especially lovely are the valley views; the Otter creek full to its wooded banks, the old-fashioned covered bridges, with streaks of sunshine lying golden across the sandy planks; the quick rise and fall and sudden turn of the road, the magnificent plumes of the elm, the rounded contours of the beech and maple, the sumach clumps, all conspire to make each drive seem more beautiful than the last.

Litchfield, Connecticut (1897)

LITCHFIELD FROM LOCUST KNOLL.

LITCHFIELD, CONNECTICUT.

By William L. Adam.

CONNECTICUT has never lacked individuality. Among the smallest of the United States, with a population less than that of Brooklyn, the fourth city of the Union, it is in some respects not unlike a wide-spread municipality. Its public men and its politicians know one another intimately and thoroughly. The representation in its lower legislative body is by towns, not by population, thus giving its little hamlets equal weight with the larger boroughs and cities, though there is but one of the latter that numbers one hundred thousand souls. Its narrow valleys are teeming hives of labor. The home of great insurance corporations and of varied industries, it contains the two model manufacturing establishments of New England, whose equal, with one exception, our more than two score states cannot furnish. It was the first community in history to give to the world a written constitution organizing a form of government in which its powers are defined, a model which to this day stands substantially unimproved. It is the seat of institutions of learning of national and world-wide reputation.

High up on the western hills of this "Land of Steady Habits" sits Litchfield, shire town of the county whose name it bears. The village, with twin parks or public enclosures at its centre, reaches out in its South Street and its East, its West Street and its North. The last is a magnificent way, broad and straight, with ample plats of grass, bordered by fine old houses with spacious yards, the ideal of a New England street, while its southern contin-

99

OLIVER WOLCOTT, THE ELDER.

nation curves gently past houses of much the same sort and once the homes of distinguished men and women. At an altitude of more than twelve hundred feet above the sea, it lies on the very crest of the ridge of high land which runs north and south through the town, making it literally a village, if not a city, set upon a hill. Its lofty position gives to the passer through its streets the exhilaration born of the upper air. The streets, seemingly level with the horizon, are swept by every breeze that blows, and at some seasons of the year by much more than a breeze,—for on one of the outlying ridges the local stage driver once told me, with Yankee keenness, a man might shave of a winter's morning without soap.

Of the Litchfield of the present I shall have but little to say. It is now best known as a town of summer residence and resort, after the fashion of its northern neighbor, Lenox. It is worthy of its reputation. Its handsome houses, both ancient and modern, the attractive drives, to Bantam

Lake nestling at the foot of the hill, to Goshen on the north over the perfection of a country road, to Cornwall on the west, the short stroll eastward to the summit of Chestnut Hill, crowned by the neat Quaker colored barns of the Echo farm, made famous by Mr. Starr's superb herd of Jersey cattle,—all these will charm the visitor.

But we would now rather direct our steps toward that remote New England town which the Rev. Dan Huntington, called in 1798 from his position as tutor in Yale College to the pastorate of the Congregational Church in Litchfield, described as "a delightful village on a fruitful hill, richly endowed with its schools, both professional and scientific, and their accomplished teachers, with its venerable governors and judges, with its learned lawyers, and Senators and Representatives, both in the National and State departments, and with a population enlightened and respectable." Mr. Huntington added to his description the remark, "Litchfield was now in its glory." It is without doubt true that at this time the isolated village, remote from the metropolis of New York and far away from the bustling, headstrong capital of New England, contained a population certainly not excelled, if indeed it were equaled, in intelligence, education and culture on this side of the Atlantic. Seventeen of its heads of families were college graduates, sixteen of the seventeen having taken their degrees at Yale, seven had been captains in the Continental army, four of them rising to the rank of general officers, four served their state in Congress, two became chief justices, and two governors of Connecticut. Nor

MRS. OLIVER WOLCOTT.

were its capable and accomplished women a whit behind their husbands and their fathers. In Washington's second administration, no woman in public life was more marked for the charms of her mind and her manner than was Mrs. Oliver Wolcott, the wife of the Secretary of the Treasury. Said the British minister, Mr. Liston, one day, to General Tracy, then United States Senator from Connecticut and one of the most brilliant men of his time, "Your countrywoman, Mrs. Wolcott, would be admired even at St. James's." "Sir," replied the doughty general, "she is admired even on Litchfield Hill!"

The town had before this time played no inconsiderable part in the affairs of our infant nation. Owing to its position it had been chosen as a place of safe keeping for the military stores needed by the colonists in carrying on the war of the Revolution, and its comparative inaccessibility led to its selection as a suitable spot for the confinement of royalist prisoners. As many as twenty or thirty of the latter, varying in rank, were some-

THE WOLCOTT HOMESTEAD.

times to be found at once in the Litchfield jail. The most distinguished of them were David Matthews, the royalist mayor of New York, sent thither in 1776, but al-

OLIVER WOLCOTT, THE YOUNGER.

lowed to stay in Captain Seymour's house, where he was under watch for months, and the Hon. William Franklin, royal governor of New Jersey. The latter was a son of Benjamin Franklin and had been governor of New Jersey from 1763 up to the time of his capture in 1776 by the Whigs, who sent him for custody to Governor Trumbull of Connecticut, a bird of a decidedly different feather. By Trumbull's order, he was confined at Middletown and Wallingford, but in 1777, by order of the Council of Safety of Connecticut, he was conveyed under guard of the sheriff of Hartford County to the Litchfield jail and there confined, "without pen, ink, or paper." In the records of the Council mention is made of two orders for one hundred pounds each, toward the expense of the guard over the governor. Here he remained till 1778, the same year that his distinguished father went as our minister to France, when an exchange was made in his favor for Mr. McKinley, president of Delaware.

After the capture of New York by the British, Litchfield became a principal station on the highway leading from Hartford to the Hudson. Here were erected a storehouse for the provisions of the Continental army, a depot for other military stores and a workshop. At each of these places, as well as at the jail, guards were on duty night and day, and a general military air pervaded the town. Most of the general officers of the army were here at various times, Lafayette among the number, while General Washington himself more than once enjoyed the hospitality of its pleasant homes. On one of his visits, he was a guest at the house of Oliver Wolcott, one of the most notable houses in the town, the resort of "Brother Jonathan," Washington's favorite, Governor Trumbull, and the house to which were brought the leaden remains of George III., pulled from their resting place on the pedestal in the Bowling Green in New York, and molded by the daughters of Governor Wolcott and various fair friends of theirs among the village maidens into bullets for the Continental forces. Some of these bullets were used by the troops who opposed Tryon's invasion, causing a facetious writer of that day to declare that the King's troops had melted majesty fired at them. Litchfield also gave to the Revolution one of its most picturesque characters; for, although he removed to Cornwall early in his life, Ethan Allen must be added to the long list of distinguished sons and daughters who have brought renown to this their native town, causing it to claim "to have been the birthplace of more noted men and women than any other place of its population in the country." Its population need not have been limited if all its daughters had proved as fruitful as one, the headstone of whose grave bears this inscription: "Here lies the body of Mrs. Mary, wife of Dea. John Buel, Esq. She died November 4, 1768, aged 90, having had 13 children, 101 grandchildren, 247 great-grandchildren, and 49 great-great-grandchildren; total 410. Three hundred and thirty-six survived her."

MARY ANN WOLCOTT.

The Rev. Mr. Huntington remained

THE PORCH OF THE WOLCOTT HOUSE, SHOWING THE ORCHARD.

the man in whose presence, whenever I met him, I always felt so small as in his. Settled in an obscure corner, remote from all the world, he soon burst forth in his sermons on 'Dueling' and 'The Government of God Desirable,' with a power that startled the land. There was an inward spring that drove the machine with a power often sublime, always effective, and wonderful in results." This is a delineation of one who for full half a century was a power in the land, and who for forty years of it was, "if not the ablest, the most noted clergyman in America." "Very pleasant," says one, "are the chapters in which the daughters of Lyman

in his pastorate about eight years, to be followed, in 1810, by that sturdiest of New England divines, Lyman Beecher, who for sixteen long years lived and wrought and preached in Litchfield as only Lyman Beecher could live and work and preach. Here, too, were born the most widely known of his children, and here was reared that family which, whatever may be the eccentricities of its members, can certainly never be accused of being tame nor commonplace, and whose abilities combined in the filial work of reproducing the story of their father's career "could make the life of a plain country minister as interesting as a novel and as instructive as a work on moral philosophy." In 1820, John Todd, then a junior in Yale College, driven from New Haven by ill health, journeyed northward, bearing a letter from Professor Goodrich to "Mr. Beecher of Litchfield." His first impressions he never forgot, and years afterwards he recorded his ideas concerning this marvelous personality: "Lyman Beecher was a thunderbolt. You never knew where it would strike, but you never saw him rise to speak without feeling that so much electricity must strike. I have his memoir lying on my table. No other man could sit for such a portraiture. . . . I have never yet met

THE FIRE DEPARTMENT BUILDING.

Beecher, after an interval of almost half a century, narrate their reminiscences of life in Litchfield, and the chapter in which Harriet Beecher Stowe gives her early reminiscences of the life there reads like an idyl." Here Lyman Beecher's character matured and developed, from that of the young man of thirty-five whose coming the quiet town saw, into that of the intellectual giant of fifty who left it. I doubt not that these sixteen

In 1826, in the old meeting-house **on** the north side of the green, **were** preached the famous "Six Sermons on Intemperance," whose effect, **when** published, was greater than that **of** almost any other series of discourses ever delivered in the American pulpit. The same ceaseless worker, in 1812, organized here the first auxiliary **of** the American Board. Thus **from** year to year his ceaseless task **was** wrought, till eighteen years beyond

SITE OF THE LYMAN BEECHER HOMESTEAD.

years had no pleasanter predecessors or followers in the life of that keen, restless, dauntless soul. It was while living here that Mr. Beecher's attention was turned toward the question of intemperance, which had then hardly been agitated in America. He was chairman of a committee of the General Association appointed to consider the matter and drew up the report himself. It is hardly necessary to say that it was a stirring one. He declared that it was the most important paper which he ever wrote.

the allotted life of man failing powers of mind and body set their fatal seal upon a life which had else known no rest.

Very conspicuous is the part which has been played in Litchfield life and history by Governor Oliver Wolcott and his family. The son of Roger Wolcott, himself governor and chief justice of Connecticut, young Oliver came to Litchfield at the age of twenty-five, having already commanded a company of volunteers in the war against the French, pursued

LYMAN BEECHER.

the usual course of medical studies and begun the practice of his profession in Goshen. Like his sons after him, he was a graduate of Yale, a college so preëminent for the number of men which it sends forth equipped for public life. On the organization of the county of Litchfield in 1751, the legislature appointed him to the office of high sheriff, a position he held for more than twenty years. Hence his removal from Goshen to the shire town, which for forty-six years was to claim him for her own. The local historian says of him, "With a commanding personal appearance, dignified manners, a clear and cultivated intellect and a character for integrity far above the reach of suspicion, it is not to be wondered at that he became a favorite of the people among whom his lot was cast."

Between the windows in the south room of Judge McCurdy's historic house in Lyme stands a handsome round table, once the property of Ursula Wolcott. The daughter of Governor Roger Wolcott and the sister of Governor Oliver Wolcott,

this woman was not the least distinguished member of her illustrious family. Visiting in Lyme, she became aware that her second cousin, Matthew Griswold, was not insensible to her many charms. But Matthew was diffident and reserved, and, having already met with one disastrous adventure in his love affairs, was less disposed than ever to take the aggressive. One day, as she met him on the stairs, she asked, "What did you say, Cousin Matthew?" "I did not say anything," was the short reply. Not long after she met him again, and again the same question, "What did you say, Cousin Matthew?" Still the same reply. One morning she met him upon the beach and again queried, "What did you say, Cousin Matthew?" Once more came the same words, "I did not say anything." "It is time you did," was the quick, emphatic response. Something he did say, and thus Ursula Wolcott was able to gather about this round table and to introduce to us more of her immediate relatives and connections who were chief magistrates of their state than it has fallen to the lot of any other woman to do in this country, whose boast it is that it has no royal

THE CONGREGATIONAL CHURCH.

family. Her father was Governor Roger Wolcott; her brother was Governor Oliver Wolcott; her nephew was the second Governor Oliver Wolcott; her husband was Governor Matthew Griswold; and her son was Governor Roger Griswold.

Like John Adams and his son in Massachusetts, Oliver Wolcott and his son in Connecticut were men whose lives were passed almost without intermission in the service of the public. Gifted with capacity for

discharged for twenty-three years. In the meantime he was a judge of the Court of Common Pleas for thirteen years and a member of the Continental Congress for seven. On the fourth of July, 1776, his name went forth to the world subscribed to the Declaration of Independence. Early in the Revolution he was commissioned a brigadier general, and he was also a commissioner of Indian affairs, by appointment of Congress. He was major general of the militia of his state, and in 1786 was elected

WEST STREET.

affairs, they never shrank from the faithful performance of any task imposed upon them. Besides his activity in the affairs of his church and of the town of his adoption, serving the latter as moderator, selectman and committeeman, as occasion required, Oliver Wolcott the elder found time, in addition to his duties as sheriff, to represent Litchfield five times in the legislature. He was next a member of the Council or Upper House for fifteen years. Shortly after the beginning of this term he assumed the duties of judge of probate, which he

its lieutenant governor, and annually reëlected to that office for ten years till, in 1796, he was chosen by his fellow citizens to the highest office in their gift, the governorship. His son, Oliver, filled the gubernatorial chair for ten years, having previously been comptroller of his state, auditor and secretary of the United States treasury, judge of the United States Circuit Court and president of the Constitutional Convention of Connecticut. No wonder the historian of Litchfield prints the name of Oliver Wolcott in large letters in his record.

There is now perhaps no school of its kind for girls so well and so widely known as Miss Sarah Porter's school in the pleasant Connecticut sister town of Farmington. But even more widely known, perhaps, was Miss Sarah Pierce's school in the Litchfield of one hundred years ago, the first institution of its sort in the country. Begun in 1792, it gathered to itself in the forty years of its existence nearly fifteen hundred young women, the flower of the land. Its fame now lives only in the memory of their descendants; but to this school

The more one learns of it and the more one considers it, the more one wonders at the astonishing success of this school. In 1772, Tapping Reeve, then fresh from his studies and his tutorship in Princeton College, removed to Litchfield and began the practice of the law. His young wife, whom he married shortly afterwards, was Sally Burr, daughter of Rev. Aaron Burr, president of Princeton and granddaughter of the renowned Jonathan Edwards. Her brother, the notorious Aaron Burr, was for a time a student in the office

NORTH STREET.

and the visits of the parents and friends of its pupils was due no small part of the social life and splendor which blazed forth in this celebrated town during the early years of the republic.

Litchfield Hill is the Mecca of American lawyers. No educational institution in the country, considering the number of its students, can compare in the results of its teaching, I think it is not extravagant to say, with the Litchfield Law School, which like its neighbor, Miss Pierce's Seminary, was the first in the land.

of his brother-in-law, but before any systematic course of teaching was begun. The outbreak of the Revolution found young Burr all ready to swing into the current of excitement, and Litchfield saw him no more as a resident. Mr. Reeve at once took high rank as a lawyer, and twelve years after his coming he began the practice of taking students into his office to instruct them in the science of which he was so thorough a master. Up to the time of his appointment to the bench in 1798, more than two hundred of his pupils thus

THE OLD COURT HOUSE AND MANSION HOUSE.

tion, till failing powers compelled him to give up his chosen task. The school was simplicity itself. It was never incorporated and had no buildings of its own. Each judge lectured in his law office, a building in his own dooryard, and the students boarded where they could. The Hill is now, alas! a Mecca without a shrine, for both offices have since been removed, and nothing now remains of this institution but its fame, a fame, however, which has made the name of Litchfield known in every state of the Union.

instructed had been admitted to the bar. Finding then the duties too heavy to be borne alone, he associated with him James Gould, a former pupil, a graduate of Yale, where he had held a tutorship, and a man who was destined to become one of the most profound lawyers and jurists of his day. Together these two masters in law conducted this successful school till 1820, the year of the founding of the Cambridge Law School. Judge Reeve then retired, but Judge Gould for thirteen years more continued his work of instruc-

During the fifty years that the Litchfield Law School flourished, about one thousand students were graduated from its two small offices, a number not so large as that now to be found in any one year in the catalogue of more than one of our larger institutions of learning. But a list which includes such names as those of Woodbury of New Hampshire, of Seymour of Vermont, of

NEW COURT HOUSE AND MANSION HOUSE.

UNITED STATES HOTEL.

profession such a work as Gould's "Pleadings in Civil Actions." To Judge Gould's instructor and the founder of the school, Mr. Hollister, the Connecticut historian, pays this deserved compliment: "He was the first eminent lawyer in this country who dared to arraign the common law of England for its severity and refined cruelty in cutting off the natural rights of married women and placing their property, as well as their person, at the mercy of their husbands, who might squander it or hoard it up at pleasure. All the mitigating changes in our jurisprudence which have been made to redeem helpless woman from the barbarities of her legalized tyrant may be fairly traced to the author of the first American treatise on the Domestic Relations."

Ellsworth and Hubbard of Connecticut, of Clayton of Delaware and Mason of Virginia, of Morton and Metcalf of Massachusetts, of Hunt of New York and of John C. Calhoun is a marked list. Of this comparatively small number of students, sixteen became United States Senators, fifty members of Congress, forty judges of higher courts, eight chief justices of states, two justices of the Supreme Court of the United States, five cabinet ministers, several ministers to foreign countries, and one a Vice-President. Such were some of the careers of those who studied under a man whose mind took such delight in the intricate mysteries of special pleading, and who gave to his

BANTAM LAKE.

Why was it that this little country town became so noted? Of wealth, as we count wealth, there was but little. Of manufactures there are not and never have been any worth the name. Litchfield's most successful merchant, Julius Deming, a native of Lyme, accumulated a handsome fortune for his day. He made arrangements to import goods directly from the European markets. What merchant in a hill town, sixty miles from tide water, as Litchfield is from New Haven, and more than one

tury began. A great, square house, with broad halls, fine old wood work and pleasing proportions, it is to my mind the best kind of dwelling yet designed for our New England climate, one that will still be pleasing when its Mansard and Queen Anne successors shall have grown shabby and disreputable.

To live in a hill town is an advantage. The old New England fashion of putting the meeting-house on the highest land in the village was a good one. It was a misfortune to

SOUTH STREET.

hundred from New York by railroad, would now think of doing that? Part of the fortune so made was invested, in 1793, in a house which is still standing and, to my thinking, has been the chief ornament of the beautiful North street. It is said that the sum of two thousand dollars was spent upon its foundations before a timber was laid; and that was a far larger sum of money in 1793 than it is in these luxurious days one hundred years later. The lines of the house are as straight and its timbers apparently as sound as when this cen-

Williamstown that a quarrel caused the ugly brick structure at the foot of the slope in the President's yard to take the place of the old church at the head of the street. Fancy the Lenox meeting-house plumped down among the buildings of the village, its white spire peering up over the brick walls of Curtis's Hotel! Think you that Fanny Kemble would then have wished to be buried in its churchyard? The men and women of Litchfield did not have the strong characters they possessed because they were born or lived upon a hill; but living upon that hill gave to those characters a moral vigor and freedom not born of any crowded, lowland town, a vigor and freedom unconsciously absorbed with the very air they breathed.

The society of Litchfield was a democratic aristocracy,—using aristocracy in the best sense of the word. It was a society in which mind, not material things, was the ruling force. There was intelligence, learning and education of no common order. The people were wholly practical, useful and unselfishly devoted to the

Confederation, Congress and the bench, they were equipped, trained, efficient, and made their influence felt with a power not to be mistaken.

Litchfield was a creature of the times which gave it birth. No preceding age could have produced it. No future days may see its counterpart. It is true that many of its children have gained their fame by work not done in the historic town. The stamp of Horace Bushnell's distinctive individuality is set upon Hartford. It was in New York that Charles L. Brace did such splendid

SOUTH STREET IN WINTER.

public good. The men were all in politics and in politics for a purpose, not afraid of soiling their hands with political work and not afraid of being called practical politicians. Nor were they men who shunned public office. The Wolcotts, father and son, were perhaps the most conspicuous examples of this; but many of their neighbors differed from them only in degree. These men were willing to do hard, earnest work in town meetings and in the affairs of their school districts; and because they were thus willing, when called to the wider duties of the colony, the state, the

Christian work for children. But the day has passed when any town so small, even if it have the good fortune to be the birthplace of men and women of so much ability, can hope to keep so many of its noble sons and daughters within its borders and to attract so many of equal ability from abroad.

Within our own day a congressman, a governor and a chief justice of Connecticut have been near neighbors on South Street. But the political power of Litchfield has now well-nigh vanished. The town is no longer the seat of any institution of

LITCHFIELD FROM CHESTNUT HILL.

learning; the Wolcott house is now rented to strangers; the blood of Tapping Reeve flows in the veins of no descendant; the family of James Gould is widely scattered; no memorials mark the spots where these men taught so long and so well, —it is even difficult to obtain a catalogue of their school; only the elm trees now shade the ground where flourished Miss Pierce's Seminary; the corner where stood the dwelling of Lyman Beecher lies vacant; the house itself, moved from its old site, is now the wing of an asylum; the church which Beecher made historic long ago gave place to another, and even this, also moved from its old foundations, is no longer a house of worship. All is now tradition. But Litchfield is still a town of delightful memories, tinged with the melancholy induced by the thought of its departed glories; it is a place to which many still love to turn in summer days; and it is and will remain one of the most beautiful of old New England towns.

THE CASINO.

Manchester,
New Hampshire
(1897)

Manchester New Hampshire

By J. W. Fellows.

THE city of Manchester is located in the valley of the Merrimack, about fifty-five miles north of Boston. Its site is mainly upon a tableland about a hundred feet above the bed of the river, rising gradually to the hills on the north and east, but widening out into a comparatively level country on the south, while the Uncanoonucs and "Joe English Hill" present a bold and picturesque outline upon the western horizon. The city is well shaded, mostly by elms, and has sometimes been called the "Elm City of New England." It is properly styled the "Queen City of New Hampshire."

The early history of the city is interesting, from the many legendary and romantic stories of the Indians who occupied the country along the river from Nashua to the lakes on the north. There is no doubt that the powerful tribes over which Passaconaway is said to have ruled inhabited all this country, and that the stories oft repeated in prose and poetry of their skill in capturing the beautiful salmon

HON. SAMUEL BLODGETT.

117

VIEW OF MANCHESTER.

and the "gamy shad" at the Falls and their w a r l i k e achievements as well as their slight approach to the pursuits of civilization are well founded in fact. But while the romantic character of their history and the interest which dwells upon their hunting grounds, their wigwam villages and their savage prowess are fascinating and attractive, it is of the origin, growth and present industries of Manchester that we prefer to write.

Although Manchester has but recently celebrated her semi-centennial, there is much in her history to be proud of. Few cities have achieved a more honorable record in national and state affairs or accomplished greater work in the pursuits of peace and industry. Proud of her history and of the great events which have given her renown, Manchester is prouder still of her industrial prosperity and her preëminence as a commercial and manufacturing community; and as she looks with admiration upon the busy Merrimack flowing at her feet and catches the din and rattle of the loom and the hum and whir of the spindle as they reach the ear from her sister cities down the river, mingling with her own, she may realize truly that "Peace hath her victories no less renowned than war." She has a population of about fifty-five thousand people, active, industrious, energetic, engaged in all the various pursuits of life and characterized by the noble purpose of earning a livelihood by honest labor and discharging the duties of enlightened citizenship.

The first settlements within

GENERAL JOHN STARK.

number of people was 285, and in 1790, 362.

Derryfield had been represented at Bunker Hill, at Bennington and at Saratoga. Her gallant and intrepid Stark, with his neighbors and comrades, had rendered valiant service in the cause of freedom, and when peace and independence were achieved it took years of toil and hardship before the dawn of prosperity shone upon this little community. An uneventful period followed. Nothing of note seems to have occurred until 1794, when Samuel Blodgett, destined to perform a most important part in the building of Manchester, projected the great undertaking of constructing his canal around the Falls.

It is not known at what time the idea of building mills in Manchester and utilizing the power of the Merrimack first took form. Throughout the earlier history the Amoskeag Falls are frequently alluded to as being of great importance. In 1731 they had attracted the attention of Governor Belcher and several of "His Majesty's Council," who came to this part of the country for a "reconnaissance." Their report runs thus: "His Excellency was much pleased with the fine soil of Chester, the extraordinary improvements at Derry and the mighty Falls at Skeag." The Falls were, however, generally spoken of as valuable for fishing purposes, but were regarded as an obstruction to commerce

the boundaries of Manchester are said to have been made in 1722, by John Goffe, Benjamin Kidder and Edward Lingfield, near the Cohas River, in the southern part of the town. A few more families came in the succeeding years, and in 1733 Archibald Stark, John McNeil and John Riddle settled upon farms near the Amoskeag Falls. Other settlements were made in the vicinity, but the increase was slow. In 1751 the charter of the town of Derryfield was granted by Governor Benning Wentworth. The grant comprised parts of Chester, Londonderry and Harrytown. A year later the remaining portion of Harrytown was added to the original grant, and in 1853 portions of the towns of Bedford and Goffstown were annexed to the city, making about thirty-four square miles of territory.

There was no particular attraction to bring settlers into Derryfield, and in those early years the increase of population was not rapid. In 1775 the

THE OLD STARK HOMESTEAD.

THE MONUMENT TO GENERAL STARK.

perseverance and firmness of character. We cannot here say what is due to his memory, but the celebrated canals which bear his name and the great work which is being done in the manufactories of the city where he spent his life and fortune are far more eloquent than any eulogy. Truly "he builded better than he knew."

The work upon the canal was prosecuted with varied success for several years by Mr. Blodgett, until his private means were entirely exhausted. He pursued his undertaking against obstacles which would have disheartened the ordinary man. Freshets washed away his works; enemies maligned his character and threw every possible hindrance in his way. At one time he was cast into prison for debt, and those whom he had regarded as friends deserted him at the time when he was in the greatest need. But he persevered, never doubting that his final success would be complete. In 1798 he obtained a charter. At several times the privileges of a lottery were granted by the legislatures of New Hampshire and of Massachusetts to raise money for his work, and other expedients were resorted to.

In the meantime, the Middlesex canal in Massachusetts having shown a favorable record for business, parties

and the transportation of merchandise to the settlements along the river. It seems that the first thought of a canal which took form in Mr. Blodgett's mind was for the purpose of "locking lumber" around the Falls. He did not then dream of the future Manchester, and had no conception of the immense power waiting so long to be utilized for countless industries and the founding of a great city.

Mr. Blodgett was a man of natural ability and varied attainments. He was somewhat famous as a soldier and as a jurist, was possessed of considerable financial ability, and was noted for great

WEAVING ROOM IN THE AMOSKEAG MILLS.

BIRD'S-EYE VIEW OF THE AMOSKEAG MILLS.

interested there were encouraged to sustain his efforts. In presenting the subject to the public, he speaks enthusiastically about the advantages of commercial intercourse with the inhabitants of Massachusetts; and it is curious to note that emphasis is laid upon the fact that nine thousand and five tons of merchandise passed through the Middlesex canal in one season. Further aid was obtained from the Massachusetts legislature, and the locks were finished in the Blodgett canal in December, 1806. The first of

E. A. STRAW.

the following May was appointed for the grand opening, and the originator of this noble work, then more than eighty-three years of age, passed, upon a raft with a few friends, from the head of his canal through the locks into the Merrimack River. The full importance of this event was comprehended by no one, but the work laid the foundations of the city and inaugurated that splendid career which has given her high rank among the great manufacturing communities of the world.

In 1810 the name

REV. CYRUS WALLACE.

ticking was obtained. A new building was erected upon the island for a machine shop, and several boarding houses, stores and other business places were built in the village of Amoskeag. The goods manufactured soon acquired a reputation, and the "A. C. A." ticking, now known the world over, became a staple product.

The immense hydraulic power afforded by the Falls was now fully appreciated. Large tracts of adjacent land were purchased and it was soon determined to commence manufacturing upon a more extensive scale. In 1831 the charter of the Amoskeag Manufacturing Company was obtained and the company organized, and the proprietors engaged in the enterprise with energy and activity. In 1835, it having been determined that the east side of the river was the most desirable for extensive works, they acquired all the lands which seemed necessary for the purposes of the corporation, and obtained control of the

JUDGE SAMUEL D. BELL.

of Derryfield was changed to Manchester. It is said the name was suggested by Mr. Blodgett from the idea that the city would be the Manchester of New England, rivaling her sister manufacturing city across the Atlantic.

The manufacture of cotton upon the Merrimack was started at Amoskeag Falls in 1809 by Mr. Benjamin Prichard and others, who erected a saw mill in that part of Goffstown now included within Manchester. The name of the mill was "The Amoskeag Cotton and Wool Factory." No very marked success attended this enterprise. The mills changed owners several times, and were operated with little or no profit until about 1825, when a new company was formed by capitalists from Boston, which commenced business immediately. Mr. Oliver Dean, one of the principal owners, was chosen agent, and under his management additions were made and machinery for making

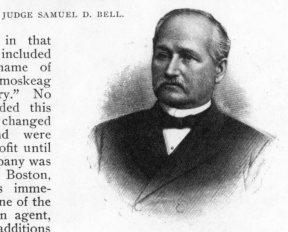

EX-GOV. JAMES A. WESTON.

THE RESIDENTIAL PORTION OF ELM STREET.

water power in Manchester, Hooksett and Garvin's Falls in Concord, also a controlling interest in the locks and canals.

In 1831, Mr. E. A. Straw, a native of Salisbury, New Hampshire, was temporarily engaged by the

THE SOLDIERS' MONUMENT.

Amoskeag Company as a civil engineer. At the time of his engagement no mills had been erected upon the east side of the river, and no improvements whatever had been made on the present site of the city. Mr. Straw soon became the permanent engineer of the Company, in which capacity he laid out the streets of the city, superintended the building of the upper canal and the dam, and other works of the Company. In 1851 he became the agent of the Land and Water Power Company, in 1856 agent of the mills, and in 1858 he assumed the entire management of its operations. It would be a pleasure to speak of the many able and distinguished men who in those early days contributed to the prosperity of the city by their intelligence, their integrity and their zealous participation in the work of building the mills in Manchester and carrying on the great enterprises contemplated by them; but the briefest history of our city would be sadly incomplete if special mention were not made of the life and services of E. A. Straw. No man had so great an influence upon its welfare, its growth and its permanence. He filled many positions of a civil character, was governor of the state, and could have had anything within the gift of the people which he desired. But his eminence as a business man exceeded any distinction which could have resulted from civil office. To his liberality in shaping the policy of the Amoskeag Company, Manchester is largely indebted for her parks or commons, lots for public buildings, and the beautiful Valley Cemetery. Many churches also obtained lands gratuitously, and others at nominal or greatly reduced prices. The same liberality has always characterized the policy of the corpora-

tory, in good times or bad, in the days of war as well as of peace, it has maintained its high rank as one of the most reliable and successful business institutions in existence. It has sixteen mills, which contain forty-five acres of floor space—some of them being immense and independent manufactories themselves. The company employs on the average about 7,500 operatives, representing a

PICTURESQUE VIEWS NEAR MANCHESTER.

tion toward the city and its religious, educational and charitable institutions.

The Amoskeag Manufacturing Company is the great central figure in the business interests of Manchester. From this immense corporation flow the means of livelihood in a countless number of ways into the homes of one-third of the whole city. It is undoubtedly the largest textile manufacturing company in the world; and throughout its his-

population of over fifteen thousand people. It supplies its employees with tenements and boarding houses, numbering in all about five hundred, mostly solid brick buildings, making comfortable homes for its people to a very large extent. In addition to the water power which it uses, the company has an immense steam plant, the combined power being eighteen thousand horse power. It has about 10,000 looms and 275,-000 spindles, and manufactures in

CITY HALL.

round numbers about 117,000,000 yards of cloth annually. Its disbursements for wages alone are about $200,000 per month. The business of the company has never been disturbed by strikes nor affected by flurries in the commercial world, but has moved steadily forward. Mr. T. Jefferson Coolidge of Boston is the treasurer and has the general management, and Mr. Herman F. Straw is the agent and executive officer of the company. Mr. Straw was "to the manor born." He is the son of Hon. E. A. Straw, and his experience and accurate practical knowledge of

all the departments of the company qualify him to an unusual degree for his important position.

The Stark Mills will be regarded as the second most important and extensive corporation in Manchester. It really was the first one to engage in mill work, having begun in 1838–39. Its plant is something more than a thousand feet in length, and it owns in adjacent localities about sixteen acres of land, upon a portion of which have been erected, for the accommodation of its employees, 136 boarding houses and tenements. Probably no company has a more comfortable class of tenements for its employees; they are supplied with modern im-

THE GOVERNMENT BUILDING.

provements, and are furnished at the lowest possible rates. The corporation owns six mammoth mills, containing 80,000 spindles and about 2,500 looms. It employs about 1,650 operatives, and manufactures about 27,000,000 yards of goods annually. The pay roll amounts to $40,000 monthly. The Stark Mills are furnished with the most improved machinery, and all appliances which modern invention can supply. The company's product is a high grade of cotton goods, mostly sheetings and drillings. It manufactures also the

THE KENNARD BUILDING.

JOHN B. CLARKE.

operatives, and manufactures annually about 32,500,000 yards of cloth. Its monthly pay-roll is about $83,000. The president of the company is Aretas Blood, and the agent is Charles D. McDuffie, both residents of Manchester. Mr. McDuffie is a man of high standing among the manufacturing institutions of New England. This corporation also owns a large number of tenement buildings of substantial and comfortable character, furnished to its employees on much the same plan as those of the Amoskeag Company and Stark Mills.

The Amory and Langdon Manufacturing Company is comparatively a new company, having commenced its operation in 1879–80. Its mills are among the finest in the city. It employs about 1,400 operatives, has about 3,000 looms and about 120,-000 spindles. Its products consist of high grade cotton goods, sheeting, shirting and jeans. It manufactures about 23,500,000 yards of goods annually, and disburses about

seamless grain bag, having been the first corporation to manufacture and introduce them. In this latter product it has no rival. The agent of the company is Mr. Stephen N. Bourne, who stands high among the successful manufacturers of the country.

The Manchester Mills, comprising both manufacturing and print works, is another of Manchester's great manufacturing institutions. It has very extensive buildings in both of its departments. Its capital is $2,000,000. The goods which it has manufactured have taken a high rank. The product includes print cloths, worsted dress goods, and cashmeres. The works contain about 4,000 looms and about 75,000 spindles. The corporation employs about 3,500

THE MANCHESTER AND STARK MILLS.

$35,000 monthly for the payment of wages. It has been very successful in its manage-

THE AMOSKEAG FALLS IN WINTER.

ment. It is largely owned by the same people who compose the Amoskeag Company.

The Devonshire Mills, employing about 140 people, add much to the

THE ELLIOT HOSPITAL.

prosperity of the south part of the town.

To the outside world which utilize the millions of products of these great mills, the details of their manufacture are often as foreign to their knowledge as though they were on another continent. It is of interest to know that when the power is applied, by a single hand, throughout an immense building containing perhaps 1,000 looms or 100,000 spindles, and all of the machinery connected with them is set in motion, several hundred people are engaged in a moment in their daily work. The writer once heard an operative say, concerning a certain loom which he had run a long time,

that he regarded it as a twin brother. The people who operate this great and complicated machinery become interested in it, and in a certain sense are a part of it. It is interesting to see in the morning, or at noon or night, when the help are moving from their homes to the mills or returning, perhaps 10,000 people pouring through the gates to or from their labor, and to realize that they are the producing element of a great and prosperous city, generally occupying comfortable homes and receiving a sufficient compensation to maintain themselves and families in a respectable manner. While some of them are unthinking people, there are many of the most intelligent and active minds to be found in any employment. It is common to hear them discussing the nice points of

THE BIRTHPLACE OF HORACE GREELEY ON
THE ROAD TO AMHERST.

ELM STREET.

difference between one kind of machine and another, which they have operated, pointing out the superiority of an American invention over an English, or vice versa, and discussing in a scientific manner the principles involved in the various inventions which have been practically successful or otherwise. The average intelligence of

have a better understanding of the wants of the consuming masses, than almost any other class of people.

The Olzendam Hosiery Company, established in 1846 by the Hon. A. P. Olzendam, is one of the most extensive hosiery manufactories in the country, manufacturing all kinds of hosiery and knit goods, and employing about 350 people. The founder of this company was one of the most scientific men engaged in the business, and his thorough understanding of all the technical requirements enabled him to place his company in the front rank.

ON THE MERRIMACK RIVER.

the operatives in these great mills will compare favorably with that in any other realm of our life. The men are usually better posted upon the markets,

A GROUP OF MANCHESTER CHURCHES.

Among the industries of Manchester which contribute largely to its prosperity is the manufacture of paper and pulp. The P. C. Cheney Company is one of the largest concerns in the state engaged in this business. They make all kinds of paper and board, glazed paper, cardboard, and every kind of waterproof paper stock and box goods, also paper for book and newspaper printing. They own the Excelsior Paper Stock Works located at Goffstown, which manufactures the sulphite fibre, in which there is a very extensive trade. They also own and operate the great Bay Pulp Mills at East Tilton and the Cherry Valley Mills at Washington, N. H. Their plant at Manchester is a very extensive one. The president and principal owner of the works is ex-Governor Person C. Cheney, whose reputation is national, and who is one of Manchester's most public-spirited

LAKE MASSABESIC.

citizens. The Amoskeag Paper Mills occupy a large brick structure fitted with the most approved machinery for the manufacture of book papers of a superior quality.

The Elliott Manufacturing Company in East Manchester, engaged in the manufacture of women's and children's knit goods, is one of the several institutions which began business in a somewhat remote part of the city within a few years. It furnishes employment for about 300 operatives, and bids fair to be one of the prominent industries in the city. The Kim-

ball Carriage Company, the Hoyt Shoe Factory, the Kimball Shoe Factory and the Eureka Shoe Factory have all been recently established in the same newly-developed section beyond East Manchester.

The extensive plant of the Manchester Locomotive Works is located in the northerly part of the city, and covers about six acres of ground. The works are second to none in their substantial construction, machinery and equipment, and their locomotives sustain a reputation equal to those of any company in the country. The

THE NEW BRIDGE OVER THE MERRIMACK.

company has already made more than 2,000 locomotives, and the works have an annual capacity of 150. This company also build the famous steam fire engine which has acquired such a high reputation in the great cities of the country. This latter enterprise it developed under the skillful management of the late N. S. Bean, who was distinguished as one of the most competent experts in steam fire engines and apparatus in the country. The construction of this steam fire engine was brought by him to such a high degree of perfection that it has

England, South America, Mexico, and all parts of our own country.

The James Baldwin Company, whose works are located in West Manchester, is engaged in the manufacture of bobbins, spools and shuttles, and is one of the most successful and best known corporations in the city. Its goods are unrivaled; it has almost a monopoly of the business.

The Manchester Street Railway has

VIEWS ON THE MERRIMACK LOOKING TOWARDS THE FALLS.

over twenty miles of track, and the company has plans and franchises for further extensions. The line extends to

come to be the best known machine now in use. The Manchester Locomotive Works employ about 700 skilled mechanics. The agent and director is Mr. Aretas Blood.

The S. C. Forsaith Machine Company probably has a broader business in the line of machinery, stationary engines, portable saw mills and mill supplies than any institution in the country. Its works cover about three acres of land. Its products are shipped to all parts of the world. It has trade in Japan, Russia, Germany,

Massabesic Lake and south and west nearly to the limits of the city. Nearly the entire stock of the corporation is now in the hands of Gen. Charles Williams, who has adopted every late appliance and improvement. During the last year the road has carried two and a half million passengers.

The Manchester Gas Light Company was organized in 1851. The People's Gas Company was organized later, and now, having leased the plant of the former company, controls the

INTERIOR OF THE PUBLIC LIBRARY.

whole business. This company is eminently successful, paying the old company a dividend of thirty-four per cent annually, dividing a fair income among its stockholders, and supplying its customers at rates much below the average. Its rivals, however, the Electric Light companies, are rapidly encroaching upon its domains and if the signs of the times do not fail will soon become the controlling factor in lighting the city. The Manchester Electric Company is composed largely of Massachusetts capitalists. It is making many improvements and extensions and rapidly preparing one of the best equipped electric plants in the country. The Union Electric Light Company, which supplies both power and light, owns a valuable plant in West Manchester.

Massabesic Lake, the source of Manchester's water supply, about four miles distant from the central parts of the city, is a beautiful body of water of pure quality. This lake is the property of the city. Attention was called to the subject of the water supply as early as 1844, and after surveys and examination Hon. E. A. Straw made a report that this lake was the

only sufficient source. In 1860 Hon. James A. Weston, Hon. Jacob F. James, both civil engineers of great experience, and Rev. William Richardson, a man of most excellent judgment, made several surveys. All this time there was active opposition to the proposition in favor of Massabesic. Eminent engineers decided that Massabesic was the only available source of supply. In 1871 the water works commission was or-

HON. NATHAN PARKER.

ganized. Hon. Samuel D. Bell, prominently identified with our early history, was one of our foremost and far-seeing citizens. He clearly saw that Manchester's water supply must come from Massabesic. The history of his skillful management in obtaining a legal title to this lake would be exceedingly interesting. At his decease the lake became the property of his sons, who conveyed it to the city. To Judge Bell's high legal

lion gallons per day, sufficient for ninety thousand people.

The fire department of Manchester contains ten companies, comprising about 165 members. The department for many years has been under the direction of Thomas W. Lane, chief engineer, who has brought it to a high state of discipline; and its membership is composed largely of prominent citizens. The city has suffered but few disastrous conflagrations, the last one occurring in 1869.

While there have been a great number of newspapers scattered through the history of Manchester, there are now only two which are worthy of notice:—the *Daily Mirror and American,* with its weekly edition, called the *Mirror*

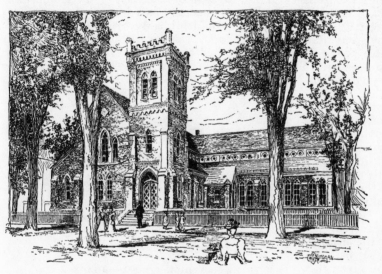

THE PUBLIC LIBRARY.

attainments and deep interest in the undertaking we are largely indebted for its success. But to Ex-Governor James A. Weston more than any other man should be given the credit of its accomplishment. He had been mayor several terms, and governor twice, and his careful training as an engineer enabled him the better to exert a powerful influence. The waterworks were completed in 1874, and the first water was pumped into the reservoir July 4th. Recently a second pumping station has been erected and a large reservoir constructed on Oak Hill and separate service provided for the east and higher part of the city. The full capacity of both systems is nine mil-

and Farmer, published by the John B. Clarke Company, under the management of Col. Arthur E. Clarke, and the *Manchester Union* (daily and weekly), published by the Union Publishing Company, whose manager is Gordon Woodbury. John B. Clarke began his newspaper work in 1852 as editor of the *Manchester Daily Mirror* and the *Weekly Mirror*, which were purchased by him soon after. In 1863 he bought the *Daily and Weekly American* and the *New Hampshire Journal of Agriculture;* and all these papers with two or three others were united. The *Mirror* is in many respects the leading Republican paper in New Hampshire. Its founder was one of the most promi-

THE FIRST SCHOOL.

nent and influential citizens of Manchester. He was a man of wonderful energy and sagacity. His broad knowledge of men and affairs coupled with a remarkable power of generalization made him a leader. The newspapers are now owned substantially by his family. The *Manchester Union* is the outgrowth of the *Union Democrat,* first published in 1857, of which James M. Campbell was the editor and subsequently the proprietor. It is the largest and most influential Democratic paper in New England, outside of Boston.

In reviewing the history of Manchester, a passing glance should be given the "Old Mammoth Road." It was completed in 1831 and, being before the days of railroads, was like all great highways an important institution in the development of the country. The building of this road was projected in 1823. It was to be the main thoroughfare or mail and stage route from Lowell to Concord, passing through the thickly settled part of the city. The undertaking was opposed by Manchester and, although "sometimes voted up and sometimes voted down," it was not until the Court issued an order upon the city to proceed and build it that the controversy ended. The opposition to the road cost the city much money and retarded her growth materially. The blowing of the horn announcing the coming stage and the changing of

mails was to the citizens of those days a notable event. The old "Falls" road also still remains in the recollection of the older people. It was a part of the stage route from Lawrence to Concord. The stage line and the turnpike are now becoming forgotten, but they were indispensable to the development of the country.

The valuation of property in Manchester for the purpose of taxation is about thirty million dollars. The system of taxation in New Hampshire is generally based upon what property would probably bring if put upon a forced sale for cash, and this is usually rated at about seventy per cent of its ordinary value. The recent average

THE NEW HIGH SCHOOL BUILDING.

annual increase has been about a million a year.

In 1810, about the time manufacturing was begun, the population was 615. For the next ten years there was only 147 increase, and in the next decade 125; but from 1830 to 1840 the number went up to 3,235. This was the period when the influence of the mills began to be felt. In 1846 the population numbered 10,125; in 1850, 13,933; in 1860, 20,108. Soon the war showed its effect, and the growth of the city ceased for a while. In 1870 we had 23,586; in 1875 the number was some over 30,000; in 1880, 32,630; in 1890, about 45,000; and in 1896 it is estimated at about 55,000. The increase of our population has kept pace with the building of new mills by the large corporations, almost in direct proportion.

There are twenty-seven Protestant and seven Catholic churches in Manchester. Many of them date back, of course, to the early days of the city. It was not a very uncommon thing for societies sixty years ago to hold meetings in barns, and often in private houses at the "Center." In those times the churches were under legal management. It would be a curious proposition now to insert in the warrants for town meetings articles to see if the meeting would vote to call a certain minister for the ensuing year, and to fix his compensation in potatoes, corn, pork and hay; and again "to see what method the town will take to provide singing." It would amuse the people of the present day to find recorded in some ward clerks' books the following: "Voted that Captain Perham set the Psalm"; "voted that John Goffe read the Psalm,"—whereby it would become the duty of Captain Perham to select the psalms, and John Goffe to read or line them during the year; yet such was the practice in old Derryfield.

Rev. C. W. Wallace was pastor of the First Congregational Church for about thirty-four years. He resigned in 1873, but supplied the pulpit for some time after. He was one of the ablest men of his time, and distinguished as a preacher and a citizen. His fearless defense of the cause of temperance and his bold stand in favor of every moral reform gave him great influence, and his advocacy of whatever cause he espoused was emphasized by his singularly pure life and exalted character.

Rev. Samuel C. Bartlett was pastor from 1852 to 1857 of the Franklin Street Congregational Church. He was president of Dartmouth College from 1877 to 1892. He has a national reputation as a man of profound learning, great natural ability, and unflinching devotion to whatever he believes to be right. Rev. Dr. William J. Tucker, the present president of Dart-

mouth College, was also pastor of the Franklin Street Church from 1867 to 1875. He is among the most accomplished scholars of the age. His ministry in Manchester was highly successful.

Rev. Arthur B. Fuller was pastor of the First Unitarian Church from 1848 to 1853. His impassioned oratory, his liberal views and generous and sympathetic character gave him a strong hold upon his congregation and made him a powerful factor in the community. He became chaplain of a New Hampshire regiment in the war, and at the battle of Fredericksburg took his place in the ranks and fell with his musket in his hands.

Rev. J. M. Buckley, editor of the *Christian Advocate*, was pastor of St. Paul's Methodist Church in 1863-64. Dr. Buckley's distinguished career as a writer and preacher has placed him among the first clergymen in the country, and his friends and admirers in Manchester, who have watched his great success with pride, are not surprised.

Rev. William McDonald was pastor of St. Anne's Roman Catholic church and one of the most highly esteemed and widely known clergymen of his time. He came to Manchester in 1844. The population contained more turbulent elements then than now, and the feelings of hostility between the native and foreign born population were easily excited. Mr. McDonald throughout a long and eventful period in our history exercised a powerful influence and managed the affairs of his people with wonderful tact and ability. Manchester owes much to him.

The Roman Catholic Cathedral is the largest church in the state and has one of the largest congregations. Rt. Rev. Dennis M. Bradley, bishop of the diocese, is the pastor. Bishop Bradley is a native of Manchester and as the head of this diocese is a man of great influence. But it is not from his commanding position that his strength mainly comes. He is an eminent scholar and an eloquent speaker. His watchful care over every interest of his people and his wise and faithful management of their affairs have gained for him their confidence and affection and the esteem and respect of the citizens of Manchester.

In the centre of Merrimack Square, in the business part of the city, is our Soldiers' Monument. The corner stone was laid on Memorial Day in 1878, by the Louis Bell Post of the G. A. R., with impressive ceremonies; and in September of that year it was dedicated by the Grand Lodge of Masons of the state. No event in the history of the city has ever attracted more widely the attention of the people of New Hampshire. The Masonic and military display was grand and imposing; and the oration by Hon. J. W. Patterson was one of that brilliant orator's noblest productions. "Here, in the midst of the crowding industries of the people whose patriotism is to be inspired and sustained by its daily contemplation, the city has erected this monument to the valor and devotion of the twenty-eight hundred men who filled its quota in the war of the rebellion." Manchester is proud of this testimonial to her citizen soldiery. The patriotism, the sacrifices and noble deeds of those who went from among her people into the ranks of the army, and whose breasts received the spears that were aimed at the heart of their country, the shaft is erected to commemorate. Manchester would not fail to honor those who bore high rank or won distinction; but she remembers most tenderly the private soldier who tented on the open field and made the weary march and bore the brunt of battle.

Manchester is not largely interested in clubs and club life. The Derryfield and the Calumet clubs, however, are particularly worthy of mention. The Derryfield club was organized in 1875 and has a local membership of about one hundred and fifty, comprising many of the most prominent people in the city. It occupies an elegant building on Mechanic Street. Its non-resident membership is quite large, and the clubhouse is the favorite resort of distinguished gentlemen from all parts of the state; and many a plan has been laid in the Derryfield that has had much to do with the affairs of the state, if not of the nation. The Calumet club is composed largely of the younger men of the city. It is one of the notable social centres and its clubhouse is one of the architectural ornaments of the city.

The Gymnasium is an institution that should not be overlooked. It has an active membership of about three hundred. Its well furnished establishment is in charge of competent instructors, and affords an excellent opportunity for physical training. It is well patronized and is doing a great good.

The Manchester Athenæum was established in 1844. A small library association under the name of the Proprietors of the Social Library in Derryfield existed from 1795; but the people taking little interest in its continuance, in 1833 the books were divided among the proprietors. The Athenæum began with a library, museum and reading room. It was favored with very liberal donations from the Amoskeag Company, the Stark Mills, the Manchester Print Works and many prominent citizens. In 1856 it was nearly destroyed by fire. In 1854 it contained about three thousand volumes, and its circulation was rapidly increasing. In his inaugural address of that year, the mayor, Hon. Frederick Smythe, suggested the propriety of establishing a city library. The suggestion was favorably received by the city government, and the property of the Athenæum was transferred to the city. In 1871 the library was removed to the new building, a permanent brick structure on Franklin Street costing originally about thirty thousand dollars, upon a lot donated by the Amoskeag Company. It has been greatly enlarged and improved, and now has a capacity sufficient for every purpose for many years. By the conditions of the transfer of the Athenæum the city became bound to appropriate a sum of not less than a thousand dollars annually for books. There is also a fund of about fourteen thousand dollars, the income of which may be expended for books, etc. The library is growing rapidly in size and usefulness. Under the efficient and popular management of Miss Kate E. Sanborn, the librarian, many improvements have been introduced and the best methods of library management adopted. The library now contains over forty thousand bound volumes and a vast number of pamphlets and periodicals. Its average daily circulation is nearly three hundred volumes, and its reading room is utilized by the public to an extent that shows its great appreciation. Upon its walls hang portraits of its founders and patrons, and in the centre of the reading room is a statue of President Lincoln, in sitting posture, presented by the distinguished sculptor Rogers, a native of Manchester.

Manchester has two public hospitals. The Elliot hospital was founded by a donation from Mrs. Mary E. Elliot, widow of the late Dr. John S. Elliot, one of the eminent physicians of our city, a portion of whose fortune, obtained in the successful practice of his profession, has thus descended and become a fund to benefit the sick and suffering. It is a thoroughly appointed institution, a costly and elegant structure standing on high ground in the southeast part of the town. It is managed by a corps of able and experienced physicians. It has an emergency department, situated in the central portion of the city.

The commodious Hospital of the Sacred Heart, under the liberal and philanthropic management of Bishop Bradley, is one of the greatest blessings of Manchester. It is in the immediate charge of the Sisters of Mercy. Patients are admitted and cared for with or without charge, according to their circumstances.

The Gale Home for Aged and Destitute Women was established in 1890, endowed with bequests by Mary G. Gale and David R. Leach. It owns a very valuable lot, upon which it has provided a Home sufficient for present needs. The income of a portion of the fund is set apart for its support, and it is the design of the corporation to erect extensive buildings when accumulations from the remaining part of the fund and other sources shall warrant the outlay. The Home is comfortably furnished and very pleasant for its inmates.

The Manchester Women's Aid and Relief Society is doing a great work in its care and aid rendered the suffering and destitute. It was established in 1873 by Mrs. Aretas Blood and other prominent and wealthy women of the city. Its Home and grounds cost nearly fifty thousand dollars. The Home is large enough for about forty persons and is usually full. The devotion and wisdom which have been shown by Mrs. Blood in the maintenance and conduct of the Home have gained for her the gratitude and reverence of the city of Manchester.

The Children's Home is another institution worthy of high commendation—a home for children who, by reason of being orphans, or from want and destitution, need support. It was erected from the contributions of the charitable people of the community. The late Mrs. W. W. Brown was the first president, and it was largely through her generous donations and wise management that it was established. At her decease it became one of the residuary legatees of her estate and will receive a large bequest in the near future.

At the Centennial Exposition at Philadelphia the public schools of

Manchester won the highest awards for excellence in nearly every department, and they possess equal merit now. The high school building recently erected is one of the best in the country. It will cost, when completed, about $135,000. There are five thousand pupils in the public schools and four thousand in the parochial schools. The St. Mary's Academy for young ladies and St. Anselm College are Roman Catholic institutions of great merit.

Manchester has been exceedingly fortunate in her banks. The Manchester Bank, now the Manchester National Bank, was organized in 1845. During nearly forty years it was practically under the management of Hon. Nathan Parker, first as cashier and then as president, and its successful career is evidence of his wisdom and integrity. Mr. Parker died in 1894, and his son, Mr. Walter M. Parker, succeeded him as president of the bank. Mr. Nathan Parker was also treasurer of the Manchester Savings Bank for about forty years, his son succeeding him too in this position. The deposits of this bank have reached the immense sum of over seven million dollars. The Amoskeag Bank began business in 1848. Hon. Moody Currier was cashier until its organization as a national bank, when he was elected president. Its prosperity and high reputation are largely due to his ability and fidelity in conducting its affairs. He was succeeded as president by Hon. Geo. B. Chandler. Mr. Currier was treasurer of the Amoskeag Savings Bank for thirty years. In 1883 he was elected its president and Mr. Henry Chandler became the treasurer and practically manages its business. The deposits of this bank are about five million dollars. The People's Bank is also conducted in connection with the Amoskeag. It is organized upon the guaranty principle and has been highly successful. The City Bank was organized in 1853 and the City

Savings Bank a little later. Hon. E. W. Harrington was for many years cashier of the former and treasurer of the latter. The Merchants National and the Guaranty Savings Bank, organized by Hon. J. A. Weston, are the successors of those institutions and are managed in a very conservative and intelligent manner. The Merrimack River Bank, now the First National, and the Merrimack River Savings Bank were organized in 1855 and 1858 respectively, with Frederick Smythe as cashier of the former and treasurer of the latter; and they have maintained relatively the same important positions as the other banks. The Second National and the Mechanics Savings Bank, which have been very successful, were organized about the same time—with Mr. Josiah Carpenter as cashier of the one and treasurer of the other. The Bank of New England, with much improved prospects, is arranging to do a loan and discount business.

Looking back to the beginning of Manchester we see that down to the time when national banks came into existence there were four banking houses in the city. The Manchester, the Amoskeag, the City and the Merrimack River banks, together with the several savings banks connected with them, began business within a very short time of each other. These great institutions, which had such a remarkable influence upon the prosperity of Manchester, were respectively conducted by four justly distinguished financiers: Hon. Nathan Parker, whose name was a synonym for integrity and fidelity; Governor Currier, who bore almost identically the same relations to the Amoskeag banks as did Mr. Parker to the Manchester, and to whose discriminating judgment and superior ability the Amoskeag banks owed their prosperity; E. W. Harrington, whose faithfulness, energy and sagacity kept his banks abreast with his competitors; and ex-Governor Smythe, who made the Merrimack River Bank and the Merrimack Savings Bank model institutions. The entire community has the utmost confidence in their successors in the banking business and in the newer institutions which have risen to keep company with the older.

The Manchester Board of Trade, composed of about 300 prominent and influential citizens, has been very efficient in promoting the business interests of the city. It has induced new enterprises to locate here and new capital to engage in industries already established, and it has exercised its influence in many ways in behalf of improvements in railroad facilities.

Manchester has one prominent insurance company which it claims as its own, the New Hampshire Fire Insurance Co. It was organized by Manchester people in 1869, and has now a capital of nearly a million dollars.

The railroad service for the city of Manchester is highly satisfactory. Recently a very extensive freight station has been erected, and plans are now being completed for a magnificent new passenger station. The railroads which run to Manchester are the main line of the Concord and Montreal, the Manchester and Lawrence, the Concord and Portsmouth, and the Manchester and North Weare. These roads with their many connections run out like the spokes of a wheel and afford communication with all sections of the state. The Boston and Maine Railroad has a lease of and operates all these roads. The late Mr. Crowningshield, then president of the Boston and Lowell Railroad, one of the most far-seeing men of his time, made the remark when once addressing the stockholders of that company that probably "there were people then listening to his voice who would live to see a line of railroad completed from Boston to Montreal." There were people in that meeting who pronounced the statement "one of the wildest of dreams"—and that was less than sixty years ago!

On September 8, 1846, the Manchester city government was established; and three days of September, 1896 were devoted to the celebration of our semi-centennial. It was looked forward to with great interest. The programme for each day was so arranged as to give every group of interests full opportunity in the exercises. People who were here fifty years ago were brought together and had their memorial exercises. The schools had their day, and six thousand pupils mingled their voices in the grand chorus of rejoicing. The trades' procession, miles in length, celebrated in a magnificent manner the countless industries carried on within the city; and the civic and military companies united in a grand display never before equaled in the state. The occasion was deemed an auspicious one to lay the corner stone of the monument in honor of ex-Governor Weston, one of Manchester's most beloved citizens; and the Grand Lodge of Masons of New Hampshire performed the ceremony, the whole Masonic display attracting greater attention than any similar event ever known in the state. In all respects Manchester was at her best. The people vied with each other in making the celebration a grand success. Our young mayor, Hon. William C. Clarke, worked unceasingly, and his zeal animated all the people. We cannot better close this brief account of the "Queen City" of New Hampshire than by a few words from the eloquent address by Hon. Henry E. Burnham, the orator of anniversary day:

"To-day, with united front, proud of our city and her grand achievements, proud of her mighty industries which, now diversified, are stronger than before, and proud of the illustrious names and deeds of her sons and daughters, who have given to her an immortality of honor, we are marching forward, with our banners streaming in a prosperous breeze and inscribed in letters of golden light with the word "Progress."

The Old Middlesex Canal (1898)

THE
New England Magazine.

NEW SERIES.   JANUARY, 1898.   VOL. XVII. No. 5.

THE OLD MIDDLESEX CANAL.

By Arthur T. Hopkins.

THE observant traveller on the Lowell railroad between Woburn and Wilmington, Massachusetts, may see a broad ditch filled with a sluggish stream of water. He is told perhaps that this was once a portion of the Old Middlesex Canal. With the words comes a swift vision of a silvery ribbon of water lying between cultivated meadows and bordered by velvety lawns and shaded woodland. On its bosom he sees the canal-boat, moving forward with easy, quiet dignity, appropriate to the time when leisure was still allowable. The vision is quickly dispelled by the rush and roar of the train, sweeping on to its destination, as the canal itself was obliterated by the growth of steam power. It may perhaps help to an appreciation of the vast changes which accompanied this transition if we will remember that, roughly speaking, the Middlesex Canal belongs to the first

half of the nineteenth century, while the railroad belongs to the latter half of that period.*

In the month of May, 1793, a certain number of gentlemen met together, for the purpose of "opening a canal from the waters of the Merrimac, by Concord river, or in some other way, through the waters of Mystic river to the town of Boston." There were present at this meeting the Hon. James

*The writer wishes to acknowledge his indebtedness to the many friends who have assisted in this interesting research, and particularly to Professor George L. Vose, Mr. Lorin Dame, Mr. J. Morris Meredith, Professor Alfred E. Burton, Mr. Henry Brooks and Hon. Parker L. Converse.

KING'S TAVERN, BILLERICA.
Beside the old canal.

THE CANAL IN NORTH BILLERICA.
Reproduced from a drawing made by Wm. Barton in 1825.

Sullivan, who was at this time attorney general and later governor of Massachusetts, and in whose fertile mind the idea originated; Benjamin Hall, Willis Hall, Ebenezer Hall, Jonathan Porter, Loammi Baldwin, a leader in the enterprise and the superintendent of construction, Ebenezer Hall, Jr., Andrew Hall and Samuel Swan. A charter was obtained from the General Court, incorporating James Sullivan and others, by the name of the Proprietors of the Middlesex Canal, bearing date June 22, 1793, and signed by His Excellency, John Hancock, Governor of the Commonwealth. There were then elected for officers: Hon. James Sullivan, president, Loammi Baldwin, Esq., first vice-president, and Hon. John Brooks, second vice-president, with the following named gentlemen in addition as directors: Hon. Thomas Russell, Hon. James Winthrop, Christopher Gore, Joseph Barrell, Andrew Craigie, Captain Ebenezer Hall, Jonathan Porter, Ebenezer Storer, Caleb Swan and Samuel Jaques.

The company being thus duly organized, the next step was to begin "the necessary surveys for the most eligible route." A primary examination of the ground was made in the summer of 1793 by Samuel Thompson of Woburn. He appears to have done his work carefully; but he was not provided with instruments of sufficient

RATE OF TOLL

ON THE

MIDDLESEX CANAL......UNTIL FURTHER NOTICE.

APRIL 4, 1808.

	Dolls. Cts.
ON all articles (excepting thofe which follow) by weight at 6¼ cents a ton, each and every mile, the whole diftance being 27 miles	1,68¾
Timber { Oak—per mile, 6¼ cents a ton	1,68¾
Timber { Pine—per mile. 4 cents	1,08
Pine Boards, Pine Plank, reduced to board meafure } 6¼ cents	1,68¾
Clapboards—4 cents a thoufand	1,08
do. freight in the Proprietors' Boats—64 cents a thoufand	
Shingles—1 cent a thoufand	
Oak Plank, 2½ inch—6¼ cents for 600 feet board meafure	1,68¾
Afh Plank, 2½ inch—6¼ cents for 700 feet board meafure	1,68¾
Staves, Barrel—6 cents per thoufand	1,62
do. Hogfhead—12 cents	3,24
do. Pipe—18 cents	4,86
do. Butt—25 cents	6,75
Hoops, Hogfhead—8 cents per thoufand	

precision for the accurate determination of elevations. An attempt was then made to obtain the services of Samuel Weston, a distinguished English engineer then in this country working on the Potomac canals. A survey was made by Mr. Weston in July, 1794, in company with Loammi Baldwin and Samuel Jaques on the part of the proprietors, and the route reported was adopted. Agents were at once appointed to carry on the work; and the first turf was removed on the tenth of September in the same year. The season being so far advanced, but little could be done until the following year, except in the securing of land, settlement of claims, purchase of materials and conclusion of contracts for future work. The compensation for the land taken ranged from $150 per acre in Medford to $25 per acre in Billerica.

The work was prosecuted with great vigor, under the direction of Loammi Baldwin, until the year 1803, when the canal was so far completed as to be navigable from the Merrimac to the Charles river, the first boat, however, being actually run over a portion of the canal on April 22, 1802.

The canal as thus built was 27 1-2 miles long, 30 feet wide at the surface, 18 feet wide at the bottom, and 4 feet deep. The locks were 11 feet wide and 75 feet long, with an average lift of about 7 feet, some being built of wood and others of stone. In the wooden locks the outside walls were of stone,

the space between the inner and outer walls being packed with earth. In this way expensive masonry was avoided, though the cost of maintenance in after years was increased. Altogether there were 7 aqueducts over rivers and streams, 50 bridges spanning the canal, and 20 locks. Four of the levels were five miles each in extent, the rest of from one to three miles each. The total cost, to 1803, was $528,000, of which one-third was for land damages. As will be seen, the amount was afterwards doubled in repairing and rebuilding the canal. Much of the work was done by contract. Laborers received about $8 per month wages, carpenters from $10 to $15 per month.

The route of the canal was crossed in Billerica by the Concord river, which at that point was 107 feet above tidewater at Boston, and 27 feet above the Merrimac at Chelmsford. The river was thus at the summit of the canal and able to supply water in both directions. It will be seen later how this fact was further utilized in the attempt to form an aqueduct of the canal. The charter also allowed the use of the Concord river, for 23 miles, through Billerica, Carlisle, Bedford, Concord and Sudbury, as a canal. This formed a portion of Governor Sullivan's far-reaching plan for inland water-ways, extending well into the interior of Massachusetts, and by way of the Merrimac river to Concord, N. H., thence through Lake Sunapee to the Connecticut river, at Windsor,

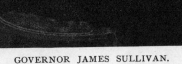

GOVERNOR JAMES SULLIVAN.
By the courtesy of J. Morris Meredith.

BRIDGE AT WEST MEDFORD SHOWING STONE PIERS OF THE CANAL AQUEDUCT.

quaint old houses, erected by the proprietors for the use of their *employés* — and through the long swamp to River Meadow brook, also crossed by acqueduct. Thence it was continued to North Billerica, at which place there are very extensive remains.

Vermont, and thence to the St. Lawrence river. It seemed a good and practical plan, and if the railroad had been delayed ten years would undoubtedly have been realized.

The canal began at Middlesex village, on the Merrimac river, in the town of Chelmsford, and was lifted through a connected flight of three locks, the depression for which is plainly seen in one of the accompanying illustrations, together with the tiny house which served formerly as the canal office. It passed under the main street, over an aqueduct across the brook—near which are some

The canal is still used by the Talbot Mills for the supply of water for power, and in this connection they have retained one of the lock gates, thus saving for us one of the best preserved and most interesting features of the old canal. At this point the Concord river was crossed at grade, a floating bridge serving as towpath, and the tow swinging clear in the waters of the river. The picture, from an old pencil sketch, well illustrates the condition of things. The boat is the *General Sullivan* packet boat. It will be noticed that the horses in the picture differ in

THE CANAL IN WEST MEDFORD.

PHOTOGRAPH BY E. B. CONANT.

some essential characteristics from those of the present day.

On the south bank of the Concord river an extensive cutting through rock was necessary. The Shawsheen river flows through a deep and narrow valley, and the stone-work for the aqueduct constituted perhaps the most imposing structure on the canal. Two end abutments and a central pier, all of stone, supported a wooden trunk or box about 180 feet long, elevated 30 feet above the river, and of sufficient width and depth. The abutments and

travellers on the canal. There were many of these, and Nichols's was a favorite place for dinner or for a night's lodging.

In Wilmington the canal passed through wide boggy meadows, where the bed sank some 60 feet before the completion of the canal; crossed the Maple Meadow brook by another aqueduct, of which the ruins are very picturesque; and then made an abrupt bend around the foot of a hill. This bend was called the Oxbow. A mile further south the canal entered the

PHOTOGRAPH BY E. S. CONANT.

BRIDGE OVER THE OLD CANAL ON THE BROOKS ESTATE, WEST MEDFORD.

pier remain undisturbed to this day, with some decaying fragments of the oaken trunk still clinging to the pier. The highway and electric car line pass within a few feet of this monument.

Half a mile further south was Nichols' lock, a portion of which still remains as part of a cellar wall. Mr. Nichols had charge of this lock for a great many years. He was a successful farmer, and in addition kept an excellent inn for the accommodation of

town of Woburn, passing within a short distance of the house of Loammi Baldwin. Just to the north of Woburn station a picturesque view of the canal may be had from the railroad. The canal has here been transformed into a duck-pond, the width being preserved, but each end of the pond being formed by a dam and the railroad embankment. The canal crossed the swampy meadows, great quantities of earth being sunk in forming the bed and side banks, passed to the rear of

the present public library building, and so on to Horn pond or Stoddard locks in Woburn, of which we are enabled, through the courtesy of Judge Converse of Woburn, to present a pen sketch by the eminent engineer, the late Marshall Tidd. Mr. Tidd served, while a lad, as gate-tender at these locks, and the sketch shows the tavern, lock and canal boat, as actually existing at that time.

In the Stoddard locks we have one of the principal engineering features of the canal. At this point a descent of fifty feet was made by three sets of double stone locks, the middle set being separated from the others by a basin-like expansion of the canal, which allowed for equalizing the water in locking. These locks were so near Boston, the journey thither in the packet boat *General Sullivan* was such a pleasant one, the view of canal and lake was so picturesque and interesting, that the place speedily became a popular resort. Pleasure boats plied the lake, Kendall's Boston brass band and the Brigade band of Boston rendered sweet harmony, and the crowds wandered from the groves to the lake and back to the canal, where shots of lumber-rafts and canal boats laden with cargoes were continually passing through the locks. So popular did the place become that in 1838 the Horn Pond house was leased for $700 for that year.

The canal continued on down to Horn Pond brook, crossing it at grade by means of waste weirs, which remain to this day in a fair state of preservation. In Winchester the towpath has been converted into the highway for a considerable distance. At Mystic lake a stone aqueduct carried the canal over the narrow upper arm of the lake. The bed of the canal is plainly visible here. It is to be hoped that these interesting remains will remain untouched during the alterations now being made on the shores of the lake by the Park Commissioners.

It is interesting to observe that the Metropolitan sewer occupies the bed of the canal for some distance, thereby affecting a considerable saving in excavation for grade. For something over a mile the canal lay within the grounds of the Brooks estate. We are indebted to the courtesy of Mr. Henry Brooks for two photographs, one of the handsome elliptical stone arch, built by George Rumford Baldwin, son of Loammi Baldwin, to convey a farm road over the canal, and considered by engineers to be one of the most graceful structures of the sort in New England; and the other a picture of such beauty and charm that one must ever regret the sacrifice of this bit of the old canal by the Park Commissioners.

Half a mile further south were Gibson's lock and the aqueduct over the Mystic river. The present Boston avenue bridge rests directly on the piers of the aqueduct, slightly built up to suit the change in grade.

SLUICEWAY, HORN POND BROOK.

The canal turned to the east at this point—the Lowell railroad passing over it by a bridge, of which the wing walls are yet plainly visible—and on past the Royal house, where the canal passed under Main street and sent off a branch to the river, for the benefit of the shipyards of Medford and Charlestown; and so on through the Mystic trotting park to the base of Winter Hill. From this point the canal followed the line of the high land around to the sharp bend in the Mystic river, where Dunning's coal wharf is at present located; then to the south, through nearly the centre of the Broadway park; around the base of Mount Benedict; across the foot of Austin street, where the gate house may still be seen; then nearly parallel to Main street to the Neck, where it passed under Main street, through a lock and into the Millpond. Most of the cargoes were loaded here, but for those wishing carriage to Boston there was a lock with double gates working either way, according to the state of the tide, for admission into the Charles river. Once in the river it was an easy matter to reach any of the city wharves; but there was also an extension of the canal, through the area

THE CANAL IN WOBURN.

FIRST INN AT HORN POND LOCK.

on which the old Boston & Maine depot has recently stood (Canal street being directly alongside), across Haymarket square, following nearly the line of Blackstone street, to the harbor, near what is now North Market street. Nearly all of the stone for Quincy market was brought over this route.

The freight boats were flat-bottomed, with square ends and parallel sides, and were between 40 and 75 feet in length, and 9 and 9 1-2 feet in width. The sides were three feet deep at the middle, but decreased to about one foot in depth at the ends, thus giving a somewhat rounded bottom. A load of twenty tons would give a draught of two feet to the boat, leaving the ends just out of water. Only half of this load might be carried in summer when the water was low. The boats were built of two-inch pine planks, spiked on to small oak cross-timbers and knees, and at each end had heavy oak cross-ties, with one for the mast thwart, a little forward of the centre. On this mast could be raised a small square sail for use on the rivers.

During the passage of the canal the towline was fastened to a shorter mast put in its place. The rudder was a long steering oar, with blade ten feet long, eighteen inches wide, pivoted on the centre of the cross-tie, and trailing behind the boat in the water. Three large scull-oars, sixteen feet long, and three setting poles for use up the rapids of the Merrimac completed the outfit. In the canal proper the boats were towed by horses, frequently without a driver, in which case the man at the rudder kept a small pile of stones or green apples ready for the encouragement of the horse. On the river a skipper and two bow-men were needed.

The entire trip, from Boston to Concord, N. H., and return, took from a week to ten days. Between Boston and Lowell the usual time for freight boats was eighteen hours up and twelve hours down, while the passage boats made the trip in twelve and eight hours, the freight boats making two and a half miles per hour and the passage boats four miles.

Of the passage boats there were at first two, one running up and one down daily. Fifty cents was the fare, no tickets being issued. Later, when the amount of travel proved insufficient to warrant two boats, one was removed, and the *General Sullivan* ran alone. This was a boat on the style of the Erie canal boats, though somewhat lighter, with a covered cabin over the whole length, except for the standing room at each end. The cabin was provided with seats and was upholstered much as the horsecars of a decade ago. In its day the *General Sullivan* was considered a model of comfort and elegance. All boats were numbered and lettered; and private boats, of which there were many, were painted with such designs as to be easily recognized, as in the

THE CANAL BED IN WILMINGTON.

case of freight cars of to-day.

A large amount of lumber was being used during this period by the shipyards on the Mystic river, nearly all of it being rafted down the canal. By the "regulations," these rafts could not be larger than seventy-five by nine and one-half feet; but a number of rafts could be banded together by slabs pinned between them. A band of seven to ten rafts required five men, including the driver; four rafts required four men, and three rafts three men. These rafts were unpinned and sent separately through the locks, and then again united. The rafts were

drawn by yoked oxen, a single yoke drawing no less than one hundred tons of timber, a load requiring eighty teams on the common road. The company's charter allowed a toll of one-sixteenth of a dollar per mile for every ton of goods carried in the boats and the same for every ton of timber floated in rafts. The actual rates ranged from one to two dollars per gross ton for the twenty-seven miles from Boston to Lowell.

According to the "regulations," boats of the same class going in the same direction were not allowed to pass each other. Repair boats had the precedence over everything, then came passage boats, freight boats, and lastly rafts. Landing and loading places were established at the Millpond in Charlestown, in Medford, Woburn, Wilmington, Billerica and Chelmsford. No goods were allowed to be loaded or unloaded at any other place without a special permit from the agent, — this being a precaution against damage to the banks.

No boats were allowed to pass through any lock after dark, — that is, seven o'clock in the spring and autumn and nine o'clock in summer; but on moonlight nights they might pass until ten o'clock, but not after that, nor before daylight at any season. Considerable damage having been done to the lock gates by the bumping

THE CANAL IN BILLERICA.

of canal-boats on entering, a fine of ten dollars was imposed upon any conductor who allowed his boat to enter the lock with sufficient headway to reach the gate. When a boat approached the lock, notice was given by the blowing of a horn, and prompt attention was thus secured. But due respect was paid to the religious sentiment of New England. The passage boat being permitted to run on the Sabbath, "in consideration of the distance from home at which those persons using it generally are, it may be reasonably expected that they should not disturb those places of public worship near which they pass, nor occasion any noise to interrupt the tranquillity of the day. Therefore it is established that no signal horn shall be used or blown on Sundays."

The methods of receiving, transporting and delivering freight were very similar to those of the present. A waybill or "passport" accompanied the goods. Freight

charges were paid on removal of the property, and in case of delayed removal, a wharfage or demurrage charge was added.

The proprietors seem to have been considerably disturbed by the discharge of rubbish into the canal. They therefore declared that "no carcass or dead animal or putrid substance of any kind shall be thrown into the canal or any basin connected therewith, under fine of ten dollars." Even more troublesome was the burrowing of muskrats, eels, etc., for this endangered the canal itself. The following is a copy of a handbill in possession of the Woburn public library:

CANAL BED, BILLERICA.

"Bounty
On Musquashes and Mink
Taken in the Middlesex Canal.
If within 2 rods of the Canal, 50 cents.
quarter of a mile,   30 cents.
half of a mile,   10 cents.
1 mile   5 cents.
Application to be made to Mr. Cyrus Baldwin, Mr. Nathan Mears, Col. Hopkins, Mr. Isaac Johnson, Mr. Elijah Peirce, Mr. Samuel Gardner, Mr. Joseph Church, whichever of them

NICHOLS'S LOCK, AT EAST BILLERICA.

lives nearest the place where the animal may be taken.

If the person applied to is satisfied of the facts, his certificate or verbal declaration thereof to the subscriber will entitle the applicant to the bounty. The applicant must produce the Musquash or Mink entire to one of the above-named persons. He may then take the skin.

(Sig.)   J. L. Sullivan.
March, 1809."

So far as can be ascertained, there was but one tow-path for most of the line, and that was on the west bank. The tow-path served many purposes. It was the preferred path of foot passengers; it was the "Lovers' Lane" for the young people of the villages on Sunday afternoons and evenings; and it served as an excellent seat for tired skaters in the winter, when the canal also served as the best of skating ponds.

What boy who has read of Hans Brinker and his silver skates would not wish that he too had lived in a time when he might skate away for miles in one direction? An elderly gentleman in Medford informed the writer that he purchased his house, in the forties, because the canal bordered the garden at the rear and the constant passing was enjoyable for the "women folks." Even to this day, in the swampy regions between Billerica and Middlesex village, the tow-path is frequently used by pedestrians, as

CELLAR WALL MADE FROM NICHOLS'S LOCK, EAST BILLERICA.

its well-trodden condition witnesses.

Ordinarily there were some sixteen men, lock-tenders, carpenters, etc., three clerks and an agent employed, at a total expense of about $8,000 per annum, in addition to the boatmen. In 1830 the boatmen were receiving $13 per month.

SHAWSHEEN RIVER AQUEDUCT.

Embargo and war of 1812 kept on increasing, until in 1816 they were $32,000. In 1819 the first dividend was paid, the assessments at that time amounting to $1,455.25 per share on 800 shares, a total expense of $1,164,200. From this time until the Lowell railroad went into operation the receipts regularly increased, so that the dividends grew from $10 to $30 per share, and in a few years would doubtless have given a handsome interest on the original investment. The year the Lowell railroad went into operation, however, the revenue was reduced by one-third, and when the Nashua & Lowell railroad went into operation, five years later, in 1840, the revenue was further reduced by another third. This killed the canal. When the bill

The affairs of the canal were in bad shape between 1803 and 1807. Constant expense was being incurred in the repairing of damages from breaks and the settling of the bed. Four directors were in charge, no one of them with full authority; tolls were uncollected; and canal-boats were detained, for weeks sometimes, till the owners were ready to unload them.

Finally, in 1808, Governor Sullivan and Loammi Baldwin died. It seemed the end of things. But at this critical juncture John Langdon Sullivan, son of the governor, a stockholder in the company and an engineer and business man, was made agent. He compelled the payment of tolls in cash before goods were delivered, charged demurrage on goods not promptly removed, caused repairs to be promptly and thoroughly made, and so improved the business that in 1810 receipts rose to $15,000 and despite the

TOWPATH, EAST BILLERICA.

for the incorporation of the Lowell railroad was presented before the legislature, the directors of the canal presented a remonstrance, which forms interesting reading by the light of subsequent events. We quote:

"There is a supposed source of revenue to a railroad *from carrying passengers.* As to this the remonstrants venture no opinion, except, to say . . . . that the use of a railroad *for passengers only* has been

In 1843 Boston had a population of about 100,000, and was still dependent on wells for its water supply. Most of these wells were badly contaminated, some being little short of open sewers. One of these wells long bore a high reputation as a sulphur spring, until Dr. Jackson analyzed it and found three per cent of putrescible organic matter. It was then discovered to be connected with a neighboring drain, — and its glory departed suddenly. There was a lively agitation at this time for a better water supply, and Caleb

LOCK AT TALBOT MILLS,
NORTH BILLERICA.

CANAL AT TALBOT MILLS.

tested by experience, nowhere hitherto; and that it remains to be known whether this is a mode which will command general confidence and approbation, and that, therefore, no facts are now before the public which furnish the conclusion that the grant of a railroad is a public exigency, even for such purpose. The remonstrants would also add that so far as they know and believe there can never be a sufficient inducement to extend a railroad from Lowell westwardly and north-westwardly to the Connecticut, so as to make it the great avenue to and from the interior, but that its termination must be at Lowell."

Business grew rapidly less with the canal after the Nashua & Lowell railroad opened. The country merchants fully appreciated the speed and certainty of the railroad, in spite of the somewhat higher freight rates.

Eddy, the agent for the canal, accordingly appeared before the legislature with plans for the conversion of the canal into an aqueduct for the Boston water supply. The water of the Concord river was analyzed by Dr. Charles T. Jackson, Professor John W. Webster of Harvard University, S. L. Dana of Lowell, and A. A. Hayes of Roxbury, and by all declared to be pure, soft and eminently suitable for the purpose. Mr. Eddy's plan consisted in abolishing the levels between Billerica and Middlesex village and

BOATMEN'S HOUSES AT MIDDLESEX VILLAGE.

boat was run on the canal, by Joel Dix of Billerica; and on October 3, 1859, the Supreme court declared that the proprietors had "forfeited their franchise and privileges by reason of non-feasance, non-use, misfeasance and neglect."

Woburn and Charlestown, conducting the water of the canal from Woburn by thirty-inch iron pipes to a reservoir on Mount Benedict in Somerville, thence to be distributed over Boston and possibly Charlestown and Cambridge. The scheme fell flat, however. Nothing further could be done. In 1846 the canal was practically discontinued. In the same year the property was sold for about $130,-000 and the amount divided among the stockholders.

On April 14, 1852, the last canal-

AGENT'S HOUSE AT MIDDLESEX VILLAGE.

The Building of Minot's Ledge Lighthouse (1896)

THE

NEW ENGLAND MAGAZINE.

NEW SERIES.   OCTOBER, 1896.   VOL. XV. NO. 2

THE BUILDING OF MINOT'S LEDGE LIGHTHOUSE.

By Charles A. Lawrence.

THE erection of the lighthouse upon the formidable reef of Minot's Ledge stands as one of the most stupendous tasks of its kind. It is the finest example of a true sea-rock lighthouse in existence, its only imitation being the tower upon Spectacle Reef, Lake Huron, which is very like it in appearance and for which it served as a model. Probably few of those who scan the noble pillar from the decks of passing steamers ever give a thought to the method of its construction, still less to the disheartening obstacles presented to its builder. Similar in location and outward appearance are several famous lighthouses in British waters, as the great Eddystone, the Wolf Rock, the Skerryvore and the Bell Rock. But the foundation rock in each of these cases is above low water level for a considerable space of time, and in at least one instance is above mean high tide level, while at Minot's reef the bed rock upon which the circle of the base of the tower was struck is for most of the year below the level of low tide.

The Cohasset Rocks, of which the Minots are a part, are a series of submerged reefs lining the Massachusetts coast from a point just above Cohasset town down the coast to some distance beyond Scituate, the next neighbor on the south. Not above four or five miles in length, they creep out from the shore for an average distance of two miles; and no captain in his senses would think of crossing them by any but the one tortuous channel which leads between White Head and the Glades into the snug cove of old Cohasset. A cruise among them in a small boat is sometimes calculated to give one the shivers, for they lie anywhere from twelve inches to a fathom below the surface and seem to rise of a sudden with the intent of grazing the keel of the unwary boat. It is doubtful whether the oldest skipper of the South Shore would care to tack across them in moderately rough sailing, save in the smallest and snuggest craft known to "the cove," and then it would be with deep misgivings. An old mariner of North Scituate, called one of the best "natural" navigators sailing out of the harbor, who has followed the sea for the best part of his ninety years and over, recently grounded his passenger sloop on one of these hidden spines in the middle of a sunny August day, and no one thought of discounting his seamanship. In a stormy sea this hideous gridiron seethes and sizzles, a boiling sheet of foam, from its seaward limit to the wild fury of surf that lashes the beaches into furrows. Well might Boston-bound mariners hold the place

THE FIRST TOWER ON MINOT'S LEDGE.*

difficulties of the undertaking and describes the various steps of the interesting task. Doubtless the eyes of the eastern seaboard were upon him, but he seems nothing daunted by this or any other incident of his heroic undertaking.

The Minots are bare only at three-quarters ebb-tide,—their highest point was 3½ feet above extreme low water,—and upon the outer Minot, the one upon which both towers have been built, there is seldom a space exceeding twenty-five feet in diameter exposed at one time, and never a space above thirty. The rock was found to be granite with vertical seams of trap rising through it. Accurate observations made from Boston Lighthouse from June 7 to October 27, 1847, gave results concerning the tides as follows:

Rise of Highest Tide . . .	14 feet 7 inches.
Mean Rise and Fall of Tides .	9 " 4 "
" " " " Spring Tides	10 " 8 "
" " " " Neap Tides	8 " 3 "

Eight holes were driven into the rock, to the depth of five feet, at the points of a regular octagon, with a ninth in the centre; and in these were fixed the nine iron piles that were to form the skeleton of the tower, the central one being eight inches in diameter at the base and six at the top. The outer ones were but four and one-half inches at the top, but all were of the same diameter below the surface of the rock, a uniform size of ten inches. As the rock was uneven, while the piles must all rise to a uniform height, their length varied from 35¼ to 38¾ feet. Sockets or couplings of gun metal were keyed to the tops, and from these sprang smaller piles

in abhorrence, and the cunning of the skilled engineer be early called upon to lessen its terrors for those who do business in the great waters.

The story of the first tower, its short period of usefulness and its tragic end, is a household tale throughout New England; yet comparatively little that has been written about it has dealt at all with the details of its construction. As a result there has sprung up the error and injustice of the belief that it was a structure culpably inadequate to the purpose for which it was designed. As a matter of fact, engineers of eminence believe that it might be standing to-day but for the lack of foresight displayed by the keeper.

Capt. W. H. Swift of the United States Engineering Corps, strongly impressed by the successful application of Mitchell's mooring screws to the forcing of iron posts into sand as a framework for iron skeleton lighthouses, built the first lighthouse in the United States upon this plan, a beacon at the entrance of Black Rock Harbor, Connecticut. Following this successful overture he designed and erected the first tower upon Minot's Ledge. In his official report of November, 1848, he sets forth the

* This and other pen and ink drawings are from photographs by J. W. Black.

ZACCHEUS RICH.
One of the Model Builders.

extending clear to the lantern. From the rock at the base, and indeed from the very bottom of the holes, the piles slanted inward towards a common centre, so that at 60 feet above the base of the middle pile they came within the periphery of a circle 14 feet in diameter; and here a castiron cap was bolted and keyed. The outer piles were tied to the central one and to each other by braces like eight spokes of a wheel, and later on were braced by cross rods, two between each pile, like a huge letter X. The first series of horizontal ties were placed 19 feet above the rock, the second 19½ feet above the first, and the third 8¼ feet below the cap. They were of 3½, 3, and 2½ inch iron, respectively. The keepers' house and the lantern were fairly above the reach of the average storm seas; but this was not the case with a lower platform which the overconfident keeper had built upon the second series of rods and tie braces, nor with that fatal 5½ inch hawser which he led from the lantern deck out to an anchorage 50 fathoms inshore.

As this structure left the hands of the builders it was thought to be adequate to its mission of warning and fit to survive as severe storms as that which early wrought its ruin, with no more than the usual damage done by a great storm to even the strongest of buildings; and there are engineers who still maintain that a similar structure upon a larger scale, if built upon these rocks, would defy the storms of years. The real defect of the first tower was insufficient magnitude. It was built at a time when appropriations from Congress were all too small for such gigantic undertakings. Captain Swift says of the structure: "The outer piles being inclined toward the centre and the piles and braces being inflexible, it is clear that so long as the braces remain in place the piles cannot be withdrawn from the rock, for the whole structure acts as an immense lewis; either the braces must be ruptured or the rock itself must yield before a pile can be displaced."

Well might he feel confident of a structure of whose minutest detail he was the parent and projector. The bare drilling of the holes in the bed rock occupied the best of two seasons, and three years were occupied in preparing the rock for the masonry. The tower was begun in 1847 and

GENERAL JOSEPH G. TOTTEN.
Late Chief Engineer of the United States.

finished in November, 1848. In 1849 was begun the process of still further strengthening the tower against vibration by the multiplication of braces and rods,—a work, alas, which was never finished. The end came, in storm and fury and darkness; and the seas in a gale still whoop an echo of their wild laugh of triumph from that awful daybreak of April 17, 1851.

Congress recognized the necessity of immediately rebuilding, and the

model constructed, the monster antitype of which has proudly buffeted the storms of over a quarter of a century.

Captain Barton S. Alexander of the engineer corps was chosen to superintend the construction, and for the various trades employed in the task old Cohasset gave of her trained and tried sons. The very table upon which the plans were drawn was specially constructed, a massive piece of mahogany with a top leveled and

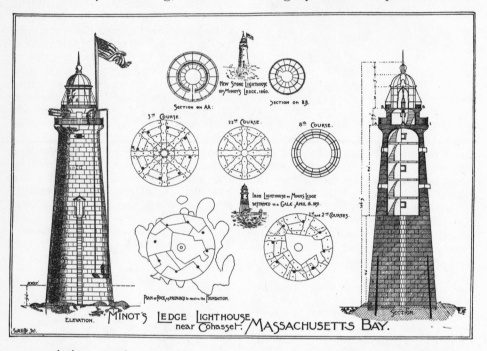

MINOT'S LEDGE LIGHTHOUSE near Cohasset. MASSACHUSETTS BAY.

appropriation made at this time seems to have been sufficient—a lesson in economy learned at bitter cost. The work was intrusted to the Topographical Bureau, who upon advertising received sixteen proposals, but before further progress was made, the new Lighthouse Board was created and the work was referred to the late chief engineer of the United States, General J. G. Totten, who brought to it a mind and heart equal to the apparently disheartening obstacles. He determined to build it of stone. From his design plans were drawn and a

squared to a nicety. The building of the model itself occupied the best of two winters, and the old shop still stands near the head of Cohasset Cove where Richard Bourne and Zaccheus Rich toiled upon this important toy. The scale employed was one inch to the foot, and the model, which was to be seen in the United States Government Building at the Chicago exposition, is stone for stone a counterpart of the granite tower out in the Atlantic.

A lightship had in the meantime done duty as a beacon, and anecdotes

THE BUILDING OF THE LIGHTHOUSE ON GOVERNMENT ISLAND.

are told of the superb Newfoundland dog who lived aboard and acted as carrier for the news bundles thrown out from passing vessels. Crowds would gather at steamer rails to witness his fearless plunge into the sea, where he would dart here and there until he had his mouth so full of news that barking was no longer possible, when he would swim for his floating home.

The actual labor of building the present tower upon the ledge might be likened to holding at bay a wild beast robbed of its prey. The action of sea waves upon and about hidden or partly sunken ledges will at times defy the judgment and skill of the oldest sea dog afloat. Ever varying, always erratic, a swell pouring over a reef seems animated by a distinctly malignant power; and woe to the dory caught disabled in its grasp! From Cape Ann to Boston, from the Graves to Cape Cod, at Thatcher's, Straitsmouth, Egg Rock or Minot's, the records of the sea rock

lighthouses are dotted with overturns of small craft of all classes in the simple attempt at landing.

In the face of this malevolent spirit of unrest, the Cohasset men sailed forth under Captain Alexander to conquest and achievement. The first step was to remove the stumps of piling which still adhered to the rock. "Three things," said Captain Alexander, "were necessary, a perfectly smooth sea, a dead calm, and low spring tides. This could only occur six times during any one lunation, three at full moon and three at the change."

A party sailed from the cove and under these conditions grappled for the ruins. A Scandinavian who passed under the name of Peter Fox,

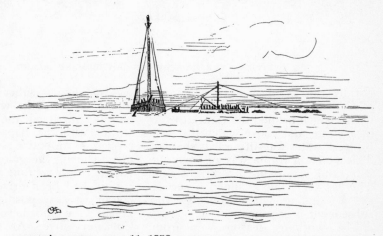

MINOT'S LEDGE, JULY 11, 1858, WHEN THE LOWEST STONE WAS LAID.

a fearless fellow and an accomplished swimmer, would locate the iron which had been carried into deeper water, then diving with a light tackle would hook on to the fragment and strike out for the surface.   In this way, and by wrenching from the rock-bed those fragments which still remained fixed, the ledge was cleared; and a new iron framework was inserted in the holes

the following January another fearful gale obscured the ledge; and when the seas moderated it was seen that the work had shared the fate of the first tower. Even Captain Alexander's dauntless spirit was shaken. The labor of two seasons was cast aside like a toy house. "If tough wrought iron won't stand it," said he, "I have my fears about a stone tower."

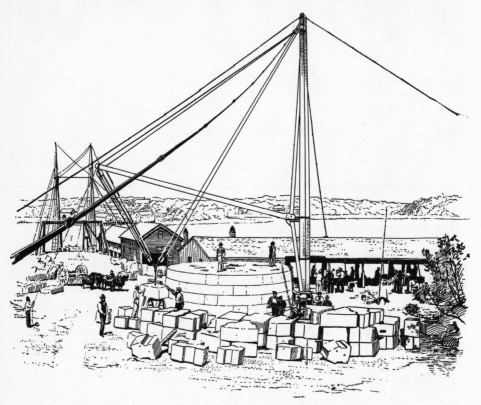

FITTING THE MASONRY ON GOVERNMENT ISLAND.

left by the wrecked tower, pile for pile, all save the central shaft, the cavity for which formed the centre of the base circle, and above which the well for fresh water was afterwards shaped. This skeleton frame was of wrought iron, and was painted a bright red. The "spider" which capped it served as a landing stage during the subsequent proceedings.

The working season was from April 1 to September 15. During

A boat load of sober men rowed out to the scene of the wreck and thoroughly inspected the work of the storm, with the happy result, as it proved, of an entire revulsion of feeling.   During the gale, a bark-rigged vessel, the *New Empire,* loaded with cotton, had been driven ashore, and lay in an easy position near White Head, the northern buttress of Cohasset Cove.   At the suggestion of Captain John Cook, a famous Co-

MINOT'S LEDGE LIGHTHOUSE.
From a photograph by Milton H. Reamy, the keeper of the light.

hasset rigger, the party visited the disabled craft and inquired whether during the storm any unusual shock had been felt. No one had noticed any, but as the visitors turned to go home, a sailor came to the side and claimed the contrary,—and at the same moment a pair of sharp eyes discovered several faint traces of red upon the dark side of the hull. The evidence was weak, but undeniable; and when the *Empire* was dry-docked at Boston her hull was found pierced in several places, and embedded among her cotton bales were some fragments of the piling.

Again was the work taken up—this time to meet with unqualified success. The rock was first cut to a succession of levels, determined by its natural structure, that which is termed the zero being one foot and nine inches above the mean low water level. Outside of a diameter of thirty feet the rock was found to be too soft to be safely worked, and a circular base of that diameter was therefore agreed upon. An eyewitness thus describes the scene:

"Captain Alexander had constructed two large, staunch row boats, naming one *Deucalion* and the other *Pyrrha*,—for he was a droll fellow, full of dry wit. The *Deucalion* was painted red, and this was more especially for his own use, while the *Pyrrha*, a green painted craft, was to carry the men. We would watch the tide from the cove, and just as soon as the ebb had reached the proper stage we would start out with it, and at the moment a square yard of ledge was bare of water out would jump a stone cutter and begin work. Soon another would follow, and as fast as they had elbow room others still, until

CHARLES PRATT.
Superintendent under Captain Alexander.

the rock would resemble a carcass covered with a flock of crows. The high-sounding names for the boats piqued the curiosity of the men not a little, until one finally inquired of Captain Alexander, 'What on airth it meant.' 'Oh,' replied he, '*Deucalion* was a giant who went through Greece of old, picking up stones and throwing them out of the way, and *Pyrrha* was his wife who ate them,'—with which mixed definition the questioner was forced to be content."

From the time when, on Sunday, the first day of July, 1855, the stroke of a hammer first rang out upon the summer air, until the rock was ready to receive the first cut stone, was nearly three years—years wrenched from the sullen power of old ocean. New dowels were inserted in the rock and successfully carried to a height of nearly twenty-five feet, or to where the twelfth course of masonry was afterwards laid. And now began the real work,—the laying of the courses; and this, executed in a comparatively short period of time, proved, as has many another noble superstructure, the value of the long, tedious preparation, a task whose re-

RICHARD BOURNE.
One of the Surviving Builders.

sults were destined to remain forever unseen. During the year 1855 work upon the foundation pit could only be performed one hundred and thirty hours; in 1856, one hundred and fifty-seven; and in 1857, in excavating and in laying four stones, one hundred and thirty hours and twenty-one minutes, the remainder of these years to be relinquished to the savage sea! During 1858 a small gain was made, when the last of the cutting and the laying of six courses of stone was accomplished in two hundred and eight hours. It was important that none but the best of granite should be employed, and samples from many localities were submitted to the severest tests. Of stone taken from Rockport, Cohasset and Quincy, that of the last-named place was proven to be "finest of grain, toughest, and clearest of sap."

Visitors to Cohasset invariably wish to visit Government Island, which seems scarcely an island at all, so narrow is the deep, rocky tide-way which separates it from the main land. Upon a level spot at the northern shore are two circular pavements of granite, as level as a ball room floor, grass-grown and soil-covered at the edges, but exquisitely laid. It was here that the tower for Minot's Ledge was first constructed. Stone sheds were erected; and for many months the island presented a busy scene. From many Cohasset homes a later generation can look out to the distant tower that dots the ocean beyond the Glades, or to the nearer heights of Government Island, with honest pride in the craft of hands which have now, most of them, forever laid the tools aside. Cohasset will not soon forget them; and their names deserve to be blazoned beside those who have stood between their country and her foe, for their work is enduring and multiplies in blessing as the years go by.

There was Captain John Cook, a famous rigger of the days when seventy sail went out of Cohasset and Scituate, whose ability with a rope and block was something marvelous. He died only this last summer. He made the model for the derrick which was used in raising the stones in the lighthouse. A prize was offered for the most practical plan for this derrick, and his was accepted. The massive granite blocks were teamed to the cutters by Clark Cutting, unassisted save by his sturdy oxen. It is said he never had occasion to shift a stone twice.

THE LIGHT KEEPERS' HOMES.

MINOT'S FROM THE ROCKS OFF COHASSET.

Captain Nicholas Tower,—a proud old Cohasset name, that of Tower!— one of a family of noted skippers, captained the first vessels used to carry the finished stones out to the ledge. Howland Studley and Elijah Pratt are remembered as men of cool judgment and skilled hand; while of the many others employed, none could have felt their responsibility more keenly than Wesley P. Dutton and George Reed, the latter of Quincy, who superintended the selection of the stone.

Not the smallest detail of preparation escaped the watchful eye of Captain Alexander; and down to the very pulley-blocks of the derricks, with their specially forged straps, everything was constructed with a view to prevent the slightest mishap. These derricks were the pride of the sparmaker's art; and the perfect-running, flawless pulley-blocks of lignum vitæ were from the careful hands of Richard Bourne, one of the model builders, who first laid out the circumference of the ground-plot at the ledge. Mr. Bourne, now a resident of Clinton, Mass., is still hale and hearty, and enjoys with a keen relish the recollection of this splendid undertaking of his native town.

The Quincy cutters avowed that such chiseling had never left the hand of man; and a closer look into the manner of joining the tower will prove that the need was of the first order. The first few courses bear no semblance to regular masonry. The lines of junction formed by the juxtaposition of the various rock-levels trace out the most erratic curvings, and suggest a snarl of wire loosely confined within a circle. As the courses grew, however, clearing first one and then another of the points of rock, they began to take shape and to admit of a radial arrangement, until, reaching the third, the last of the bed rock was covered, and the courses proceeded with regularity and greater speed. When it is considered that each stone must be cut to fit its neighbors above, below and at either side, and exactly conform to the next inner row upon the same level; that eight iron piles, tapering as they ascended, must be allowed for in certain of the stones; and that those of the innermost row, the ends of the eight great "headers," must be finished each as a fragment of the bore of the well that drills its way from the first floor nearly to the bed rock, it will be seen that nothing short of perfect cutting and flawless joining could be tolerated. Each stone was secured to the course under it by two or more bolts or dowels of three-inch gun-metal, that material having been selected from a variety of metals which had received an under-water test of more than a year. The hole in the undermost stone was drilled flaring at the bottom, and the bolt, its end split into two tiny clefts, was spread and clinched when driven home. Strap-iron inserted between the courses kept the stones apart

CAPTAIN COOK, THE FAMOUS COHASSET RIGGER.

sufficiently for the flowing in of Portland cement, which becomes almost literally a part of the solid stone. Each stone is dovetailed to those upon either side. This process holds good up to the twenty-third course, which, forty-four feet above the rock, serves as the first course of the "shell" or hollow portion containing the keepers' rooms. Here each course is "joggled" by a middle annulus to the course which it rests on. At the top the interior is arched over, and upon the outside the top course flares outward in a severely plain but shapely cornice.

As the hammers clinked ashore, the busy chisels were slowly reducing the ledge to a condition to receive the fitted stones; but the progress out at sea was of necessity tedious and protracted. "Frequently," says Captain Alexander, "one or the other of the conditions would fail, and there were at times months, even in summer, when we could not land there at all." But once well above the hungry water, the difficulties of the task were lessened, and the last 26 courses were laid in 377 hours during the year 1859.

Captain Cook loved his joke, and upon one occasion, while in charge of the men at the ledge, he solemnly inquired of a recent comer, a lank stripling from Vermont, "Can you swim, sir?"

"No, sir, I cannot. Why do you ask?"

The mischievous skipper looked nervously around and replied: "Well, if Captain Alexander knew you were at work here and unable to swim, I— I should be a little afraid he might discharge ye. Now, just you strap one of these life preservers on to you, and if you get washed off we'll pick you up."

A number of the clumsy old "hourglass" style of life preservers were lying upon the deck of the schooner which attended the cutters, and throughout part of one day the luckless youth labored with his ungainly incubus strapped, bustle-fashion, to his back. Presently some one announced, "Red boat coming"; and what excuse the master joker ad-

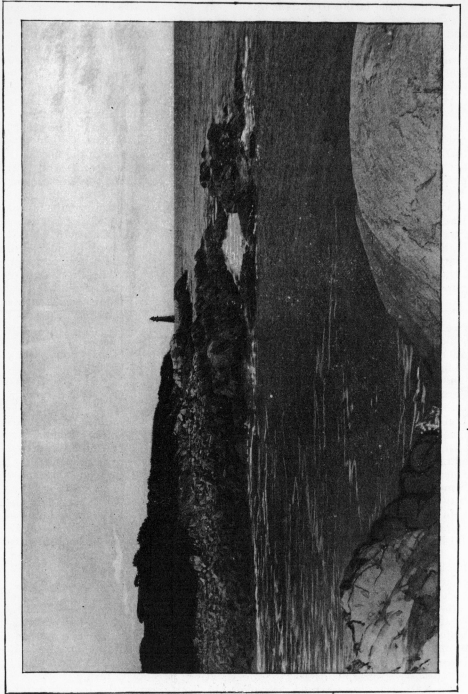

MINOT'S LEDGE LIGHT, FROM THE SHORE.

vanced for the removal of the bustle, or how the young man settled with him ashore, is not stated.

The work was photographed in various stages by James Wallace Black, of Boston, then of the firm of Whipple and Black, who till a very recent time was still busy with his cameras, a veteran of his art, at 333 Washington Street. He has just passed on to join the silent majority. He wrote:

"The photographs were made at the instance of Captain Alexander, who, let me say, was an agreeable gentleman of the old school. It was one of the great works of his life, and he was absorbed in it. It was but a short time that the men could work even at the lowest tides, and the difficulty of making the photographs was very great, it being done in the early history of the art, long before the present quick dry process came about, and when we had to take our materials to prepare plates upon the spot, as well as to fix, wash and preserve them from injury when done. This was no easy task in a tossing boat; but we had plenty of help,—though even this did not make it inviting to stand on slippery rocks trying to steady the camera while making the exposures. We had to work lively, as our time was measured by *minutes,* and the uncertainty of the work in those days can only be realized by the older men of the profession. But for the time they were quite good pictures, and as I did all the work I may be pardoned for feeling a pride in them."

Each stone having been approved, and the courses actually laid upon the island, the work at the ledge was simply a repetition, although the conditions out upon the bosom of the heaving Atlantic must have given a rare zest to the undertaking, not to be found ashore. The shaft is purely a frustum of a cone, the useless tree shape at the base being discarded.

Like a page of fiction runs the anecdote of one Noyes, who was employed upon both the iron and granite towers. Owing to some petty official friction he ceased work and for a time disappeared. During the Rebellion a fine clipper ship, the *Golden Fleece,* with Cohasset men aboard of her, fell a prey to the marauding *Alabama.* As the men filed aboard their conqueror, one glanced up the side, and there, leaning over the poop rail, in the uniform of a Confederate naval officer, was the renegade Noyes.

The tower was finished September 15, 1860, just in time for the autumnal fury of the Atlantic to accord a full test to its right of existence. The total cost was about $300,000. Of rough stone there was used 3,514 tons, of hammered stone 2,367 tons, and from this amount were produced 1,079 separate blocks. The first cut stone was laid July 9, 1857, and the lowest block July 11, 1858. The entire time consumed was 1,102 hours, 21 minutes.

The dimensions are not realized from a distant view of the tower. From the lowest stone to the top of the pinnacle is 114 feet, 1 inch. The height of the focal plane above the lowest point is 96 feet, 1 inch, and above mean high water mark, 84 feet, 7 inches. The diameter of the first full course, the third from the bottom, is 30 feet, and that forming the granite floor, or the top of the twenty-second, is 23 feet, 6 inches. Its completion must have seemed to the builders like the finishing touch to a pedestal, for such it was, to the lighter yet no less important work which grew, course by course, above it. The lantern parapet rises four courses above the cornice of the tower proper, and is crowned by the lantern itself, strapped and bolted to the unyielding stone. High guards of iron railing encircle both the cornice and the parapet, and from this dizzy height the curving outlines of the awful reefs can be traced for many a fathom.

What an ocean graveyard is guarded by the gray old tower, its foot streaked slimy and green with the

MINOT'S FROM THE LIGHT KEEPERS' HOMES.

washings of the tides! The stanch pilot boat *Lawlor* has within the past twelvemonth added her bones to the bleaching skeletons of oak which strew the bottom between the Minot's and the dreaded Harding's,—"somewhere within two or three miles," says her survivor; and about the same "somewhere" from the light, perhaps nearer, the *Allentown* went down in the blizzard of 1888, a fine iron steamer sinking with all on board. It is said that in one spot the ledge runs evenly but a few feet below the surface for several fathoms, parallel with the shore, with its outer wall a sheer drop of nine fathoms!

The keepers and their monotonous life have been thoroughly introduced to a public which has only of late begun to remember the pride with which this noble triumph of peace was at the time received.

The day of the cornerstone oration, with no less a personage than Edward Everett for orator of the day, still lives, a vivid memory in the minds of the people of the South Shore.

The powerful light of the second order has for more than thirty years sent its aggressive rays out upon the ugly expanse of black ocean which nightly encircles the tower with its vast cold plain. But of late a change has come over the staid old sentinel. Weary with his quarter-century vigil, has he given up the struggle and tossed his superb torch hissing into the restless waters that chafe his foot? There is black darkness upon the ledge, although the stars fleck the very horizon and the shore lights twinkle in radiant perspective from Cohasset to Strawberry Hill, and the unquenchable fire of Boston Light sears a pathway of shriveled silver as its powerful beam wheels slowly around in its faithful circle. But, ah! —from the blackness above the dread Minot's there leaps, bursts, a mighty outpouring of light! It quivers, throbs, and is gone. A space of darkness—and again the unbearable flash,—once, twice, four times,— and again darkness, and a tremendous relay of power. Then—one, two, three—and the number of the Minot's station has been spelled out in splendid telegraphy upon the ebon scroll of night.

Block Island
(1876)

BLOCK ISLAND.

By CHARLES LANMAN.

MOHEGAN BLUFF.

AS the poet Dana made Block Island the scene of his fascinating story called the "Buccaneer," we may with propriety begin our description with the opening verses of his famous poem :*

"The island lies nine leagues away.
  Along its solitary shore
  Of craggy rock and sandy bay
  No sound but ocean's roar,
Save where the bold, wild sea-bird makes her home,
Her shrill cry coming through the sparkling foam.

"But when the light winds lie at rest,
  And on the glassy, heaving sea
  The black duck, with her glossy breast,
  Sits swinging silently—
How beautiful! no ripples break the reach,
And silvery waves go noiseless up the beach."

Its exact position, at the junction of Long Island Sound and Narraganset Bay, is longitude 71° 30' west, and latitude 41° 8' north, and it is washed by those waters of the Atlantic which are perpetually blue. From Newport it is, indeed, just "nine leagues away," less than five from Point Judith, eight from Watch Hill, and seven from Montauk. The island is between eight and nine miles long, and from two to four in width. At its northern extremity, where stands a light-house, a sandy bar shoots out for a mile and

a half under water, upon the end of which people now living allege that they have gathered berries, and from which at least two light-houses have been removed in the last fifty years on account of the encroachments of the sea. Clay bluffs, rising to the height of one and two hundred feet, alternate with broad stretches of white beach in forming its entire shores. Its surface is undulating to an uncommon degree, and almost entirely destitute of trees. The highest nill, lying south of the centre, rises more than three hundred feet above the sea; and by way of atoning for its want of running streams, it has two handsome lakes, one of which is of fresh-water, and the other of salt-water, with an area of about two thousand acres. Small ponds fed by springs are numerous, and of great value to the farmers. The only harbor on the island lies on the eastern side, nearly midway between the two extremities, and the contrast presented by what are called the Old Harbor and the New Harbor is very striking. At this point also is the only collection of houses that approaches to the dignity of a village. Here the Block Island fleet, the fish-houses appertaining thereto, a relief station, one big and one smaller hotel, and several boarding-houses, half a dozen shops, one church, and two windmills, are scattered about in very

---

* The entire poem was reprinted, with illustrations, in *Harper's Magazine* for October, 1872.

much of a helter-skelter fashion. One of these windmills was built upon the main shore at Fall River sixty years ago; twenty years ago it stood near the Old Harbor, at which time we made a sketch of it; and to-day it is a conspicuous landmark in the interior of the island. From this village, branching out in every direction, are many winding roads, most of them private and blocked up with gates, upon which are located the snug habitations of the islanders, numbering in all about thirteen hundred souls, three-fourths of whom are thrifty farmers, while the balance are supported by the harvests of the sea. Barring the massive and interminable stone walls which intersect the entire island, the inland landscapes are almost invariably composed of undulating pastures, studded with picturesque homes and barns and hay-stacks, the most of them commanding glimpses of the sea. From the height of land already mentioned, and known as Beacon Hill, the ocean presents nearly a complete circle, broken only by one hill, and well-nigh every house upon the island may be distinctly seen, as well as about two hundred sails per day during the summer months. Other prominent landmarks are Clay Head, a lofty and solemn promontory pointing toward the northeast; Pilot Hill, also in the northeastern part; Bush Hill, near the Great Pond; the Great Bathing Beach, which is two miles long, and as fine as any on the Atlantic coast; and the southern cliffs, which are the crowning attraction of the island, next to the sea air and the ocean scenery. These great bulwarks are both imposing and beautiful, and it is in keeping with the fitness of things that the highest of them should be surmounted by a first-class modern lighthouse, which, though near the brow, can not be seen from the beach below. Their formation is of clay interspersed with bowlders, and hence we find here a greater variety of colors than at Mount Desert or the Isles of Shoals. The profiles of the cliffs are both graceful and fantastic, and when looming against a glowing sky or out of a bank of fog, they are imposing to the last degree; and while you may recline upon a carpet of velvety grass at their summits, you have far below you the everlasting surf of the Atlantic, dashing wildly among the bowlders, or melting in peace upon the sandy shores. But to enjoy this cliff scenery in its perfection, you must look upon it under various aspects — in a wild storm, when all the sounds of the shore are absorbed in the dull roar of the sea coming from afar; in a heavy fog, when the cliffs have a spectral look, and the scream of the gulls is mingled with the dashing of the unseen breakers; at sunset, when a purple glow rests upon the peaceful sea and the rolling hills; at twilight, when the great fissures are gloomy, and remind you of the dens of despair; and in the moonlight, when all the objects that you see and all the sounds you hear tend to overwhelm you with amazement and awe.

But the air and the ocean, after all, are the chief attractions of Block Island—the air, bland and bracing in summer, pure and delicious as nectar in the sunny autumn, and not without its attractions even in the winter and early spring; and the ocean, in conjunction with the sky, making glorious pictures, thus leading the mind from sublunary things to those that are eternal in the heavens.

The aborigines of Block Island were a part of the Narraganset nation, and they gloried in the fame of their three great chieftains, Canonicus, Canonchet, and Miantonomoh, the first of whom it was who sold Aquidneck, now Rhode Island, to the English. It was about the year 1676 that the last two of this trio were slain, one of them at Stonington and the other at Sachem's

OLD WINDMILL.

Plain, in Connecticut, and with them the Narraganset power virtually expired. When the white men first visited Block Island, they found there about sixty large wigwams, divided into two villages, adjoining which were two hundred acres of land planted with maize; and while the records do not state when these Indians finally left the island, the presumption is that it was soon after the whites had fairly obtained possession of their new domain.

In colonial times the land-owners were comparatively few; their estates were large, and houses somewhat pretentious; they were waited upon by slaves, and in the habit of exchanging formal visits with the great proprietors on the Narraganset shore. In modern times, however, we find the land so cut up and subdivided that a farm of one hundred acres is rather a novelty, while the largest proportion range from two to forty acres, and the largest on the island contains only one hundred and fifty acres. Contrary

OLD LIGHT-HOUSE.

to the common belief, about three-fourths of the inhabitants are farmers, and the remainder fishermen. The houses of the inhabitants are generally after the old New England model, one story and a half high, always built of wood, and nearly always painted white; the barns, however, which are neat and well kept, are frequently built of wood combined with stone walls; the stone fences which surround or cross and recross the plantations are noted for their substantial character; and the grazing lands, on account of their neatness and beauty, are invariably attractive.

A more complete colony of pure native Americans does not exist in the United States than is to be found on Block Island. They are a clannish race; think themselves as good as any others (in which they are quite right); they love their land because it is their own; their ambition is to obtain a good plain support from their own exer-

tions, in which they are successful to a man; they are simple in their habits, and therefore command respect; they are honest, and neither need nor support any jails; they are naturally intelligent, and a much larger proportion of them can read and write than is the case in Massachusetts, the reputed intellectual centre of the world; they are industrious, and have every needed comfort; and kind-hearted to such an extent that they do not even laugh at the antics of those summer visitors who have a habit of making themselves ridiculous. In their physical appearance the men are brown and hardy, as it becomes those who live in sunshine, mist, and storm even from the cradle; and the women are healthy, with bright eyes and clear complexions, virtuous and true, and as yet without the pale of the blandishments and corruption of fashion.

While storing away, with a liberal hand, a supply of all the necessaries of life for their own consumption, the Block Islanders have an eye to trade, and send over to Newport and Providence, to Stonington and New London, large supplies of cattle, horses, sheep, hogs, grain, poultry, and eggs, as well as cod livers for oil, and large quantities of sea-moss, receiving in return not only money, but all the necessaries of foreign growth or production.

The fishermen of this island live and appear very much like their brother farmers, but naturally have more intercourse with the outside world. Very frequently, indeed, we find individuals who are both farmers and fishermen. They are a quiet but fearless and hardy race, and what they do not know about the ocean—its winds and storms and fogs—is not worth knowing. All the boats in their possession at the present time would not number one hundred, and the majority of these are small, but they suffice to bring from the sea a large amount of fish annually. The two principal varieties are the cod and blue fish. The former are most abundant in May and November, and although not any better by nature than the Newfoundland cod, they are taken nearer the shore, and cured while perfectly fresh, and hence have acquired a rare reputation. There are three banks for taking them, ranging from five to ten miles distant. The blue-fish are taken all through the summer and autumn, are commonly large, and afford genuine sport to all strangers who go after them. The writer of this once saw sixty boats come to shore in a single day, every one of which was heavily laden with blue-fish. Another valuable fish taken is the mackerel, and when they are in the offing in June, the Block Island fleet, joined to the stranger fishermen, sometimes present a most charming picture. And as they anchor at night, to use the language of another, under the lee of the island, the lights in the rigging, the fantastic forms of the men dressing the fish, the shouts of old shipmates recognizing each other, the splash of the waves, the creaking of the tackle, the whistling of the wind, the fleecy clouds flying across the face of the moon, conspire to make a picture that seems more like a fairy vision than reality.

But the sea-faring men of Block Island are not all purely fishermen. Many of them do a profitable business as pilots. A goodly number of them, too, are called wreckers, and their business is to lend a helping hand, and not to rob the unfortunate, when vessels are driven upon the shore by stress of weather or lured to destruction by the deceitful fogs. And it occasionally happens that we hear of a Block Islander who becomes curious about the world at large, and obtaining command of a ship at New Bedford or New London, circumnavigates the globe; but they are always sure to come back to their cherished home, better satisfied with its charms than ever before.

This island was discovered by the Florentine Giovanni di Verazzano in 1524, while upon a voyage along the coast of North America under a commission from the French king. The name that he gave to it was Claudia, in honor of the king's mother; but as he did not land upon it, and never saw it afterward, the island was utterly forgotten for well-nigh a century. After the Dutch had founded New Amsterdam, some of them sailed for the northeast, on a visit to the Pilgrims at Plymouth, and they saw the island also; and it was one of the white-haired race, Adrian Blok or Block, who rediscovered it, and whose name it has ever since borne. Its original owners, the Narraganset Indians, named it Manisses.

In 1636, while Roger Williams was planting the standard of civilization and Christianity on the spot where the city of Providence now stands, a certain Boston trader attempted to establish a business arrangement with the Indians on Block Island. "The cause of our war" (according to a writer in the Historical Collections of Massachusetts) "against the Block Islanders was for taking away the life of one Master John Oldham, who made it his common course to trade among the Indians. He coming to Block Island to drive trade with them, the islanders came into his boat, and having got a full view of his commodities, which gave them good content, consulted how they might destroy him and his company, to the end they might clothe their bloody flesh with his lawful garments. The Indians having laid their plot, they came to trade, as pretended; watching their opportunities, knocked him in the head and martyred him most barbourously, to the great grief of his poor distressed servants, which by the providence of God were saved. This island lying in the roadway to Lord Sey and the Lord Brookes's plantation, a certain seaman called John Gallop, master of the small navigation, standing along to the Mathethusis Bay, and seeing a boat under sail close aboard the island, and perceiving the sails to be unskillfully managed, bred in him a jealousy whether that island Indians had not bloodily taken the life of our own countrymen and made themselves master of their goods. Suspecting this, he bore up to them, and approaching near them, was confirmed that his jealousy was just. Seeing Indians in the boat, and knowing her to be the vessel of Master Oldham, and not seeing him there, gave fire upon them and slew some; others leaped overboard, besides two of the number which he preserved alive and brought to the Bay. The blood of the innocent called for vengeance. God stirred up the heart of the honored Governor, Master Henry Vane, and the rest of the worthy Magistrates, to send forth one hundred well-appointed soldiers under the conduct of Captain John Hendicott, and in company with him that had command, Captain John Underhill, Captain Nathan Turner, Captain William Jenningson, besides other inferior officers." The result of the expedition was, "having slain fourteen and maimed others, the balance having fled, we embarked ourselves and set sail for Seasbrooke fort, where we lay through distress of weather four days; then we departed." Captains Norton and Stone were both slain, with seven more of their company. The orders to this expedition were "to put the men of Block Island to the sword, but to spare the women and children."

Soon after that event the island became tributary to Massachusetts, and Winthrop informs us that on the 27th of January, 1638, the Indians of Block Island sent three men with ten fathoms of wampum as a part of their tribute, and by way of atoning for their wicked conduct. In 1658 the General Court of Massachusetts granted all their right to Block Island to Governor John Endicott and three others, who in 1660 sold it to a certain company of persons, and the first settlement was commenced in the following year. The story of that sale was duly written out at the time, and after the settlement had been effected was placed on record among the files of the island, where it is to be found at the present time.

In 1663 the island was annexed, by the charter of Charles II., to the colony of Rhode Island. In 1672 it was incorporated as the town of New Shoreham, and so named, it is supposed, because some of the prominent settlers had come from the town of Shoreham, in Sussex County, England. From the start, it had conferred upon itself more ample powers of self-government than had been conferred upon any other town in the colony, for the reason that "they were live-inge remote, being so far in yᵉ sea," and because of "yᵉ longe spelles of weather," which sometimes rendered it difficult to reach the island.

When war was proclaimed between France and England in 1689, Block Island came in for rather more than its share of attention from the enemies of England. In July of that year, as we learn from the records of Massachusetts, three French privateers came to Block Island, having among their crew one William Trimming, who treacherously decoyed and betrayed those he met at sea, pretending they were Englishmen, as he had a perfect use of the English tongue. He was sent on shore, and, by plausible accounts, succeeded in obtaining a pilot to conduct the vessels into the harbor, whereupon the people, who imagined no treachery, were immediately made prisoners of war. They continued on the island a week, plundering houses, and stripping people of their clothings, goods, etc., and destroying their bedding. This same Trimming was afterward shot dead on the spot (it was thought through surprise) by Mr. Stephen Richardson, of Fisher's Island, lying near New London, where he had gone with others of the crew on a similar expedition, he having his gun partly concealed behind him, and not laying it down when commanded. Mr. Richardson was much blamed at the time for it.

In 1690 the French again landed upon the island, plundered it, and carried off some of the inhabitants. Other attacks were made from time to time during that and the subsequent wars between England and France, viz., in 1744 and 1754, as well as during the Revolutionary war and that of 1812, the island having been, from its position, peculiarly exposed to them, and it did not obtain a lasting peace until after all hostilities were ended.

Mr. W. H. Potter, while discussing the hostile demonstrations alluded to above, gives us this information: "In 1775 H.B.M. man-of-war *Rose*, Captain Wallace, with several tenders, was stationed to guard the island, lest the islanders should transport their stock and stores to the main-land, these being wanted to supply the British ships. Notwithstanding the vigilance of Commodore Wallace, the authorities of Rhode Island, under the superintendence of Colonel James Rhodes, brought off the live stock from Block Island, and landed them at Stonington, whence they were driven into Rhode Island. It was to punish Stonington for this raid that Wallace, it is supposed, bombarded Stonington Point in the fall of 1775. I have conversed with a person who was present when the *Rose* made her attack on Stonington, and he said of her destination, 'The next day the *Rose* set sail for her station off Block Island, where, I understood, she was stationed to prevent the cattle of the island from being removed.' As Newport was in possession of the enemy, the Block Islanders had their full share of trials." That the people were intensely loyal to the colonies is abundantly shown by the old records, but, as subsequent events proved, they paid for their patriotism by suffering much persecution. From a communication sent to us on this and one or two other topics by Dr. T. H. Mann we cull the following:

"In August of 1775 the General Assembly ordered all the cattle and sheep to be brought off the island, except a supply sufficient for their immediate use, and two hundred and fifty men were sent to bring them off to the main-land, and such as were suitable for market immediately sent to the army, and such as were not, sold at either public or private sale. Total number of sheep and lambs removed was 1908, and the amount paid to the inhabitants for the same was £534 9s. 6d. out of the general treasury. By an act of the General Assembly of May, 1776, the inhabitants of New Shoreham were exhorted to remove from the island, but there is no record of any general attention being paid to the exhortation; but some

STREET SCENE.

few did leave the island, and their petitions to the General Assembly for permits to return, collect the rents, and look after their property were quite frequently presented, and usually referred to the general commanding the defenses of the coast of the colony.

"There are a number of instances upon record of the abuse by individuals of the rights of neutrality. The royal forces occupied the island, or held direct communication with it, for nearly eight years, and it was not a difficult matter for the hardy boatmen, with their small open boats, to procure supplies from the main-land under cover of 'needed supplies' for their own use, and sell to good advantage to the troops who occu-

life of General Nathaniel Greene, says: 'The maiden's name was Catherine Littlefield, and she was a niece of the Governor's wife, the Catherine Ray of Franklin's letters. The courtship sped swiftly and smoothly, and more than once in the course of it he followed her to Block Island, where, as long after her sister told me, the time passed gleefully in merry-makings, of which dancing always formed a principal part.'......

"She was an intimate acquaintance of General Washington's wife, Martha, meeting her many times at army head-quarters whenever the army rested long enough to permit the officers' wives to join them. In the life of General Greene, above alluded to, we read: 'And an intimacy sprung up between her

OLD MILL.

pied the island, or touched at the island for such supplies. At several different times the boatmen lost their whole cargo by confiscation to the colonial forces, who eventually put a stop to the smuggling. There is no evidence that this kind of smuggling was carried on to any extent, only by a few individuals......

"An exchange of prisoners took place between the contending forces upon Block Island at several different times, its location making it a very convenient station for such exchanges. The island furnished several distinguished men to the Revolutionary forces, and one lady who figured very conspicuously as the wife of General Nathaniel Greene. George Washington Greene, in his

and Mrs. Washington which, like that between their husbands, ripened into friendship, and continued unimpaired through life. His first child, still in the cradle, was named George Washington, and the second, who was born the ensuing year, Martha Washington.'"

In the old times of which we are speaking the lottery was considered a legitimate means to be used for raising funds for any undertaking that required an extraordinary outlay of money. Even the stern old Puritans of this colony looked upon the lottery as legitimate when its gains were to be applied to a laudable purpose.

It has already been mentioned that the poet Dana made Block Island the scene of

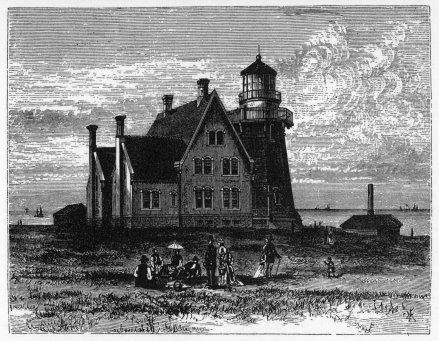

THE NEW LIGHT-HOUSE ON MOHEGAN BLUFF.

his most brilliant poem; and although his local descriptions are poetically accurate, and he makes much of a burning ship, we must question the assertion that his hero, Matthew Lee, the Buccaneer,

"Held in this isle unquestioned sway."

With equal ability, but in a different vein, the poet Whittier has also celebrated the leading romantic legend associated with Block Island, but he made the mistake of charging the Block Islanders with some acts of wickedness of which they were never guilty. We now propose to give a summary of the facts connected with the famous vessel called the *Palatine*, which we are permitted to make from an elaborate paper prepared by Mr. C. E. Perry, who is, on account of his researches in that direction, the highest authority extant.

The passengers of the *Palatine*, it would appear, were wealthy Dutch emigrants who were coming over to America to settle near Philadelphia.

There is much difference of opinion concerning the date, some placing it as early as 1720, while others suppose it to be as late as 1760. Nothing definite can be determined, but Mr. Perry's grandmother, who is now seventy-six years of age, and retains her faculties in a remarkable degree, remembers distinctly of her grandmother's telling her repeatedly that she was twelve years old when the *Palatine* came ashore.

If this reckoning can be depended on, the *Palatine* must have been wrecked during the winter of 1750–51. She came ashore, as tradition reports, on a bright Sabbath morning between Christmas and New-Year's, striking on the outer end of Sandy Point, the northern extremity of the island.

The unfortunate passengers, who doubtless commenced this memorable voyage with bright hopes of a happy future in the New World, whose attractions were at that time currently believed by the common people in many parts of Europe to vie with those of the garden of Eden before the fall, were doomed to suffer almost inconceivable miseries. For six weeks they lay off and on, skirting the coasts of Delaware, during a period of peculiarly fine and delightful weather, almost within sight of the region they had hoped to make their home, while an unnecessary and enforced starvation was daily reducing their numbers and leading the survivors to pray for death as a welcome release from further sufferings.

These emigrants, many of whom were quite wealthy, had with them money and valuables, and the officers of the ship, headed by the chief mate, the captain having died or been killed during the passage, cut off the passengers' supply of provisions and water, though there was an ample sufficiency of both on board. The pangs of hunger and thirst compelled the unarmed, helpless, starving wretches to buy at exorbitant prices the miserable fragments that the crew chose to deal out to them. Twenty guilders for a cup of water and fifty rix-dollars for a ship's biscuit soon reduced the wealth of the most opulent among them, and completely impoverished the poorer ones. With a fiendish atrocity almost unparalleled in the annals of selfishness, the officers and crew enforced their rules with impartial severity, and in a few weeks all but a few who had been among the wealthiest of them were penniless.

Soon the grim skeleton starvation stared them in the face, and as day succeeded day the broad waters of the Atlantic closed over the remains of those who a few weeks before had been envied for their good fortune and their fair prospects.

At last even the brutal officers, whose villainy no words in our language can adequately express, became satisfied that they had got all the plunder that was to be had, and left the ship in boats, landing perhaps on Long Island, to make their way to New York, carrying with them undoubtedly a remorse which preyed upon their souls, as hunger and thirst had gnawed at the vitals of their hapless victims. The famished, dying remnant of the once prosperous and happy company had no control over the ship, and she drifted wherever wind and tide might take her. How long she drifted, with the wintry winds whistling through her cordage, and the billows breaking around and across her, we shall never know. We may picture to ourselves these dying immigrants in their helpless journeying over a waste of strange waters.

Drifting here, drifting there; land always in sight, yet always inaccessible; some dying from weakness and despair, some from surfeit when the crew had gone and the provisions were left unguarded, all more or less delirious, and some raving mad. When the ship struck on Sandy Point, the wreckers went out to her in boats, and removed all the passengers that had survived starvation, disease, and despair, except one woman, who obstinately refused to leave the wreck. These poor miserable skeletons were taken to the homes of the islanders and hospitably cared for. Edward Sands and Captain Simon Ray were at that time the leading men on the island, and it was to their homes that most of these unfortunate people were taken; and on a level spot of ground at the southwest part of the island, which then formed part of Captain Ray's estate, are still to be seen some of the graves where those who died here were buried. Edward Sands was Mr. Perry's grandmother's great-grandfather, and when the survivors of those who were taken to his house had sufficiently recovered to leave the island, one of them insisted upon his accepting some memento of their gratitude for the kindness shown to them during their stay, and gave to his little daughter a dress pattern of India calico. Calicoes or chintz patches, as dress patterns of the Eastern calico were then called, were rare in those days, even among the wealthy classes; and a little Block Island girl could not easily forget her first calico dress, especially when the gift was connected with circumstances so unusual and peculiar. Mr. Perry's grandmother has often heard her grandmother speak of this dress and relate its history. This anecdote, simple and unimportant as it may seem, has a bearing on the subject, for it

OLD ICE-HOUSES ON BLOCK ISLAND.

disposes of the supposition that none of the *Palatine's* passengers ever left the island. Where they settled, or where their descendants may be now, is one of those mysteries that hover like a dark cloud over the whole subject, and seem to preclude all hope of its ever being completely unraveled. One, and one only, of the passengers that lived to tell of their living death on board this prison-ship remained permanently on the island.

This passenger was a woman whose original surname is not known. Her given name was Kate, and owing to her unusual height, she was commonly spoken of as Long Kate, to distinguish her from another woman of the same name, who was generally known as Short Kate. Both women were more frequently called "Cattern," a corruption of Catherine.

Long Cattern married a colored slave belonging to Mr. Nathaniel Littlefield, and by him had three children—Cradle, Mary, and

sea, one of the wreckers set her on fire. The object of this act is not now apparent, but it is very improbable that he intended to destroy the unfortunate woman who persisted in remaining on board. No motive for such a horrible design can be imagined, and he doubtless supposed that she could be induced to leave the wreck when she discovered that it had been set on fire.

That she did not do so, and that she was not removed by force, only add two links to the inexplicable chain of circumstances that already perplex and embarrass us. The ship drove away into the gloom and darkness of a stormy night, while the hungry flames crawled up her spars, crackled through her rigging, licked up the streaming cordage and loosened sails, and settled at last to the hull, where it finished its cruel task. So ends the material *Palatine*. So ends the life of her last unhappy passenger. So, doubtless, would have ended the story of her voyage and her wreck, to the outer

A ROYAL VISITOR.

Jennie. These all died on the island. Jennie never had any children. Cradle had five children, but none of them were ever married. Mary also had a large family, but they all moved away, with the exception of two sons, whose children moved away, and a daughter Lydia, who married, and left several children, one of whom, familiarly known as Jack, still lives on the island. Long Cattern had her fortune told before she sailed, by a seer of her native land, who prophesied that she would marry a *very* dark skinned man.

The *Palatine*, it would seem, merely grounded on the extreme edge of the point, and as the tide rose she floated off, and the wreckers, making fast to her in their boats, towed her ashore in a little bend farther down the beach, now known as Breach Cove. An easterly wind springing up, and appearances indicating that, in spite of all the efforts that could be made, she would drive out to

world at least, had it not been for that remarkable phenomenon that has served to perpetuate her memory, and to stimulate research into her history.

Tradition tells us that her shrieks of despair and agony could be plainly heard on the shore, growing each moment fainter and fainter until death or distance finally ended them.

"But the year went round, and when once more
  Around their foam-white curves of shore
  They heard the line storm rave and roar,

"Behold again, with shimmer and shine,
  Over the rocks and seething brine,
  The flaming wreck of the *Palatine*."

Little wonder that the great sachem, with the superstitious awe common to the Indian character, went raving mad whenever that strange light appeared in the offing.

There are various versions of the *Palatine* or fire-ship story, but the facts collected by Mr. Perry are undoubtedly the most authentic. The names of many respectable people, natives of Block Island and others, are in our possession who have declared that they had frequently witnessed the appearance of a burning ship off the shores of the island, and there are very few of its inhabitants who do not believe in the romantic legend. Several persons have attempted to account for the phenomenon on scientific principles. One of them, Dr. Aaron C. Willes, who was formerly a prominent physician on Block Island, wrote a letter in 1811, in which he asserted that he had seen this radiance himself a number of times, and after describing its peculiarities, but without hazarding any speculations, he makes this remark: "The cause of this roving brightness is a curious subject for philosophical investigation. Some, perhaps, will suppose it depends upon a peculiar modification of electricity; others upon the inflammation of hydrogenous gas. But there are probably many other means, unknown to us, by which light may be devolved from those materials with which it is latently associated, by the power of chemical affinities."

A full account of the shipwrecks that have happened on its shores would take more space than we can now spare. During the last twenty years, however, there have been not less than sixty, and the records show that they have been quite frequent during all the years of the present century. The loss of property has, of course, been great, but the lives lost have not been as numerous as some would imagine. In 1805 a ship called the *Ann Hope* came ashore on the south side, and three lives were lost; in 1807 the ship *John Davis* was purposely driven ashore by the captain, when the steward was murdered for fear that he would tell tales. Not long afterward three vessels came ashore in one night, but no lives were lost except those of one captain and his son, whose bodies were washed ashore clasped in each other's arms.

In 1830 the *Warrior*, a passenger packet running between Boston and New York, and accompanied by another vessel of the same line, anchored off Sandy Point one evening, in a calm. During the night the wind sprung up, leaving both vessels on a lee shore. The other vessel got under way and went out, signaling the *Warrior* to follow; but it is supposed the watch on board the *Warrior* were asleep; and when they awoke, such a gale of wind was raging that they could not get under way, and that morning she dragged her anchors and went ashore, and every soul on board was lost. The captain, who was an expert swimmer, got ashore, and brought his little boy with him; but the child's hat blowing off, he ran back after it, and the sea coming in rapidly, they were both lost.

The wreck of the steam-ship *Metis* off the shores of Watch Hill during the latter part of August, 1872, is well remembered, together with the fearful suffering and loss of life there sustained. During the morning of August 31 the drift from the wreck commenced driving up on the west shore of Block Island. A large amount of the drift consisted of fruit and other articles of a perishable nature. The property was carted up in heaps on the beach. There were many cart-loads of tea, soap, flour, boxes of butter, cheese, kegs of lard and tobacco, barrels of liquors, crates of peaches, boxes of lemons, barrels of apples, cases of dry-goods, boxes of picture-frame mouldings, and a large quantity of drift-wood, broken furniture, and general *débris*. A large, fine-looking horse was washed up with the halter still fastened to the stanchion to which he was tied. About twelve o'clock on the same night the body of an infant apparently about six months old was found, and immediately carried to a house near, where a coffin was procured, and the next day the child was buried. The night clothing which was upon the child was carefully preserved for identification, but its father nor mother ever came to shed a tear over the little grave, as they had probably gone down with the ill-fated vessel.

Two life-saving stations have been recently built upon the island, one at its eastern extremity and the other at the western. These stations are supplied with mortars for throwing lines across shipwrecked vessels, and with life-boats calculated to ride out safely any sea that may be raised, and all other necessary apparatus for rescuing the lives of mariners who may be wrecked upon the shores. The buildings will furnish shelter, lodging, and victuals to those who may be unfortunate enough to be wrecked upon the island. During the winter season and stormy weather a crew of six men to each station is in constant readiness to meet any emergency.

The stories and legends of the wreckers so often told and written are calculated to leave very erroneous impressions of the humane exertions of the wrecking bands scattered at intervals along our whole Atlantic coast. Although many of these bands have become quite wealthy in their avocation, it is just as true that they have saved millions upon millions of dollars to the owners of wrecked property, which, without the aid of the bold wrecker, would have been entirely lost. There being two "gangs" upon the island, it naturally follows that considerable rivalry exists between them, which redounds to the advantage of the owners of any vessel which chances to become a wreck on the coast.

From shipwrecks to religion the transition is not only natural, but should be profitable; and so a little information on the churches of Block Island will not be out of place in this paper. There are two church societies and two churches. They are both of the Baptist persuasion, and founded in 1772; prior to 1818 they were united, but about that time one Enoch Rose dissented from some existing opinions, whereupon a "war of the Roses" was commenced, which ended in two parties, the Associate and the Free-will Baptists; and whether this Rosy war was any more beneficial than some others of like character, is a question that can not now be settled. One thing, however, may be asserted with safety, and that is, that the islanders are a church-going people, and have generally been fortunate in having good and capable men as religious teachers. During the summer of 1875 an extensive eating-house was established at the Harbor for the convenience of transient visitors the keeper of which is an ex-preacher, who takes delight in devoting his establishment to religious services on Sundays.

Block Island is entirely without wild animals — not even a rabbit or a woodchuck will ever appear to startle the tourist on his rounds. The traditionary lore has gone so far as that the oldest inhabitant once saw a fox, but that individual was found to have come over from Point Judith on floating ice in a severe winter. Thanks to St. Patrick, there are no snakes, but any number of toads and frogs. Wild fowl, such as geese, brant, ducks, and others, were once numerous in the spring and autumn, stopping here to rest while migrating, but they have been frightened away by the roar of civilization, which has already got thus far out to sea. Loons in large numbers sometimes winter in the bay that lies between Clay Head and the Harbor. They arrive in the autumn, soon lose their wing feathers, when they are for several weeks unable to fly, and can only escape from their enemies by diving; and it is a singular circumstance that one winter a great many hundreds of them were caught by a field of floating ice, and driven toward the shore, where they were easily killed by the native sportsmen.

CLEMENCE.

THE air among the pines that day seemed heavenly to Paul Ashford, where, deep in fragrant shade, he lay upon the mellow carpet of fallen leaves, his ears filled with a sea-like murmur, his eyes upturned to the blue sky of late June.

Such a contrast to turbulent Gotham, whose never-ending whirl of business and pleasure, thronged pavements and noisy streets, made the green and quiet of this New Hampshire village little short of paradise to weary eye and worn-out nerve! For the glad life which abounded here was not that of restless humanity, but of vegetation, bird, and insect, with here and there a group of lazy, large-eyed cattle.

Upon Paul Ashford fortune had bestowed that golden mean implied in the philosopher's prayer, "Give me neither poverty nor riches." To one of his temperament, however, this was an injury rather than a benefit. The possession of greater wealth would have afforded scope for the exercise of his generous impulses and cultivated tastes, or the stimulus of poverty might have aroused his dormant energies to develop more fully the gifts with which Nature had endowed him.

For that partial dame had chosen to make Ashford a glaring instance of her favoritism, and the curse that lurks, as cynics say, in every blessing rendered this versatility his chief drawback. In literature, art, and music he was "clever," when in either path alone, with the aid of a little adverse criticism, he might have risen to eminence. But his book had been pronounced a success, his sketches full of promise, his tenor at amateur concerts faultless, and having taken his place as an "Admirable Crichton," he had become nothing more. So his great natural gifts had achieved for Ashford little beyond that social celebrity which is the result of such accomplishments, when united with a good temper and a handsome person.

Possessing a comfortable income and no incentive to action, he might be likened to the nicest, brightest of engines, finished within, polished without, lacking only—steam. And, as a consequence, at twenty-five he fell a prey to *ennui*.

"You need a thorough shaking up," declared his physician, not sorry for the opportunity. "Leave off your make-believe life a while. Don't visit Saratoga or Newport, but take a pedestrian trip to the mountains, and end your campaign by two months in some place much as God made it. Don't come back till your face is browner and your eyes brighter. And go without your friends, to make the change complete."

Which advice Ashford first laughed at, then pondered, and finally followed.

Amidst the grandeur of cloud-cutting summit and deep ravine, the clear mountain air had filled him with fresh life, while sun and wind had left their wholesome ruddiness upon his cheek. *Ennui* had slipped off like an old garment long before the delicious afternoon when he had thrown himself down to rest a little, before resuming his tramp, under the pine-trees in the outskirts of Hillburn, a hamlet nestled amidst that Alpine scenery.

He took a book from his knapsack, only to find that reading accorded less with the place than dreaming; and before he fairly knew it, his dreams were genuine, for he was fast asleep.

Whittier's
New Hampshire
(1900)

THE

NEW ENGLAND MAGAZINE.

NEW SERIES.

AUGUST, 1900.

VOL. XXII. NO. 6.

WHITTIER'S NEW HAMPSHIRE.

By David Lee Maulsby.

THE fashionable world has elected to make its summer pilgrimage to the White Mountains; and to this day the Presidential range and its neighborhood are the objective points for most admiring tourists in New Hampshire. But Whittier's favorite haunts were to the south of the parallel belonging to Sandwich Notch, through which, one autumn day, "the west wind sang good morrow to the cotter"; and "Chocorua's horn" was to him, so far as his pages show, more impressive than the rocky summit of Mount Washington. It is true that during the last twelve years of his life the Quaker singer was from time to time a summer guest at Intervale; but these later years have left small record in his verse. It is also true that, near the beginning of his poetical career, his rather long poem, "The Bridal of Pennacook," was written in northern New Hampshire, in order, characteristically enough, to soothe the waking hours of an invalid girl. The name of Passaconaway, the Indian chief whose daughter is the heroine of this poem, is now associated once for all with the beautiful dome-like mountain of the Sandwich range. Clearly this Indian chief was a favorite hero of Whittier's, for "Passaconaway" was the title of a prose tale that he wrote before 1839, the scene of which was laid on the banks of the Merrimac River.

It was in the valley of the Pemigewasset that N. P. Rogers lived, whom Whittier visited with pleasure when only twenty-six years old, and who later entertained the famous English antislavery agitator, George Thompson. In Concord, New Hampshire, it will be remembered, Whittier and his English friend, after a speech by the latter, were threatened with death by a bloodthirsty mob. In his appreciative sketch of Mr. Rogers, Whittier makes many loving references to New Hampshire scenery; for example: "One can almost see the sunset light flooding the Franconia Notch and glorifying the peaks of Moosehillock, and hear the murmur of the west wind in the pines, and the light, liquid voice of Pemigewasset sounding up from its rocky channel, through its green hem of maples."

Related to the same vicinity is the beautiful apostrophe to the summits of the North, in "Mountain Pictures." The boldness of the following lines, afterwards tamed into acceptable conformity at the suggestion of another, is noteworthy:

"Last night's thunder-gust
Roared not in vain; for where its lightnings
    thrust
Their tongues of fire, the great peaks seem
    so near,
Lapped clear of mist . . ."

Mrs. Fields tells sympathetically of a visit paid her in Campton in 1865,

From a photograph copyrighted by H. G. Peabody.

CHOCORUA LAKE AND MOUNTAIN.

when the poet, beginning with Emerson's pregnant lines upon "The Sphinx," discoursed upon the mysteries of spiritual existence, and ended by recounting a vision concerning the outcome of the civil war, described in writing by an old man of Sandwich a quarter of a century before the event.

Another region of New Hampshire connected with Whittier's writings is the southeastern part, near his Amesbury home, and bordering upon the ocean. Whittier's associations with the Isles of Shoals have already been described in the NEW ENGLAND MAGAZINE.* The "Ramoth Hill" of that heart-revealing poem, "My Playmate," was in Hampton. In the same place General Moulton used to live, a legend connected with whose family appears in "The New Wife and the Old." The ancestors of the Hugh

Tallant who planted "The Sycamores" came from Ireland to settle in New Hampshire. At Seabrook lived Elizabeth Gove of peaceful memory.

> "Her path shall brighten more and more
>   Unto the perfect day;
> She cannot fail of peace who bore
>   Such peace with her away."†

It was at the house of Sarah Gove, at Hampton Falls, that at last the tired singer gently slipped away from life.

But Whittier's memory, as did his love, clings most closely about that part of New Hampshire which lies, on the map, below Campton and above Laconia. And, indeed, when full recognition is given to his affection for the part of the Granite State which is nearest to his Massachusetts home, and when all is said in due praise of the giant mountains of the north, it is

*In the article, "In Whittier Land," by W. S. Kennedy, November, 1892.

† "The Friend's Burial."

THE SANDWICH RANGE AND LAKE CHOCORUA.

From a photograph copyrighted by H. G. Peabody.

From a photograph copyrighted by H. G. Peabody.

THE BEARCAMP RIVER.

not surprising that Whittier dearly loved the milder central region. For the country about Lake Winnepesaukee, if it does not lie stretched at the feet of great mountainous masses of towering height, is yet full of the calmer beauty of hills and vales diversified with sheets of water, now placid as a mirror, now white-capped by the breeze. In sight, too, from favorable points are many of the eminent sentinels of time—half the horizon, it may be, rimmed with distant peak behind peak. Thus, from a convenient high point on the stage road between Moultonboro and Sandwich, one can see Chocorua, Paugus, Passaconaway, Wonalancet, Whiteface, Tripyramid, Black Mountain (sometimes inappropriately called Sandwich Dome), and Mount Israel, to say nothing of the less conspicuous Squam Mountains, extending toward the west. The reader of early American war ballads will recall that rude description of Lovewell's fight, when Paugus, chief of the Pigwacket Indians, was attacked by "worthy Cap-

JOHN G. WHITTIER.

tain Lovewell." But one's pleasure in the view need not be complicated with historico-literary associations. Let him rather turn to the left, where Red Hill lifts its several summits to heaven.

"So seemed it when yon hill's red crown,
  Of old, the Indian trod,
And, through the sunset air, looked down
  Upon the Smile of God."

Or he may turn to the right, where Ossipee Mountain, with its Black Snout, shows its long ridge.

"The shadows round the inland sea
  Are deepening into night;
Slow up the slopes of Ossipee
  They chase the lessening light."

"Tired of the long day's blinding heat,
  I rest my languid eye,
Lake of the hills! where, cool and sweet,
  Thy sunset waters lie!" *

Red Hill might conveniently be encompassed in half a day's good driving; but the roots of Ossipee extend in so many directions that one with the best horse could hardly encircle all of them in a single sweep, should one travel from sunrise till the fall of even-

* "The Lakeside."

ing. Even Black Snout is celebrated, as the reader may see if he will turn to the third stanza of "A Letter," published anonymously during the heated political contest of 1846, when John P. Hale of New Hampshire was elected to the United States Senate to the joy of the abolitionists.

What wonderful changes the poet saw pass over his beloved mountains; what shadows of clouds on their breasts, while the concealed sun spread broad fields of light below; what mists lazily rose from slope to slope, or clung like a wreath upon the half-hidden hoary head! What sunsets painted their fascinating or grotesque shapes of color, while the land lay slumbering in a tender radiance, as of a life well spent and drawing to its peaceful close! There was something congenial to Whittier's disposition in the tempered boldness of this landscape, its glimpses of possessing beauty, its virile restraint.

Of the score or more of poems suggested to Whittier while he was in the Granite State, the greater part represent one or another of three localities, —the Bearcamp River, Asquam (or Squam) Lake, and Lake Winnepesaukee. All three of these regions may

THE OLD BEARCAMP HOUSE.

THE STURTEVANT FARM NEAR CENTRE HARBOR.

be included in a square, the side of which measures twenty-five miles. For many happy summers the inn at West Ossipee was the accustomed place of meeting for Whittier and his friends, among whom Lucy Larcom may be particularly mentioned as a fellow worker in letters. Here the poet, with his group of associates, young and old, gathered about the evening fireside, would listen with zest to the tale of the day's adventures, and join heartily in the merriment of the hour. For among his intimate friends, Whittier's reputation as a teller of stories and a maker of pleasant talk almost equals his reputation as a poet. The name of the hostelry thus made fragrant with happy memories was the Bearcamp House, although Whittier, in his prefatory note to the "Voyage of the Jettie," speaks of it as the "Wayside Inn." It was burned down in 1881, much to the poet's regret. All that is now left of it is the cel-

lar-place, overgrown with a tangle of bushes. But the peaceful street of the village remains, and over it one of the two new inns hangs out its picturesque sign-board of Revolutionary fashion, while the other extends to the visitor the welcoming arms of its broad piazza. The Bearcamp River winds along the roadway in its stony channel, and can be traced in its meandering for many miles. Of literary interest is the traditional spot near the covered bridge, whence the *Jettie*, named in honor of "the Bay State's graceful daughter,"

THE WELL ON THE STURTEVANT FARM.

SQUAM LAKE AND SHEPARD HILL.

THE WOODLAND PATH AT THE STURTEVANT FARM.

"All the pines that o'er her hung
    In mimic sea-tones sung
        The song familiar to her;
    And the maples leaned to screen her,
    And the meadow grass seemed greener,
        And the breeze more soft to woo her!"

"Dies now the gay persistence
    Of song and laugh in distance;
        Alone with me remaining
    The stream, the quiet meadow,
    The hills in shine and shadow,
        The sombre pines complaining."

Mrs. Jettie Morrill Wason, was launched.

"On she glided, overladen,
    With merry man and maiden
        Sending back their song and laughter,
    While, perchance, a phantom crew,
    In a ghostly birch canoe,
        Paddled dumb and swiftly after!"

At the request of the same lady, who also first sang it, was composed the love song, "The Henchman," by no means so much read as it deserves. It is hard to resist the impression that

THE WHITTIER PINE, ABOVE SQUAM LAKE.

the unfulfilled love which found expression in "My Playmate," and in "Memories," and which perhaps is hinted in the concluding stanza of "Maud Muller," was also the inspiration of this mediæval picture of a self-effacing lover, forever faithful, seeking no sign that his lady shares his passion.

There are other unpublished poems relating to the shores of the Bearcamp, and at least two such poems that have been published. "How They Climbed Chocorua" belongs to the former group, and humorously celebrates the adventures of seven of

Of the two published poems that relate to the Bearcamp country, one deserves a word by itself. The inquisitive sojourner in West Ossipee is likely to find himself confused in his attempts to discover historical basis for that popular narrative poem, "Among the Hills." Surely Whittier never wrote a better bit of description than this:

> "The locust by the wall
> Stabs the noon-silence with his sharp alarm;"

and the rest of the prelude is note-

Photograph by Arthur M. Comey.

MOUNT WHITTIER FROM TAMWORTH.

the poet's young friends, who spent the night on the horned mountain. The Knox brothers, who were accustomed to furnish bear steaks to the inn, acted as guides in this adventure, and the poem celebrating the ascent was read by Lucy Larcom at a husking in the Knox barn, not far from the inn, soon after the party returned. The poem was read as coming from an unknown writer, although everybody knew that Whittier, who sat silently by, must be the author. As a reward, the poet was presented with the bear skin that was then stretching on the barn door.

worthy as containing a plea for beauty in the humblest life. The body of the poem, as many readers will remember, begins with the description of a brilliant autumn day, presaging winter, while filled with memories of June.

> "Above his broad lake, Ossipee,
> Once more the sunshine wearing,
> Stooped, tracing on that silver shield
> His grim armorial bearing."

In the afternoon of this glorious day, made more resplendent by contrast with the preceding weeks of rain, the poet is driving, "my hostess at my side," on an errand that takes them to a certain white farmhouse,

"Where taste had wound its arms of vines
    Round thrift's uncomely rudeness."

"The sun-brown farmer in his frock
    Shook hands, and called to Mary:
Bare-armed, as Juno might, she came,
    White-aproned from her dairy.

"Her air, her smile, her motions, told
    Of womanly completeness;
A music as of household songs
    Was in her voice of sweetness."

The farmer straightway falls in love with the beautiful city maiden, who playfully puts aside his advances until his passionate rejoinder convinces her that his life happiness depends upon her answer. Then she gracefully avows that she loves him. The result is a marriage that establishes the maiden among the mountains, a centre of refinement and a revealer of nature's loveliness to those who have hitherto been unseeing.

THE LAUNCHING PLACE OF THE "JETTIE."

On the way home the hostess tells how this cultivated wife came to be in the honest farmer's home:

"From school and ball and rout she came,
    The city's fair, pale daughter,
To drink the wine of mountain air
    Beside the Bearcamp Water!"

She tells how her step grew firm and cheeks blooming.

"For health comes sparkling in the streams
    From cool Chocorua stealing;
There's iron in our northern winds,
    Our pines are trees of healing."

"The coarseness of a ruder time
    Her finer mirth displaces,
A subtler sense of pleasure fills
    Each rustic sport she graces.

"Her presence lends its warmth and health
    To all who come before it.
If woman lost us Eden, such
    As she alone restore it."

The farmer becomes prosperous, and in due time is sent as representative to the General Court.

The verisimilitude of such details naturally provokes inquiry. "Who was the sun-brown farmer?" Who in real life was the city bred "Mary"

Photograph by Arthur C. Smith.

THE OSSIPEE MOUNTAIN.

that he wedded, each thus experiencing, in their perfect union, "the giving that is gaining"? And who was the "hostess," who told the story so circumstantially to the poet, as he drove at evening by her side to buy some butter from the proud housewife? More than one student has tried to answer these questions, and has weighed the probabilities which attach to the legend each one of the neighboring farmers who married maidens from the city. Now and then, some misguided questioner, by letter or by personal interview, has made inquiry of those patient women, who, at one time or another, served as hostess of the old Bearcamp River House. Some wielders of the modern camera have even carried off in triumph a photograph of house or gravestone, hugging it as an au-

Photograph by Arthur C. Smith.

LAKE WINNEPESAUKEE.

thentic memento. But, so far as the heroine of the poem is concerned, Whittier's own words set the matter forever at rest. In a letter written shortly after the burning of the Bear-camp House he says: "The lady of the poem 'Among the Hills' was pure-ly imaginary. I was charmed with the scenery in Tamworth and West

ST. MARY'S ARCH, OSSIPEE PARK.

Ossipee, and tried to call attention to it in a story." This letter is given at page 669 of Mr. Pickard's biography, to which friends of Whittier must always be deeply indebted. In the earliest version of the poem, the land-lord, not the landlady, tells the story.

Before leaving the region of West Ossipee and Tamworth, it is worth remarking that three mountains have, at one time or another, laid claim to Whittier as godfather. As one may see on recent maps, the two noble hills in South Tamworth, whose bases may be said to meet, while their sky-lines are quite distinct, are called Whittier and Larcom, and thus fitly typify the friendship and fellowship of their namesakes. Formerly the mountain now called Lar-com was called Whittier. But the late Mr. M. F. Sweetser, who named this mountain for the Quaker poet, consented to the change of name proposed by the Appalachian Club, and when the matter was left to a vote of the people of Tamworth, in town meeting assembled, they approved the new name, "Larcom," which, in con-sequence, as it now ap-pears upon the maps, is sufficiently authorized, while "Whittier" appro-priately designates the larger and loftier of these two neighboring moun-tains. The third claimant of the poet as godfather is a pretty hill in West Os-sipee, whose ascending path starts not far from the launching place of the *Jettie.* Once up the hill, the climber, gets an en-trancing view of the valley of the Bearcamp, such as might well suggest a lov-ing description like that in "Sunset on the Bear-camp":

"A gold fringe on the purpling hem
    Of hills, the river runs,
As down its long green valley falls
    The last of summer's suns.
Along its tawny gravel-bed
    Broad flowing, swift and still,
As if its meadow levels felt
    The hurry of the hill,
Noiseless between its banks of green
    From curve to curve it slips;

Photograph by Mabel E. Anderson.

OSSIPEE LAKE.

The drowsy maple-shadows rest
  Like fingers on its lips."

"Touched by a light that hath no name,
  A glory never sung,
Aloft on sky and mountain wall
  Are God's great pictures hung."

The local tradition is that Whittier used to climb the hill, by no means an impossible task for an active man of sixty-nine; but the Quaker bard was a semi-invalid during his successive summers in this place, and at the date of the poem was accustomed to let his younger friends go mountain climbing without him.

Several summers were spent in part at the Asquam House, in Holderness, on the summit of Shepard Hill. It was at the Asquam House that the lines on the death of Longfellow were written in a volume of his poems. It was from the veranda of the house that Whittier watched the progress of the tempest limned in powerful lines in his "Storm on Lake Asquam," and it was from the same inn that the following letter was sent to Mrs. Fields:

"Thy dear letter comes to me here, and I have read it where this beautiful but unhistoric lake stretches away before me, green-gemmed with islands, until it loses itself in the purple haze of the Gunstock Mountains, whose summits redden in the setting sun. . . . . . I left Amesbury yesterday in a hot southerly rainstorm; but just as we reached Alton Bay the wind shifted to the north-northeast and blew a gale, scattering the clouds, and by the time our steamer passed out of the bay into the lake the water was white-capped, and waves broke heavily on the small islands, flinging their foam and spray against the green foliage on the shores. It was pleasant to see again the rugged mass of Ossipee loom up before us, and the familiar shapes of the long Sandwich range come slowly into view. To-day the weather is perfect,—clear

Photograph by E. D. Holmes.

LITTLE MOUNTAIN AND MOUNT LARCOM.

BOAR'S HEAD, HAMPTON BEACH.

"Moosehillock's woods were seen,
With many a nameless slide-scarred
   crest
And pine-dark gorge between.
Beyond them, like a sun-rimmed cloud,
   The great Notch mountains shone,
Watched over by the solemn-browed
   And awful face of stone!"

Our shy poet abandoned this wide prospect only when the crowds of curious visitors became annoying to him.

It may seem strange to those who have visited but one of these places that Whittier preferred the Asquam lakes to the outlook from Ossipee Park, high up on Ossipee Mountain. The lofty plateau is commanding, the sight satisfying of Winnepesaukee and its dotting islands, with perchance a glimpse of the lake steamboat, the *Mount Washington*, tiny in the distance, emitting its ribbon of smoke. Grandly impressive is the rocky gorge, carved by the streams of centuries, spanned by many rustic bridges, which overlook cascades and silent stony pools. When Whittier visited Ossipee Park in 1884, he was too feeble to climb up and down the steep pathways, and could not have gone so far as the chief cataract. Nor did he thrust his hand into that rocky

keen sunshine, and cool, bracing wind. The season is rather late, and the sweetbrier roses are still in bloom, and these often parched hill slopes are now green as your English downs."

The Gunstock Mountains mentioned above, or "peaks of Gunstock," as the twin summits were otherwise called, are now united as Mount Belknap.

At Asquam Lake, Whittier met gladly some of General Armstrong's teachers from the Hampton Institute in Virginia, and to this region he would urge his friends to come to visit him ere it should be too late. He never tired of the Asquam Lakes, in storm and sunshine, and speaks of them as "the loveliest lakes of New England." Again, he says: "Such a sunset the Lord never before painted." The summit of Shepard Hill, upon which the Asquam House stands, affords outlook to the horizon on every side. In "The Hilltop," one aspect of the view is thus described:

"There towered Chocorua's peak; and west,

THE GOVE HOUSE AT HAMPTON FALLS, WHERE WHITTIER DIED.

cave known as "the devil's den," in which His Satanic Majesty might still take refuge, if he were now no larger than the serpent that tempted Eve. But there was a seat the Quaker poet loved, where he could muse upon a waterfall as it slipped from pool to pool, under a leaning leafy birch near "Mary's Arch," and there still hangs a painted piece of wood bearing the year and day of his reverie.

It may have been this ascent of Ossipee Mountain that he had in mind when he said that he had once looked down upon the scene from another mountain and found that it had lost its charm. But it is certain that the lake whose Indian name he had written meant "the Smile of God," was a lasting source of rest and inspiration. It is commemorated in at least four of his poems: "The Lakeside," "Summer by the Lakeside," "A Summer Pilgrimage," and "A Legend of the Lake." Whittier, in his later years, used to like the hotel at Centre Harbor, partly because of its earlier associations with his sister Elizabeth. No doubt there are "summer people" at Centre Harbor, who, treading the shores of Winnepesaukee, pass the site of the deed celebrated in the last-named poem without being aware of it. On the other hand, scarcely a week of the summer goes by without some one stopping at the home of " 'Squire Dow" to ask if this really is the dwelling that was once on fire, and into which rushed the half-crazed man, determined to save from the flames the prized armchair of his dead mother. The house now standing was built by its present occupant on the very spot of the dwelling thus destroyed in the winter of 1853-4, and is of the same general plan. The victim was a man of legal education, well informed, but dissipated. In vain his neighbors tried to dissuade him, then an elderly man, from entering the burning building. He plunged into the fire as if to atone for all his shortcomings by one final and commanding act of self-sacrifice.

It is possible to visit Sturtevant Farm by driving up the long steep hill that leads out of Centre Harbor. Here can still be seen the room which Whittier used to occupy during the seven consecutive years of his visits, and the old four-poster in which he used to sleep, originally the property of Robert Fowle, the first Episcopal rector at Holderness. Here, too, is the desk at which Whittier wrote. Across the hall one is shown the bedchamber of Lucy Larcom, for she did literary work in this very room. At the rear of the house is a charming woodland path of shade, along which Whittier used to wander, past the little family burying ground, until he came to the great pine and its prospect over Lake Asquam.

"Alone, the level sun before;
   Below, the lake's green islands;
Beyond, in misty distance dim,
   The rugged northern highlands."

Under this spreading tree many social hours were spent with books and conversation, and one evening in 1885 Whittier surprised his friends by reading to them, in sonorous tones, his "Wood Giant,"

"Dark Titan on his Sunset Hill,
   Of time and change defiant!"

Is there not something of personal reference in the fancies awakened by the great pine tree's mystic rune?

"Was it the half unconscious moan
   Of one apart and mateless,
The weariness of unshared power,
   The loneliness of greatness?"

White-spired Melvin Village, although on Lake Winnepesaukee, and the scene of "The Grave by the Lake," was probably never visited by Mr. Whittier. This is the opinion of the inhabitants, and it also helps to explain the inaccuracies of the poem, which assumes that the spot where bones of a giant were unearthed is identical with that traditionally regarded as a tribal grave of the Ossipee Indians. There is no "great

mound" such as the note prefatory to
the poem declares to be "at the mouth
of the Melvin River." Mr. C. W.
Davis of Melvin, who first visited the
traditional mound forty-five years
ago, has in his possession "A Gazet-
teer of the State of New Hampshire:
by John Farmer and Jacob B. Moore:
embellished with an accurate Map of
the State, and several other engrav-
ings: By Abel Bowen. Concord: published by Jacob B. Moore, 1823."
On page 191 of this interesting old
book, under the heading "Moultonborough," occurs the following passage:

"On the line of Tuftonboro, on the
shore of the lake, at the mouth of
Melvin River, a gigantic skeleton was
found about fifteen years since, buried
in a sandy soil, apparently that of a
man more than seven feet high—the
jaw bones easily passing over the face
of a large man. A tumulus has been
discovered on a piece of newly cleared
land, of the length and appearance of
a human grave, and handsomely
rounded with small stones, not found
in this part of the country; which
stones are too closely placed to be
separated by striking an ordinary
blow with a crowbar, and bear marks
of being a composition. The Ossipee
tribe of Indians once resided in this
vicinity, and some years since a tree
was standing in Moultonborough on
which was carved in hieroglyphics the
history of their expedition."

It is easy to see how a reader
might assume that the first two sentences of this extract refer to the
same place. As matter of fact, the
skeleton was found a mile and a half
from the place where the "tumulus"
used to be known to the boys of
the neighborhood as the Indian
grave. Apparently Whittier, naturally
enough, confused the two objects, and
transferred the giant skeleton to the
Indian burial mound.

Colonel Higginson, in his "Contemporaries," has referred to Whittier's surpassing claim to the laureate-
ship as poet of New England. If one

should need further witness to Whittier's love for New Hampshire, in particular, the published correspondence
and other prose writings will be found
to contain many incidental touches
betokening his interest in "the wild
and lonely hills and valleys" he knew
so well. Always there is the tone of
joy in the prospect of visiting these
beloved scenes, if he is away from
them, or of perfect contentment if he
is face to face with their satisfying
charm. To Emerson he writes: "I
must go up among the New Hampshire hills, away from the sea." Perhaps the most striking single passage
illustrating Whittier's transcendent
regard for external nature is put into
the mouth of Doctor Singletary, a
character on the lines of Ian McCla-
ren's Doctor MacLure and Whit-
comb Riley's "Doc Sifers." To the
good doctor heaven would be welcome, should it bear the familiar
aspect of earth. He says to a friend:

"Have you not felt at times that our
ordinary conceptions of heaven itself,
derived from the vague hints and
Oriental imagery of the Scriptures,
are sadly inadequate to our human
wants and hopes? How gladly would
we forego the golden streets and
the gates of pearl, the thrones, tem-
ples and harps, for the sunset lights of
our native valleys; the wood-paths,
whose moss carpets are woven with
violets and wild flowers; the songs of
the birds, the low of cattle, the
hum of bees in the apple blossoms,
the sweet, familiar voices of human
life and nature! In the place of
strange splendors and unknown music, should we not welcome rather
whatever reminded us of the common sights and sounds of our old
home?"

For a third of a century the poet of
New England's life and various
moods found recreation and stimulus in the sweet mid-region of New
Hampshire. Here he met his friends
in that intimate converse that he
dearly loved. Here he talked, and
read, and wrote, while the wind

played its melodies through pine and maple, or rippled the bosom of the shining lake. Here he found on page and tongue the legends that the people knew, and turned them into song. Here his humor found vent in youthful sallies that vied with the spirits of his younger companions, or took shape in some impromptu rhyme that might be incorporated into the letter he was writing, or might be repeated to some laughing listener as too slight to be set down upon paper. It was of the New Hampshire hills that he said, "Nature never disappoints me," a sentence uttered more than once and of more than one place, so that it may be said to comprehend his feeling for the great world of earth and sky, which has moved so many poets to rapturous expression, as it has entered into the soul of many another man whose heart has felt although his lips are dumb.

Nantucket in the Revolution (1905)

Nantucket in the Revolution

By Arthur H. Gardner

THE decade preceding the Revolutionary period had been a prosperous one for Nantucket. In the century which had elasped since John and Richard Gardner had migrated thither from Salem and cast in their lot with Thomas Macy, Edward Starbuck, Tristram Coffin, Peter Folger and others of that little band of pioneers, a thrifty township had sprung up on this island wilderness and held high rank—third it was claimed—in commercial importance among the maritime ports of the colonies.

From its remote and isolated location, its circumscribed limits and other natural conditions, it early became apparent to the settlers of Nantucket that their chief resources must be drawn from the ocean rather than the soil, and they applied themselves to the development of an hitherto untried industry—the whale-fishery. Beginning by pursuing in boats from the shore occasional whales which ventured in sight of land, they later employed small vessels to go in search of the leviathan at greater distances and encouraged by the success of these early undertakings, gradually fitted out larger craft and extended their voyages until Nantucket's whaling fleet numbered upwards of one hundred and fifty vessels manned by more than two thousand men. The prosecution of the business on this extensive scale necessarily carried in its train and tributary to it numerous other industries. Rope-walks, candle-works, coopers' shops, and sail-lofts were hives of industry, blacksmiths, boat-builders, carpenters, painters, draymen, in fact, all classes of artisans and mechanics found steady employment, the air resounded with the hum of activity and the town was prosperous and thriving.

Such was the condition of Nantucket when the clouds of political discontent, aroused by the oppressive acts of the Mother Country, began to gather in the colonial horizon. Ere long rumblings of the approaching conflict were wafted across the waters. Of the three tea ships whose cargoes were unceremoniously dumped into Boston Harbor on that memorable night in December, 1773, the "Dartmouth," Captain Hall, and the "Beaver," Captain Hezekiah Coffin, were owned by William Rotch of Nantucket, and thither they returned immediately, bringing the disquieting news. Of the fate of these two famous ships it may be interesting to know that in April, 1774, the "Dartmouth" was sent to London with a cargo of oil and foundered at sea on her return trip in November of that year. The "Beaver" went to Brazil Banks, filled with oil, and in 1774 sailed for London, where Captain Coffin died and the ship was sold. The "Beaver" was built on North River in 1772, about the same time as the "Bedford," another Nantucket whaler owned by Mr. Rotch, and destined to become equally famous in

connection with events incident to the struggle for Independence, and of which mention will be made later.

One of the earliest acts particularly affecting Nantucket was the passage by the English parliament in 1774 of the "Massachusetts Bay Restraining Bill," the operation of which was to prevent trade to any save British ports, and to prohibit the Newfoundland and other American fisheries. On petition of English Friends, or Quakers, representing the bad effect of this rigorous law on Nantucket, the island was exempted from its provisions, whereupon the Colonial congress, to prevent the Newfoundland fishery being supplied with provisions through Nantucket, passed an act prohibiting the exportation of provisions to that island from any of the colonies save that of Massachusetts Bay, and on the 7th of July, 1775, further ordered

"that no provisions or necessaries of any kind be exported from any part of this colony to the Island of Nantucket until the inhabitants of said island shall have given full and sufficient satisfaction . . . that the provisions they have now by them have not been and shall not be expended in foreign but for domestic consumption."

Of course the effect of this order was to kill the Newfoundland fishery and deprive the islanders of one of their means of support.

Meantime the war cloud which had hovered over the colonies had burst, and open hostilities begun. Blood had been shed at Lexington and Bunker Hill. While the echoes of that "first shot heard round the world" reverberated over the country and quickened the enthusiasm of the colonists, they carried consternation and dismay to the inhabitants of Nantucket, a large proportion of whom were Quakers and opposed on religious principles to bearing arms. The situation of the island was peculiarly unfortunate. Lying thirty miles from the mainland, exposed to inroads of either belligerent and with neither able to protect her, cut off from supplies and with all business at a standstill, a common distress fell upon all her brave hearts. The whaling fleet, representing a large part of the wealth of the island, was necessarily much at sea, liable to capture, while there was scarce a family but had some member on shipboard, for whose safety the keenest anxiety was felt. Most of the whalers, however, arrived home in safety, the English government directing their efforts in the early part of the conflict to land operations, and neglecting until later to send out their cruisers in great numbers. Each whaleship which arrived, however, added to, rather than lessened the embarrassment of the islanders, since it increased the number of consumers of their rapidly decreasing stores, while furnishing no means of replenishment.

In September, 1775, the Selectmen of Sherburne addressed a letter to the General Court, setting forth the distress occasioned by the order cutting off their sources of supplies and requesting that it be so far modified as to suffer the necessaries of life to be brought them. Whereupon a resolve was adopted authorizing the committee of correspondence for the town of Falmouth to grant permits to the inhabitants of Nantucket to purchase supplies in specified quantities. The resolve also made the members of the committee a kind of spies to watch over the islanders. In December the General Court became suspicious that the islanders were importing more provisions than were needed for domestic consumption and supplying the same to the enemy, whereupon they called for an accounting and ordered the withholding of any further of provisions, fuel or necessaries, and the printers of the colonies were instructed to publish this order in their newspapers. As a result of this public proscription great suffering ensued among the islanders, who were brought to the verge of famine. Early in 1776 the Selectmen of Sherburne succeeded in satisfying the General Court that their suspicions were unfounded and the prohibitive order was suspended.

Whaling having now ceased, the wharves and shores were lined with vessels stripped to their naked masts. The necessities of the inhabitants compelled them to turn their attention to developing such resources as were within their immediate reach. Some engaged in farming, others in fishing near the shore in boats. Cut off from all kinds of imported goods, they dispensed with those that were not absolutely essential, while necessity invented substitutes for others. Little advantage from their fishing could they derive without salt, while the difficulty of importing it rendered its price almost prohibitive. To meet this exigency salt works were established at various points on the island and its manufacture attempted after a crude fashion. A considerable quantity was thus obtained, but not enough to compensate for the expense incurred, and the attempts were finally abandoned. The failure was attributed to the prevalence of fog keeping the air moist and preventing the water from evaporating as rapidly as required.

Meantime the merchants, whose ships and commodities were lying idle, conceived the idea of clubbing together and dispatching a few vessels to the West Indies laden with oil, candles, etc., for which good returns were certain could they elude the enemy, and by a number joining in loading one vessel the individual loss in case of capture would be less severely felt.

By order of the Provincial Congress, all vessels sailing to foreign ports without colony permits were lawful prizes if captured by privateers. From the records in the office of the secretary of state it appears that some six or eight applications for permits were filed by Nantucket merchants early in 1777, and orders were issued to the Naval Officer of the port of Nantucket to allow these vessels to proceed on their voyages, they being manned wholly by Quakers. The few which returned in safety made very profitable voyages, but the risk of capture finally became so great in consequence of the increasing number of British vessels which thronged the American coast, that the enterprise became too hazardous to continue, not so much on account of pecuniary loss, as of the sufferings of those who were captured, many of whom languished and perished in English prison ships established on the coast. Cut off from this meagre source of supply, and rendered desperate by privations and sufferings which daily grew more and

more intense, a number of the inhabitants ran open sailboats to Connecticut and elsewhere to procure provisions, making their trips by night, and selecting dark and stormy ones even in winter to pass the ports held by the enemy, preferring the danger of foundering at sea to falling into the hands of the British and incarceration in the dreaded prison ships.

By these means and with what bread stuff was raised on the island the distress of the inhabitants was in a measure relieved, though many were barely saved from death. The risk attending the trips was great and many lost their lives in them. Even then provision was scarce and dear. Corn was frequently $3 a bushel and sometimes more. Flour was $30 a barrel and other breadstuff in proportion. The suffering for clothing, however, was inconsiderable throughout the war, for immediately on being cut off from the supply of English manufactures the women in each family engaged in weaving cloths of various kinds for their own household. Twelve or fifteen thousand sheep roamed over the island, subsisting on the herbage which its soil produced and they furnished wool in abundance, which was carded, spun and woven. A considerable quantity of flax was raised yearly, dye stuff was readily obtainable, and by the industry of the women the members of each household were thus kept supplied with comfortable homespun clothing.

Prior to the war the inhabitants had depended on the mainland for their wood. This source being now cut off, recourse was had to such fuel as was obtainable on the island. Several swamps outside the town were found to abound with peat, and general permission was granted by the owners for the public to dig therefrom, without charge. Many availed themselves of the privilege, while others went up harbor in boats to Coskata, some six or eight miles from town, and cut firewood, while still others used the scrub oaks on the "commons" or brush from the swamps. All these were hard, tedious and laborious methods of procuring fuel, but the inhabitants eagerly and thankfully availed themselves of them.

Meantime the island was often visited by English cruisers who would threaten to sack or burn the town, and this kept the inhabitants in a state of constant apprehension, although the enemy never carried their threats out to any considerable extent until one day in the early spring of 1779. On the sixth of April a fleet of eight vessels came down to the bar, where all but two anchored. The latter entered the harbor and made fast to the wharf. About a hundred armed men landed and proceeded to plunder the stores and commit other depredations. They were expostulated with by leading citizens and finally desisted, but not until they had destroyed and carried away property to the value of $50,000 or more.

The inhabitants now determined to no longer submit without protest. A town meeting was convened and it was voted to apply to the General Court for permission to send a committee to the British commanders in New York to represent the situation at Nantucket and solicit redress and protection. Permission was granted and Benjamin Tupper, Timothy Folger, Samuel Starbuck and William Rotch were appointed. So well did they execute their mission that written orders were issued by Sir George Collier, commander-in-chief of the English naval forces, forbidding any further molestation of the inhabitants of Nantucket under severe penalties. Sir Henry Clinton fully united with these orders and gave verbal assurance to the committee that they should be obeyed.

Meantime the colonial government, though unable to protect the helpless islanders, watched with jealous eye for the least symptoms of disloyalty. Early in 1778 a resolve was adopted by the General Court of Massachusetts "for making enquiry relative to supplying the enemy by way of Nantucket." What was the result of this does not appear, but the action of the town in memorializing the British commanders was duly reported to General Gates, who called it to the attention of the Massachusetts legislature with severe strictures. Thereupon that body, notwithstanding it had sanctioned the procedure, went through the farce of an investigation, and adopted the following resolution June 23, 1779, the very day that the order exempting Nantucket from British aggression was issued at New York:

It appearing by sundry intercepted letters that Several Inhabitants of the island of Nantucket have been discovered in a design to carry on a correspondence and trade in an unjustifiable manner with the British troops at Newport and New York to the injury of the cause of the United States. And the town of Sherburne as a town on said island appears in some measure guilty of a violation of their fidelity to said States by sending a committee to convey their Memorial in an unwarrantable manner to the British troops at Newport and New York, ... the said inhabitants are hereby strictly forbidden to send any memorial or have any communication with the enemies of these United States without first obtaining leave of this General Court.

Following close upon this reprimand and injunction by the home government came the disquieting information that a squadron of English armed vessels was preparing to leave New York for Nantucket for the purpose of sacking and plundering the town, and of burning it should any resistance be made. It was soon learned that the fleet had arrived at Martha's Vineyard and was waiting a change of wind, then at the eastward, to proceed on its mission of destruction. Consternation reigned. There seemed to be nothing to prevent the coming of the enemy but the continuance of the prevailing east wind. Meantime the inhabitants improved the 'opportunity to secure a portion of their property. Carts, boats and men were employed day and night carrying goods out of town, or depositing them in scattering houses which it was supposed might escape the conflagration. Some buried their valuables. A constant look-out was kept in anxiety and dread for the appearance of the fleet, but day after day the wind remained unchanged. At length the commanding officers of the fleet wrote to the people of Nantucket, under date of September 16, 1779, charging them with having signalled an approaching vessel, thus preventing her capture by an English cruiser lying in wait for her within the harbor, and

of having molested and hindered his Majesty's servants on divers occasions in the discharge of their duties, and they threatened that unless immediate and sufficient explanation was made to commence operations against them. To each and every charge (despite the prohibition of the Provincial Government against holding communication with the enemy) the town, through its committee, returned a full and explicit denial, supplementing the same with a statement of unprovoked injuries and insults to which the inhabitants had been subjected. On their return the committee reported that they

"found the gentlemen much dissatisfied but on a thorough inspection of the matter and our producing to them the votes of the town of Sherburne, disavowing every such proceeding, they were satisfied so far as to commence no proceeding against the town without the future conduct of the inhabitants should make it necessary."

During all this time, and until the fleet returned to New York, the wind continued to the eastward, which it is probable alone prevented the immediate execution of the enemy's designs, and many people were inclined to regard it as a miracle wrought by Divine Providence in behalf of the islanders.

In July, 1780, the town forwarded another memorial and petition to the British authorities, setting forth their distressed condition and asking permission for twenty fishing boats to fish around the island, four vessels to be employed whaling and ten small craft to supply the island with wood and provisions. This petition ultimately resulted in securing in part the desired relief, though not until it had been several times renewed. Toward the latter part of 1781 a number of whaling permits were issued by Admiral Digby, the British commander at New York.

When it became known that some kind of indulgence had been granted by the enemy to the people of Nantucket it created considerable dissatisfaction in some quarters, but the colonial government, knowing the situation there, inclined to condone rather than condemn the acceptance of favors from the British. Several vessels whaling under these permits were taken by American privateers, and carried into port, but in every instance when it was found that the permits were used for no other purpose than that for which they were granted and that the vessels had not been engaged in any illicit trade, they were immediately released.

At the time of the Revolution Nantucket had fifteen London packets. One of these—ship "Somerset," Captain Alexander Coffin—was on her passage from London when she was captured by Commodore Paul Jones. Captain Coffin had dispatches from Franklin to the Continental Congress announcing the treaty and alliance with France, and these papers were subsequently forwarded by Jones.

Despite outward show of neutrality and public disavowal of acts in violation thereof, the people of Nantucket at heart were in sympathy with the colonists in their struggle for Independence. Indeed, in March, 1775, before hostilities had actually begun, two donations, one of £26—16—9 from the Congregational parish, and one of £90—9 from persons unknown, supposed to be the Friends' Society, an aggregate of over $500,

were forwarded from Nantucket for the relief of the inhabitants of Boston and Charlestown "suffering from the operation of that cruel act of the British Parliament, commonly called the Boston Port Bill," and during the war, by a preconcerted arrangement of the mill vanes on the hill, many a vessel which would otherwise have fallen a prey to British cruisers in the harbor was warned of their presence by wireless telegraphy.

While prudence dictated the policy of neutrality and non-resistance generally observed by Nantucket, it was in accord with the Quaker principles which prevailed. There were, however, not a few restless spirits, whose hearts, fired by patriotism or stirred by indignation, chafed under the restraint imposed by the more sober-minded majority. Some of these joined the Continental army, others engaged on board privateers. Among the latter was Captain Benjamin Bunker, who early in the war enlisted as an armorer in a South Carolina privateer, was captured by the British and confined in the Jersey prison ship. After his release he returned to Nantucket. One day an English privateer which lay off the Bar sent two boats to intercept an in-coming schooner. The crew of the latter succeeded in beaching her and cut away her mainmast before the boats captured her. Captain Bunker hastily manned two whaleboats, retook her and made prisoners of her captors. Returning to the wharf, he took a small schooner, put all his men below but two to navigate her, and ran out to and alongside the privateer, when his men swarmed aboard and captured her without striking a blow. Captain Bunker also captured another privateer in the Cod of the Bay near Great Point. Running down to her with a small vessel and a four-pound gun, before the Englishman could comprehend the situation, the gun was fired, killing one man and smashing a boat, and the privateer was grappled, boarded and taken. Captain Bunker conveyed all his prisoners in safety to the continent and delivered them to the colonial authorities.

Just how many Nantucketers entered the American service can never be ascertained for the reason that many enlisted to the credit of towns on the mainland or otherwise concealed their identity out of consideration for the avowed neutrality of Nantucket, but it is known that at least twenty-one men were enrolled at one time under Captain Paul Jones on the "Ranger" in 1777, and many of them followed him through the war, or until they fell in action—one of them, Reuben Chase, being the "Long Tom Coffin" of Fennimore Cooper's "Pilot." So far as is known not a man entered the British service. Many captured seamen were given their choice of joining a British vessel or confinement in the prison ships, and invariably chose the latter, despite the horrors in store. It was Captain Nathan Coffin of Nantucket who, when captured by a British admiral and told that he must go into His Majesty's service, or go into irons, made that memorable reply recorded by Bancroft: "Hang me if you will to the yard arm of your ship, but don't ask me to become a traitor to my country."

Heavy taxes were imposed on Nantucket by the colonial government, but owing to the impoverished condition of the people, but a small portion was collected, and the balance was remitted after the war. In addition, requisitions for supplies for the continental army were made from time to time. In 1777 Nantucket was required to furnish 59 blankets. In 1778, and again in 1779, 158 pairs of shirts, shoes and stockings. In 1780, 111 shirts, pairs of shoes and stockings, 55 blankets and 77,292 pounds of beef. In 1781, 88 shirts, pairs of shoes and stockings, 44 blankets and 20,976 pounds of beef. It has been stated that Nantucket was exempted from military drafts, but I find from Colonial records that on January 25, 1782, the town of Sherburne having signified its readiness to procure another man to fill the place of one furnished the previous December, who had proved to be a deserter, was granted ten days in which to do so and the state treasurer was directed to suspend his execution accordingly. Again, on a Resolve adopted March 7, 1782, for raising 1,500 men to serve in the Continental army three years or during the war, Nantucket's apportionment is designated at sixteen men.

Near the close of 1782 the old Quaker merchants of Nantucket received private information that peace was coming. Among the whaling fleet in the harbor was the ship Bedford, before alluded to. She had been one of the last of the whaling fleet to arrive during the war, returning from Brazil Banks in March, 1777, full of oil, and had lain at Nantucket ever since. She was immediately fitted for sea and dispatched to London, and was the first vessel to carry the American flag into a British port. She arrived off Trinity, February 6, 1783, flying the stars and stripes, and her appearance caused such comment and excitement as probably no other vessel ever did, before or since. Her arrival was thus chronicled by an English magazine of the day:

The Bedford, Capt. Mooers, belonging in Massachusetts, arrived in the Downs the 3d of Feb., passed the Gravesend the 4th and was reported at the Custom House the 6th inst. She was not allowed regular entry until some consultation had taken place between the Commissioners of the Customs and the Lords of the Council, on account of the many Acts of Parliament yet in force against the rebels in America. She is loaded with 488 butts of whale oil, is American built, manned wholly by American seamen, wears the rebel colors, and belongs to the Island of Nantucket in Massachusetts. This is the first vessel which has displayed the thirteen rebellious stripes in any British Port.

About the same time William Rotch dispatched sloop "Speedwell" to St. Domingoes. She was taken by the British and carried into Jamaica but immediately released when it was learned that the war was over, and she showed that the first United States flag there On her return to Nantucket she was loaded with candles and sent to Quebec, where she was the first vessel to display the stars and stripes to the wondering gaze of the Canadians. Thus it will be seen that Nantucket's vessels were the first to proclaim in foreign ports that England's American daughter had cut loose from her mother's apron strings and set up house-keeping on her own account.

At the beginning of the war there were more than 150 vessels belonging to Nantucket navigated by the youth and manhood of the island. Fifteen were lost at sea and 134 were captured. Of the crews, some perished miserably in prison ships, others lingered years in confinement and returned, broken in health and ruined in fortune to destitute families. Macy's history estimates that over a thousand lost their lives in consequence of the Revolution, but perhaps so large an estimate is not warranted. At the close of the war there remained only a few old hulks and the town resembled a deserted village. Colonial paper currency had been freely taken by the islanders and the failure of the government to redeem it still further impoverished them and added to their distress.

Thus it will be seen that Nantucket, though she furnished no regiments to swell the Continental army, fitted out no privateers to harass the enemy at sea, and witnessed no sanguinary conflicts within her borders, paid as dearly for the Independence of our country as any place in the Union.

Ten Days in Nantucket (1885)

TEN DAYS IN NANTUCKET.

By Elizabeth Porter Gould. [1]

One night in the early part of July, 1883, as the successful real-estate broker, Mr. Gordon, returned to his home from his city office, his attention was arrested by a lively conversation between the members of his family on the wonders of Nantucket. The sound of this old name brought so vividly back to him his own boyish interest in the place, that almost before he was aware of it he announced his return home to his family by saying: "Well, supposing we go to Nantucket this summer? It is thirty-four miles from mainland, and so free from malaria there is no better place for fishing and sailing, and there would be a mental

EARLY MORNING, NANTUCKET.

interest in looking around the island which would be instructive and delightful, and, perhaps, profitable for me from a business point of view."

Mrs. Gordon, who had of late years developed a keen interest for the historic and antique, immediately seconded her husband in his suggestion; and before the evening closed a letter was sent to Nantucket asking for necessary information as to a boarding-place there, for at least ten days, for a party of five, — Mr. and Mrs. Gordon, their daughter Bessie, twenty years of age, their son Tom, fifteen years, and a favorite cousin of

It is scarcely necessary to say that few schools have ever been established upon such a basis of conscientiousness and love, and with such adaptability in its conductors, as that at Eagleswood ; few have ever held before the pupils so high a moral standard, or urged them on to such noble purposes in life. Children entered there spoiled by indulgence, selfish, uncontrolled, sometimes vicious. Their teachers studied them carefully ; confidence was gained, weaknesses sounded, elevation measured. Very slowly often, and with infinite patience and perseverance, but successfully in nearly every case, these children were redeemed. The idle became industrious, the selfish considerate, the disobedient and wayward repentant and gentle. Sometimes the fruits of all this labor and forbearance did not show themselves immediately, and, in a few instances, the seed sown did not ripen until the boy or girl had left school and mingled with the world. Then the contrast between the common, every-day aims they encountered, and the teachings of their Eagleswood mentors, was forced upon them. Forgotten lessons of truth and honesty and purity were remembered, and the wavering resolve was stayed and strengthened ; worldly expediency gave way before the magnanimous purpose, cringing subserviency before independent manliness.

Then came the war. In 1862 Mrs. Weld published one of the most powerful things she ever wrote, — "A Declaration of War on Slavery." We have not the space to follow the course of the sisters' lives farther ; and, were it otherwise, the events narrated would be all too familiar. Sarah, after a somewhat prolonged illness, died on the 23d of December, 1873, at Hyde Park, Mass. The funeral services were conducted by the Rev. Francis Williams, and eloquent remarks were made also by Wm. Lloyd Garrison. On the 26th of October, 1879, Angelina passed quietly away, and the last services were in keeping with the record of the life then commemorated. We close this writing with a passage from the remarks which Wendell Phillips made on that occasion. No words could possibly be more touching or more eloquent : —

When I think of Angelina there comes to me the picture of the spotless dove in the tempest, as she battles with the storm, seeking for some place to rest her foot. She reminds me of innocence personified in Spenser's poem. In her girlhood, alone, heart-led, she comforts the slave in his quarters, mentally struggling with the problems his position wakes her to. Alone, not confused, but seeking something to lean on, she grasps the Church, which proves a broken reed. No whit disheartened, she turns from one sect to another, trying each by the infallible touchstone of that clear, child-like conscience. The two old, lonely Quakers rest her foot awhile. But the eager soul must work, not rest in testimony. Coming North at last, she makes her own religion one of sacrifice and toil. Breaking away from, rising above, all forms, the dove floats at last in the blue sky where no clouds reach. . . . This is no place for tears. Graciously, in loving kindness and tenderly, God broke the shackles and freed her soul. It was not the dust which surrounded her that we loved. It was not the form which encompassed her that we revere; but it was the soul. We linger a very little while, her old comrades. The hour comes, it is even now at the door, that God will open our eyes to see her as she is : the white-souled child of twelve years old ministering to want and sorrow; the ripe life, full of great influences; the serene old age, example and inspiration whose light will not soon go out. Farewell for a very little while. God keep us fit to join thee in that broader service on which thou hast entered.

theirs, Miss Ray, who was then visiting them, and whose purse, as Mr. Gordon had so often practically remembered, was not equal to her desire to see and to know.

In a few days satisfactory arrangements were made, which ended in their all leaving the Old Colony depot, Boston, in the half-past twelve train, for Wood's Holl, where they arrived in two hours and a half. From that place they took the steamer for a nearly three hours' sail to Nantucket, only to stop for a few moments at Martha's Vineyard.

While they were thus ploughing their way on the mighty deep, Nantucket's famous crier, "Billy" Clark, had climbed to his position in the tower of the Unitarian church of the town, — as had been his daily custom for years, — spy-glass in hand, to see the steamer when she should come in sight. Between five and six o'clock, the repeated blowing of the horn from the tower announced to the people his success, and became the signal for them to make ready to receive those who should come to their shores. Just before seven o'clock the steamer arrived. While she was being fastened to the wharf, Tom was attracted by this same "Billy," who, having received the daily papers, was running up the wharf toward the town ringing his bell and crying out the number of passengers on board, and other important news, which Tom failed to hear in the noise of the crowd. A few minutes' walk brought the party to their boarding-place. When Mrs. Gordon spied the soft, crayon likeness of Benjamin Franklin on the wall, as she stepped into the house, her historical pulse quickened to such an extent that she then and there determined to hunt up more about the Folgers; for was not Benjamin Franklin's mother a Folger and born on this island? Then, as she saw about her some old portraits and copies of the masters, and, above all, a copy of Murillo's Immaculate Conception in the dining-room, she was sure that the atmosphere of her new quarters would be conducive to her happiness and growth. The others saw the pictures, but they appreciated more fully, just then, the delicious blue-fish which was on hand to appease their hunger.

After a night of restful sleep, such as Nantucket is noted for giving, they all arose early to greet a beautiful morning, which they used, partly, for a stroll around the town. Of course, they all registered at the Registry Agency on Orange street, where Mr. Godfrey, who had entertained them by his interesting guide-book on Nantucket, gave them a kind welcome. Then they walked along the Main street, noticing the bank, built in 1818, and passed some quaint old houses with their gables, roofs, and sides, all finished alike, which Burdette has described as "being shingled, shangled, shongled, and shungled." Tom was struck with the little railings which crowned so many of the houses; and which, since the old fishing days' prosperity did not call the people on the house-tops to watch anxiously for the expected ships, were now more ornamental than useful. They passed, at the corner of Ray's Court, a sycamore tree, the largest and oldest on the island, and soon halted at the neat Soldiers' Monument, so suggestive of the patriotic valor of the island people.

Later they found on Winter street the Coffin School-house, — a brick building with two white pillars in front and a white cupola, — which was back from the street, behind some shade trees, and surrounded by an iron fence. As they looked at it Miss Ray read aloud the words inscribed on the front : —

FOUNDED 1827 BY
ADMIRAL SIR ISAAC COFFIN, BART.
ERECTED
1852.

They were also interested to see, near by, a large white building, known as the High School-house. As they neared home Tom's eyes noticed the sign of a Nantucket birds' exhibition, and a visit to that place was made.

During the walk Mrs. Gordon had been particularly interested in the large cobble-stones which the uneven streets supported in addition to the green grass, and also the peculiar Nantucket cart, with its step behind.

On their return to their boarding-place, they joined a party that had been formed to go to the Cliff, a sandy bluff about a mile north from the town, where they were told was to be found the best still-water bathing on the island. Soon they were all on the yacht " Dauntless," which hourly plied between the two places ; in twenty minutes they were landed at the Cliff; and fifteen minutes later they were all revelling in the warm, refreshing water. Bessie declared that in all her large bathing experience on the north shore she had never enjoyed anything like this. Miss Ray felt that here in this warm, still water was her opportunity to learn to swim ; so she accepted the kind teaching of a friend ; but, alas, her efforts savored more of hard work to plough up the Atlantic ocean than of an easy, delightful pleasure bottling up knowledge for some possible future use. While Miss Ray was thus struggling with the ocean, and Bessie and Tom were sporting like two fish, — for both were at home in the water, — Mr. Gordon was looking around the Cliff with his business eye wide open. As he walked along the road back from the shore, and saw the fine views which it afforded him, he admired the judgment of Eastman Johnson, the artist, in building his summer-house and studio there. A little farther on, upon the Bluffs, the highest point on the island, he noted the house of Charles O'Conor with the little brick building close by for his library ; he then decided that an island which could give such physical benefit as this was said to have given to Mr. O'Conor, would not be a bad one in which to invest. So the value of the Cliff or Bluffs he placed in his note-book for future use.

At the same time that Mr. Gordon was exploring the land Mrs. Gordon was in the office of two gallant young civil engineers, exploring the harbor ! In fact she was studying a map of the surroundings of the harbor, which these young men had made to aid them in their work of building a jetty from Brant Point to the bell-buoy. As she examined it she found it hard to believe that Nantucket had ever stood next to Boston

VIEWS IN NANTUCKET, MASS.

and Salem, as the third commercial town in the Commonwealth. She sympathized deeply with the people of the years gone by who had been obliged to struggle with such a looking harbor as the map revealed, and said that she should go home to learn more of the " Camels," which she honored more than ever. When they told her that probably three years more than the two that had been given to the work were needed to finish the jetty, and that there was a slight possibility that another one would be needed for the best improvement of the harbor, she thought her interest in the matter could be better kept alive if she should hunt up her old trigonometry and learn that all over again ! With this idea she left the young men, whose kindness to her she fully appreciated, and went to find her party. She soon found, on the yacht ready to go back to town, all but Miss Ray ; she had chosen to take one of the many carriages which she had noticed were constantly taking passengers back and forth from the town to the Cliff, at the rate of ten cents apiece.

Later in the afternoon their attention was arrested by another one of the town-criers, — Tom had learned that there were three in the town, — who was crying out that a meat-auction would be held that night at half-past six o'clock. When they were told that these meat-auctions had been the custom of the town for years, they were anxious to attend one ; but another engagement at that hour prevented their so doing, much to Tom's regret.

The next day was Sunday. As Bessie and Tom were anxious to see all of the nine churches of which they had read, they were, at first, in doubt where to go ; whereas their mother had no questions whatever, since she had settled in her own mind, after having reduced all sects to the Episcopal and the Roman Catholic, that the Episcopal Church was the true historic one, and, therefore, the only one for her personal interest, that she should go to the St. Paul's on Fair street. Mr. Gordon usually went to church with his wife, although he often felt that the simplicity of the early apostolic days was found more in the Congregational form of worship. This day he yielded to Tom's desire to go to the square-steepled Congregational Church on Centre street, to hear Miss Baker, who had been preaching to the congregation for three years. He entered the church with some prejudice ; but soon he became so much interested in the good sermon that he really forgot that the preacher was a woman ! Miss Ray and Bessie went to the Unitarian Church on Orange street, to which the beautiful-toned Spanish bell invited them. After an interesting service, on their way out they met Tom, who wished to look into the pillared church of the Methodists, near the bank, and also into the " Ave Maria" on Federal street, where the Roman Catholics worshipped. Miss Ray, being anxious to attend a Friends' meeting in their little meeting-house on Fair street, decided to do so the following Sunday, if she were in town ; while Bessie said that she should hunt up then the two Baptist churches, the one on Summer street, and the other, particularly for the colored people, on Pleasant street. Their surprise that a town of a little less than four thousand inhabitants should contain so many churches was modified somewhat when they remembered that once, in 1840, the number of inhabitants was nearly ten thousand.

In the afternoon the party visited some of the burying-grounds of the town, six of which were now in use. The sight of so many unnamed graves in the Friends' cemetery, at the head of Main street, saddened Miss Ray; and she was glad to see the neat little slabs which of late years had marked the graves of their departed ones. They strolled around the Prospect Hill, or Unitarian Cemetery, near by, and wished to go into the Catholic one on the same street; but, as Mrs. Gordon was anxious to see some of the old headstones and epitaphs in the North burying-ground on North Liberty street, and their time was limited, they went there instead. When Tom saw her delight as she read on the old stones the date of 1770, 1772, and some even earlier, he said that she must go out to the ancient burial-ground on the hill near the water-works and see the grave of John Gardner, Esq., who was buried there in 1706. As he said this one of the public carriages happened to be within sight, and she proposed that they take it and go immediately to that sacred spot. When they arrived there her historic imagination knew no bounds; her soliloquy partook of the sentiment — in kind only, not in degree — which inspired Mark Twain when he wept over the grave of Adam. In the mean while, Mr. Gordon had gone to the Wannacomet Water-works, which supplied the town with pure water from the old Washing-pond. He there noted in his note-book that this important movement in the town's welfare was another reason why investment in the island would be desirable.

As they started to go back to town from the burial-ground Tom wished that they could drive to the south-west suburbs, to see the South and also the colored burying-grounds, for he should feel better satisfied if he could see everything of a kind that there was! But Mrs. Gordon had seen enough for one day, and so they drove to their boarding-house instead.

The ringing of the sweet-toned church bell the next morning at seven o'clock reminded Miss Ray of her desire to visit the tower which contained it. She had noticed how it rang out three times during the day, at seven, twelve, and nine o'clock, and, for the quiet Nantucket town, she hoped that the old custom would never be dropped. And then this bell had a peculiar attraction for her, for it was like the one which was on her own church in Boston, the New Old South. She had been greatly interested in reading that this " Old Spanish Bell," as it was called, was brought from Lisbon in 1812; that it was stored in a cellar for three years, when it was bought by subscription for about five hundred dollars, and put in this tower. She had read, further, in Godfrey's guide-book, that " some little time after the bell had been in use, the sound of its mellow tones had reached the Hub; and so bewitching were the musical vibrations of this queenly bell (e) of Nantucket to many of the good people of the renowned ' City of Notions,' that the agents of the Old South Church negotiated with the agents of the Unitarian Church, saying that they had a very fine clock in their tower; that they had been so unfortunate as to have their bell broken, and wished to know at what price this bell could be procured. The agents of the Unitarian Church replied that they had a very fine bell in their tower, and would like to know at what price the Old South Society would sell their clock. The bell weighs one thousand five hundred and seventy-five pounds; the Boston gentlemen offered one dollar a pound for it, and upon finding they could not get it at any price, they asked where it came from; and having ascertained its history, sent to Lisbon to the same foundry and procured that which they now have." And she had been told further that this same bell had been removed to the new church on the Back Bay. With all this pleasant association with the bell of her own church, of course she must pay it a visit. So at about nine o'clock, after Mr. Gordon and Tom had gone off with two gentlemen for a day's blue-fishing, she, with Mrs. Gordon and Bessie, started out for their morning's sight-seeing. In a half hour's time they had climbed the stairs to the tower, and were admiring the fine new clock, — a gift from one of Nantucket's sons, now living in New York, — which had been first set in motion two years before, to replace an old one which had told the time for over half a century. A little farther up they saw the famous bell, and Miss Ray did wish that she could read Spanish so as to translate the inscription which was upon it. A few steps more brought them into the dome itself. Here, then, was the place where " Billy " came to sight the steamers; and here was where a watchman stayed every night to watch for fires. Whenever he saw one, Bessie said his duty was to hang a lantern upon a hook in the direction of the fire and give the alarm. She said that this had been the custom for years. As they were all enjoying this finest view which the island affords, Bessie spied the Old Mill in the distance, and as she had that painted on a shell as a souvenir of her Nantucket trip she must surely visit it. So they were soon wending their way up Orange street, through Lyons to Pleasant, and then up South Mill to the Old Mill itself. On paying five cents apiece, they were privileged to go to the top and look through the spy-glass, and also see the miller grind some corn. This old windmill, built in 1746, with its old oaken beams still strong and sound, situated on a hill by itself, was to Bessie the most picturesque thing that she had seen. She associated this with the oldest house on the island, built in 1686, facing the south, which she had seen the day before.

In the afternoon they continued their sight-seeing by visiting the Athenæum on Federal street. They found it to be a large white building with pillars in front, on the lower floor of which Miss Ray was particularly pleased to see such a good library of six thousand volumes, and a reading-room with the leading English and American periodicals, the use of which she learned was to be gained by the payment of a small sum. Bessie was attracted to the oil-painting on the wall of Abraham Quary, who was the last of the Indian race on the island. Then they examined, in an adjoining room, the curiosities gathered together for public inspection. Here they found the model of the "Camels," and also the jaw of a sperm whale, seventeen feet long, with forty-six teeth and a weight of eight hundred pounds. Bessie said that the whale from which it was taken was eighty-seven feet long and weighed two hundred tons. When Mrs. Gordon learned that this very whale was taken in the Pacific Ocean and brought to the Island by a Nantucket Captain, she became as much interested in it as in the "Camels," for surely it had an historical interest. After an hour spent in this entertaining manner, they returned to their boarding-place in time to greet the gentlemen who had come back with glowing accounts of their day's work, or rather pleasure, for they had met with splendid success. Tom's fingers were blistered, but what was that compared to the fun of blue-fishing!

What particularly interested the ladies was a "Portuguese man of war" which one of the gentlemen had caught in a pail and brought home alive. This beautiful specimen of a fish, seen only at Nantucket, their hostess said, and seldom caught alive, was admired by all, who, indeed, were mostly ignorant of the habits or even the existence of such a creature. Bessie wondered how such a lovely iridescent thing could be poison to the touch. Tom promised to study up about it when he should begin his winter studies, whereupon his mother said that if he would tell her what he should learn about it she would write it out for the benefit of them all.

The next morning they all started from the wharf at nine o'clock in the miniature steamer, "Island Belle," for Wauwinet, a place seven miles from the town. Miss Ray had become interested in the pretty Indian names which she had heard, and was struck with this, which she learned was the name of an old Indian chief who once controlled a large eastern part of the island. In an hour they landed on the beach at Wauwinet. They found it decorated with its rows of scallop-shells, some of which they gathered as they walked along. Some of the party made use of this still-water bathing, while others ran across the island, some three hundred yards, to enjoy the surf-bathing there. Tom was delighted with this novelty of two beaches, separated by such a narrow strip of land, that he was continually going back and forth to try the water in both places. He only wished that he could go up a little farther where he had been told the land was only one hundred yards wide, — the narrowest part of the island. After a shore dinner at the Wauwinet House, and another stroll on the beaches, they started for the town on the yacht "Lilian," which twice a day went back and forth. The wind was unfavorable, so they were obliged to go fourteen miles instead of seven, thus using two hours instead of one for the sail. On their way they passed the places known as Polpis, Quidnet, and Coatue. Mr. Gordon was so much impressed with the advantages of Coatue that he noted the fact in his note-book; while his wife became so much interested in the nautical expressions used that she declared that she should get Bowditch's "Navigation," and see if she could find those terms in it; she must know more of navigation than

she did.   As they landed at the wharf they heard "Billy" Clarke crying out
that the New Bedford band would give a grand concert at Surf Side the
next day.   Now, as this kind of music had been the chief thing which they
had missed among the pleasures of Nantucket, of course they must go
and hear it.   So the next afternoon, at two o'clock, they were on the cars
of the narrow-gauge railroad, bound for the Surf-Side Hotel, which they
reached in fifteen minutes, passing on the way a station of the life-saving
service department.   They spent an hour or two seated on the bluff overlooking the grand surf-beach, and enjoying the strains of music as they
came from the hotel behind them.   It must be confessed that Mr. Gordon
was so interested in noting the characteristics of this part of the island with
an eye to business, that he did not lose himself either in the music of
the band or the ocean.   On his way back to town, when he expressed his
desire to build a cottage for himself on that very spot, Surf Side, Mrs.
Gordon would not assent to any such proposition; for she had settled in
her own mind that there was no place like Brant Point, where she
and Bessie had been that forenoon; for did not the keeper of the light-
house there tell her, when she was at the top of it, that on that spot was
built the first light-house in the United States, in 1746?   That was enough
for her, surely.   The matter was still under discussion when Miss Ray
told them to wait until they had visited 'Sconset before they should
decide the question.   As for her she could scarcely wait for the next morning to come when they should go there.   And when it did come it
found her, at half-past eight o'clock, decorating with pond-lilies, in honor
of the occasion, the comfortable excursion-wagon, capable of holding their
party of eight besides the driver.   By nine o'clock they were driving up
Orange street by the Sherburne and Bay View Houses, on their way to
Siasconset, or, 'Sconset, as it is familiarly called.

As they passed a large white building known as the Poor Farm,
Tom was surprised that a town noted for its thrift and temperance should
be obliged to have such an institution.   Bessie was glad to learn that they
were going over the old road instead of the new one, while Miss Ray
would rather have gone over the new one, so as to have seen the mile-
stones which Dr. Ewer, of New York, had put up by the wayside.
They met the well-known Captain Baxter, in his quaint conveyance,
making his daily trip to the town from 'Sconset.   As they rode for
miles over the grassy moors with no trees or houses in sight, none of them
could believe that the island had once been mostly covered with beautiful
oak trees.   Soon the village, with its quaint little houses built close together on the narrow streets, which wound around in any direction to
find the town-pump, its queer, one-story school-house, its post-office,
guarded by the gayly-colored "Goddess of Liberty," was before, or
rather all around them.   They had all enjoyed their ride of seven and a
half miles; and now, on alighting from the carriage, the party separated
in different directions.   Miss Ray insisted upon bathing in the surf-
beach here in spite of its coarse sand and rope limitations, since it was the

farthest out in the Atlantic Ocean. Her experience with the strong
undertow in its effects upon herself and upon those who watched her is
one, which, as no words can portray it, Tom has decided to draw out for
some future Puck; for he thinks that it is too good to be lost to the public.

Mrs. Gordon and Bessie walked among the houses, noticing the peculiar names which adorned some of them, and, indeed, going inside one
of the oldest where a step-ladder was used for the boys of the household to
get up into their little room. They crossed the bridge which led them to
the Sunset Heights where some new houses, in keeping with the style of
the old ones, were being built. They were pleased to see this unity of
design, rather than the modern cottage which had intruded itself upon
that coast. In their walk they learned that about eleven or twelve
families spent the winter at 'Sconset. The air was intensely invigorating,
so much so that Mrs. Gordon, who was no walker at home, was surprised at herself with what she was doing without fatigue. Later they
found Mr. Gordon looking at the new church which had just been
completed, and which he had ascertained was built for no sectarian purpose, but for the preaching of the truth. They all met at noon for their
lunch, after which they went a mile and a half farther to visit the Sankaty
Head light-house, the best one of the five on the island. The keeper
kindly escorted them up the fifty-six steps to the top, where they learned
that the point of the light was one hundred and sixty-five feet above
the level of the sea. He gave them some more facts relative to the light,
interspersed with personal experiences. Tom said that he should
remember particularly the fact that he told him that this light-house
would be the first one that he should see whenever he should come home
from a European trip.

Two hours later they were relating their pleasant experiences in the dining-room of their boarding-house, while enjoying the delicious blue-fish
which gratified their hunger. As for Miss Ray her anticipations had been
realized; and that night she wrote to a certain young man in Boston that
she knew of no place in America where they could be more by themselves and away from the world, when their happy time should come
in the following summer, than at 'Sconset.

The next afternoon found them all listening to Mrs. McCleave, as she
faithfully exhibited the many interesting curiosities of her museum, in her
home on Main street. Mrs. Gordon was very much interested in the
Cedar Vase, so rich with its "pleasant associations," while Bessie was
delighted with the beautiful carved ivory, with its romantic story as told
by its owner. Miss Ray considered Mrs. McCleave, with her benevolent
face, her good ancestry, and her eager desire to learn and impart, a good
specimen of the well-preserved Nantucket woman.

Through the courtesy of their hostess they were privileged, on
their way back, to visit the house of Miss Coleman, on Centre street,
there to see the wonderful wax figure of a baby six months old, said to be
the likeness of the Dauphin of France, the unfortunate son of Louis XVI.

When Mrs. Gordon learned that this was brought to Nantucket in 1786, by one of her own sea-captains, she became very much excited over it. As she realized then that her knowledge of French history was too meagre to fully understand its historical import, although she appreciated its artistic value, she determined that another winter should be partially devoted to that study. So she added " French history " to " Camels," " Light-houses," " Navigation," and " Indians," which were already in her note-book. She had added " Indians " the day before when her interest in them had been quickened by some accounts of the civilization of the early Indians in Nantucket, which seemed to her almost unprecedented in American history. After supper Mr. and Mrs. Gordon went out in a row-boat to enjoy the moonlight evening, Tom went to the skating-rink, Miss Ray spent the evening with some friends at the Ocean House near by, while Bessie went out for a moonlight sail with some friends from a western city, whom, she said, she had " discovered, not made." Her appreciation of a fine rendering of her favorite Raff Cavatina by a talented young gentleman of the party, soon after her arrival, had been the means of bringing together these two souls on the musical heights, which afterwards had led to an introduction to the other members of the party, all of whom she had enjoyed during the week that had passed. And now, with these newly-found friends, on this perfect July evening, with its full moon and fresh south-westerly breeze, in the new yacht " Lucile," she found perfect enjoyment. Pleasant stories were related, and one fish-story was allowed, to give spice to the occasion. After a little more than two hours' sail they found themselves returning to the Nantucket town, which, in the moonlight, presented a pretty appearance.

The next day, Saturday, Mr. Gordon and Tom started early to sail around the island, with an intention of landing on the adjoining island, Tuckernuck. Tom had calculated that it would be quite a sail, for he knew that Nantucket Island was fourteen miles long, and averaged four miles in width; and his father had decided that such a trip would give him a better idea of the island's best points for building purposes. On their return at night they found that the ladies had spent a pleasant day, bathing, riding, and visiting some Boston friends who were stopping at the Springfield House, a short distance from them. Bessie had found more pleasure in the company of the young musician and his friends, having attended one of the morning *musicales* which they were accustomed to have by themselves in the hall of the Athenæum. Tom and his father had much to tell of their day's pleasure.

Mr. Gordon, for once in his life, felt the longing which he knew had so often possessed his wife, to go back and live in the years gone by; for if he could now transfer himself to the year 1659, he might buy this whole island of Thomas Mayhew for thirty pounds and two beaver hats. What a lost opportunity for a good business investment! As it was, however, some valuable notes were added to his note-book, suggested by the trip, which time alone will give to the world. He was more and more convinced that the future well-being of Nantucket was more in the hands of real-estate brokers and summer pleasure-seekers, than in those of the manufacturers, agriculturists, or even the fishing men as of old. He could see no other future for her, and he should work accordingly. His chief regret was that the island was so barren of trees.

They spent the next day, Sunday, in attending church, as they had planned, and in pleasant conversation and rest preparatory to their departure for Boston on the following morning. They expressed gratitude that they had not been prevented by sickness or by one rainy day from carrying out all the plans which had been laid for the ten days. Mrs. Gordon very much regretted that they had not seen the famous Folger clock which was to be seen at the house of a descendant of Walter Folger, the maker of it. She should certainly see it the first thing, if she ever were in Nantucket again; for she considered the man, who, unaided, could make such a clock, the greatest mechanical genius that ever lived. She felt this still more when she was told that the clock could not be mended until there could be found a mechanic who was also an astronomer.

At seven o'clock the next morning they were all on board the steamer, as she left the old town of Nantucket in the distance. Mrs. Gordon looked longingly back at Brant Point, which she still felt was the best spot on the island; while Bessie eagerly watched for the little flag which a certain young gentleman was yet waving from the wharf.

At half-past one they were in Boston, and an hour later at their suburban home, all delighted with their short stay in Nantucket. They felt that they had seen about all that there was to be seen there, and they were glad to have visited the island before it should be clothed with more modern garments.

Golfing
Around the Hub
(1899)

BY GEORGE H. SARGENT.

S O firm a hold has the Scotch game taken upon the people of Boston and its vicinity, that within a radius of twelve miles from the Boston City Hall, no less than twenty-nine links may be found, comprising in their circuit every variety of hazard known to man. An imaginary round would take one over courses varying from five to eighteen holes in length, and over many kinds of turf, from unkempt raggedness to velvety green. The Boston golfer who starts out on a round of the Hub has many miles of golf ahead of him, and he surely will not lack for variety ; yet if all the courses were made into putting greens for one gigantic links the most noticeable thing that would strike the Brobding-nagian golfer who essayed the round would be the preponderance of short holes.

The golf clubs of the Boston district almost encircle the city, the only break being where the waters of the harbor separate the promontory of Winthrop on the northwest from the long arm of Nan

tasket which runs up toward it from the southeast.

The natural starting point of a golfing pilgrimage about Boston would be one or the other of these two points. Whichever it be, the golfer will start with a voyage. A pleasant half-hour's sail down the harbor brings one to Hull, where, on a high bluff known as Telegraph Hill, is a sign which proclaims to the world of summer visitors that here the Hull Golf Club lives and moves and has its being. Like several other golf clubs, this grew out of a yachting organization, the members of the Hull Yacht Club having taken up the game on other courses, and become so interested that a course of their own became an imperative necessity. So the Hull Golf Club was organized and links laid out on this point, not far from the yacht-club house. While the course is new and rough, it affords the yachtsmen an opportunity to combine the pleasures of yachting with golfing ; and the club boasts a unique hazard in the form of a government fortification

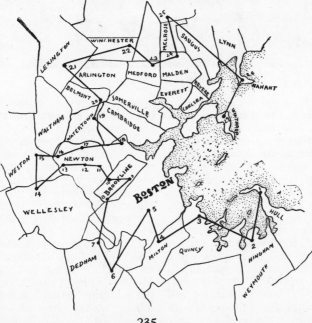

erected for the defence of Boston Harbor in the late war with Spain. From the ninth green of the course, the last hole, may be seen the ocean-going traffic of Boston, as the ships and steamers pass out the main channel, close by the frowning headland. The course abounds in short holes, and has a total length of 2,429 yards. But as the Hull Yacht Club has recently consolidated with the Massachusetts Yacht Club, and the latter organization brings an increased membership, more funds for the improvement of a pretty little course will be available another year.

From Hull, across an arm of the harbor, is another short and pleasant sail to the little course of the Crow Point

the turf is much like that of the Myopia links, wearing well and healing readily. Last year this was noted as one of the best-kept courses in New England. Wollaston has a pre eminent claim to possessing "links," for its situation at Norfolk Downs is upon actual "downs" or "links" like those which gave the word to golf language as a synonym for "course." Last fall the club membership had reached such proportions and the club's position in the golfing world was so well established that a tract of some seventy acres was secured by outright purchase; and nine additional holes were laid out this spring to make a full course by joining with the old one. It is the intention to lay out nine more

OVER THE POND AT ALLSTON.

Golf Club in old Hingham. This, like the Hull, is a new club, and there is a keen rivalry between the two, leading to a series of interesting team-matches when the summer colonists invade both places.

Leaving this course and making his way up the south shore toward Boston, the next to be visited is that of the Wollaston Golf Club, at Norfolk Downs, in Quincy. This club is rapidly assuming a place among the most important in New England, for before this season ends the members will be playing upon an eighteen-hole course. Organized in 1896, the Wollaston Golf Club played on leased land which was naturally well adapted to golfing, for the quality of

holes next year, when the club will give up its lease of the land covered by the original nine holes and have an eighteen - hole course, all on its own acres. The course is over beautifully-rolling country in Milton and Quincy, not so very far from the original Merry Mount where Wollaston's roistering Episcopalians were taken captive by the scandalized Miles Standish, before 1630.

One reluctantly leaves Wollaston's fine turf and its beautiful surroundings to turn to other golfing fields. The Hoosic Whisick Golf Club in Milton, a little farther inland, is largely a family affair, most of the club members being

Bostonians of leisure, who make their summer homes in this charming village, away from the sound of locomotives. Scenery is not a necessary concomitant of golf, but the views from parts of this course are superb. The course itself is somewhat short, but it has some "sporty" hazards; and in spite of the varying lengths of the holes, from 120 to 390 yards, it was here that Alex. Findlay, the professional, made his famous record of twenty consecutive holes in exactly four strokes each, a record which is believed to be unique.

From Milton the golfing pilgrim goes tained ever since as professional and greenkeeper, and here he gives lessons to hundreds of beginners who crowd the course—often uncomfortably—in pleasant spring and fall weather. The Park links are indeed the beginner's delight. Here he may cut divots to his heart's content, and freely does he avail himself of the privilege. The course is nearly two miles in circuit, and has only one short hole—120 yards—while there are holes of 498 and 542 yards, giving splendid opportunity for practice with the brassy. There are two streams and a narrow pond to be crossed, but as

SEAWARD FROM THE SIXTH TEE, HULL.

directly into Boston, for a round upon the public links in Franklin Park. In October, 1896, acceding to an increasing demand, the more readily, perhaps, because two members of the Board of Park Commissioners were golfers, the city of Boston established a public course —the second in the United States. Willie Campbell laid out what was then the longest nine-hole course in the country, on a tract of some sixty acres, uncrossed by roads or paths, in what is known as the Country Park section of Franklin Park. Campbell has been re-

yet no artificial hazards have been provided. Players on the course must secure permits from the Park Commission, and a charge of fifteen cents a round, or two rounds for twenty-five cents, is made.

On public holidays and on Saturday afternoons in summer the links are closed, for experience has shown that there are yet many Park visitors who know nothing of the game, and, therefore, fear nothing from standing fifty yards in front of the duffer, whose ball may fly anywhere should he be fortunate enough to hit it. One golfer who played at the Park tells of a choleric old gentleman who persisted in walking directly in the line of play on the long hole. "Fore!" shouted in stentorian tones, had no effect upon him. So the player waited until the old gentleman was well ahead, and then, with a cry of "Look out!" he drove the ball, which landed almost at the visitor's feet. The old man walked on, and, after another wait, the player repeated the experience. On the third stroke the old gentleman turned, and declared he would have the golfer arrested if he persisted in driving that ball at his head. The golfer explained, as well as he could, that he was trying to make that hole in five, and he merely wished his rights. "That's all right," exclaimed the old man fiercely, "but

was organized in the spring of 1897, and a course of nine holes laid out near Islington station of the New England Railroad. Most of it was old pasture land, on which the turf was close and hard, requiring little to be done on the fair green. There are ponds and, of course, stone walls, but these may be made into useful hazards. The links run over a picturesque country, with a splendid view of the lowlands in the distance. So well has the club prospered since its organization that the Bostonians who compose most of its membership contemplate extensive improvements.

Dedham's other golf organization—the Dedham Golf Club—is an outgrowth of the Dedham Polo Club, to which many of its members belong. The bold riders whose prowess is known

ALLSTON OVERLOOKING THE CHARLES RIVER.

don't you dare hit me!" Obviously, with such people on the course, play on the public links becomes less and less pleasant as one becomes proficient, and Campbell notes that each season a new crop of golfers come up. Those who play one season learn enough of the game to appreciate the advantages of less crowded links, and join some of the clubs near at hand. So firmly has golf become established as a public institution in Boston, however, that better accommodations for public golfers, including the erection of a club-house and work-rooms for the professional, are only a question of time.

From the public course the way of the golfing pilgrim leads southward into Dedham, where two golf courses may be found. The Norfolk Golf Club

at Narragansett Pier, Meadowbrook and Brooklyn, took up the game some three years ago, and secured a tract of land, on which a short course of nine holes was laid out and a club-house erected. It lies along the upper waters of the historic Charles River, and the roll of the surface of the country is admirably adapted to the game, while there are hazards of ravines, woods bordering the course, streams, a road, and the omnipresent stone walls. Dedham is improving, however, and as the golfers of the aristocratic old town grew in experience, the terraced "table cloth" greens gave way to broad ones, where putting could be done under less artificial conditions.

Golf thrives in Dedham, for there is also a short private course on the

THE COMMONWEALTH GOLF CLUB, CHESTNUT HILL, NEWTON.

handsome estate of Hon. Samuel Warren at "Karlstein," and with the Dedham Boat Club, the Dedham Polo Club and the Norfolk Hunt Club, all composed largely of the same people, the Dedham Golf Club was an absolute necessity to complete the quartet of sporting organizations.

"Playing to the next hole," as the sporting writers say in all their accounts

TELEGRAPH HILL.—THE LINKS OF THE HULL GOLF CLUB.

of golf matches, the drive, to continue the simile, is toward the fountain-head of golf in this part of the country, to "The Country Club," in Brookline. Not the Brookline Country Club, nor the Country Club of Brookline, but "The Country Club," for this organization of Boston's wealthiest classes, who are devoted to country life, has the right to its title by being the first "country club" in America. Its race meetings have long been famous, and some years ago it had a polo team which won on many a hard-fought field. All the best features of country sport have been fostered by this organization, and it was but natural that it should be one of the first clubs in America to take up golf. The game had been played by some of the members abroad, and on a private course which was laid out on the Hunnewell estate in Wellesley, the first golf course in New England.

In the spring of 1893 a course of nine holes was laid out on The Country Club grounds by Willie Campbell. Although well-nigh perfect in affording good lies through the green, and having excellent teeing grounds and putting greens, the necessity of maintaining a race-track and steeplechase

J. G. THORP, RUNNER-UP, CHAMPIONSHIP '96.

course over parts of which the golfers must play has hitherto kept The Country Club from having an ideal links.

So popular did the game become that last year $42,000 was paid for the Baker estate adjoining the club property, and nine additional holes were put in, giving the members an eighteen-hole course to play over this season. The total playing length is about 5,200 yards. Among the hazards on the old course, some of which have been criticized by the golfing experts, are "an avenue, steeplechase course, race track, polo fields, pigeon-shooting grounds, stone-wall jump, sand bunker and bastion, a water jump, and a vast gravel-pit or crater."

These are the hazards, by the way, which Mr. Sutphen, in Gordon G. Smith's "World of Golf," credits to the Baltimore Country Club. Most of The Country Club members would cheerfully resign them to the Baltimore Country Club, or any other organization that wants them, although they do not seriously bother the expert manipulator of the cleek or the true driver.

Golf in America owes much to The Country Club. Many a New England course can claim this as its parent organization, for wherever The Country Club members have gone to spend their summers, they have taken the game with them, and distributed greens and teeing grounds all along the north and south shores of Massachusetts Bay, and carried them inland to the mountains.

More than this, it was a leader in golf in The Country Club, who, when the two so-called "national championships" were held at Shinnecock and Newport, saw the necessity of a governing body for the game in this country. No club could occupy the position here which the Royal and Ancient Golf Club of St. Andrews held with relation to the sport abroad, and so Mr. Laurence Curtis, with the late Mr. Theodore Havemeyer and others, brought about the organization of the United States Golf Association. One of the early golfers of The Country Club, Mr. W. B. Thomas, had just been elected to the presidency of this organization, succeeding Mr. Curtis, who took the place of the late lamented Mr. Havemeyer, the first president. If golf is indebted to The Country Club for its advancement, it has paid the debt in kind; for while not all The Country Club members are interested in racing, or polo, or shooting, golf is a game in which young and old, men and women, may play with equal

zest. Golf has proved a financial tonic
to more than one country club in
America.

Two courses of limited extent, within
the town of Brookline, form the next
links in this golfing round. The Warren Farm Golf Club is an offshoot of
The Country Golf Club, always providing for overflow meetings, so to speak,
on Saturdays and holidays, while its
regular players find this six-hole course
more convenient of access than the
larger course of The Country Club.

The other, the Chestnut Hill Golf
Club, is largely social, but has links
running, as its name implies, over the
slopes of Chestnut Hill. It joins to a
succession of rather unfair greens, an
ample variety of hazards, including
trees and brambles, to meet the requirements of those who demand a more
than " sporty " course.

Chestnut Hill is on the edge of
Newton, formerly called " the Garden
City," but which might now be called
" the Golfing City," for it has no less
than five golf courses. Time will come,
and that probably soon, when a consolidation must take place, for some
of these golf courses are on building
lots too valuable to be given up to
the sport of a limited number of players. At present the difficulty in the
way of consolidation lies in the fact that
members of each course prefer the nar-
rower limits of a course near home, to
a larger field which is less easy of access. It seemed, when Newton had
only four clubs, that the golfing pro-
clivities of her citizens were well provided for, but last year another club
was organized, and this year may see
yet another. The latest is the Commonwealth Golf Club, situated near Commonwealth avenue, that artery of blue
blood which continues through Newton
after leaving Boston. Mr. Dana Estes,
the publisher, was at the head of this
organization, and after one season of
success, it has decided to enlarge and
improve its course, on which is already
a handsome club-house, from which
every teeing ground and putting green
in its nine-hole course is visible.

Newton Center comes next in order,
and here the home of the golf club of
that name is a scene of activity in summer, when the nine - hole course is
thronged with players. The erratic
player goes into three figures with cer-

LAURENCE CURTIS (COUNTRY CLUB),
EX-PRESIDENT UNITED STATES GOLF ASS'N.

tainty, for the lies are often appalling,
and even Alex. Findlay, who said he
could get around any nine-hole course
in 50, failed to do better than 57 the first
time he played on the Newton Center
links. He has since done it in 44, as has
also the Rev. E. M. Noyes, who holds
the club championship, although most

W. B. THOMAS (COUNTRY CLUB),
PRESIDENT UNITED STATES GOLF ASS'N.

THE FIRST TEE AT OAKLEY COUNTRY CLUB.

of the members look upon Mr. Noyes's score as an inspiration.

In many respects the Newton Golf Club course is like a private course, as most of it is laid out on land which has been loaned to the club by wealthy men who are members. The course was a short one, but this spring it was lengthened to about 2,520 yards, and considerable was done in cutting down trees which, however pleasing to the eye, did not add to the enjoyment of the play-

THE CLUB HOUSE, OAKLEY COUNTRY CLUB.

ers. Nature has done her part well toward providing a good course, and the opportunities have been improved so that the club limit of membership, 150, was reached last year.

Leaving Newton on the southwest to play over into the adjoining town of Wellesley, the golfing pilgrim reaches the course of the Wellesley Hills Golf Club, laid out three years ago. It is now nine holes, but the land adjoining the links is looked upon with regard to its possibilities for making an eighteen-hole course when the club is a little older. The turf, like that in the "Country Churchyard," "heaves in many a moldering heap," but with time and

well as the tiller of an unconquered yacht. Here, too, the late Governor William E. Russell frequently played. Weston maintains a club team which plays many matches with other clubs in the Boston district, and generally acquits itself with credit.

From Weston the line leads back through Newton into Boston once more. Across the Charles River, in Newton, is the course of the Woodland Golf Club, at Auburndale, where a great hotel is headquarters not only for the golfers, but for bicycle clubs, tally-ho parties and other sportsmen who come out from the city. A short course and hazardous, is this, but it is well kept, and it

"THE COUNTRY CLUB," IN BROOKLINE. THE FIFTH GREEN, LOOKING ACROSS THE POLO GROUNDS.

money good golf links have been built on many a less promising foundation.

Before leaving Wellesley mention must be made of the Wellesley College Golf Club, the only known organization where golf is compulsory. Here the young ladies of the college find it a part of the prescribed physical training, under the direction of Miss Harriet Randall, the accomplished athletic director.

Adjoining Wellesley is Weston, where the Weston Golf Club, one of the oldest in the neighborhood of Boston, numbers among its founders General Charles J. Paine, who can handle a golf club, as

had a representative at the last national amateur championship.

In Newton, too, is the nine-hole course of the Braeburn Golf Club, with an excellent variety of hazards, the natural features being admirably utilized. Here, too, the members gaze upon an adjoining tract of land and plan a possible arrangement of nine additional holes. The course of the Braeburn Club is well kept, and its open tournaments are always popular.

The Allston Golf Club, which has a nine-hole course within the city limits of Boston, is even more easy of access from the business district of the city than the public links in Franklin Park. Commonwealth Avenue street c a r s, which run directly by the course, bring golfers out from the famous subway in twenty minutes. The course is on land owned by an express company, the perambulating horses of which often form tantalizingly movable hazards. Despite its uncertainty of tenure, the club has a little club-house, and extensive improvements on the land have been made. The feature of the Allston course is its famous pond, 100 yards wide, over which a player must drive unless he prefers to work his way with a mashie through an apple orchard. The pond is fed by springs and drained by evaporation. Caddies declare that it is bottomless, but players aver that its bottom is paved with at least a million golf balls. A steep bluff furnishes admirable opportunity for practicing lofting shots, and a water-main zigzagging across the course contributes variety to the hazards. Yet the ease of access makes up for many shortcomings, and the club is one of the most popular in the Boston district.

Crossing the Charles River into Cambridge, the golfer next comes to the links of the Harvard Golf Club. This was established a few years ago as the Cambridge Golf Club, and in 1896 furnished the runner-up in the national amateur tournament in the person of Mr. J. G. Thorp, who was beaten only by the redoubtable Whigham. Last year the club was reorganized as the Harvard Golf Club. Under this title it is now a flourishing organization, with a nine-hole course in Watertown, just across the Cambridge line. Here the students indulge in a great deal of informal match-play, and here the Harvard team practiced for the intercollegiate championship, which they won at Ardsley last fall. In addition to the Harvard students and members of the team, there are members who retained their interest in the old club. It was for playing on these links on Sunday that the first Sunday golfers were arrested in this country; and as they were students in college, they preferred to pay their fines and avoid notoriety rather than, as advised by eminent counsel, take the case to a higher court.

The club which was responsible for the change in fortunes of the Cambridge Golf Club was the Oakley Country Club, organized and incorporated last year by some of the leading golfers of the University City. This club acquired the famous old Pratt estate in Cambridge and Belmont, with a colonial mansion erected in 1742 by a descendant of a Huguenot exile from France. On these grounds an eighteen-hole course was laid out, with a preponderance of short holes. The old mansion, with its oval ball-room and its fine two-story hall, with balcony and winding stairways, was converted into a club-house, and proved to be admirably suited to the purpose. The links have fine turf, and while their improvement has but just been fairly started, they have proved exceeding popular. Here, as the course is partly in Belmont and partly in Cambridge, Sunday golf players may keep on that part of the course on which the ban does not rest, and escape the blue laws.

Somehow, golf has not taken as deep root in the northern suburbs of Boston as on the south and west, although there is good turf. Probably this is for the reason that the vacant land in the immediate northern suburbs is largely near the level of tide-water. On this side of Boston the clubs are farther from the city, yet there are several within the twelve-mile radius. One of the most active of these is the Lexington Golf Club, which has a nine-hole course in that historic town. Truly the "redcoats," who were repelled so bravely in the early days of the Revolution, have now taken the town, and the "rebels" have laid down their arms and taken up golf clubs. The course has excellent turf and plenty of hazards, although the application of dynamite to some of them would improve the chance of low scoring.

To the east of Lexington there lies the golfing ground of the Winchester Golf Club, a flourishing organization formed in 1897, and having a club-house and links on Woodside Road in Winchester. The greens are excellent, and the teeing grounds are better than in most clubs of limited membership, but local rules are still necessary to provide for balls in hoof-marks and cart-tracks.

Still farther east is the Medford Golf Club, with a course of varying length. Five holes is the number generally played, but there are extra teeing grounds and putting greens, by which a nine-hole course, partly over rough ground, is possible. Most of the members prefer to make nine holes by playing twice around and combining two holes on the second round, rather than essay the task of mowing "fog" and "bent" by playing the extra holes. Changes made in the course last year, however, give the club a nine-hole course which will be in fair condition by the end of this year, with good distances and fairly satisfactory greens.

On the east of Medford is Malden, which has a golf club born last year, with a course several years old. The course was laid out on the private grounds of Hon. E. S. Converse, the philanthropist, and after being kept pri-

Nahant, which is a summer home of wealthy Bostonians, and which has been facetiously termed "Cold Roast Boston," has a golf club, for which nature has done little more than provide room for the course. The Nahant Golf Club is an outgrowth of the Nahant Club, where the social activity of the members finds a larger field than the sporting side. This club shares with the Royal Minchinhampton Golf Club, of England, the honor of having as a trophy a swallow which was killed by a driven golf ball. The ex-president of the United States Golf Association is authority for the authenticity of this remarkable shot, which demonstrates the unerring accuracy of the drives

NEWTON CENTRE GOLF CLUB-HOUSE.

vate for three years, the use of the grounds was generously given to the young men and women of Malden society, on condition that a club be formed. The condition was not hard to comply with, and was soon met by the organization of the Pine Banks Golf Club, where devotees of cleek and mashie may prepare themselves for play on longer courses.

North of Malden the Wakefield Golf Club has just been reorganized after a trying year, in which the course suffered somewhat from neglect. Under the new conditions there is a good prospect that Wakefield will take its proper place among the golfing suburbs of Boston.

made by Nahant Club members, one of whom is United States Senator Lodge.

"Home," in this round of the Boston links, takes one to the Court Park Golf Club of Winthrop, on an arm which runs down into Boston Harbor toward Nantasket, the starting point. One of the most picturesque places on the Massachusetts coast, near Boston, the course can be reached by a short sail from the city, and the links provide sport for many summer visitors. One round may satisfy the golfing pilgrim, but he who lingers late, and, after his round of all the Boston courses, sits on the deck of the little steamer, bound for Boston, and watches the flashing beacons of the har-

"THE COUNTRY CLUB" IN BROOKLINE.

bor, and the city lights twinkling afar, while the rising moon makes a broad furrow of silver on the rippling water, will feel that the pilgrimage is worth the making, and that the round ends fittingly.

While these are the golf courses of Boston and its immediate vicinity, mention must be made of other courses where the Boston golfers play, or the golfing round the Hub is not complete.

Most prominent among these are the links of the Essex County Club and the Myopia Hunt Club. The former, at Manchester - by - the - Sea, are widely known as the scene of the national women's championship of 1897. Here, in the summer time, many tournaments are held, and the course is especially popular with the women of Boston society. On the nine holes of this course there is a good variety of hazards, and the up-

THE NEWTON GOLF CLUB-HOUSE.

keep, under the direction of Mr. J. Lloyd, winner of the open championship two years ago, is not surpassed in New England. The Myopia Hunt Club, at Hamilton, where the open championship was held last year, then had only a nine-hole course, with nine additional holes under way. These were opened for play in the last of the tournaments last fall, and the members now have one of the best full courses in the East. On the links the members of the aristocratic summer colony of Boston may be found any day in summer with driver and putter; and, while half an hour's ride from Boston

THE BRAEBURN CLUB-HOUSE.

on the south shore, at Scituate, or in historic old Plymouth, where a short nine-hole course affords them opportunity to play "the only game."

Team matches, where so many clubs are found, are common, as might be expected, and there has been a Neighborhood Golf Cup competed for by Concord, Lexington, Salem and the Vesper Country Club of Lowell for several years. In Newton, last year, a trophy was offered by President Andrew B. Cobb, of the Newton Golf Club, to be competed for by the golf clubs of Newton.

The need of a district association of Boston golf clubs, similar to the Metropolitan Golf Association in New York, is apparent, and it is almost certain that such an association will come in due season. In the meantime, golf

FIRST TEE, BRAEBURN.

by train, the surpassing quality of the turf and the natural attractiveness of the links cause them to be opened early and closed late in the season.

Another popular course near Boston, just outside of the twelve-mile limit, is that of the Concord Golf Club, which in its first two or three years was famous for its team-play, and now for its almost universal informal match-play.

Old Salem has a good course where golfers of that old seaport indulge in the Scotch sport; and along the north shore, near the "reef of Norman's Woe," is the course of the Magnolia Golf Club, much patronized in summer by Boston players. Others find golf

FORTY ACRES OF BRAEBURN FROM THE FIFTH TEE.

THE WOLLASTON GOLF CLUB.—APPROACH TO THE SEVENTH GREEN.

interest grows constantly in and around Boston, and enthusiasts look forward to the coming of that happy day when every man may sit on his own putting green, and Boston players shall hold all the golf championships.

This purview of the conditions of the circle of the courses round the Hub brings into focus the extent of the golfing ardor that has been developed with the earnestness that characterizes the New Englander in all his undertakings.

THE CLUB-HOUSE, NINTH GREEN AND FIRST TEE, WOLLASTON.

The Lobster at Home (1881)

THE LOBSTER AT HOME.

In the spring, the lobster, who has passed the winter months in deep water, returns again inshore. He has found the deep water both tranquil and warm, while the shallower expanses near land have been troubled to the bottom by furious gales and chilled by the drifting ice. Thirty fathoms is a very fair depth for his winter home, while in summer the trap in which he is generally captured gathers in a goodly number if sunk in a depth of five fathoms, or even less. A few lobsters burrow in the mud and in a manner hibernate, but

A LOBSTER-POT.

A LOBSTERMAN'S HOME AND IMPLEMENTS.

gradually shelves for a moderate distance, but presently drops off into deep soundings. An indented coast is much more advantageous. So great a stretch of shoals and shallows as exists along the north-east of New England, from Yarmouth in Maine to Cape Sable, the lower point of Nova Scotia, will hardly be found elsewhere. It presents an endless series of promontories which have barely escaped being islands, and islands which have barely escaped being promontories. With the innumerable resulting bays, coves, sounds, estuaries, and straits, hardly does the water deepen from one shore before it shoals again to another. As a consequence, the Maine coast has become the best lobster-fishing ground in the world, and the industry of taking and introducing the lobster into commerce has extended to great proportions.

The awkward crustacean, when snared, is either sent fresh to market in smacks containing wells, or he is boiled at some central establishment, and sent in open crates, or, finally, he is put up in hermetically sealed cans. The first two processes continue all the year round, but a law of the State of Maine prohibits the canning of lobsters except between the first of March and the first of August. There are various theories about their unsuitableness for this purpose after August first. It does not seem to be quite clear whether the law is for the protection of the purchaser, to whom the flesh is said to be at times poisonous, or of the lobster, to prevent its too rapid destruction by indefatigable pursuit.

The typical lobsterman lives at the bottom of a charming and remote cove. The

the ordinary aspect of those taken in winter shows that their habits at this time differ little from what they are at any other. The migratory impulse seizes upon all about the same moment, and they come in in regular columns, the stronger members in the front, the weaker in the rear; and though there is hardly a more quarrelsome animal, whether at large or in a state of captivity, than the lobster, they postpone, for the time, the manifestation of their habitual temper.

A straight line of sea-coast furnishes but a limited area of feeding-ground for the lobster, even should it contain the desirable kind of food. The bottom in such a coast

HAULING TRAPS.

shores rise in bold, gray crags, but he has a strip of sand on which to beach his boat. He is a fisherman in other branches and a farmer as well, for lobstering need not take the whole of any one's time. His buildings, seen at the top of a rising ground, are weather-beaten gray and red. At the shore he has fish-houses, a great reel on which nets are wound up, and in a cleft of the rock smokes a large iron kettle, wherein is brewing a decoction of tar and rosin for water-proofing the rope-work of his lobster-traps. The traps themselves have the appearance of a pile of mammoth bird-cages. The structure is four feet long, two feet wide, and two feet high, with a semicircular section. It is made of slats, with wide intervals between, to afford the proposed victim a clear view of the baits arranged on a perpendicular row of hooks within. A door opens in the circular top, through which access is had for preparing the baits and removing the contents. The trap is sunk to the bottom by a ballast of stones, and a billet of wood at the other end of the rope serves as a buoy. The ends are closed only with tarred rope-netting, and in one there is a circular opening of considerable size. The bait used is a cod's head, or sometimes a row of cunners.

FACTORIES AT SOUTH SAINT GEORGE.

The lobsterman has, perhaps, one hundred and fifty such traps, set in eligible locations. He visits them every morning, and sometimes the circuit of buoys marked with his name is five or six miles in extent. He lays hold of the submerged rope, covered with a green, beard-like weed, lifts the trap, removes what it contains, and drops it again to the bottom. The occupation presents its most picturesque aspect in winter, when the fishing is in deep water. The lobsterman then, with his dory filled with a pile of the

LOBSTER-FACTORY AT MOUNT DESERT.

LOBSTER-FACTORY AT DEER ISLAND.

curious cages which he has taken up for repairs or is going to set in new places, ventures far out to sea, often at no little personal risk. Sometimes a particularly violent gale will drive the traps with it, and wreck them in the breakers. One lobsterman on the island of Monhegan lost over fifty in this way in one night.

A mature lobster should measure, without the claws, from one to two feet long, and weigh complete from two to fifteen pounds, but smaller sizes are so common that a length of ten and a half inches, without reference to weight, has been made a standard for certain calculations. It is claimed that the average size, as well as the profits of the business, is being steadily diminished by the industry with which the pursuit has been lately followed up. The shores teem with traps, and the competition is so fierce that whereas a lobsterman once made four or five dollars a day, he now regards himself lucky if he makes but one. Occasional prodigies in size turn up to astonish and delight their

captors. Lobsters have been taken as heavy as twenty-five pounds, in a "line" (twenty-eight fathoms) of water. At South Saint George, below Rockland, hangs the claw of a lobster which in life weighed forty-three pounds. At Friendship, not far distant, there is authentic record of a certain *white* lobster of formidable development. The normal color is black, or greenish-black, turning to vivid scarlet by boiling. The hard shell is incapable of expansion, and, if it were not for a special provision, would prevent all growth. Relief is found in the periodical shedding of the shell. It splits in two along the back, and is sloughed off and replaced in time by a new one formed underneath. This change takes place in many lobsters, though not in all, some time about the first of August, and, undoubt-edly, one of the objects of the canning-law was the protection of the "shedders"; for without a shell the lobster is defenseless from enemies, and is obliged to take refuge in crevices and under stones to avoid them; by October the new panoply is in good order, and by December his condition is at its best.

If we are to accept the theory of a veteran lobsterman whom we met at Mount Desert, the lobster may attain to the age of man. The first shedding of the shell, he tells us, occurs at the age of five years. After this, he confesses his inability to fix the periods of renewal. The mother is often seen surrounded by baby lobsters a few inches in length, who take refuge under her tail in case of danger, and sometimes the little ones are found stranded in conch-shells, into which they have crawled near the shore. At the end of the third year the young are

UNLOADING THE SMACK.

perhaps four inches long, and at the end of the fourth hardly more than six. At such a rate of progress it appears that something in the neighborhood of five years must elapse before they attain the length of eight or ten inches, at which size they are first found in a soft condition. Our lobster-man's theory of longevity is based upon his observation of this slowness of growth.

Fineness of organization would not seem to be the strong point of the lobster any more than beauty of form, yet he moves about his chosen feeding-grounds with a very respectable set of endowments for picking up his living. He has his sense of smell at the base of one pair of his numerous feeler-like antennæ and his sense of hearing at another; his eyes are located at the end of flexible peduncles and have an extended range of observation, and two long, fine antennæ meander cautiously over everything in his vicinity with a delicate sense of touch. His principal power resides in the great pair of anterior claws, which have force sufficient to crack a clam. His prey (clams and mussels, and such fish as the

CANNERS.

sculpin, flounder, and cunner) is seized and held fast by the sharp teeth between the thumb-and-finger-like grasp of the larger claw, then held in the duller small one while he sucks away the substance at leisure. His locomotion is very rapid and by preference backward, the cunning peduncle eyes no doubt having first taken the requisite bearings. Curving his many-jointed, wide tail inward, he moves with a velocity for which those who have only seen him in the market-stalls would never give him credit.

Thus equipped, the lobster approaches the trap set for his inveiglement. The dull, big eyes of the cod's head in the trap stare sagely out at the bloodless victim. The bead-like optics of the lobster, in the flurry of this cold temptation, peer cunningly in. As to the attractiveness of the morsel there can be no question, and the way to reach and take possession of it through the passage in the net-work seems ample. With a few deft strokes he is within. Why does he not return in the same way? Whoever understands the defective logical processes of the lobster's mind can alone explain. It does not occur to him to turn around, and

as to going out forward, the great claws, now spread out, render it difficult, though the opening is in no way more contracted than before. Nor does the fate of one deter the entrance of others. When the trap is lifted it contains from one to a dozen of all sizes, and with them a few "five-fingers" (star-fish), and perhaps a blundering, large-headed sculpin, who is much surprised at being brought so suddenly to light. Whether or not a loss of appetite be occasioned by the discovery of his situation, the lobster does not disturb the baits to any considerable extent. A large one will eat a piece hardly larger than one's finger, though he may have been in the trap with the bait for hours.

"It is a cheap-livin' fish," a lobsterman tells us, with an air of confidence, almost of giving away the secret of the business. "Nothin' is ever found inside of him. He kin eat barnacles, sea-weed, mud,—anything. He kin live five and six months in the well of a smack on what he finds there, and come out all right,—unless they chaw each other up," he adds. "They're most always a-doin' that. It don't seem as though it hurt 'em no gre't, nuther. You find lots of 'em with their claws broke off in fights, but they grow out ag'in jest as good. Some think they lose 'em off in thunder-storms, too. I dunno how that is, but they do say that they're pretty considerable frighted."

The grip of a lobster's claw, which can crack a clam easily, is strong enough to take off a man's finger, and there has even been a story of the death of a Maine hotel-keeper from the clutch of a lobster. The experienced are usually cautious in handling them. At Deer Island, a man told us that he had been caught while opening a trap beside his boat, and held in a most painful position for nearly half an hour, supporting the weight of the trap as well as the weight of his tormentor, who, at last, not being interfered with, let go of his own accord. Another lobster-fisher went ashore with a particularly fine specimen slung over his shoulder, and stopped to scare with it a young girl he met on the way. Inadvertently putting back one of his hands, it was savagely gripped by the dangling claws; the other, hastening to its relief, was seized also, presenting the joker to the object of his attentions in a highly unfavorable light. She was obliged to bring assistants with hammers and knives to break the claws.

For lobster-catching on a smaller scale, two kinds of nets, and a hook with a ten-foot handle not unlike a mackerel-gaff, are occasionally used. One is an ordinary dip-net, lowered by ropes and with a bait in the bottom; when the lobster enters, the additional weight is felt and the net pulled up. The other is a circle of wire, playing in equal halves on an axis; a rope is attached to each side, and it is lowered like the other; by pulling the ropes the parts shut together, inclosing whatever rests within.

The first destination of the captives is the lobster-car. This is a great floating box, perhaps twelve feet long by eight wide, by two and a half deep, submerged to the water's edge. Here they are preserved till the arrival of the smack. The Portland or Boston or New York smack comes once a week, to carry off the larger ones fresh in its

CRACKING LOBSTERS.

well; the factory smacks come for the smaller ones, to be canned, every day or two. The smack runs down to the lobster-car and luffs up alongside. The owner stands on its slippery surface, and dips out the contents into the iron-bound scoop of a fine large weighing-tackle, rigged to the throat-halliards. The skipper keeps the tally on a shingle. The large, bold implements, the free attitudes, the strongly characteristic dresses, offer the artist plenty of material.

The arrival of the smack is an important event in the cove. The skipper brings the news of the trade and the personal gossip of his circuit, and executes many small commissions for the household. An ordinarily prosperous factory, as that at Green's Landing, Deer Island, has three such small vessels in its employ, attending upon, perhaps, one hundred and fifty lobstermen in all. The skipper endeavors to attach to himself his special gang, or *clientèle*, and to make it as large as possible. To insure that they shall fish for him and no other he uses all the arts of a commercial traveler. He makes a slightly more favorable price here, relies upon an exhibition of jolly good-fellowship there, and again appeals to long-established usage and relations. He must be able, too, to fit a client out here and there on credit with the necessary gear for the campaign. By every means in his power

BOILING-ROOM.

he assures him that he will not do better with any other living skipper, and begs him not to forget it. His own compensation is sometimes a salary, but more often a commission on the amounts brought in. His cabin is six feet by four, by a height sufficient to stand erect in. It has a couple of bunks with squalid calico quilts on them, a rusty iron stove, and a table-leaf letting down from the foot of the mast, at which he sits casting up his accounts on the shingle— that universal record-book—as he cruises in and out of the small harbors, past the reefs with their singular beacons and the little light-houses of the poorer class.

" Do you see yonder light ? " our skipper says, as we sail near South Saint George. " Well, there was a feller appointed keeper from somewheres in the State onct, what had never see the water afore, I guess—a regular p'litical job. Well, after he'd been there a little there was complaints ag'in him, and he was hauled up before the board.

"'What time do you put your light out?' says the board.

"'Nine o'clock,' says this here p'litical keeper. 'That's when I turns in myself, and I supposed all decent folks was to hum by that time, or ought to be.'"

The smack nowadays runs alongside the wharf of the lobster-factory. From the land side, the first seen of the skipper is a pair of brawny hands on the string-piece. They are followed, as he climbs up the side, by his sou'-wester, his patched woolen round-about, and his cowhide boots covering his trowsers to the knee. The great weighing-scoop is again rigged, a tub, with a rope and stake handle, is lowered from a small crane at the corner of the wharf, the shingle is resumed, and the live freight, clutching and flapping viciously, begins to be as unceremoniously transferred with shovels as though it was only coals.

The lobster-factories are very numerous, and can hardly escape the notice even of the fashionable visitor to Maine. He is confronted by one, for instance, at the landing of Harpswell, the principal island of Casco Bay, another at the historic old town of Castine, another at Southwest Harbor, Mount Desert, besides the one at Green's Landing. Deer Island has factories at Oceanville and Burnt Cove, forming part of a series, twenty-three in number, which belong to one firm, and stretch all the way down to the Bay of Fundy. They cannot be called intrinsically inviting, owing to their wholly utilitarian character, although they are apt to have redeeming features in an occasional touch of the picturesque.

The factory opens at one end on the wharf, close to the water. Two men bring in the squirming loads on a stretcher and dump the mass into coppers for boiling. At intervals the covers are hoisted by ropes and pulleys, and dense clouds of steam arise, through which we catch vistas of men, women, and children at work. Two men approach the coppers with stretcher and scoop-nets, and they throw rapid scoopfuls, done to a scarlet, backward over their shoulders. The scarlet hue is seen in all quarters—on the steaming stretcher, in the great heaps on the tables, in scattered individuals on the floor, in a large pile of shells and refuse seen through the open door, and in an ox-cart-load of the same refuse, farther off, which is being taken away for use as a fertilizer.

The boiled lobster is separated, on long tables, into his constituent parts. The meat of the many-jointed tail is thrust out with a punch. A functionary called a "cracker" frees that of the claws by a couple of deft cuts with a cleaver, and the connecting arms are passed on to be picked out with a fork by the girls. In another department, the meat is placed in the cans. The first girl puts in roughly a suitable selection of the several parts. The next weighs it, and adds or subtracts enough to complete the exact amount desired (one or two pounds). The next forces down the contents with a stamp invented especially for the purpose. The next puts in a tin cover with blows of a little hammer. Then a tray is rapidly filled with the cans, and they are carried to the solderers, who seal them tight except for minute openings in the covers, and put them in another tray, which, by means of a pulley-tackle, is then plunged in bath caldrons, in order that the cans may be boiled till the air is expelled from their contents through the minute openings. Then they are sealed up and are boiled again for several hours, when the process of cooking is complete.

In the packing-room the cans are cleaned with acid, painted a thin coat of green to keep them from rusting, pasted with labels displaying a highly ornamental scarlet lobster rampant against a blue sea, and placed by the gross in pine boxes to await the arrival of the company's vessel, which cruises regularly from factory to factory,

THE BELLE OF THE LOBSTER-SHOP.

collecting the product. Nine-tenths of the supply at present goes to the foreign market. On "loaf-days," the hands occupy themselves with making the neat cans which it is their ordinary business to fill.

The solderers, each with his little sheet-iron furnace, bristling with tools, on the table beside him, and the white light of one of a long row of small windows playing over him, give the suggestion of alchemists. Over their heads in a prominent place is a placard: "NOTICE! HOW TO PRESERVE HEALTH: LET THESE TOOLS ALONE!!!" There must be a little history of mischief-making attached to this. Who could have interfered with the honest solderers' tools? Could it have been yonder pretty girl, certainly the belle of the lobster-shop? She stands at the end of a long table, in a check apron bound with pink, her arms bare, her brown hair with threads of auburn in it hanging down her back in a braid. She is of the robuster Yankee type, about which there is no suspicion of consumption. Near her, by the partition, is a disused dory on a heap of coarse salt, which forms a sort of beach for it, and overhead other dories are sandwiched between the rafters. She is very steady, they tell us, and engaged to a young man who sails in the company's freight-smack; and, indeed, we see him come in, in a linen duster over a suit of ready-made clothes, and shake hands with her and his friends and acquaintances round about. When we ask her if we are at liberty to draw her picture, she says she "don't know as it makes any odds," and is evidently not displeased with the proposition. Still, it appears by a certain nervousness in her manner that it does make "odds," for she inquires presently how check "takes," and after that, inventing a plausible pretext for delay, hurries home and returns with her hair discouragingly smoothed down by wetting, and arranged around the front in crimps.

The solderers are paid from twelve to fifteen dollars a week, ordinary men from seven to ten, and the girls no more than three and a half. Yet even at this price a respectable class of female labor is engaged. Some of the young women have taught school in their time. This is not so remarkable when we say that common report has it that there are towns on this coast where, by the excessive shrewdness of rural committeemen, the wages of school-keeping have been reduced to two dollars a week.

The minor employés are generally gathered from the neighborhood. The more skillful are brought in for the season, and have successive engagements at different points. The solderers are in particularly active demand, owing to the extent to which the business of canning has been extended, and seem to have in their vocation a substantial means of livelihood. The sweet-corn season opens as soon as the lobster season closes, and soon after the first of August the solderers will be found making ready to hurry to the country back of Portland, where corn-canning is an industry of great magnitude.

The corn-factories and lobster-factories are owned to a large extent by the same companies, and one may chance to hear it charged that the lobster-law was procured with special reference to this natural connection of the two crops.

"It aint in the interest of the lobster nor yet of the public, the law aint," said an informant who holds this theory. "They say the meat is p'is'n after such a time, but the smacks keeps on catchin' of 'em up and puttin' in ice all summer—that don't look much like it. The parties wants the sawderers down to Freeport and Gorham for cannin' the corn—that's how it is; and they don't want no one else a-goin' on with lobsters when they aint at it. But what was your object in knowin'?" he interrupts his discourse to ask, not readily conceiving a merely speculative interest in these matters; "was you thinkin' of startin' a lobster-factory?"

Early Milford
(1899)

THE CONNECTICUT MAGAZINE.

VOL. V.   MARCH, 1899.   NO. 3.

EARLY MILFORD.

BY M. LOUISE GREENE.

Illustrated from photographs by E. B. Hyatt,

I.

"In this place there is but one Church, or in other words but one steeple—but there are Grist and Saw Mills, and a handsome Cascade over the Tumbling dams."—
Washington's Diary, October 17, 1789.

ONE hundred and fifty years earlier, another traveller, a pioneer in the wilderness, had noticed the picturesque cascade, and his keen eye had marked its utility, with the result that, a year later, in March, 1640, the Second General Court of Milford agreed with the first William Fowler "that he should build a mill and have her running by the last of September;" and further that if the town thought proper, it should take the building off the miller's hands at a valuation of £180. To encourage him, he was given thirty acres of land or "Mill Lot" in Eastfield,* rate free during his life and also the "perpetual use of the stream." This mill, the first in New Haven Colony, was duly completed. It was a grist mill, but soon there was added to it a saw-mill. So valued was this property, that after a freshet in 1645, the town empowered its owner to go through the village and to call upon each man for one day's labor in repairing damages, and to do this whenever such help was necessary. The town fixed the miller's rates at three quarts out of each bushel of grain.

For over two centuries and a half the water turned the mill-wheels of successive generations as each William Fowler in turn to the ninth generation of him who first chained the stream, measured the grist or told the tale. Stage-coach gave way to railway while the old mill still held its own. Each building became in time the "old mill"† until the fifth and last, built about 1884 and closed some ten

---

*See map.

†The small old building next the new mill is a part of the plant, dating from 1845, when a great freshet swept away both grist and saw mill.

years later. With its long, slender hooks making immense Roman "V's" upon its western end, with its "Ye Fowler's Mills Established in ye year 1639," above the door, it stands an ancient landmark, (it was the oldest business house of its kind in the country), by right of long existence demanding that the road make a sweeping curtsy in passing. Looming upon the traveller, who is about to cross the stream, it is almost an integral part of the new Memorial Bridge. In very truth, a part of that historic sentiment which built the bridge and which speaks from

hewn blocks of granite, bearing the names of the first settlers. There are ten blocks on the south and twenty on the north coping. At each end of the former is a stone four feet wide by five and a half high. Two inscriptions, on their curved and polished surfaces, recite briefly the services of the colony's first guides. One is dedicated to Thomas Tibbals, who led the people along the tortuous Indian trail from New Haven to Wepowagee, and is " in consideration of his helpfulness at the first coming to Milford to show the first comers the

THE MEMORIAL BRIDGE.

every stone. This memorial was the united effort of town and people. For the construction of the bridge proper, Milford town voted $3,000. The tower and inscriptive ornament are gifts from descendants, (whether Milfordites or not), of the settlers whose lives are thus commemorated.

The stone bridge is simple in design, its broad copings surmounted with rough

place."* The second is in memory of the Reverend Peter Prudden

" First Pastor in Milford
Obit 1656,
The Voice of one crying in the
Wilderness, Prepare Ye
The way of the Lord, make His Paths
Straight.

The text is that of his first sermon preached in New Haven Colony, and in

---

*From the land records recording his grant of land. Captain Thomas Tibbals in 1635 had chased the fleeing Pequots into the Fairfield swamps, and at that time became acquainted with the surrounding country.

New Haven, on the afternoon of April 18, 1638, beneath the branches of a big oak tree which stood near the present northeast corner of George and College streets. Along the southern coping runs the inscription " God sifted a whole nation that He might send choice grain into the wilderness."

The glory of the bridge, architecturally, is the round tower at the northwest end, with roof of Spanish tile, with ancient lantern, and buttress trending northward, ye old mill-wheel at its foot, making for the wayfarer an attractive seat. This old stone is reputed to be the

bridge there is a second seat formed by the stone reading :

IN MEMORIAM
JONATHAN LAW
GOVERNOUR OF THE COLONY OF
CONNECTICUT
FROM 1742 TO 1750.
THIS STONE ONCE HIS DOORSTEP.

Returning to the tower, we find below the lantern two inscriptions by the Wepowage Lodge, one commemorating that Indian tribe whom the first settlers of Milford found so friendly, and the other bearing their chieftain, Ansantuwoe's

THE BRIDGE TOWER AND MILL.

one, which the first William Fowler hewed roughly from a near-by quarry and made to serve him until a better stone could be obtained. On the buttress, in rising order, are graven the fundamental virtues of society; Law, Order, Morality, Liberty, Charity. This stone work frames the inscriptive tablet to Governor Treat,—of whom more hereafter,—while at the northeastern end of the

mark, while over the key-stone of the arch above the door leading into the tower, and also the arches of the bridge beneath which flows the Wepowaug river, ideal Indian heads stand out in high relief. On the oaken door, sunk within the portal of the tower, is an ancient knocker from the house upon whose porch, in 1740, Whitefield preached that memorable address which later caused secession from the First Society and the formation of Plymouth Church. Above this door are the wrought iron figures 1639, the date of the settlement of Milford.

From the bridge one can reconstruct the early time. Topographically, one will omit the houses close to the river on either side. That ground was open. So too was the lower part of Broad street to the harbor, and on this vacant ground the train band manoeuvred six times a year.* The river also was open to the sound, and vessels swung at anchor at Fowler's little dock but a short distance below the mill. Mr. William Fowler's home lot and mill (41)† extended seven acres and three rods. Next to him, moving northward along the river, came the Rev. Peter Prudden's house lot (40)† of the same dimensions. Later, in 1700, this house was fortified to resist any attack, because of the increasing unfriendliness of the Indians. At the southeast corner of the pastor's garden, on a clear day, could be dimly seen the low mounds of those whom death, as early even as 1744, claimed,

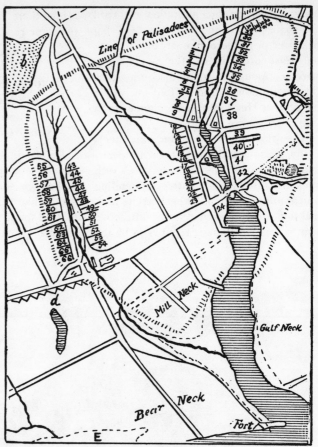

MAP OF MILFORD IN 1646.

Scale 3 miles to the inch.

b.—Dreadful swamp or Great Dreadful Swamp.   *c.*—Eastfield common line fence.   *d.*—Westfield common line fence.   *e.*—Great meadow extending to the shore.

First Congregational Church opposite 9.   Second Congregational Church opposite 38.   Town House opposite 15   Episcopal Church opposite 17.

The best house lots were listed in 1676 at 25s. per acre ; the worst at 20s. "Impropriated" (improved) land, counting that improved by tillage, mowing or English pasture was divided one-fourth of the whole to list at 20s; three-fourths at 10s ; and all unimproved land at 12d per acre.

Stephen Stone House, Wharf St., near harbor, 1689.

when a little son of William East's passed away on June 18th, and thus began in the little town the long muster roll of

---

{ March,
{ April,
{ May,
{ September,
{ October,
{ November,

Company comprised every male from 16 yrs. to 60. Each villager under fine of 5s was compelled to have on hand, 1 lb. powder, 2 lbs. shot, and 2 fathoms of match.

†See Map for numbers in brackets.

centuries. For over a hundred years there was but one meeting house, and that a few rods south of the present First Church. It was a queer, box-like structure *thirty* feet square, with a roof like a huge candle extinguisher, surmounted by a belfry from which the bell-rope hung down into the middle aisle. From the guard seats within, the watch could look across the river, past Sachem's Island just below the present Episcopal Church, or from the doorway they could sweep the horizon, could scan the harbor, the mills, the New Haven road (sixteen rods wide), or could follow the line of palisades, and watch the two bridges, the meeting-house bridge and Fowler's, now replaced by this memorial to the pluck and character of him and his associates. During troubled periods, sentries were maintained on each of the four sides of the meeting-house, and the train-band went heavily armed to church.

THE FIRST MEETING-HOUSE.

A few rods west of the meeting-house stood the country tavern from 1644 until about 1828. It was first kept by Henry Tomlinson and later it was owned by the Bryans, and kept for a long term of years

ALONG THE RIVER.

THE FIRST CONGREGATIONAL AND PLYMOUTH CHURCHES.

by them. It was here that General Washington stopped on his New England tour of 1789. In his journal are frequent complaints of the poverty of the inns with which he met. Tradition says that at this, then Clark's inn, disappointed in his supper of boiled meat and potatoes, he called for a bowl of bread and milk, which was set before him with a broken pewter spoon. Upon remonstrance, his host declared the house had no other. Thereupon, His Excellency gave the servant two shillings with the command to go to the minister's and borrow a silver spoon.

By the bridge below the miller, (42), was the home of Thomas Lawrence, with but one acre of ground; while diagonally across the river to the southwest, the smallest allotment of all, (24) only three rods, held a little lean-to house with rent oak shingles, its small square windows divided into many diamonds by leaded glass. Here the light burned latest in the village. Here lived one of the most honored men in the little settlement,

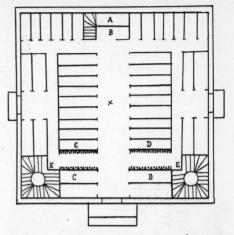

PLAN OF FIRST MEETING HOUSE 1641–1727.

a—Pulpit. *b*—Deacon's seat. *c* and *d* (on women's side) Guard seats. Dots—Gun racks. *x*—Bell rope. *e*—Gallery stairs: gallery added 1697, side galleries were added in 1707 and 1709.

Jasper Gunn, sealer of weights and measures, "equal to the standard used at New Haven, which was brought from the Bay"—feared by every dishonest merchant and trader; Jasper Gunn, teacher, more or less dreaded by boys and girls in those days of harsh discipline; Jasper Gunn, physician, known as far as Hartford and revered among the villagers. Among the memorial blocks upon the bridge is one bearing his name and that of his faithful consort, Sarah.

From the bridge in the farther western distance, smoke from chimneys showed the whereabouts of the twelve families settled on either side of West End Brook. The nearest chimney,

THE CLARK HOUSE.
(Courtesy of Mrs. Nathan Pond.)

that of Widow Martha Beard, (54) to whom, for her courage in continuing on into the wilderness with her three sons and three daughters after the death of her husband at sea on the passage over, the town made a liberal grant of land both at the original allotment and later divisions. Her eldest son James died unmarried, and his was the first estate administered upon in Milford. Her son Jeremy died without issue. John rose to be captain. Her

could not squeeze between them, enclosing about a mile of country, and bounding on the west the home lots of the settlers on the further side of West End Brook. In 1645-46 the Indians came up to this palisade daring the white men to come out and taunting them that they were " shut up all one as pigs." Among the West End villagers, was William Roberts (57) whose grave is marked by the oldest legible stone in the

FIRST CONGREGATIONAL CHURCH.

daughters married well. " Ensign John Stream, obit 1685. Martha Beard his wife " and " Martha Beard (widow)" is the lettering of one of the blocks on the south coping. The Beard home lot included the land on Broad street from " Charles A. Tomlinson's corner to the large elm in John G. North's place."*

From the bridge the eye could follow the palisades, so thickly set that a man

present cemetery. There, too, was Deacon George Clark Sr.,(65)carpenter,† and Farmer George Clark, (43). In 1700 the house the deacon built was, like Mr. Prudden's, a fort of refuge. But before that time, the deacon had built himself another house outside the palisades. For the courage thus displayed, the town made him a grant of forty acres of land in Westfield. This house, known as the

---

*N. G. Pond.

†Father of Ensign George Clark 1647-1734.

Clark or Pond house, was long occupied by the late Mr. Nathan G. Pond, historian and genealogist, who made of it a very mine of colonial treasures. The hipped roof of the house was added in recent years.

The people from West End Brook came across from West Town street to River street by a foot path to the meeting house, maintained with convenient stiles. "The stiles," the records say, "to be maintained by bro: Nicholas Camp at West End, and by bro: Thomas Baker at the meeting-house (for the outside stiles ;) and for the inner fences, each man shall maintain his stile in the most convenient place ; and the passage over Little Dreadful swamp in John Fletcher's (12) lot shall be by a long log hewed on the upper side." It is to be remembered that at this time there was much common land,* where each man's initials on a post stood for his share of the four foot ten inch fence which he was required to keep in repair. If notified of a break he was to repair it within sixteen hours under penalty of five shillings. The gates to these enclosures were kept by individuals whom the town paid in grants of land, rate free during such keeping. It was rather necessary that fences should be in good repair if only for the reason that for a century, the town kept a flock of from 1000 to 1500 sheep. These were pastured more or less at large, and though they were in the care of shepherds hired to watch them, sheep, then as now, had a way of stampeding. The profits arising

from the flock went to meet the town's expenses. Hogs abounded in such numbers that in 1657 the Milford people petitioned the General Court of New Haven Jurisdiction to consider some method of limiting the number.

From the bridge, was seen the roof of the common-house where now the chimneys of Baldwin's straw shop rise. At the settlement the people had come over the hills from New Haven, driving their cattle before them, while they sent their goods and the materials for their common house around by sloop. Within the year separate homes were built, but at first they must have shared the common-house, and, doubtless, beneath its roof were held the earliest public meetings.

At the First General Meeting, November 20, 1639, they met to organize themselves into a theocratic republic, and it was

"Voted that they would guide themselves in all their doings by the written Word of God, till such time as a body of laws should be established."

"That five men should be chosen for judges in all civil affairs, to try all causes between man and man; and as a court to punish any offenses and misdemeanor." (This Court was known as the Particular Court.)

"That the persons invested with magistracy should have power to call a general court (or town meeting) whenever they might see cause or the public good require."

"Voted that they should hold particular courts once in six weeks, wherein should be tried such causes as might be brought

---

*1. Eastfield, enclosing the gulf neck, was divided among the settlers on Mill River and was known as the first division abroad.

2. Westfield, south of the town between Milford turnpike and the great meadow to Milford Point, or Poconoc was divided among those of West End.

3. Mill Neck, the land between Wharf Street and Bare-Neck Lane was divided among settlers from both ends of the town. This, and the apportionment of land toward Dreadful Swamp, equalled the second division at home. Always, at each division, land was set aside for the minister and elders of the church. At first, each settler was given a piece of meadow-land, either in the great East River, or harbor meadows. Each settler paid a tax of 4 s. for each acre of house lot and meadow land.

before them, they to examine witnesses upon oath as need should occur.''

''Voted and agreed that according to the sum of money which each person paid toward the public charge, in such proportion should he receive or be repaid by lands, and that all planters who might come after, should pay their share equally for some other public use.''

The judges chosen were William Fowler, Edmund Tapp, Zachariah Whitman, John Astwood and Richard Miles— to hold office to the following October— and to pass upon the admission of inhabitants and the division of lands. These five men with the addition of Rev. Peter Prudden, Thomas Buckingham and Thomas Welch constituted the seven pillars of the original Milford church, organized August 22, 1640, at New Haven.

Of these seven names, all but Astwood's occur among the memorial blocks. Richard Miles later moved to New Haven. His Milford lands became the property of his son Samuel, to whom Milfordites, with the exception of the David and Mary Carrington Miles branch (coming from another son of Richard's, Capt. John), trace their descent.

On February 12, 1639, three of these men, William Fowler, Edmund Tapp and Zachariah Whitman together with Benjamin Fenn and Alexander Bryan–(names also memorialized)— bought of

Ansantaway (his [mark] mark)

Arracowset (his [mark] mark)

Anshuta (his [mark] mark)

Manamataque (his [mark] mark)

Tatacenacouse (his [mark] mark)

the land lying between the East River and the Housatonic, the sea with the island south and the two-mile Indian path to Pangusset or Derby. The deed was taken in trust for the body of fifty-four planters, and in consideration of '' 6 coats, 10 blankets, 1 kettle, 12 hatchets, 12 hoes, 2 dozen knives and a dozen small glasses'' (mirrors) was solemnly confirmed by Ansantaway's passing over to the white men a piece of turf wherein he set a twig to symbolize his surrendering of the soil and all that grew thereon. Various purchases extended the town's limits far beyond the present boundaries. The sale of territory to help piece out the surrounding towns reduced its dimensions to the present triangle of about six miles.

The Milford men came in two bodies, those of 1639 and those of 1645. Most of them were from the English counties of Essex, Hereford and York. There were fifty-four heads of families or approximately two hundred settlers. Some came from New Haven, others from Wethersfield, following Rev. Peter Prudden who had ministered there between the formation of his own church at New Haven, August 22, 1639, and his ordination as pastor of the Milford church, April 18, 1640, after which Mr. Prudden took up his residence in Milford.

The second mill built in the town (1675), the first fulling-mill, was also visible from the bridge. It was near the meeting-house, and was built by Major Treat, later Governor Treat, Lieutenant Fowler, son of William Fowler, and Thomas Hayes. It was a fulling and saw-mill. Thirty years later, a grist-mill, near by, was added, with two sett of stone, one for English and the other for Indian grain, and ''a good boult, so yt men, if they wish, may boult ye own flour.'' The saw-mill gave place in 1836 to the woolen factory of Townsend, Dickinson & Co. In 1689, a second fulling mill was built on Beaver River. This in turn gave way to a flour mill from about 1783 to 1828. Cloth was not commonly sheared or pressed until after the Revolution. A kind of worsted stuff, known as everlasting, sheepskin or buckskin were used for breeches.

Commerce early went far afield from Fowler's dock. As the river filled up, vessels moored farther and farther down the stream. The names of Bryan and Camp suggest that of their partner, William East. Ensign William East had another between Richard's and the house of Miles Merwin, tanner. In 1675, the three men owned two brigs for West Indian commerce and a sloop for coasting-trade. In Boston, Ensign Bryan's notes of hand passed current as freely as do our bank-bills to-day. A fourth store-house was built in 1685 by Nicholas Camp in the West End. Staves, cattle, horses, beef, pork, flour, and corn were exported in exchange for rum, molasses and European goods. In 1714,

ACROSS THE BRIDGE.

liam East. Ensign Alexander Bryan as early as 1640 sent a vessel to Boston laden with furs to exchange for goods needed by the planters, either for themselves or for trade with the Indians. In ten years, trade increased to require a warehouse or store 60 x 20 feet. For it the town granted him land on the west corner of Broad street and Dock or Bryan lane, at the foot of which he built, in the same year, his own wharf. In 1655 Richard Bryan built opposite his father's, a warehouse of about half the size. Ser-

Samuel, son of Deacon Clarke, bought Richard Bryan's warehouse and land (2r. 13 ft. x 31½ ft. wide) on the east side of the highway for £16.

Shipbuilding, in the old yard a few rods below the mill (Fowler's) had already begun. Bethuel Langstaff had built in 1690 a brig of 150 tons for Alexander Bryan; another in 1695 for Boston parties. The "Sea-Flower" for Richard Bryan was launched in 1717. The "Isabella," an East Indian, sold in New York in 1818, was the last built at Milford.

During the period of the industry, coasters and an occasional merchantman, were built for shippers of Milford, New York and Boston. Most of these were built at the town yards though a few were constructed at Wheeler's Farms on the Housatonic.

Milford commerce did not last quite two centuries. It crashed with the big failure of Miles, Strong and Miles, in 1821. Among her early traders and merchants was John Maltbee, 1670; Mungo Nesbitt, enrolled a citizen and given the freedom of the town in 1696; Edward Allen, shipbuilder and importer, 1700. There were also the two great merchants of French extraction, Peter Pierett, who built the town wharf in 1730; and Louis Lyron, 1640. (The stones in the old cemetery record their virtues and attest their wealth.) In the middle of the last century, trade with Holland was carried on by John Gibbs. In its closing years, a wharf was built at the Gulf by the firm of Charles Pond & Co., large shippers.

But a short way up the street from the Memorial Bridge, one comes yet again face to face with reminders of the earlier time, pleasantly woven with memories of the letters Cadmus gave, of other lands and other days, commingling with the mighty interest of the pressing time. As the "Taylor Library" greets the eye one recalls the old English song:

" Oh, for a book and a shadie nooke
    Eyther in door or out,
With the green leaves whispering overhead
    Or the street cryes all about,
Where I maie reade all at my ease
    Both of the newe and old,
For a jolly goode booke wherein to looke
    Is better to me than golde.''

Augusta,
The Capital of Maine
(1898)

AUGUSTA, THE CAPITAL OF MAINE.

By Ewing W. Hamlen.

THE earliest predecessor of the modern city of Augusta of which history has any record is the Indian trading post which was established near the spot where the capital of Maine now stands, and which was called by the Indian name of Cushnoc. The large tract of land on both sides of the river Kennebec, from Merrymeeting Bay to its source, was occupied by the powerful tribe of Indians named Canibas; and this land was granted by the Council of Plymouth to William Bradford and his associates in 1629. Bradford traded up the Kennebec, more or less, and one of the principal gathering points of the Canibas tribe was Cushnoc.

In 1640 the Kennebec patent was surrendered by Bradford to the New Plymouth Colony; and in that year the council established a trading post at Cushnoc. This post was maintained by the council until 1660, but in that year the patent passed into other hands. Some sort of a post seems to have existed at Cushnoc most of the time, but no attempt was made to erect a settlement here until about a hundred years after the post was given up by the New Plymouth Council. In 1692 the remains of the old trading post were still to be seen; but it was not till 1732 that Governor Belcher contemplated the founding of a settlement and the establishment of a mission at Cushnoc. This idea was never carried into effect, and when the first settlement actually was founded in 1754 it was on no such peaceful basis as that designed by Governor Belcher.

There was an Augusta in Maine as early as 1714; but it had nothing in common with the present city except the name, and its life was very short. It was a small settlement founded in 1714 by Dr. Oliver Noyes, who was then part owner of the Pejepscot patent, embracing lands near the mouth of the Kennebec; and the remains of the stone fort and fishing settlement which he made on the shores of the Alliquippa harbor at Small Point, and named Augusta, are still to be traced. This Augusta had been deserted when the Plymouth Company in 1754 erected a fort on the eastern bank of the Kennebec River at Cushnoc, which they named Fort Western. This fort was situated close to the river bank, and consisted of a palisade of timber, with a square block house at each of two diagonally opposite corners, and a main building containing the store and dwelling houses. This main building is still standing in good preservation, near the east end of the present Kennebec bridge at Augusta. The fort was garrisoned by twenty men, and four cannon were mounted in it. A road "fit for the passage of wheeled carriages" was built to Fort Halifax, eighteen miles up the river, by order of Governor Shirley, and a series of expresses, by means of whale boats, was arranged between Fort Halifax and Falmouth, calling at Fort Western, the trip up or down the river being made in from twenty to twenty-four hours.

In 1755 the war with the French and Indians broke out; but Fort Western

THE OLD SECOND MEETING HOUSE.

tween two and three hundred whites. The town of Hallowell was incorporated in 1771, and included in its limits the present city of Augusta, the town of Chelsea, and a large portion of the towns of Farmingdale and Manchester. The towns of Vassalborough, Winslow and Winthrop, farther up the river and more inland, were incorporated in the same year.

James Howard may be considered as being the first settler at Cushnoc. He was appointed commander of Fort Western by Governor Shirley when it was built, and after the war he settled down, receiving a large grant on the east side of the Kennebec. This property he increased by purchase from time to time, and on the incorporation of Hallowell he was elected one of the first board of selectmen. The Howard family were the first regular traders in the new settlement; as early as 1763 James Howard was licensed to sell tea and coffee, and in 1765 his son, Samuel Howard, was in command of a trading sloop plying between Cushnoc and Boston.

was left in comparative quiet and did not suffer much. In 1760 large grants were made of the land below Cushnoc bordering on the Kennebec, Dr. Sylvester Gardiner and Benjamin Hallowell respectively taking large grants in the towns now bearing their names. In 1762 the first grants were made to the settlers at Cushnoc, and in the following year these grants were extended farther up the river. The peace of 1763, by which France renounced all claim to Canada and other possessions in North America, brought in its train a most favorable change in the condition of things along the Kennebec valley. With the end of the war the colonists settled down to their more peaceful vocations, strengthened their civil organization, and increased their trade.

It was not till after the fall of Quebec, in 1759, that any buildings were erected at Cushnoc outside of Fort Western; but five years later a census showed that there was a population in Gardinerstown and the settlements at Cobbossee, Cushnoc and Fort Halifax of be-

The rough state of the surrounding country as late as 1776 is shown by the vote passed in that year by the town of Winthrop, that there be paid to Rev. Mr. Shaw "four shillings which he

OLD FORT HOUSE.

paid for a pilot through the woods" when he went there to conduct services.

In the fall of 1775 Benedict Arnold came up to Fort Western on his expedition against Quebec. He established his headquarters at James Howard's, and remained there eight days. Capt. Daniel Morgan of Virginia commanded the riflemen of this expedition; Capt. Henry Dearborn, who was afterwards Secretary of War, commanded a company; and Aaron Burr, then a young man, was a volunteer. The disastrous end of this expedition is told in history, and has nothing to do with Augusta.

While there were undoubtedly a number of Tory sympathizers in the neighborhood at the time of the Revolutionary War, the town of Hallowell took its part in the military organization recommended by the Provisional Congress, and in 1776 sent a draft of men to join the Continental army. In 1777 the town seems to have been in a bad way, for we read that it voted to stop for the time being "the raising of any money for preaching or other uses," but voted to improve its roads by "one day's work laid upon the polls, and eighty days upon the estates."

Among those whose estates were declared forfeit by the law of 1778, as absentee Tories, we find the names of Sylvester Gardiner, Benjamin and Robert Hallowell, and William and John Vassal. These men were among the most important of the first settlers, as is well evidenced by their names

THE WILLIAMS MANSION.

having been given to the towns of Gardiner, Hallowell and Vassalborough. Owing to the law's delay and by the intervention of the signing of the provisional articles of peace at Paris, November 30, 1782, these estates were not actually confiscated, as the sixth article provided that there should be "no future confiscations made"; and as these cases were still pending at that date and this article was held to be a stay to the proceedings, the estates were retained by their owners.

During the twenty years between the Revolutionary War and the separation of Augusta from Hallowell, the settlement prospered. The first meeting-house was erected in 1782, and money was voted from time to time "to procure preaching." In 1784 a census showed the population to be six hundred and eighty-two; but the settlement was still very much in the rough, for of the thirty-eight houses in town, only twenty were reported as being "anyways comfortable or convenient." Among the names of the new settlers during this period we find those of Samuel and Daniel Cony and Seth and Asa Williams, whose families have since that time been foremost in the affairs of the place.

Separation from Massachusetts was a prominent subject of argument at this time; but the establishment of courts at Pownalborough and Hallowell tended to allay the excitement and to render the people of Maine more content with the existing condi-

THE HOME OF JAMES G. BLAINE.

Fort," were then in office as senator and representative respectively, so that "The Hook" was somewhat handicapped at the start. After a bitter contest the legislative committee decided, in view of the fact that "The Fort" was at the head of navigation on the river, that the bridge should be built there, and not at the lower point. Although it is hardly probable that anyone realized it at the time, this decision was the turning point in the fate of the two villages. Owing to the better communication with the rest of the country on the east of the river the village of "The Fort" has grown apace, and has now completely overshadowed "The Hook." The termination of the contest for the bridge brought to a crisis the feeling of "The Hook" against "The Fort"; and the town of Hallowell was in 1797 divided by act of the legislature. The charter of incorporation was granted to the new town February 20, 1797, under the name of Harrington; but the name did not prove acceptable to the townspeople, and in June of the same year, on petition to the legislature, the name was changed to Augusta.

Augusta at its incorporation con-

tion of things. At various times the town sent a representative to the General Court at Boston, but sometimes it was too poor to be able to afford this luxury and remained unrepresented.

In 1790 there were two well settled villages in the town of Hallowell, one called "The Fort," around Fort Western, and the other "The Hook," which is the present Hallowell, two miles down the river. In this year also another well known name appears for the first time, when James Bridge was elected town agent. By this time the town had grown to a considerable extent, and two or three ventures were made in the publishing of newspapers, only one of which, the *Kennebec Intelligencer,* lasted more than one year.

The fight between the two villages of "The Fort" and "The Hook" in regard to the building of a bridge across the Kennebec came before the legislature in 1796. Daniel Cony and James Bridge, both of "The

tained about two-thirds of the territory, about half the population, and about half the valuation of the old town of Hallowell. The building of the bridge was completed in 1797, and from that time the business of the new town steadily increased. Hallowell still held most of the trade with the district to the west, but nearly all the business from the eastern side of the river came to Augusta. The latter town did a considerable shipping business, and during the War of 1812 and for a few years preceding that war, she suffered more than her parent and rival from depression of trade.

The first meeting-house in town was built in 1782, before the incorporation of Augusta.

THE JAIL.

There was a good deal of dispute as to the location of this building, and after considering the matter for two or three years the town voted in 1781 "to reconsider all the votes that ever have been passed in this town in respect to building a meeting-house, and to begin all anew,"—which was certainly comprehensive. The house stood on what is now Market Square in Augusta. It was nothing but a rectangular barn, with a small porch. Early in the present century the town had completely outgrown the accommodations of the old meeting-house, and in 1809 the second building was erected on the edge of the steep hill overhanging the business part of the city, on the site where the third build-

ing now stands. The old first meeting-house was taken down in 1810, as it had then become an obstruction on Water Street, in which it partly stood, and the materials were used to build a town-house on Winthrop Street. The second meeting-house, of which a view is given, was struck by lightning and burned to the ground in 1864. The present granite church was built on the same site in the following year.

During the years of prosperity at the beginning of the century, besides the

COURT HOUSE.

second meeting-house just mentioned, Augusta built her first grammar school, a new court house, and a new stone jail, to replace the old one burned in 1808. The Augusta bank, which was the first established by Augusta capital and under Augusta management, was started in 1814, with Judge James Bridge as president. After his death in 1824, this office was held successively by Daniel Williams, Thomas W. Smith and Samuel Cony, the latter being in office when the bank surrendered its charter in 1864.

The Cony Female Academy was built by Judge Daniel Cony in 1815, and endowed by him for the free instruction of such "orphans and other females under sixteen years of age" as should be found worthy. This academy continued its useful career until 1857, although in 1844 its needs required the purchase of a new building.

THE WATER FRONT.

When the present High School was built a few years ago on the same site, the old building was moved down the hill near to the bridge, and is now used as a cabinet-maker's shop and harness store.

The first Kennebec bridge fell on the morning of Sunday, June 23, 1816, and a second bridge, covered, was built in 1818. This bridge was burned in 1827, when a third bridge, also covered, was erected. The third bridge lasted till half a dozen years ago, when it was removed to make way for the present steel structure.

Upon the separation of Maine from Massachusetts, Daniel Cony, Joshua Gage and James Bridge were elected delegates from Augusta to the convention at Portland to frame a constitution for the new state. This constitution was approved by the people in December, 1819; and by the Act of Congress of March 3, 1820, the state of Maine was admitted to the Union from and after the fifteenth day of that month.

The first number of the *Kennebec Journal* was published on January 8, 1825, the proprietors being Messrs. Eaton & Severance. In 1831 the Democratic newspaper, *The Age,* was

MAINE CENTRAL RAILROAD BRIDGE.

started; and in 1833 the *Journal* was enlarged in order to cope with its rival. Passing through various hands, the *Kennebec Journal* came eventually into the proprietorship of James G. Blaine and John L. Stevens, late minister to Hawaii. Mr. Blaine

HIGH SCHOOL.

gave it up in 1857, and after being owned by several other people the paper was purchased in 1868 by Messrs. Sprague, Owen Nash, who in 1870 successfully issued it as a daily paper. It is now owned by Messrs. Burleigh Flynt, and is one of the best daily papers in the state.

In 1827 the legislature, then meeting in Portland, after a committee (appointed in 1822) had visited and reported upon Portland, Brunswick, Hallowell, Augusta, Waterville, Belfast and Wiscasset, and after years of debate, decided upon Augusta as the seat of government for the state of Maine. In the same year Congress authorized the construction of an arsenal at Augusta, and Kennebec Arsenal was built in the following year. The buildings of the Arsenal are of

granite, and stand to-day as they were originally erected. Major John R. Maginnis, of the U. S. Ordnance Corps, is the present commandant.

The present Court House was built in 1829, of granite, the front having an arcade, the square pillars of which support the more slender columns of the gallery above. The Court House was enlarged a few years ago, to meet the growing needs of the county.

The corner stone of the new State House designed by Charles Bulfinch, the architect of the State House at Boston, was laid in the same year, and the legislature met within its walls for the first time in 1832. The situation of

POST OFFICE.

the capitol was certainly well chosen. It stands on a knoll between the old Hallowell road and the new or river road, facing the east. Situated at the extreme south of the town, it overlooks almost the whole of Augusta. Away to the north stretches the Kennebec, until it is lost not far above the dam behind the bluffs forming the west bank at that point. Covering both banks of the river is the town itself, the houses being for the most part veiled by the magnificent old trees which are

THE BANGS FACTORY.

plentiful throughout her streets. Directly to the east, across the river, are the Arsenal and the Insane Asylum; and to the south the view extends down the river to Hallowell, Gardiner and the lower Kennebec valley. To the west the capitol is backed by a round and well wooded hill, which in the autumn is one mass of glowing color. In the course of years the State House was found to be too small for the increasing requirements of the legislature, and in 1889 a large addition was made by throwing out a wing to the rear. The architecture of

the new part is in perfect keeping with that of the old, and the addition has much improved the appearance of the building.

Undoubtedly the most important improvement in the history of Augusta was the building of the dam across the Kennebec. The Dam Company was incorporated in 1834, but owing to the unfavorable report of an engineer the scheme languished and came near being abandoned. In January, 1835, however, the corporation took another start, and the four men who then composed it set to work to carry the project through.

RESIDENCE OF HON. JOSEPH H. MANLEY.

All the other incorporators had dropped out, and Daniel Williams, Edmund T., James and Horatio Bridge were the energetic men who still held to their intention of erecting the dam. Reuel Williams came in soon after, and a plan was made by the new engineer, Col. William Boardman, of Nashua, N. H. Immediately after the making of this plan, the shares of the company began to go up, and enthusiasm revived. In the same year the construction of the dam was begun, and was

THE KENNEBEC DAM.

continued through 1836 and 1837, with James Bridge as agent. The dam was completed and the lock formally opened, October 12, 1837. Luther Severance, at that time editor of the *Kennebec Journal,* and afterwards the first United States minister to the Sandwich Islands, was one of the first to see the possibility of a dam, and was one of the strongest supporters of the scheme from its very inception. At the banquet given after the

granite, but it was not for several years that granite quarrying was developed to any extent. About 1836, however, many companies were organized, and the granite business continues to this day one of the chief industries of Augusta. The Hallowell granite is well known in the East, and among other large buildings built of it are the Equitable Building, and the new fifteen-story American Surety Company Building, both on Broadway,

LOOKING UP THE KENNEBEC. THE ARSENAL AT THE RIGHT.

completion of the dam, in honor of Colonel Boardman, the engineer, one of the toasts, given by Gen. Rufus C. Vose, was "Old Kennebec, its *perseverance,* its dams, and its *Bridges!*" Up to this time the water power of Augusta had been derived from the little Bond's Brook, on the banks of which the saw, fulling and grist mills of the town were situated.

It was about this time that the first systematic efforts were made to utilize the granite that lay in such profusion around Augusta and Hallowell. The State House was built of Hallowell

New York. The Granite Bank was organized in the year last mentioned, and is the oldest of the banks now doing business in Augusta.

In the spring of 1839 a freshet occurred, which practically ruined those who had put their fortunes into the construction of the dam. During the year which had elapsed since the completion of the work, ten saw mills had been contracted for, and a canal and basin had been built for their accommodation. Some of the mills had also been erected, and prospects were bright. But disaster was at hand.

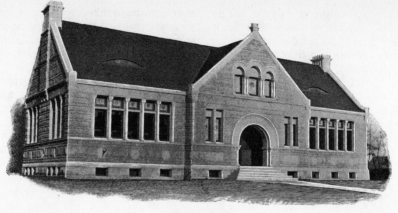

PUBLIC LIBRARY.

On May 30, 1839, came a freshet of unusual height, and the water made its way through the west wall of the dam, which had been damaged by a freshet in January of the same year, and burst in all its fury into the canal on the west bank of the river. The bank wall of the canal gave way under the strain, carrying with it the newly erected mills. So great was the freshet that the water undermined the bank of the river, and the mansions of Judge Bridge and Edmund T. Bridge fell into the roaring torrent and were washed away. The river had cut out a new channel for itself around the western end of the dam, and in doing so had swept away no less than seven acres of land. When the flood subsided the dam was left high and dry and, with the exception of its western end, practically uninjured.

From this crushing blow the citizens of Augusta rallied nobly, and in 1840 the dam was extended across the river to the new western bank. Saw mills were erected, and in 1845–6 the first cotton mill was built. The population of the town in 1840 was 5,314, and after the starting of the new mills it increased at a still more rapid rate.

Steamers were now running regularly on the Kennebec, and the competition between the rival lines from Augusta to Boston was very keen. At one time as many as five steamers from Boston were lying at the Augusta wharves. The fare to Boston was put down to fifty cents, but, notwithstanding this, one steamer came out at the end of the season of 1845 with a clear profit of nearly ten thousand dollars. The river was dredged between Augusta and Gardiner in order to permit the passage of steamers at any stage of the tide, and for this purpose the town voted to tax itself to the extent of $10,000.

One of the three Presidents of the United States who visited Augusta (the other two being Grant and Harrison) was President Polk, who came there in the summer of 1847. He arrived by the steamer *Huntress* at Hallowell, landing there about one o'clock on the morning of Saturday, July 3, and, together with the committee appointed to receive him, drove to Augusta in carriages. The President's arrival in Hallowell was announced by the firing of a gun, and cannon and the ringing of all the bells in town welcomed him to the capital of the state. The town had been illuminated all the evening, and the appearance of it when the President entered was most festive. A torchlight procession escorted him through the town to the house of Hon. Reuel Williams on Cony Street, where he and several of his friends spent the remainder of the night. In the morning he held an informal reception on the lawn south of Mr. Williams's house, and then drove in an open barouche, escorted by a formal procession, to the State House, where he made a speech from the balcony and afterwards had a great number of the citizens presented to him. Among the gentlemen who accompanied the President on this visit was James Buchanan, then Secretary of State. After midday dinner the President drove to Gardiner, where he stopped for a short time at the house of Robert Hallowell Gardiner, taking the steamer for Portland in the early evening.

In 1849 Augusta became a city, and Gen. Alfred Redington was elected her first mayor. The population in the next year was 8,232, and the valuation of the city was $2,337,138. The Portland & Kennebec Railroad, the con-

ton; her dam provided water power for a large cotton mill, some half a dozen saw mills, a grist mill with six sets of stones, and one or two other mills; her business was in good condition; and her material prosperity was every day increasing.

Immediately upon the declaration of war, the legislature authorized the raising of ten thousand volunteers, and Henry G. Staples was appointed to organize a company in Augusta. This company was fully recruited within two days, and a second company was raised by Moses B. Lakeman in a similarly short time. Six weeks later, on June 5, 1861, these two companies, with the Hallowell company, went to Washington on active service. It is not necessary here to give the history of Augusta during the war. That she acquitted herself with honor may be

THE CAPITOL.

struction of which was begun in 1847, was completed to Augusta by 1851, and great rejoicings greeted the arrival of the first train on the 29th of December of that year. In 1857 a railroad was completed to Skowhegan; and soon after the railroad to Bangor was finished. At the outbreak of the Civil War, the city was connected by railroad with Portland on the one hand, and with Skowhegan and Bangor on the other; she had steamers plying direct between her wharves and Bos-

gathered from the fact that by August, 1862, she had sent out more than four hundred men out of a total of sixteen hundred in her limits between the ages of seventeen and fifty years.

In September, 1865, occurred Augusta's great fire, by which almost the whole of her principal business street was destroyed. Eighty-one buildings were completely burned. The Post Office, two hotels, every bank, lawyer's office, dry goods store, shoe store and clothing store in the city

SOUTH PARISH CHURCH.

UNIVERSALIST CHURCH.

are a large number of houses, the Arsenal and the Insane Hospital. In common parlance, Augusta is divided into four parts, viz., "The Street," "The Hill," "Frenchtown" and "The East Side."

Water Street is undoubtedly one of the finest business streets to be found in a city of the size of Augusta. The solid brick and stone blocks on both sides of the long street are occupied on their lower floors by stores and shops, and in the upper parts by offices, halls, etc. The regularity and substantial nature of these buildings give a well-to-do air and businesslike aspect to the street. At the south end of Water Street are the old *Kennebec Journal* office, the new Masonic Temple, the Post Office and the Opera House. The Masonic Temple was erected a year ago, and has added much to the beauty of the street at that point. It is a handsome red brick block, the first floor of which is occupied by large stores. Half of the second floor is taken up by the Abnaki Club, a flourishing social club which recently came into existence. The

were destroyed, and the total loss was half a million dollars. In the next year most of the burned buildings were replaced, generally by stone or brick structures. The appearance of Water Street, which is the main business street of the city, was greatly improved by the class of buildings erected after the fire, and the character of the street has steadily improved, until at the present time there is but one wooden building in the main part of it, all the others being of brick or stone, and three stories or more in height.

Augusta at the present day has spread out her wings over the steep banks of the Kennebec, and the heart of the city is Water Street, lying parallel with the river, close to the western bank. Several streets, all very steep, lead westward to the upper part of the town, where the majority of the citizens have their houses. To the north, still on the west side of the river, lies the French colony, on the slope of Cushnoc Heights; and across the river on the east bank, scattered over the still steep but more gradually rising hills,

EPISCOPAL CHURCH.

upper floors are devoted to the fine Masonic rooms.

The old Granite Hall, which stood at the corner of Market Square, on the site of the present Opera House, was burned to the ground in the winter of 1890, and the following spring operations were begun on the erection of the present building. The Opera House is one of the best, if not the very best, in Maine; the interior is decorated in white and gold. The Post Office, which stands on the water side of the street, opposite the Opera House, is a

sent out. But one of the principal businesses of Augusta is the publishing of family papers, so called. The late Mr. E. C. Allen was one of the first to take up this business and to introduce it into the city. He was a man of great energy and industry, and by his own exertions created a business in his particular line which was unparalleled. Since his start in business other firms have taken up the family paper, and have also been successful. The principal firms now publishing these papers in Augusta are the Gannett &

COBBOSSEE GREAT POND.

fine structure of granite. It was built during the term of office of Hon. Joseph H. Manley, and is a credit to the town.

A thing to note in connection with the business of the Augusta Post Office is the fact that Augusta stands seventh of the cities in the United States in the amount of mail matter transmitted, being surpassed only by New York, Chicago, St. Louis, Philadelphia, Boston and Cincinnati. It would at first sight appear very strange that a city of twelve thousand inhabitants should take such a high place in the tables of tonnage of mail matter

Morse Concern, and Messrs. Vickery & Hill. There are one or two other smaller publishing firms in the city, but these two do by far the largest share of the business. It is in consequence of the business of these publishing houses that from ten to fourteen tons of second-class mail matter is shipped from Augusta every day. Every morning an empty mail car is put on the siding just below the station, and every night the mail train stops long enough for the engine to run down and pick up the same car, now filled with mail.

This publishing business gives em-

UNITARIAN CHURCH.

ployment to a large number of people, the majority of the hands being girls, who are engaged in folding and preparing the papers for mailing, etc. The Vickery & Hill Company occupies a large building on the hill, and has just put in, in addition to the old presses, a new three-decker press, capable of turning out some five thousand twenty-four page papers per hour. The Gannett & Morse Concern have their place of business on the East Side, near the river. A few months ago they had the misfortune to have one of their buildings burned, but with the enthusiastic help of their employees they were able to get off their publications with only a few hours' delay. A new building was erected within a week, and other and more permanent ones will be put up in the spring.

In the upper floors of the Post Office building is the Pension Department. On the fourth day of each March, June, September and December these offices are crowded to overflowing with veterans, each patiently waiting for his small share of the $750,000 which is paid out at this office every quarter. The sight of these old veterans of the Civil War brings freshly to mind the thought of what they have gone through for their country's sake, and even the most unpatriotic cannot but be affected by the sight. As they throng in and out of the government building, and gather in groups at the banks of the city, or in its shops and stores, the thoughtful of the present generation cannot help experiencing a deep feeling of thankfulness that the lines are cast unto them in pleasanter places than they were to the generation of thirty years ago.

Next to the Post Office is the slope leading down to the Kennebec & Boston Steamboat wharf; and on the other side of Water Street is Market Square, where in the winter the heavy sleds from the surrounding country districts gather with their loads of fir boughs, hay or cord-wood, waiting for customers. In the summer the square is filled every morning with the farmers' wagons, loaded with all the produce of the farms and gardens. Here, too, the travelling fakir takes his stand and discourses to the crowd gathered around him on the all-powerful virtue of the particular balsam which he has for sale, or invites the strong men in the crowd to try their strength of swing with the sledge on his machine with the lofty scale and sliding indicator. On the selfsame spot now occupied by the Italian woman with her little cage of birds, beseeching every passer-by to have his fortune told, stood at the beginning of the century the first meeting-house of Augusta. Those were the days when

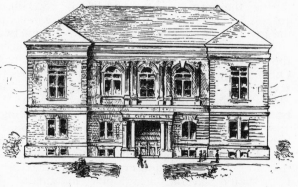

NEW CITY HALL.

one had to go to church or run the risk of being publicly reprimanded by the constituted authorities for the neglect, and when our modern fakir might have been ducked as a quack or put in the stocks as an idler; the little Italian woman in still earlier days might have been hanged as a witch.

From Market Square to the bridge is the busiest part of Water Street. Among the many fine buildings, the newest one, which stands out as the handsomest and best, is a commodious block, with a marble and granite

STATE INSANE ASYLUM.

THE NEW BUILDINGS.

pillared front, built recently by Mr. P. O. Vickery. There is an appearance of prosperity about Water Street which is always most encouraging. Even in the bad year of 1893, when the most depressing reports were coming from every part of the country, a look at Water Street cheered one up and seemed to show that here, at least, things were in a prosperous condition. Whether it was from the canny conservatism of the Maine merchants in their methods of doing business, or from some other reason, true it is that Maine generally, and Augusta in particular, suffered less from the bad times than any other part of the country.

From the bridge northward Water Street winds its way toward "Frenchtown," under the bridge carrying the

Maine Central Railroad's main line to Bangor, and passing by the gigantic cotton mills of the Edwards Manufacturing Company. Just before reaching the Edwards Mill a road turns off to the left, and going westward threads the valley of Bond's Brook. It was on this brook that some of the earliest mills were built; and there are still one or two on the lower part of it. This little valley is one of the most picturesque places in the city, and it is hard to say when it is most beautiful,—in the early summer, when the woods covering its sides are in their freshest green; in the fall, when these same trees are ruddy with all the thousand tints of that most lovely season, or in the winter, when the snow covers the ground and the only green things to be seen are the tall fir trees standing in solemn groups around the mill ponds, and when the course of the stream can be traced only by the ice upon it.

Going back to Market Square, and climbing the old Jail Hill, now known as Winthrop Street, we pass the end of the Maine Central passenger station, and at the top of the hill reach State Street, the chief avenue on the plateau lying parallel with the river on the west. At one corner is the new Lithgow Library, recently opened as a public library. The building is of granite, gray, rough hewn, and the roof is of red tile. The combination of color gives the building a striking appearance. In the library have been placed a number of beautiful stained glass windows, commemorative and

SOLDIERS' MONUMENT.

illustrative of prominent incidents in the early history of the town, which are likely to be of permanent value.

On the corner diagonally opposite is the Court House, and next to it stands the jail, both of granite. The latter is one of the best in Maine, and kept in perfect condition within and without. Shutting one's eyes to the heavy iron bars which guard its windows, it looks like anything but a prison, and altogether has a most imposing appearance.

All the churches in the city are grouped on or close to State Street, half a dozen of them being within a stone's throw of the new library. For half a mile up the hill to the west lies a network of streets, bordered with magnificent old trees, on which are the houses of the majority of the citizens of Augusta. All the houses are good; none of them are ostentatious. One of the best features of Augusta society, speaking broadly, is the moral atmosphere pervading it which precludes the idea of the rich vying with each other in outshining their poorer neighbors. The central idea which may be gathered from the character of the houses of the people is that all should live comfortably and none extravagantly. The cause of this is largely to be found in the direct or indirect influence of the many remaining members of the numerous old families who came here when the settlement was young, and who have lived in the town and for the town ever since. They have modified the stern Puritanism of our forefathers, and have adopted the modern comforts and luxuries, but they have always discountenanced extravagance and empty show. This simplicity tends to make the tone of Augusta society less conventional than that of many other cities of similar size. Augusta's hospitality to the stranger is well known; and one has only to be a stranger and have his lot cast among her people, to find out the reality and warmth of that hospitality.

Away at the south end of State Street is the house of the most distinguished man who ever made his home in Augusta, the late James G. Blaine. The public life of Mr. Blaine need not be touched upon here. In private life he was simplicity itself. Saddened as his last years were by the death of three of his children, in his bereavement he had the sympathy of all his fellow-townsmen. The Blaine house, like most of the houses of the better class in Augusta, is not pretentious in any way. Originally it was a good deal smaller, but the size of his

THE EDWARDS COTTON MILL.

family forced Mr. Blaine to enlarge it by building an addition at the rear. In the garden south of the house Mr. Blaine loved to lounge and walk. In the summer time now his grandchildren may be seen there romping about with a multitude of dogs. The present members of the family are devoted to their canine friends, and when they come to Augusta bring with them everything from a ratting terrier to a mastiff.

Just across the street from the Blaine house is the State House. Every second winter this is the scene of bustle and activity, consequent upon the assembling of the biennial legislature. In legislative winters every hotel in town is crowded to overflowing. Gaieties are continuous in the town, and Augusta people vie with their visitors in hospitality. The halls and lobbies of the capitol are thronged with members of either House, councillors, officers of the state, and the ubiquitous lobbyist. The latter figures most prominently, perhaps, in cases of town division. The state of Maine has not yet resolved herself into her final units, and at every session of the legislature there come up petitions for the division of some town or other and the incorporation of a new one. These battles are the most bitterly fought of the many that are waged each session; for in a town fight there are but two sides, and these are taken and held with a pugnacity and a tenacity characteristic of the Maine people when once fully roused. There is little speaking for effect in the Maine legislature. Most of the members are hard-headed business men, and the business of the state is conducted in a businesslike way. Impassioned oratory makes but little impression, and is somewhat discountenanced when it springs up, although a thoroughly good speech receives the most courteous hearing.

Near the centre of the upper part of the town lies the little park, with the Soldiers' Monument in its centre, a polished granite column, on a triangular plinth, surmounted by a bronze figure of Fame. Descending again to Water Street, the Kennebec bridge is reached. The view, looking up the river, shows, first, the steel bridge of the Maine Central Railroad; farther up the river, on the left, is the Edwards Mill, an immense brick building, a quarter of a mile long; still farther up is the dam, with the lock, now filled up, at the right of it; beside the lock is the pulp mill of the Cushnoc Fibre Company. During the summer months the river is full of floating logs, lumber driving being the principal industry on the Kennebec. The mill of the Augusta Lumber Company, on the east bank below the bridge, is now the only saw mill in Augusta, and save the Millikens' mill at Hallowell, is the lowest on the river. During the open season schooners are always being loaded at their wharf, and it is no uncommon thing in the summer to see ten or a dozen lying at the wharves on the west side of the river loading or discharging cargoes of lumber, granite or coal.

Close by the river bank at the east end of the bridge stands the new City Hall, now in the course of erection. The architect is Mr. John C. Spofford of Boston. The building is being erected by a corporation, from whom the city will lease it with an option of purchase at cost after ten years. In this building all the offices of the city officials will be located, thus bringing all the departments under one roof. One of the features of the new building will be a hall large enough for any state convention, so that in future Augusta can be reckoned as one of the places where large conventions can be conveniently held.

Hardly fifty yards from the new City Hall is the old main house of Fort Western, now degraded to the position of a tenement house of the lower class. The two block-houses and the palisades have long ago disappeared, but the old store and dwelling house, with its twelve-inch timber walls, still stand in good preservation, a memorial of the troublous times of the early settlement.

One of the most interesting houses in Augusta stands on Cony Street, at the top of the hill leading from the bridge. This is the old Williams mansion, which was built in the first years of the century by Col. Arthur Lithgow, then sheriff of Kennebec county, and which was purchased a few years later by Hon. Reuel Williams. The front of the house is toward the south, and the back toward the street. This is said to be owing to a quarrel which the builder had with Judge Cony, who had a brick house on the opposite side of the street, which also stands to the present day. In the Williams house things have been left pretty much as they were when it was first built; and the furniture and wall-papers are the delight of the antiquarian. The south parlor is octagonal, and its walls are still covered with the original paper, which was brought from England at great expense. The design of this paper represents the voyages of the redoubtable Captain Cook, and the figures on it are pictured about half life size. It was in this house that President Polk stayed when he visited Augusta in 1847 and was entertained by Mr. Williams.

Not far from the Reuel Williams mansion stands the present commodious High School building. On a quiet little street close by is the house of Mr. James Bridge, who was one of the prime movers of the Kennebec Dam Company, and in 1836–7 agent for the corporation in the construction of the dam. Mr. Bridge died January 8, 1896, in the ninety-second year of his age, and prior to his death shared with Hon. James W. Bradbury, who is now ninety-three, the distinction of being one of the oldest men now living in Augusta. Mr. Bradbury graduated from Bowdoin College in 1825, and was a classmate of Nathaniel Hawthorne and Henry W. Longfellow. He was United States senator from Maine from 1846 to 1853, having as some of his companions in the

Senate such men as Webster, Clay, Calhoun, Douglas and Cass. Opposite Mr. Bridge's house is the old Daniel Williams mansion. Mr. Daniel Williams was a prominent man in the affairs of Augusta in the early part of the century, and his son, Gen. Seth Williams, distinguished himself in the Civil War, becoming Adjutant General under General Grant.

On the road which leads from the bridge to the State Insane Hospital, known as Hospital Street, stands the home of the Hon. Joseph H. Manley, one of the most prominent politicians in Maine. Mr. Manley has twice been postmaster of Augusta. He is at present secretary of the National Republican Committee, and chairman of the Executive Committee.

Just beyond, stretching down to the river, is the United States Arsenal, and still farther on is the Asylum. The main buildings of the latter are of stone, but large brick wings have been added from time to time. The grounds of the Asylum are beautifully laid out, and from them one can get the best general view of the city of Augusta.

Augusta is surely a beautiful city. In the summer, when the trees which line all the streets are in full leaf, it is at its best. Through the hot weather the people take full advantage of the noble river which flows through their midst. The scenery on the Kennebec from Augusta to the sea is very fine, and a sail on the *Kennebec* or *Sagadahoc* is worth taking. At Merrymeeting Bay, where the Androscoggin joins the Kennebec, the sheet of water has the appearance of a lake, and the outlet is hard to find. In the summer, too, many of the inhabitants of Augusta betake themselves to the cottages at Hammond's Grove on Lake Cobbosseecontee, some four miles away. Cobbossee Great Pond, as the lake is sometimes called, is about ten miles long, and affords fine sport for the fisherman. It is surrounded by woods and farms, and dotted with islands. On a number of the islands and at many points around the shores are little camps and cottages, and canoeing is a favorite enjoyment.

The principal industries of Augusta at the present time are the Edwards Cotton Mills, the pulp business of the Cushnoc Fibre Company, the sash and blind factories of Bangs Bros. and of Webber & Gage, the lumber business of the Augusta Lumber Company, the granite paving block business, and the family-paper business of the publishing firms. There are smaller factories and machine shops, all in flourishing condition, and the town is steadily growing in prosperity.

The business spirit of Augusta is not only conservative, but progressive. As the material welfare of the town may be said to have really begun with its separation from Hallowell and the building of the bridge across the Kennebec, so it is argued by the most energetic of Augusta's business men can her prosperity be increased at the present time by still further and better communication with other cities and districts. A scheme is on foot to connect Augusta by railroad with Lewiston on the west and with Camden on the east. The proposed line would connect with the Grand Trunk Railway at Lewiston, and this connection would enable merchants in Augusta to get their freight from the West at a through rate. The continuation of the line to the east would tap a section of the state not now provided with railway facilities, and would bring an increase of business to Augusta. The Board of Trade has this scheme in hand, and it is probable that before another summer has passed the matter will be brought into such shape that the railroad will be an accomplished fact within a very few years. In such ways Augusta is reaching out to make her future fruitful as her past has been.

Marblehead
(1874)

MARBLEHEAD

dinary idea of Marblehead is tolerably complete. But this idea, though not without some merit of its own, has not the merit of comporting with the facts that make up the claim of this old sea-port town for some more general interest and recognition than it has latterly received. Time was when Marblehead got its full share of these commodities without any challenge such as I offer here.

Marblehead is not on the Cape; not on any cape, in fact, but on two small peninsulas connected by a narrow strip of sand and pebble. It is northeast of Boston sixteen or eighteen miles. In going there one takes the Eastern road to Salem, then a branch road which, midway between Salem and Marblehead, touches the head of

"Three fishers went sailing out into the west—
    Out into the west as the sun went down;
  Each thought of the woman who loved him the best,
    And the children stood watching them out of the town;
  For men must work, and women must weep;
  And there's little to earn, and many to keep,
    Though the harbor bar be moaning."

THE German word *Anderheit* means "otherness." A thing passes into *Anderheit* when it becomes radically different from what it has been. A great many old New England towns are going through this process; they are very rapidly passing into "otherness." This is especially true of the seaport towns near Boston; of Portsmouth, of Newburyport, of Salem, and of Marblehead. That the place last named is near Boston will probably be news to the average man not of New England birth. It is generally supposed to be upon the Cape, *i. e.*, Cape Cod. This misconception is associated with the mental image of a sandy waste inhabited by a race of fishermen. Add the Marblehead dialect, and the figure of "Flood Oirson," as depicted by Whittier, and a group of boys "rocking" the unwary foreigner, and the or-

Salem Harbor, at high tide a lovely sheet of water, with one little "emerald isle" in it, having more the appearance of a great inland lake than of a little arm of the sea. The ride by rail is very pleasant almost all the way from Boston. At first there is a succession of dreary places, new and bare; then the conductor shouts "Revere!" and while your next neighbor is telling you that this is where the dreadful accident happened a few years ago, you glide out upon the great salt marshes, where haply the hay is being tossed into huge stacks. The marshes are not nearly so monotonous as they at first might seem. They vary with the changing seasons and the changing tides. But it is at low tide, at sunset, that they put on their most magnificent array. At such times I have seen streams of liquid gold flowing through banks of crimson and purple. After hot days in the city how grateful is the breeze that comes in from the sea between Nahant, that stretches far out on the right, and Phillips Point! When the sea is at its bluest, and the marshes are at their greenest, the train speeds all too fast, such a feast of color is

299

spread out before us. Below Swampscot, "Salem's great pasture," if it is July, gives color of another sort, the rough hills being covered with wood-wax, or "dyer's-weed," with which in splendor not even the golden-rod can compete, though that is nowhere more sumptuous than here. All the coast along here is a series of peninsulas. East Boston is one; beautiful Nahant is the next; Phillips Point, just below Swampscot, is the next; then comes "Marblehead Neck," as the outer of the two peninsulas which form the township is called; then Marblehead proper; then Salem. Between the Neck and the town proper lies the harbor, half a mile or so in width, a mile and a half long, and for depth one of the deepest on the Atlantic coast. The *Great Eastern* could swing at anchor here. But the harbor is not

"THE CHURN."

so safe as it is deep, opening as it does with a capacious mouth at the northeast. A heavy northeast storm will set adrift every vessel in the harbor. After the "Minot's Ledge storm" the beach at the head of the harbor was strewn very thick with schooners, fortunate in finding such an easy resting-place. With the exception of this beach, and several coves, the shore of the harbor is rocky and remarkably precipitous, in places almost perpendicular. The rocks on which the light-house stands at the mouth of the harbor have this character. The fishermen steer so near that one can touch them with an eight-foot oar. "Half-way Rock," called "Half Rock," is even more precipitous. This rock is three miles out, and gets its name from being about half-way from Boston to Cape Ann. It is some forty feet high, and in a heavy storm, receiving the full force of the sea, the surf is thrown more than a hundred feet in air, and the rock looks from the shore like a great fountain. It was for many years, and may be still, the custom for outward-bound fishermen to throw coppers

on this rock, for luck, as they sailed by it. And it was also the custom for adventurous boys to land here and collect such of these offerings to Fortuna as had stuck in the crevices. The adventure must have been a great deal more than the reward.

There is an ancient and popular rhyme which indicates in general terms the geological structure of the town, also that of Salem, together with some reflections on the gastronomy of Beverly and the morals of Lynn; and all this in a quatrain:

> "Marblehead's a rocky place;
> Salem is a sandy;
> Beverly's a beany place,
> And Lynn it is a dandy."

There has never been any love lost between these neighboring towns, but their bark has been worse than their bite, and in cases of emergency they have stood by each other manfully. In 1774, when Salem had her biggest fire, it was the men of Marblehead who put it out, and the records show that the Salem people were not ungrateful. They not only passed high-sounding resolutions, but they voted the Marbleheaders one hundred and thirty-two breakfasts, and I forget how many gallons of gin. The rocks of Marblehead are not so rough and jagged as those at the Isles of Shoals, but they are much more beautiful. They do not carry back the mind to such a violent commotion, not being so twisted and gnarled. Their color is a perpetual pleasure to the eye, and again, unlike the rocks at Star and Appledore, they border fields and farms of wonderful fertility. All along the shores there are dikes of greenstone worn out by the action of the sea. When a heavy sea is rolling in one can sit for hours at the head of these dikes, listening to the thunder of the waves, and watching the clouds of spray. One of these dikes, called "The Churn," which, being at the back of the Neck, is exposed to the full force of the sea, often affords a grand and lovely spectacle. The end of the dike is nearly vertical. When the waves strike it the surrounding rocks jar with the terrible concussion. The foam is tossed high up into the air, and when the light is favorable a rainbow lends its evanescent beauty to the scene. The climax of beauty is reached in the rocks upon Cat Island, sometimes called Lowell Island. Here the rocks display the loveliest colors, the most striking contrasts, the most delicate gradations. The rocks bared by the tides are rich with reds and browns; those farthest from their reach are tender with soft greens and grays, thanks to the lichens that they nourish with all needful sustenance.

Cat Island is associated with one of the most interesting episodes in the history of Marblehead. In 1773 a local excitement for some months took precedence of the great public affairs that were at that time arousing so much interest. This excitement was the "Small-pox war." It seems that Elbridge Gerry, Azor Orne, John Glover, and his brother Jonathan had bought Cat Island and established there a hospital for inoculation. The town had granted them permission, but the apprehensions of the more ignorant being excited, the permission was revoked. The proprietors, however, continued their work, and at length received and successfully treated some hundreds of people. But somehow the infection spread in the town, and the hospital was held responsible. One January night a party of men from the town set fire to it, and it was burned to the ground. The proprietors were mightily incensed, and arrested two of the offenders, who were put in Salem jail. But five hundred of their townsmen were soon battering at the doors, and before the military, which had been called out, arrived, the prisoners were on the way to Marblehead, where a promise was extracted from the proprietors of the hospital to abandon the prosecution. But the Salem sheriff, thirsting for justice as for

blood, called out five hundred Salem men to march with him to Marblehead and re-arrest his prisoners. To his dismay, he learned that six or eight hundred Marbleheaders were armed and ready to receive him. Dreading the results of an encounter, the proprietors' "bugles sang truce," and the small-pox war was over. But in those troubled times it was a terrible misfortune for the people of the town to be arrayed in opposition to their most trusted leaders, Gerry and Orne and Glover. Gerry was a representative in the General Court, and one of the famous com-

ELBRIDGE GERRY.

mittee of correspondence with Hancock and the Adamses. He threw up both positions. The letters of Samuel Adams to him at this time are full of grief and anxiety. Neither Gerry nor the town could be spared from full participation in the crisis that was pressing harder every day. And before long Gerry relented, and the local war was soon almost forgotten in the vaster interests of the war for Independence.

The principal entrance to the harbor is between Cat Island and Marblehead Rock, which is not far from the eastern end of the Neck. This rock for a long time had for a beacon an old pulpit from one of the Boston churches, and it seemed a fine touch of poetic justice that a thing from which so much noise had proceeded should be compelled to listen to the infinite noise and tumult of the sea. The other entrance into the harbor is called "Baker's Island way." Baker's Island has two lights upon it.

"Two dim ghosts at dusk they seem,
    Side by side so white and tall,
Sending one long, hopeless gleam
    Down the horizon's darkened wall.
Spectres strayed from plank or spar,
    With a tale none lives to tell,
Gazing at the town afar
    Where unconscious widows dwell."

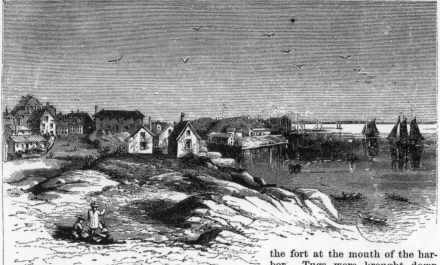

GREGORY STREET.

There is many a picturesque island and many a dangerous reef and rock here in the inner bay. The Gooseberries are not at all sour-looking, as their name suggests. The Misery Islands are called so to signalize some misery of shipwreck long ago. Pope's Head has brought disaster and chagrin to many a returning fisherman. One schooner that ran upon this rock was good enough to get off again, and, while her crew had gone up to the town to see their wives and babies, to make her way up into Little Harbor. Another was much less accommodating, for having been left there in the night, the crew, returning in the morning, found that she had given them the slip. Half-way over to Cape Cod she was picked up by a vessel that made claim for salvage, and the claim had to be allowed, "rough" as it was upon the owners and the crew. The lower part of the town is called Barnegat, and the name suggests that its inhabitants were once Barnegat wreckers; but, in truth, wrecks have been like angels' visits on this rugged coast, fortunately for those who sail the sea. Not of Marblehead, but of several other places, is the story told of a day when somebody came rushing into church in meeting-time, shouting, "A wrack! a wrack!" whereupon all the men sprang to their feet, and were making off; but the minister shouted after them, "Hold on there! Let every man have a fair start. Wait till I get to the end of the broad aisle." Only two vessels have been wrecked near Marblehead within the writer's memory. One of the wrecks was more comical than tragical—that of the old *Chusau*, which, missing stays in calm weather, went upon Jack's Rock, which is only a few rods from the fort at the mouth of the harbor. Tugs were brought down from Boston to pull her off, and cables were strained and broken, and timbers were wrenched away, but the old ship would not budge. Presently there came a storm, which got her off with ease, but in a thousand pieces, scattering along the shore her freight of gum-copal, of which every young man in the town procured a piece, with a fly in the middle, and thereof made a heart for some dear Dulcinea.

Marblehead can boast no beach of equal length and smoothness with Nantasket and Nahant. The longest is less than a mile in length, and it is heaped with pebbles far below high-water mark, and far above it. Longfellow's *Fire of Drift-wood* and Hawthorne's *Foot-prints on the Sand* had here their local birth. The beauty of the pebble compensates for any lack of sand. The porphyry pebbles, curiously veined and marked, are not less beautiful than the marbles we bring home from Rome, and they are bits of older ruins. The larger pebble is in great demand for ballast; and one of the pleasantest sights on midsummer days, while sitting on the cliffs, is the droghers rocking gently at anchor in the offing, while the men are filling the dories on the beach and running them off through the surf, up to their waists in the water.

"I sit and wonder what the cliffs would say
    If they could speak, remembering the day
When first, 'Thus far, no farther,' it was said,
    'Here thy proud waves be stayed!'

"So wondering how strange it is and still,
    Save where a mile away the droghers fill
Their battered dories with the shingly store
    Of the long-hoarding shore!"

A more exciting scene is that presented by the great yacht races. The home stretch is generally parallel with the Neck, and from the headlands it is sport indeed to see the mighty-winged things go fleeting by—

> "To watch the race with neither hope nor fear,
> Since none than other is to me more dear;
> My prize the perfect beauty of the sight—
> Unselfish pure delight."

The highest honor that the harbor knows in these degenerate days is when the New York yachts, the night before the race, come in for harborage. Then all is life and motion. A hundred dories dance around the handsome creatures that lie anchored off the wharves, whither the towns-folk come flocking down. There is much talking and swearing, and betting of the most harmless character, the stakes not being put down, and for a few bright hours the harbor seems to renew its ancient rapture, if it does not experience a keener joy than when a score of vessels bound for Bilboa were waiting for the wind to blow them fair.

There was a time when the headlands of the town and Neck were covered with a more anxious crowd than ever watched the generous rivalry of a regatta. That was the day when the *Chesapeake* and *Shannon* had their duel in the offing, when brave, foolish Lawrence, dying, pleaded, "Don't give up the ship!" The whole dreadful scene was visible from Marblehead, made more pathetic by the fact that there were men of Marblehead on board the *Chesapeake*. I have heard one of them tell of the horrors of that day, of the hope, of the desperation, of the butchery, of how he, with his board-ing hatchet, clove his man through to his clavicle. I have heard one of the mothers tell of how she left her wash-tub, and went, bare-headed and bare-armed, down to the Head to see the dreadful fray. A few days later poor Lawrence had a hero's burial in Salem, but the British flag hung at his vessel's peak, and the survivors of her crew were prisoners.

The streets of Marblehead have from time immemorial been regarded by "the stranger within her gates" with wonder and amazement. Nor are these sentiments unnatural. I have known Marblehead people so public-spirited that they would swear that every street in town is a bee-line; and this we may allow; but the bee must be no honey-laden but a honey-gathering one—a wandering, meandering, tergiversating fellow. The reason for this is evident. The strike of the syenite and greenstone ridges is in a north-east and southwest direction. The thickly settled portion of the town is made up of six or seven of these ridges, with intervening valleys. In fact, the harbor is the deepest of these valleys, and the Neck the highest of the ridges. This configuration determines the direction of all the main streets. They follow the valleys and the ridges. Sometimes the fronts of the houses are a thin veneering several stories high on the face of the great ledges, while at the back there is one story on the top of the ridge. Sometimes this order is reversed, and the stories lessen toward the front. The houses fa-

HOMES OF THE SEA KINGS.

cing "the Common"—
homes of the old sea kings
and Bilboa traders, more
than a century old—are
the best illustration of
this method. The cross
streets dodge the minor
ledges, as the main streets
follow the major ones. The
result is certainly confus-
ing to the foreigner, but it
is certainly more satisfactory to the eye than the
gridiron plan on which our
smart new towns are com-
monly laid out. The dis-
tribution of the houses is
a far greater wonder than
the sinuosity of the streets.
They remind one
of a good-natured
crowd of Irishmen
upon St. Patrick's
Day, when every
man is facetiously
planting his elbow
under his neigh-
bor's fifth rib,
or in the pit of
his stomach.
The newer por-
tions of the
town are much
more regular.
The condition
of the older
portions can
not be accounted for
without resorting in
some cases to the hy-
pothesis of "pure cuss-
edness." The windings
of the streets and the
ubiquitous ledges ac-
count for it only in part. These
circumstances doubtless set the
fashion, which, once set, like
every other fashion, was carried
to the extreme. Whatever the
cause, the effect is vastly comical. The theory of an earthquake, which shuffled a once
orderly array into the present
jumble of delicious incongrui-
ties, might be maintained successfully were it not that the
town records make no mention
of it, and the oldest inhabitants have no
tradition of it in their repertory of departed days. The appearance of the town
is changing rapidly. It is growing smart-
er-looking and more commonplace. Not
only are great shoe manufactories crowding about the handsome railroad station,
and ambitious dwelling-houses dotting
the suburbs, but the old houses are un-

LEE STREET.

dergoing a continual process of repair. Many innocent of paint for many a score of years are tasting for the first time that long-forbidden fruit of competence and self-respect. Thirty years ago the town abounded in various old houses, still inhabited, with many a broken window-pane stuffed with old hats or petticoats. The most of these have disappeared; but many are still left in tolerable repair, all weather-browned and blackened and overgrown with "dainty mosses, lichens gray." In 1820, I am told, hardly a dozen houses in the town were painted, and ruin was the average condition, the broken window-panes outnumbering the whole ones. This was when the town was still lying prostrate after the war of 1812. Now there is growing pride and almost universal neatness, with a good deal of taste, best shown in the gay little flower gardens that every where assimilate the rich juices of the soil, and convert them into the most brilliant coloring. Happy the man who is allowed to penetrate beyond these outer courts into the inner sanctuaries, into the snug sitting-rooms and the polished kitchens and the "chaney closets" of incomparable neatness and niceness. Here are to be seen heir-looms from a remote antiquity, cups and saucers out of which great-grandmothers drank forbidden tea in old colonial days, famous old desks and chests of drawers and high clocks, that "make the judicious grieve," because they are not to be bought with money.

There are a great many houses scattered through the town that are impressive monuments of the departed days of mercantile prosperity. Now there is prosperity again, and it is building its monuments, and some of them are certainly handsomer than the old ones, but they are very uninteresting in comparison with the houses that have tasted the salt air of the old town for two and three half centuries. There are scores of houses that date back as far as this, and many of them are houses that have a history, that have associations. Great and good men have lived and died in them, and their ancient walls and timbers seem to exhale the fragrance of their piety and courage. Here is the house which Parson Barnard built in 1720, or before. Here is the old "glebe" of the Episcopal church, nearly or quite as old. Here is the house where Elbridge Gerry was born, and the houses where his compatriots, Colonel Orne and General Glover, plotted against oppression. The birth-place of Judge Story is not far away, and exactly opposite is the house where Parson Holyoke lived, and where his son, Dr. Holyoke, who lived to be a fine old centenarian, was born. The parson himself left his Marblehead pulpit in 1737 to take the presidency of Harvard College. The people voted to not let him go; but the college pleaded hard, and so the people had another meeting, and called in Parson Barnard, of the First Church, to pray with them. The result was favorable to the college. "Old Barnard prayed him away," was some one's brief account of the transaction. Some of the *novi homines* have got into the fine last-century houses. But this, perhaps, is quite as it should be. The old Lee mansion-house, the finest of all, is now used for banks and offices. This is not nearly so old as many others, but it is far more capacious and more tasteful than any of its fellows. It was built in 1758 by Colonel Jeremiah Lee, and as long as it remained in the family it was graced with full-length portraits of the colonel and his wife, painted by splendor-loving Copley, in the handsome costume of the period. The original cost of the building is said to have been £10,000 sterling. There were plenty of slaves to keep its oak and brass well polished. Its great hall was wider than our city lots, its staircase in proportion. Here Washington was received by Colonel William Lee, whom he had promoted for distinguished bravery at Trenton and Princeton; here Lafayette was made "a spectacle for men and angels" on the occasion of his second visit to America. Should another hero come to town, where would he be received? But the danger is not imminent.

In one of the queerest corners of the town, called "Oakum Bay," there stands a house as modest as the Lee house was magnificent. So long as he lived it was the home of "Old Flood Oirson," whose name and fame have gone farther and fared worse than any other fact or fav y connected with his native town. Plain)nest folk don't know about poetic license, and I have often heard the poet's conduct in the matter of Skipper Ireson's ride characterized with profane severity. He unwittingly departed from the truth in various particulars. The wreck did not, as the ballad recites, contain any of "his own towns-people." Moreover, the most of those it did contain *were* saved by a whale-boat from Provincetown. It was off Cape Cod, and not in Chaleurs Bay, that the wreck was deserted, and the desertion was in this wise: It was in the night that the wreck was discovered. In the darkness and the heavy sea it was impossible to give assistance. When the skipper went below he ordered the watch to lie by the wreck till "dorning," but the watch willfully disobeyed, and afterward, to shield themselves, laid all the blame upon the skipper. Then came the tarring and feathering. The women, whose rôle in the ballad is so striking, had nothing to do with it. The vehicle was not a cart, but a dory; and the skipper, instead of being contrite, said, "I thank you for your ride." I asked one of the skipper's contemporaries what the effect was on the skipper. "Cowed him to death," said he— "cowed him to death." He went skipper

IRESON'S HOUSE, OAKUM BAY.

again the next year, but never afterward. He had been dead only a year or two when Whittier's ballad appeared. His real name was not Floyd, as Whittier supposes, but Benjamin, "Flood" being no corruption, but one of those nicknames that were not the exception, but the rule, in the old fishing days. For many years before his death the old man earned a precarious living by dory-fishing in the bay, and selling his daily catch from a wheelbarrow. When old age and blindness overtook him, and his last trip was made, his dory was hauled up into the lane before his house, and there went to rot and ruin. This solitary dory-fishing is the last resort of many an ancient fisherman. A few days ago I found one of these in his eighty-fifth year splitting up his dory for fire-wood. It was a sad job for him. He had followed the sea for seventy-seven years. He could still row and fish, he said, as well as ever, but his sight was getting dim.

One of the most persistent superstitions of the town attaches to the vicinity of Skipper Ireson's dwelling. Time was when hundreds of people were ready to aver that they had heard in this vicinity the Screeching Woman's doleful and heart-breaking cry. The story was that once upon a time a pirate crew had landed at the cove, bringing a woman with them. For one hundred and fifty years, on the anniversary of her outrageous death, at dead of night, her cries for help could be distinctly heard. But while this, with many kindred superstitions, was the staple of the old wives' evening talk, and sent a curdling horror through the young

folks' veins, it is remarkable that the witchcraft delusion which made such havoc only four miles away was here quite innocuous. One Marblehead woman was accused before the Salem courts, and suffered death for reasons too absurdly gross for ears or eyes polite.

The hoarse refrain of Whittier's ballad is the best-known example of the once famous Marblehead dialect, and it is not a bad one. To what extent this dialect was peculiar to Marblehead it might be difficult to determine. Largely, no doubt, it was inherited from English ancestors. Its principal delight consisted in pronouncing *o* for *a*, and *a* for *o*. For example, if an old-fashioned Marbleheader wished to say "he was born in a barn," he would say, "I was barn in a born." The *e* also was turned into *a*, and even into *o*, and the *v* into *w*. "That vessel's stern" became "that wessel's starn," or "storn." I remember a school-boy declaiming from Shakspeare, "Thou little walliant, great in willainy." There was a great deal of shortening. The fine name Crowninshield became Grounsel, and Florence became Flurry, and a Frenchman named Blancpied found himself changing into Blumpy. Endings in *une* and *ing* were alike changed into *in*. Misfortune was misfartin, and fishing was always fishin. There were words peculiar to the place. One of these was *planchment* for ceiling. Crim was another, meaning to shudder with cold, and there was an adjective, crimmy. Still another was *clitch*, meaning to stick badly, surely an onomatopoetic word that should be naturalized before it is too late. Some of the swearing, too, was neither by the throne nor footstool, such as "Dahst my eyes!" and "Godfrey darmints." The ancient dialect in all its purity is now seldom used. It crops out here and there sometimes where least expected, and occasionally one meets with some old veteran whose speech has lost none of the ancient savor.

A few years ago "the dismantled fort" which figures in Longfellow's *Fire of Driftwood* was the principal object of interest to the stranger. It was indeed a fine old ruin, a famous place for lovers, when the sea was lapping softly on the crags, and the moon was making a great pathway for their hopes, and the light-house opposite a little pathway for their fears, and the white sails of the boats went dancing across these pathways out of and into the darkness. The fort was called Fort Sewall, after Chief Justice Sewall, one of the great men of the town, a grandson of the first Chief Justice Sewall, of whom

"Touching and sad a tale is told,
    Like a penitent hymn of the Psalmist old,
Of the fast which the good man life-long kept,
    With a haunting sorrow that never slept,"

because he, then a junior judge, had given judgment against the Salem witches. A letter of the grandson, written in 1780, is one of the most interesting side lights of the Revolution. It describes a sad state of affairs, mainly owing to a severe winter and a great scarcity of wood. The poor went about begging and stealing it; the rich had to burn their meaner furniture. Sewall, then a young lawyer, tells how he had to warm himself at his neighbors' fires and among their pots and kettles. Seeing that not long after he married one of the wealthier daughters of the place, it may be inferred that he warmed himself at her fireside oftener than at any other. Fort Sewall's greatest day was the 3d of April, 1814. Then it really did good service, for then the *Constitution*, chased by the frigates *Tenedos* and *Endymion*, ran in to the protection of its guns. It was Sunday, but the Sabbath peace was sadly broken. Heavy cannon were sent over from Salem, the battalion of artillery in the town made ready, from the Charlestown Navy-yard assistance came post-haste, and the New England guards in Boston marched to the rescue of the brave old ship. But the *Tenedos* and *Endymion* made off to sea again without waiting to be peppered. During the late war the old fort was made over, so that now it is wholly without interest.

"Little Harbor" lies back of the fort, with a little island, Gerry's, at its mouth. On this island the first regularly ordained minister of Marblehead built him a house, and the pavement of his door-yard is still visible, and a shanty stands upon the cellar that he dug two centuries ago. The Fountain Inn was on the main-land a few rods from

THE POWDER-HOUSE, 1755.

the sea-girt parsonage, so safe from interruption at high tide, when, let us trust, the sermon was habitually written. The Fountain Inn was the first inn in the place, and a romantic interest attaches to its history. A few years ago a well belonging to it was accidentally discovered in digging a post-hole. It had been filled up, but its walls were as good as ever. It was cleared out, and is now in use again. Sweet Agnes Surriage must have drawn many a bucket of water from this well, and Sir Harry Frankland's horses must have taken a long pull at its nectar before they started off again for Boston. Dr. Holmes has made the fortunes of these two the subject of his ballad *Agnes*, but the ballad is far less interesting and poetical than the unvarnished tale as told by the learned antiquary, Mr. Elias Nason, in a charming monograph. Sir Harry was a lineal descendant of Oliver Cromwell. In 1741 he was made Collector of the Port of Boston. The next year he went to Marblehead, presumably to oversee the first erection of the fort. Stopping at the Fountain Inn, he found a lovely girl engaged in scrubbing down the steps, doubtless anent his coming.

"Bent o'er the steps, with lowliest mien,
    She knelt, but not to pray;
Her little hands must keep *them* clean,
    And wash *their* stains away."

Shoeless and stockingless, her feet showed all the prettier. Her face was found to match. And so it happened that Frankland gave her a crown to buy shoes with, and not being able to forget her, came again,

"OLD NORTH" CONGREGATIONAL CHURCH.

search of Sir Harry, who had been overtaken in the streets. At last she found him, buried under heaps of stones, but still alive. She succeeded in getting help to extricate him, her own superhuman efforts having been in vain; and he, deeply affected by these proofs of her devotion, made her his lawful wife. They were first married by a Romish priest, but on the passage to England assurance was made doubly sure by a Protestant remarriage. Lady Frankland relented when she heard the story of that dreadful day. Then came a dozen years of perfect happiness, interrupted by Sir Harry's death in 1768. Lady Agnes went to England when the rupture came between the colonies and the mother country. The old mansion-house was burned only a few years ago, but the elms the lovers planted are now twelve feet in circumference, and the box is ten feet high.

"Thus Agnes won her noble name,
  Her lawless lover's hand;
The lowly maiden so became
  A lady in the land."

and found her as before. "I keep them to wear to meeting," said she of her new shoes. This time, when Sir Harry went back to Boston, he took Agnes with him, avowedly to educate her, but with ulterior purposes soon carried out. The Boston of 1750 was not the Boston of a century before, but still it could not tolerate such open sin, and Sir Harry was driven by the social chill into a warmer atmosphere. He built at Hopkinton a stately mansion, and carried Agnes thither. Her lowly birth was not the sign of any natural inferiority, and her fine powers expanded rapidly in a congenial atmosphere, and her heart, supremely devoted to Sir Harry, went out in love and tenderness to all her household and acquaintances. Music and flowers were her two great delights, and Richardson's affecting stories often soothed her loneliness when business in the city took her lord away. In 1754 Sir Harry went abroad, and took her with him. His mother and his noble kindred generally gave her a very cold reception. They went to Lisbon, and were there when the great earthquake overwhelmed the city. When the tumult had subsided Agnes went out in

Back of the spot where stood the Fountain Inn rises a rocky hill, and back of this another, upon which once stood the first meeting-house built in the town. No church since built has occupied so fine a site, affording as it does a view of all the coast from Boston to Cape Ann, and of the immeasurable sea. The old building underwent many changes as the town increased in size, and all these were duly recorded, and can be read to-day in the town records, which are in a state of perfect preservation. One can hear in those records the rattle of the window-panes, which were fastened with nails, without putty, and the nails, it seems, were always coming out. Laths and plaster were things unknown. A century later "King Hooper," a famous merchant and aristocrat of Marblehead, had a country-seat in Danvers, and he there made some generous gift to the Episcopal church; whereupon, in token of gratitude, the vestrymen voted to lath and plaster a spot in the ceiling directly over his pew, and just the size of it. The improvement to the ancient house in Marblehead which leaves upon the records the most shining trace was the introduction of a second gallery. So strikingly did this "thing of beauty" confirm the truth of Keats's famous line that, ten years after its completion, it was voted in town meeting "that Robert Knight should be released from paying his town rates during his lifetime for his workmanship done in the meeting-house in building the galleries." This building was at length removed to a more sheltered spot, and, with still further improvements, it lasted until 1824 for religious purposes, and a year longer for the storing of fish. The society that left it built what is now known as the "Stone Church," or "Old North." Its front is of granite; its sides and back are from the ledge on which it stands. The worshipers can sit in their pews and see the rock from which these were hewn and the pit from which they were digged rising high up against the windows. One venerable church is still standing, St. Michael's, built in 1714. It has suffered somewhat from repairs, but is still a singularly quaint and interesting bit of antiquity. The second rector of this church, Rev. David Mossom, removing to Virginia, there had the distinguished honor of marrying Mr. George Washington to Mrs. Martha

Custis. Another venerable building is the Town-house, built in 1728 "on the spot where the gaol and cage now stand," so reads the vote for the appropriation. The powder-house is also venerable.

The ecclesiastical history of the town had a most pathetic beginning. August 15, 1635, there was such a storm on the New England coast as has not since been paralleled. We have various accounts of it. One by Governor Winthrop, who says that there were "two flood tides within two hours of each other;" one by Richard Mather, the first of all the Mathers, of New England fame and shame. He was caught in it at the Isles of Shoals, where, from Smutty Nose Island, a house belonging to a tailor, named Tucker, was washed away and carried entire to Cape Cod, where it was hauled ashore, and a box of linen and some papers made known where it was launched. But by far the most affecting account of the storm is that of Anthony Thatcher, also a tailor, who with his cousin, Rev. John Avery, had started from Ipswich a few days before. Avery was bound for Marblehead, where he had been invited to come and preach the Gospel. His wife and eleven children were with him, Thatcher's wife and seven children, a Mr. Elliot, and four sailors. All of these were lost but Thatcher and his wife. Thatcher's account of the disaster is too fine to be abridged, but too long for our present limits. Whittier has retold the story in one of his rarest poems. The poor tailor named

TUCKER'S WHARF—THE STEPS.

"THERE ON THE HIGHEST POINT IS A SIMPLE MONUMENT."

the rock on which the shallop struck, Avery's Fall, and the island near by, Thatcher's Woe, and they are still called Avery's Rock and Thatcher's Island.

> "There was wailing on the main-land
> From the rocks of Marblehead;
> In the stricken church at Newbury
> The notes of prayer were read;
> And long by board and hearth-stone
> The living mourned the dead."

Of all the ministers who have preached in Marblehead from the beginning the Rev. John Barnard doubtless did the greatest work, and was the man of strongest character. Until he came to the town there had been but one church; but the congregation were divided between him and the Rev. Edward Holyoke. Barnard had the majority of votes, but refused to settle unless Holyoke could come and take his friends and form another society. This was agreed upon, and carried out in 1715. In 1737 Barnard was informally invited to take the presidency of Harvard College, but feeling certain that Holyoke was the fitter man, he so advised the overseers and corporation, and his advice was taken. It is a significant fact that the town had at this time two men held to be worthy of so great an honor. In his old age Barnard wrote an autobiography, and sent the manuscript to President Stiles, of Yale College, the universal correspondent of those times, the most ubiquitous of men, forever turning up in the history of his generation. It is spiced with a considerable amount of egotism, but it is a document of inestimable value and abounding interest. The most amusing item is that for ten weeks he preached upon one leg, the other being affected with sciatica. Parson Barnard, like the famous Hugh Peters and many other preachers of

that time, was more than a preacher. He was a man of public spirit. He was a social regenerator. When he came to Marblehead there was not one foreign trading vessel in the port. "Nor could I find," says the autobiography, "twenty families that could stand on their own legs; and they were generally as rude, swearing, drunken, and fighting a crew as they were poor. I soon saw the town had a price in its hands, and it was a pity they had not the heart to improve it." He at last succeeded in stirring up a young man, Joseph Swett, to engage in foreign trade, though his first venture was only to Barbadoes. From this time the town began to export its own fish. In 1740 the town had 150 vessels engaged in fishing, and at least a third as many more in carrying them to Bilboa and other Spanish ports. The town became second in population and wealth to Boston, and when the days of trial came, its port of entry and its freest benefactor. The Revolution, the French and English wars, and the war of 1812, with the embargo that preceded it, put an effectual stop to this astonishing prosperity. To-day only a few of the men who were a part of it remain. When you find one of them you find a treasure. He has his castles in Spain, and he will talk about them by the hour as he sits sunning himself and warming his thin blood on the wharves, which, now almost deserted, he remembers when they bustled with activity. He is nearly ninety years old. He saw Lafayette and Washington when they came to town. He saw General Glover in his coffin. He has talked with Elbridge Gerry's freedman Cato, his slave before the Revolution. He was a privateersman in the war of 1812, and one of the five hundred men of Marblehead who were in Dartmoor prison at the end of that war. He has a lively recollection of that April day when the prisoners there were fired upon. He has seen the armies of Napoleon and Wellington on the Peninsula, and he is not so old but that his eye will sparkle when he tells you of the beauty and the tenderness of the girls of Spain and Portugal. An egg is not so full of meat as he is full of tales of storm and wreck and merciful deliverance. But his name is not legion, and the places that have known him will soon know him no more. *Post tot naufragia portus.*

A successor of Parson Barnard, of a less practical turn, was wont to pray for those "who go down to the sea in ships, and who do business on great waters," "may they be blessed with a perpetual calm." I fancy that without the Scriptural part of this petition no prayer was considered perfect in the good old times. Certainly it was never omitted from any prayer that I overheard from Parson Bartlett's lips when that good man was the instructor of my youth. But the prayer for a perpetual calm is now receiving a late answer. It settled down

upon the foreign traffic long ago, and now it is settling down upon the fishing. When Whitefield came to Marblehead he asked, "Where do they bury their dead?" because it was so rocky. They buried them on what is now "The Old Hill," and was originally the church-yard of the First Church, one of the rockiest hills in the whole town. There the old Puritan ministers lie buried under resounding Latin epitaphs; there the red wild roses bloom their reddest and the golden-rod its yellowest; and there on the highest point is a simple monument in memory of those lost in the gale of '46—a dozen vessels, sixty-six men and boys. To-day the Bank fishing vessels, all told, only number eighteen, and on board of these there are not a score of Marblehead men. The rest are mainly from the Provinces. Once the fish fences covered every seaward hill and many an inland one; now a few acres contain all that remain of them. For hundreds of warehouses where the fish were stored, there remain perhaps a dozen. These changes have been gradual. Little by little St. Peter's followers have become followers of St. Cris-

"WHEN I WAS WITH SNOW, IN THE 'BRILLIANT.'"

"SITTING, STITCHING IN A MOURNFUL MUSE."

pin. Twenty years ago there was a new departure. The town had its ship-yard, and four or five large ships were built, and thrice as many schooners. Those were happy days for the old veterans. They thought that verily the Saturnian days had come again. But their hilarity was brief. A deeper melancholy soon possessed their generous hearts.

And now that that old life is almost ended, it is lived over and over again in happy recollection by those who once were fairly steeped in it. Events that at the time had little pleasure in them are very pleasant to recall, as Virgil long ago suggested. A few years ago the town was sprinkled thick with little shoe shops, about twelve feet square, in which six or eight men could work. There were hundreds of these little shops. They offered great facilities for conversation, though when all were hammering at once, the voices were pitched very high. But the shoe business itself has undergone a revolution. Few of these little shops are now occupied. Dozens of them are in a melancholy process of decay. The invention of labor-saving machinery has crowded the men into large manufactories, which are not favorable for conversation of the sort we have in mind. That needs enough partakers, and no more, to insure a generous rivalry, and to cap every climax with a more exciting story. The present scene of this is the back shop of the little grocery. This back shop is an abounding and delightful institution. It must be seen in winter-time if one would see it to advantage. Then, when the floor is full of pea-nut shells and the air is thick with smoke, and the salamander is red-hot and sizzling with occasional ejections of tobacco juice, the little circle rises to the height of the occasion. Sometimes all talk at once. "When I was with Snow, in the *Brilliant*," one begins; but some heavier engine throws him off the track. He soon gets on again, and begins afresh his story in a higher key, only to be again suppressed. They have all heard it scores and scores of times. He goes off with a snort, and the rest go on spinning their yarns. Some of them have lost nothing by a hundred repetitions. If the pleasure is more in the telling than in the hearing, it is still about equally distributed. The colloquy tends rapidly to become soliloquy where one monopolizes all the talk.

Marblehead has never kept a poet, though Whittier and Longfellow and Holmes and Lucy Larcom, here the noblest singer of them all, have celebrated real or imaginary things and persons and events connected with the dear old town. If Lucy Larcom had written nothing but her *Hannah Binding Shoes*, she would have an enviable fame. I have fancied that I know the very woman who suggested that affecting ballad,

"Sitting, stitching in a mournful muse."

But there is material enough for poetry in the scenes and habits of the fast-receding time, when all the energy of the community was concentrated upon "the art preservative of all arts," if it be true that fish makes phosphorus and phosphorus makes brains. There was the bustle of preparation, the getting in of wood and salt and stores. The schooner generally went to Boston for her salt, and then we youngsters had a fine time of it, going with her to "the dim rich city," and sleeping in the cabin or the "forekistle," and making friends with the cook. Or was it better when a great ship came to Marblehead with a whole load of salt, and we were permitted to go on board of her, and to row at night under her bows and feel their awful shadow, and wonder if her stern went down till it touched the heart of the world? Then there were the home preparations, the washing and mending of the great pea-jackets and trowsers that smelled so of the sea, the packing of the chest, the making of "Harrison cake" and hard gingerbread. When the day came for sailing it was a very silent morning in the house. There was no talk at breakfast-time. The handsome thing for the skipper to do was to sail round the harbor an hour or two with the company that had collected on board, with a long string of "Moses boats" and dories dragging at the stern. Sometimes there was a treat all round from a certain little keg, which the more prudent skippers regarded with unmixed aversion. When at length the skipper shouted, "All ashore!" the last boats were always loaded to the gunnel. Then we went up on "Bartol's Head," and watched the white sails lessen more and more, till they made only a little gleam on the horizon. From that time the "Spoken" in the newspapers was narrowly watched, but with little satisfaction, until the first of the fleet returned, bringing news of nearly all the rest, and how many thousand fish they had on such a day. They used to *count* thousands, but now they guess quintals. It was a great day when some good neighbor came to the door or window, saying, "Mrs.——, your husband's coming up the harbor." Sometimes there was a rich brown face in the doorway without a word of warning; sometimes a well-known step in the night upon the gravel. There was one coming back that was different from all others within the memory of the present generation. It was after the September gale of '46. After the first news of the disaster had been brought to town there were many weeks of terrible anxiety, of alternate hope and fear. From every headland, and from the "Old North" steeple, eyes were straining into the distance to catch the first hint of a returning sail. And when one was descried, the word went from house to house all through the town, and hundreds crowded to the wharf to see what vessel it might be, and what news it brought of kindred or of friends. Only the fishermen's wives staid very quietly at home, waiting for the sign of hope or widowhood. Sometimes bad news was contradicted, and "women received their dead raised to life again, and others were tortured, not accepting deliverance." I well remember one of these returns. The wharf was packed with an expectant crowd of men and women. As the vessel came up the harbor there was none of the usual hilarity. There were no cheery shouts and answers. There was no talk about "how deep" she was, no brag that she had "wet her salt." When the crew landed, the crowd parted silently to let them through. There was hardly a word spoken. The crowd broke up as the crew separated, and followed them to their various homes. I remember walking home with my hand held in the skipper's very tight indeed, his monstrous fishing boots clumping along with what then seemed to me a very solemn sound. For myself, I was not superior to a feeling of gratification at being escorted home by so many people, though I was but a fly upon the wheel. Then followed such a day. The house was thronged with people anxiously inquiring for their friends. Children came to hear that they were fatherless, and wives to learn that they were widows. And little by little the story of the storm was told, and the story of what followed, when the sea was strewn with proofs of terrible disaster, with wood and spars and seamen's chests and bedding. In one place the masts of two vessels were found hopelessly entangled; in another a vessel lying on her beam ends, and with every mighty surge lifting her masts high up out of the melancholy waste, and then plunging them down again in a sad, hopeless way that almost broke the hearts of those who witnessed it. To a stranger in the town the monument on the "Old Hill" means little, but no monument that I have ever seen is so vocal for me with

"The still sad music of humanity."

But when the voyage had been prosperous, and there had been no general disaster to overcloud its good success, the return was quite a little jubilee. How delicately were the gradations of kinship and acquaintance-ship expressed by the different gifts which the happy children were deputed to carry round! The outer circle received only "sea-crackers," that is, crackers left over from those carried, and impregnated with the briny flavor of the sea. The next circle inward received with the crackers a bit of smoked halibut; and those still more favored, in addition to the crackers and halibut, some "tongues and sounds." To all these luxuries, for the inner circle a halibut's fin was added; and the crowning point of good-will was a "hagdon"—a sea-bird of too rank a savor to be universally enjoyed. The days for washing out were also great days for the children. The fish are now washed in a pound, which is chained against the schooner's side, then carried in dories to the beach, where the tip-carts are backed down into the water to receive them. Even now the scene is picturesque enough; but it was much more so when the washing out was done upon the beach. The fish were dumped into the water, and the men, with their "ile-skins on" and fishing boots, dashed them together, whitening the water with a more decided pickle than the average brine of the sea. On these occasions to carry dinner was esteemed a high prerogative. The dinner was contained in two tin pails, polished as nev-

UNLOADING FISH.

er door-plate was upon Fifth Avenue. One of these was full of tea; the other, with a knife and fork neatly tied to the handle, of meat and vegetables. And with what interest we youngsters watched these dainties disappear, and what nectar and ambrosia seemed the portions given to us in answer to our dog-like looks of pleading! Once there were more than fifty fish fences scattered along the shore. Now there are only two. Long may these two remain, with all their old belongings, that appeal so pleasantly to eye and nose! Here is no such disgusting odor as that which haunts the fishing houses of the Bay fishermen at Swampscot Beach, but a smell so strong and sweet that it is positively agreeable, especially if old associations mingle their fragrance with it. And pleasant it is to see the curing-men, who have caught many a quintal in their day, moving about in the long aisles between the fences, spreading or heaping up the fish, and bearing them away in their barrows to the old warehouses, that are scored all over with the tallies of fish that long ago made brains for poets and philosophers.

The methods of the fishermen have changed as well as their numbers. Twenty-five years ago all the Bank fish were caught on board the schooners. Next, huge dories were carried, in which the men rowed out in various directions, so that if the fish were not found in one place, they might be in another. Now trawls are employed at great cost, and involving harder work than ever. These changes have brought in a different form of tragedy from any formerly experienced. The men are sometimes caught out in the fog, and do not get back again for days. This very summer (1873) two were caught out in this way, and when picked up at length by a Gloucester schooner, they were fearfully exhausted. For a week they had had nothing to eat or drink. One, in the madness of his thirst, had drunk salt-water, and so increased his thirst and brought on delirium. Verily

"Stone walls do not a prison make,
  Nor iron bars a cage."

Here there is possible a form of "solitary confinement" worse a thousand times than that of the prisoner at Sing Sing.

The history of Marblehead is yet to be written. The materials for it are abundant, and they have been patiently culled by a citizen of the place, who is a lineal descendant of Gerry's coadjutor, Colonel Azor Orne, of Revolutionary fame. If ever the results of his researches are made public, they will show that the old town has a history second in interest to no other of its size in the United States. In the town records the line of progress can be traced from the time when a few Naumkeag Indians lived here among rocks and swamps and forests to the time when the annual expenses of the town, including the minister's salary, were £250, and from that time till now, when the annual expenses are $70,000. From first to last there have been a great many changes. The rocks mostly remain. But the swamps have been converted into fertile farms and gardens, and the forests long ago were built into ships and houses, or went to soften the stern rigors of an inclement coast. The town was originally part of Salem, or Salem was a part of it, for it was Marblehead that gave the name to the whole settlement. "Here is plentie of Marblestone," wrote Francis Higginson in 1629, "in such store that we have great rocks of it, and a harbour near by. Our plantation is from thence called Marble-harbour." This name was soon changed to Salem, but the old name was retained for the portion since called Marblehead till 1633, when its present name was generally agreed upon. There was no separate incorporation, however, till 1648, and for a long time after that Marblehead remained in ecclesiastical leading-strings, and though there was preaching at home, the worshipers had to go to Salem for their sacramental bread and wine, for baptism and marriage. The first settlers at Salem were a forlorn hope that followed brave old Roger Conant after the breaking up of the settlement at Cape Ann in 1626, and doubtless Marblehead had settlers from this time. The first mentioned inhabitant was Thomas Gray, who had bought Nantasket from the Indians in 1622. Thomas had evidently offended, for it was decreed by the General Court in 1631 "that his house at Marblehead be pulled down, and that no Englishman shall hereafter give house-room to him." But the man whose name on "Found-

ers'-day," if the town ever has one, will demand the highest honor is Isaac Allerton, one of the *Mayflower* pilgrims, the intimate associate of Carver and Brewster and Bradford and Winslow. His name immediately followed theirs on the famous compact signed in the *Mayflower* cabin. According to Governor Bradford's journal, "Good-wife Allerton was delivered of a son, but dead born," on the 22d of December, 1620, O. S.— a sad beginning for the settlement, for this was the first comer. Allerton was the first assistant governor, and the only one for several years. He it was who, with the redoubtable Miles Standish, "went venturously" to treat with Massasoit. Point Allerton, the first headland of Nantasket, bears his name. For a second wife he married Elder Brewster's daughter Fear. When Winthrop and his party came in 1630, the first face they saw was Allerton's, who boarded them from his shallop. He had the best head for business of any man at Plymouth, and made five voyages to England in the interest of the colony before 1631, when, falling out with his old friends, he came to Marblehead in the *White Angel*, and in the same vessel, loaded with fish, he soon after went to England again. Returning, he made Marblehead his home, building there a large fishing house, and employing many vessels. His son-in-law, Maverick, co-operated with him, and, after him, was the most conspicuous early settler. This Maverick was a good friend of the Indians—gave thirty of them

DRYING FISH, LITTLE HARBOR.

THE TOWN-HOUSE.

"Christian burial" in one day, when the small-pox was sweeping off their feeble remnant. It was Allerton who sent to Ipswich for Parson Avery the ill-fated shallop. Apparently he was the most stirring person in the vicinity of Massachusetts Bay. But as he had fallen out with the Plymouth colony, he now fell out with Winthrop's General Court, which gave him "leave to depart from Marblehead." Afterward, in New Haven and at New Amsterdam, he heaped coals of fire upon his Massachusetts enemies, by proving very serviceable to them in many ways. His only monument in Marblehead is Allerton Block, the finest building in the town for business purposes. But when it was built, a few years ago, the name was Greek to almost every body.

The impulse which Allerton had given was seconded by others, so much so that the third vessel built in New England was built here in 1636, the *Desire*, of 120 tons burden. Alas for her good fame, a part of her first cargo from the West Indies was the first slaves introduced into the New England colonies. All foreign trade was soon abandoned, and early in the next century fishing was the only business of the place. There was not even a carpenter belonging to the town. Parson Barnard reformed this altogether, and for fifty years before the Revolution there was a large export and import trade, and gold is said to have been as plenty as copper had been before. This was the period when nearly all the fine old houses in the town were built, and in which the town acquired the immense influence it evidently had in the events preparatory to the Revo-

lutionary war, and during that momentous struggle.

The ancient records contain a great deal that is laughable at this remove, though it was solemn as eternity at the time. There was the case of John Gatchell, who in 1637 was fined ten shillings for building on the town lands; but it was agreed to abate one-half the fine "in case he should" cutt off his long har off his head." There was a regulation size for dogs, above which they could not be tolerated. When the small-pox appeared in town, all under as well as all over this size were put to death, lest they should carry the contagion. In 1676 no person was allowed to settle in the town who could not give bonds that he would not become a pauper. The original settlers contended jealously for their prerogatives, and were much like the old farmer who wanted all the land adjoining his. When the first load of salt arrived in Marblehead the General Court "sat on it," and voted to send down certain men to unload it, "with power to impress others into their service." The boundaries of land were so indefinite as to become a fruitful source of litigation. "From the bramble-bush on the north, so many feet to the bramble-bush on the west," etc., was no uncommon designation. The province having appropriated five hundred and fifty pounds for the improvement of the fort, it was voted by the town, as a security against embezzlement, "that the trustees deposit the money in one chest with two different locks and keys, the chest to be left in the charge of one and the keys to be held by the others, and the chest not to be opened except in the presence of all three gentlemen." For the honor of human nature be it said, two of the trustees refused to serve on these conditions.

Until the mother country became utterly regardless of the welfare of the colonies the town was noted for its loyalty. When in 1745 Sir William Pepperell wanted men for his expedition, he found the most of them in Marblehead, and when Louisburg surrendered, great was the joy, for the town had been a constant sufferer from the French privateers that found a shelter under the guns of that fortress. The traditional sentiment of loyalty to the king was cherished long after indignation was aroused at the hard measures of his government. It was insisted, perhaps willfully, that he was not responsible for these measures. But there came a time when this theory was no longer possible for discerning minds. The conviction that he was responsible first found expression at a town-meeting held in Marblehead in a series of resolutions from the hand of Elbridge Gerry, as were all the resolutions of the period. Many were startled at this, but many months had not passed before the average public sentiment indorsed the manly utterance. There was more than one "cradle of liberty." Those were the days of town-meetings and resolutions and circular letters, and not Faneuil Hall itself resounded with more stirring eloquence or saw more resolute defiance of oppression than the old Town-house in Marblehead, which ought to stand for centuries to come as the best monument of that heroic time. Colonel Azor Orne was the orator, Gerry was the man of mighty words, employed to draft all letters and resolves. Glover, "the man of war," labored with these; but a better opportunity was awaiting him in no distant future. Sixty merchants of the town agreed to import no tea, and when one of four who had refused to sign the agreement had brought a chest to town, it went out much sooner than it came in, well pasted over with patriotic mottoes, and accompanied by a derisive and indignant crowd. When State Street, Boston, ran with patriot blood, there were fierce echoes of the firing down at Marblehead, but her own sons had bled before, and that shed in State Street was not the first blood of the Revolution. This was shed on board a Marblehead vessel, the brig *Pitt*, Captain Thomas Powers. Returning from Cadiz, she was boarded by a lieutenant and party of seamen from the British war ship *Rose*, with a view to impressing some of her crew. The attempt succeeded, but not without much labor, and the exchange of many rounds, and the death of the lieutenant, who was killed by a harpoon hurled at him by Michael Corbett, who for three hours defended himself in the fore-peak. On February 26, 1775, the tragedy of Lexington came very near being anticipated at Marblehead and Salem. On this day Colonel Leslie landed at Marblehead with from two to five hundred men, and marched to Salem, with a view to seizing there a certain piece of ordnance. There they were prevailed upon to turn back without accomplishing their purpose. As they marched back through Marblehead, the Marble-

GREAT HEAD.

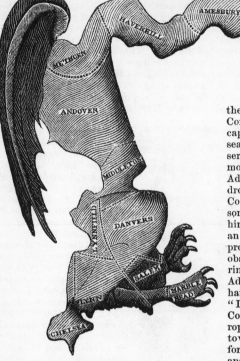

GERRYMANDER.

The Revolutionary honors of the town were divided between her own regiment (her own from drummer-boy to colonel) and her privateersmen. John Manly, of Marblehead, and not Paul Jones, was the first to run up the American flag; and Commodore Tucker, not Paul Jones, again, captured more British vessels, guns, and seamen than any other captain in the service of the thirteen States. It was a mortar captured by John Manly, if John Adams can be trusted as authority, that drove the British out of Boston. With Commodore Tucker Adams had some personal acquaintance. The commodore took him to Europe in 1779. They fell in with an enemy and a fight ensued. Adams promised to retire below, but Tucker soon observed him fighting as a common marine, and ordered him to leave the deck. Adams not doing so, Tucker laid violent hands upon him, exclaiming, as he did so, " I am commanded by the Continental Congress to carry you in safety to Europe, and I will do it." But of all the old town's naval heroes Captain James Mugford earned for himself the briefest glory and the most pathetic fame. He had been impressed on board the British frigate *Lively*, in Marblehead Harbor. His wife went on board the frigate, and stating that they had just been married, demanded his release, which soon after was granted, but not before he had heard the sailors talking about a " powder ship" which they were expecting from England. Resolving to capture her, he

head regiment was drawn up, a thousand strong, to dispute their passage if they had done any thing amiss. It was in the church at Watertown, in which the Massachusetts General Court assembled, that Elbridge Gerry proposed the first measure of defensive warfare, in the view of John Adams the most important measure of the Revolution. As representative of the town in the first Continental Congress, Gerry's voice was from the first for "independency," and his name stands among the signers of the immortal Declaration. He was perhaps the greatest man of whom the town can boast. Colaborer with Hancock and the Adamses, the bosom friend of Joseph Warren, signer of the Declaration, Governor of Massachusetts, and Vice-President of the United States, his name has been ungraciously embalmed in the word gerrymander, which hundreds use where one knows its origin. Gerry, while Governor of Massachusetts, was charged with remodeling the Essex district for political purposes. A map of the district as remodeled was not unlike some fabulous monster, to which the name gerrymander, suggested perhaps by salamander, was given. And now all remodeling of districts for party purposes is gerrymandering. Surely the unsullied patriotism of Elbridge Gerry did not earn for him any such doubtful honor.

GENERAL GLOVER.

applied for a commission, but sailed, before it came, in a small fishing smack, with a score of men from Glover's regiment, in which he was himself a captain. He captured her in Boston Bay, and carried her into Boston, at a time when Washington's stock of powder did not amount to more than nine rounds per man. A few days later, returning to Marblehead, his little vessel was surrounded by a swarm of barges from the British fleet then lying in Nantasket Roads. The fight was desperate, and Mugford was mortally wounded. But his vessel got away, bearing his lifeless body, which a few days later the marine regiment at Marblehead buried with solemn pomp.

The Twenty-first Provincial, afterward the Fourteenth Continental regiment, was oftener called the Marine Regiment than by any other name. It was composed entirely of Marblehead men. For two years after the beginning of the war it was commanded by Colonel Glover, and when he was made brigadier-general it was a part of his brigade. It was at first stationed at Beverly, and employed in fitting out the first privateers, whose crews were taken mainly from its ranks. It marched to Cambridge after the battle of Bunker Hill, and was there quartered in the noble mansion now occupied by the poet Longfellow. On the arrival of Washington it was made his head-quarters. One of his first trials was on account of the Marblehead boys, whose laughter was excited by the appearance of the Virginia regiments, and who not only derided them, but snow-balled them. The Virginians were sensitive, and got very mad, and things looked serious when Washington arrived. There were plenty of bickerings and jealousies in the camp at Cambridge, and it is said that Colonel Orne, of Marblehead, was often called upon to address the quarrelsome and discontented, and restore them to a sense of duty. Twice during the war the Marblehead regiment was assigned to a position of first-rate importance, a position that could hardly have been taken by any other regiment. On the 28th of August, 1776, Washington, defeated in battle, having decided to evacuate Long Island, Glover, with the whole of his regiment fit for duty, was summoned to take sole charge of the retreat across East River. There were but few rowboats, and until eleven o'clock the sail-boats were useless, the wind being unfavorable. At that hour, however, it changed, and, what was better, a fog settled over Long Island, and before morning the whole army, 9000 men, with all the field artillery, ammunition, provisions, cattle, horses, carts, etc., were got over. This retreat has always been considered one of the highest proofs of Washington's good generalship. But it is easy to see that it never could have been accomplished if he had not had a regiment of fish-

ermen to call upon. Nor without these could he have gained that victory at Trenton, which gave to our affairs such a new aspect that it was really the beginning of the end. Glover and his men were chosen to transport the army across the swollen Delaware filled with floating ice. The night was so intensely cold that several men were frozen to death. Snow and sleet added to the difficulty of the passage, but when it was accomplished the fishermen led the advance. A captain of the regiment, a son of General Glover, found that the arms had been unfitted for use by the storm. This being made known to Washington, he made answer in three words, " Advance and charge." And so Trenton's famous victory was won. Afterward Glover was stationed at various points in New York, and always did good service. He was one of the court-martial that tried Major André, and was officer of the day that saw his execution.

When the war was over, and Marblehead summed up her losses, it was found that, whereas in 1772 she had twelve thousand tons of shipping and twelve hundred voters, at the close of the war her tonnage was but fifteen hundred and her voters but five hundred, while there were about five hundred widows and one thousand orphans in the place. The fishing business soon revived, but the foreign trade had met with mortal wounds. It revived but partially, and the war of 1812 gave it its absolute quietus. During this war the town was not in sympathy with the prevailing sentiment of New England, which was violently anti-democratic. With more to lose by war than any inland town, her patriotism did not falter, and great was her delight when Gerry, losing the Governorship of the State by the Federalist reaction, was made Vice-President. Nearly one-fifth of her whole population was in the ranks or on board of privateers or regular men-of-war, "Old Ironsides" getting here nearly her whole crew. More than five hundred Marblehead men were in Dartmoor and other English prisons at the end of the war. After the war there came a period of terrible depression. The old people can not yet speak of it without bitterness. Gradually the shoe business came in to eke out the scanty resources of the inhabitants. When the Massachusetts troops were called out at the beginning of the late war the wine stirred in the cask again. The order came late in the afternoon. At eight o'clock the next morning the town's three companies were in Faneuil Hall. No other companies arrived so soon. A part of the Eighth regiment, they started for Washington, expecting to go through Baltimore. At Philadelphia, the story goes, one of the captains *ground his sword*, and the brave fellows wrote their names on bits of paper, and pinned them to their clothing. And now all that seems as remote as the war of 1812, or even the Revolution.

What will be the future of this quaint old town it would be hard to prophesy. Only one thing is certain, that its coves and headlands will ere long become the spoil of strangers seeking for summer residences. And nowhere can they find more wild and lovely ocean scenery or more invigorating air. Already many handsome cottages have sprung up along the shore. For several years past the Neck has been a favorite place for camping out, more than a thousand people dwelling there in tents and shanties, in rare instances in a truly " æsthetico-economical fashion." But now the Neck has been laid out in building lots, and most of the nomads have been driven away. Upon the harbor side a score or two of shanties still offend the eye with their unsightliness. But even these " abominations set up in the holy place" can not seriously mar its beauty and picturesqueness. While rocks and sea remain, and clouds and sunlight deck them with a thousand varying colors, there will be solace here for weary brains and hearts, haply made sweeter if with the natural charm there mingles some recollection of the parts which the old town once played in comedies and tragedies, which at the time were full of interest alike to actor and beholder.

Haddam
Since the Revolution
(1899)

The Connecticut Magazine.

VOL. 5. DECEMBER, 1899. NO. 12.

HADDAM SINCE THE REVOLUTION.

BY EVELINE WARNER BRAINERD.

WHAT is known to-day as "the old meeting house," built soon after the Revolution, was so truly for the succeeding fifty years the centre of the town life, that it seems a fitting point from which to begin an account of Haddam's second century. It was planned before the division of the original society into the three of Haddam, Higganum and Haddam Neck. Boatloads of parishioners then came across the river and tramped through the meadows. Ox teams brought families from Johnson's Lane near Durham and from Turkey Hill near Killingworth. In the sketch of the First Congregational Church, written by the present pastor, Mr. Lewis, there is a charming description of the structure. It stood at the head of Haddam street, crowning a hill ; surrounded by buttonballs ; "a stately building," of the dignified style of the time. Three stone steps, leading to the green on which it stood are all that now remain. Nothing of the building has this generation seen, save a few bits of the decorations, the "cookies," as the children called the mouldings that softened the terrors of the sounding board. It is

an increasing regret that with the changes in the church body, it was deemed wisest to leave the old building.

The present church, finished in 1847, is pleasant and convenient, and it may be but the glamour of the past that makes the departed structure seem the more precious. In the old church it was that Watt's Psalms and Spiritual Songs were lined off, and the tuning fork held its final sway. There sounded the clarionet, the bass viol and the fiddle. To the old church, on the death of Mr. May in 1803, came David Dudley Field, whose descendants figure in every history of American jurisprudence, literature or enterprise. Dr. Field held three pastorates in the town, two to the original church, from 1804 to 1818 and from 1836 to 1844, when he became the pastor of the church then newly formed at Higganum. During all these twenty-seven years Dr. Field's efforts for the town were enthusiastic and effective, and his interest in the place and the people to which his earliest and his latest labors were given is evinced not alone in the faithfulness of his pastoral work, but in his three volumes concerning the region ; " History of Middle-sex County," " History of the Towns of Haddam and East Haddam," and the "Brainerd Genealogy." Among those of his children born in Haddam, were David Dudley, the eminent jurist ; Stephen, long senior justice of the Supreme Court ; Matthew, who bore an important share in the successful laying of the first cable ; and Emilia, whose son, Mr. Justice Brewer, sat with his uncle, on the Supreme bench at Washington.

CONGREGATIONAL CHURCH, HADDAM.

The unpainted walls of the dwelling which the Fields first occupied, and in which David Dudley Field, Jr., was born, stood until five years ago, opposite the present schoolhouse. Further up the street was the second home, a square white house, built by Dr. Field, the site of which is yet made beautiful by the elms set out by the preacher. On Dr. Field's return for his second pastorate, he went to the new parsonage, beside the meeting house, the building noted in village an-

nals as the result of the "cold water raisin'." In those days, neighbors gathered to put up the frames of buildings. The labor was made the occasion for merrymaking and New England rum figured in the entertainment. The parsonage was built for Dr. John Marsh, the clergyman between the two pastorates of Dr. Field. Dr. Marsh was famous as a pioneer in the temperance movement that later swept over the country. No rum could be expected at the "raisin'" of his parsonage, and many were the prophesies that the timbers would never be in place on such terms. The staunch minister won however and no stouter building faces the street to-day, than that of the " Ma'sh place."

Some twenty years ago, the four sons of Dr. and Mrs. Field, proposed a memorial for their parents. A park was contemplated on the site of the church where their father had preached, and below the parsonage, but the space was small and finally, not only that was bought, but also a larger tract opening in the centre of the village and running behind the "Brainerd Academy," in the founding and success of which, Dr. Field was deeply interested. Drives wind through the grounds. Young trees and shrubs mingle with the veteran growth that stood in the pasture lots before the park was planned. Frowning on the village, Isinglass Hill rises from the midst of the lawns. Toward the street, great boulders make its end a cliff. Behind the Academy, its steep side rises, clothed in dark undergrowth and slender trees that reach upward for the sunlight. On its summit two ragged pines keep watch. Every child of the town has gathered mica from the loose stones of its steep pathway and has crept to the edge to peer venturesomely over the ledges. Each, when older grown, has returned to look on the serene sweep of the river, the low, velvety island, and the distant hills as this height shows them ; to pick out from the mass of tree tops, the peaks of familiar houses and recognize by the grey stone hall, the ancient elms, the three graces of Haddam.

It was on one of the brightest of late October days that the famous brothers came back to the home of their boyhood, to give to the town the two beautified stretches of ground "to be kept as pleas-

The New Lights, or Separatists, as they were first termed, formed the Baptist church of Shailerville. The Methodist church of Haddam centre originated in the "class" at Chapman's ferry, Shailerville, in 1815. The services have been many years discontinued, its last pastor, Rev. Henry Burton, being the grandfather of Connecticut's true poet, Richard Burton. At Haddam Neck, Ponset and Higganum, the denomination has build-

REV. DR. AND MRS. DAVID DUDLEY FIELD.

ure grounds for the people of Haddam in all time to come." David Dudley Field had delivered great speeches before great audiences, but never words more eloquent than were the few spoken on this seventy-fifth anniversary of his parents' marriage, "to those and the descendants of those whom they loved and among whom they dwelt."

From the one of early times the church organizations in the town have increased to nine with Swedish services at intervals.

ings and is well represented. Started as a Sunday School in the home of Mr. Wm. C. Knowles, the present rector, the Episcopal church in eastern Ponset is now housed in a pleasant little structure and forms a needed center for the scattered households of the region. A Roman church building has been erected at the entrance of Higganum street. The Congregational church of Higganum, a plain white edifice, crowns Big Hill, whence the surrounding slopes of lawn and pasture and forest spread in a wide picture, and from the crest of which upper Higganum seems tumbled, willy nilly, into the hollow at its feet. The little white church of Haddam Neck turns its back on the world across the river in order to face its village street. There is not a point whence the Neck can be seen that does not show the tiny spire facing unsociably to the east, with no sign of excuse, for the Neck, from the west, looks one steep hillside with here and there a farm house set in woods. The longest of recent pastorates, however, have been in the original society and no

Efforts for a town library were made as early as 1791, when a library society was formed. This was short lived but twenty-five years later a literary society owned eighty volumes. Other attempts to collect books have left traces in odd volumes bearing the marks of the different clubs, remnants of these small gatherings being now included in the twelve hundred books of the present free library. Originally the Association having the care of the library charged a fee of one dollar a year for its use. Since this fee was dropped, the circulation of the books has increased tenfold, but all support must now come from gifts, and the funds are at present nearly exhausted. Aside from the amount needed yearly (one hundred dollars) the collection has outgrown its present quarters and a building for its accommodation, making possible also a reading room, is the dream of those interested.

THE OLD FIELD PLACE.
(Birthplace of David Dudley Field, Jr.)

account of the town is complete that does not mention these. Mr. Cook, known in theologic circles for his "Theory of the Moral System" and "Origin of Evil," served some few years after the division of the society. Later came Mr. James L. Wright, the beloved pastor, in memory of whose sixteen years of beautiful service, the present communion table was given. In 1871, on the death of Mr. Wright, succeeded Mr. Everett E. Lewis, whose earnest endeavor for the welfare of the town has been through all these eight and twenty years as unflagging as it has been broad minded, thoughtful and devoted.

In ripping an old needle case, recently, the stiffening was found to be ancient ball invitations. One card decorated at the top by an olive branch and the word "Peace" reads: "Miss Zeruiah Brainerd is requested to honor the company with her attendance at the Ball at N. & J. Brainerd's Hall on Wednesday the 1st March, 1815, at three o'clock, afternoon." The windows of "N. & J. Brainerd's Hall" still look down on the village street from between the heavy hemlock boughs. The house, now that of Mr. G. A. Dickinson, is a fine specimen of the hip roof looking to-day as staunch and comfortable as on that March afternoon when its walls echoed to the figure

calls of Hull's Victory and the Virginia
Reel. Another of the cards has this
more elegant legend

" Anniversary Ball.

" The compliments of the Mana-
gers are respectfully proffered to Miss
Zeruiah Brainerd, Soliciting her attendance
at the Ballroom of Daniel Smith on Tuesday the 4th of July at 5 o'clock P. M.

" Haddam, 28, June 1815."

Probably what is known as the old
Smith house, below the school of the
centre district, was the tavern of Daniel
Smith, though no signs of such use remain ;
but, two doors further down the street,
stands a plain, peaked roofed dwelling,
where in Revolutionary days, was a tavern,
and here is still to be seen the bar window,
such as is often still in use in English
inns. At the upper end of the street,
close upon the turnpike in its days of
prosperity, but now, by the laying of the
new road over Walkley Hill, left stranded
in the fields, is the last of these hotels.
Its front is weather worn, its roof and cornice show their age, but dreariest of all,
from the upper story of the long ell, the
four windows of the assembly room, show
melancholy, never opened shutters to the
passers by. With the coming of the railroad went the stage lines, and with them

REV. DR. JOHN MARSH.

most of the call for such houses of entertainment, while within the last decade,
enactment has taken from the town, the
last encouragement to the business.

Half the suits for Middlesex County
before the Superior Court were tried at
Middletown, half at Haddam, the half-
shire-town. With the growth of the city
of Middletown, this arrangement has
grown more and more irksome to lawyers
and judges, till it has at length been done
away. The upper story
of the stone building,
standing where the
turnpike bends sharply
westward, held the
room of the Superior
Court. On the ground
floor still beats that
heart of the Republic,
the town meeting, and
here, with honesty or
with dishonor with wis-
dom or with thought-
lessness, men settle the
details of government

THE MARSH PLACE.

and in them, unwittingly, its most far reaching measures. But the courtroom above, where have spoken the greatest of Connecticut's jurists, is deserted. Here, full of pranks and raillery, remembered

among the well known names on the records of these sessions.

A memento of the one execution that has shadowed the fair place exists in a time browned pamphlet which, one must

ENTRANCE OF FIELD PARK.

by his hostess half in admiration, half wrathfully, came Brainard, the young poet, calling the law his profession. Here came John Trumbull whose "McFingal" was to touch the nation's sense of humor, and here Zephaniah Swift, compiler of the first American law treatise, sat as judge. Senator Roger S. Baldwin who so magnificently defended his State against the attack of Senator Mason of Virginia tried causes in this room, and one who was then a little girl tells how she used to run to the window as he passed for a glimpse of his fine, white features and stately carriage; Daggett, last of the top boot and knee breeches gentry, Wait, Hosmer and Storrs, Chief Justices of the State, were familiar figures. Roger M. Sherman, Leman Church, and more of recent date, McCurdy and LaFayette Foster are

confess, bespeaks as much of curiosity as horror. It is entitled,

A
SERMON
Preached at Haddam, June 14, 1797
On the day of the
Execution of
THOMAS STARR
Condemned for the murder of his
Kinsman
Samuel Cornwall
By............

and here follows a vivid description of the manner of the deed.

Quarrying, which to the present time has been the principal business carried on in Haddam centre was begun on the west side of the river in 1792 by the brothers Nehemiah and General John Brainerd. The stone is like that of the Neck and largely used for curbing, paving and foundations. In the village the house built by some of Mr. Nehemiah Brainerd's family, the town hall, the county jail, jailer's house and the academy are of the finely colored material and prove that it would be a satisfactory building stone.

In 1839 it was, that these brothers who had given business to the place gave it also its most valued possession, the Academy. With the dark side of Isinglass Hill behind, the steep, sunny slope to the street before, its grey stones were the pride of the place. We peer through the foliage of heavy trees for a glimpse of its bare windows. Its halls resound to the footfalls of the chance visitor and the green desks stand in melancholy order awaiting occupants who never come. We turn away regretfully, feeling robbed of some good thing that our fathers enjoyed. The catalogue of 1841 shows the school in its days of prosperity. One hundred and eighty-five pupils are on the roll, from Massachusetts, New York, Pennsylvania and Mississippi, as well as from its own state. Its days were numbered however, and no faithfulness of teaching could save it. The high school was taking the place of all such simple private schools. To carry it on as is the preparatory school of recent years, called for more money than its endowment furnished, so a fine building stands unused and the triumphs and the pranks of the students are but stories for the reminiscent fireside.

With the coming of the freight train the stone cutters moved to the sand by the Shailerville stations, and "General's Wharf" lies deserted. Tall elms grow from the carpet of stone chips and bits of flagging, and the sound of the water lapping the timbers is no longer mingled with the ringing of the hammers. Among the hills bluffs of broken stone peer out from the young woods and the wanderer comes suddenly on old quarries, like amphitheaters, where saplings cling to the roughly-hewn seats and steps. Arnold's, on the

CONGREGATIONAL CHURCH, HIGGANUM.

Connecticut Valley Railroad, opened for the convenience of the quarries on the west of the river, marks the passing of the original proprietors. During the ownership of Mr. Samuel Arnold, the business was carried on most successfully, giving large employment in the town. Mr. Arnold was a man of force and energy. For four terms he represented the town in the legislature and was a member of the thirty-fifth congress, serving on the committee on claims. Even a recent change of roof line, necessary to modern living, cannot rob the Arnold homestead, standing to the west of the Town Hall, of its position as the quaintest specimen of the old time structure to be found in the region.

Feldspar has been quarried in several parts of the town. Lately, in Mr. Gillet's quarry on the Neck, have been found what jewelers judge the finest of the tourmaline in greens, reds, pinks, blues, lilacs, lemons, yellows and colorless. The brown, green and black tourmaline had been

back from the main street, an apprentice was learning his trade of blacksmithing, with the finer work required for the forging of sword blades, and judging from the after skill of the apprentice, Hezekiah Scovil, whatever work was done in the little establishment was well done, well taught and well learned. When a young man Mr. Scovil went to New Haven, and there, from Eli Whitney, then a gun manufacturer for the United States Govern-

FROM ISINGLASS HILL, FIELD PARK.

found in other districts and not far from a feldspar bed on the west side of the river are these minerals in fine doubly terminated crystals. The town is known to scientists for its deposit of the rare chrysoberyl; but many other uncommon stones and more usual minerals in abundance make it a Mecca to the mineralogist, and specimens from its hills are to be found in all the leading museums of the world.

Near the opening of this century, in a shop beside the Ponset road three miles

ment, learned the welding of gun barrels. To the north of Cocaponset Brook runs another stream and, in the heart of its valley rises the round wooded hill, from which the hollow takes its name, Candlewood. The steep hillsides now bear elms, maples, oaks and tulips, but when the first dwellers beside the brook built their rude homes, pitch pine clothed the slopes, and gave torches and flaring house lamps to the new comers. At the head of this tiny valley Mr. Scovil built his factory and here, for many years, the principal business was the supplying of gun barrels to the various government arsenals. By the side of this first shop stands the wide brick house of the master. The woods are closing in on the home, the shop is gone, but the business, brought to its present prosperity by the sons who here learned every detail of the trade, has stretched further and further down the stream till the latest of its series of buildings looks on the main street. Some time before 1840, Mr. Daniel Scovil, travelling in the South was struck with the inferiority of the hoes then in use there. He proposed to his brother, Mr. Hezekiah Scovil, the manufacture of a hoe especially for the Southern market. It seems a commonplace scheme, yet, as one drives by the buildings, the oldest worn and blackened ; the next, beside a pretty pond, the hills rising steeply behind its low red walls and white cupola ; the third group, neat offices and packing rooms ; the fourth and largest, with the well known look of the busy factory ; all linked by wooded stream, smiling pond and foaming dam, all bearing the marks of slow growth, thrift and precise neatness, it is easy to read into manufacture the charm of true romance. It was thirty years ago that the gentle seeming water grew through a long storm to a growling flood. The saw-mill dam, far up the stream, gave way, and the water tore through the valley taking down the lesser buildings in its path and carrying away one life with a frail old structure.

Since the death in 1881 of Mr. Daniel Scovil, the work has been carried on entirely by Mr. Hezekiah Scovil, the firm

name remaining. The hoe without those methods of introduction and advertising now deemed necessary, supplanted the poor tools in use at the south and the Scovil name on a hoe is a guarantee of its worth. An old negro, criticising the tool on which he leaned, said to a Haddam man, then living at the south, " I wish I could git 'nother hoe such ez I hed befo' de war. It cum frum de Norf. I dunno whar, but it wuz a Scovil an' it was the best hoe ever I see." Lately another gratuitous compliment has strayed northward. This comes from the negroes on

N. & J. BRAINERD'S HALL.

a fruit farm. The owner, tried in vain to introduce another hoe. " They were using the Scovil," he remarked in telling of the failure, " I could not get them to change."

Such a manufactory as this of Mr. Scovil's, prosaic though its output be, should have been the delight of William Morris. It bears in every department the stamp of personality, to which, in such establishments, we are unaccustomed. Every part of the work is known accurately to the chief. In every process he is the master workman. His men are trained under his eye. He, himself has worked out the machinery from its conception to its finish. Each autumn Mr. Scovil has been wont to spend a day in the woods, selecting trees from which to make trip hammer handles. Whenever fitting trees were found they were bought, the handles made and stored till six years should have seasoned them to their best estate. Little wonder, under management at once so detailed and so broad, that the hoe works have succeeded.

Higganum holds another large manufacturing plant; that for the making of

THE TOWN HALL.

farm machines, and now, principally of the "cut-away" harrow. The business has been carried on with many fluctuations of success for thirty years, in its most prosperous days, employing one hundred and fifty men. High among the hills, a short distance back of Higganum Hollow, lies the reservoir of this company, a pretty sheet of water, shut in so naturally by the soft slopes, that it would never be thought an artificial lake.

Of lessers attempts at manufacturing, there is early mention of tanneries, cotton gins, carding machines; while in late

years, a button factory on Well's brook, cotton and hardware shops in Higganum, hardware and steam heater manufactories in Shailerville have had shorter or longer periods of activity.

In Haddam as everywhere in Connecticut the War of 1812 met with cool response. There was one Sunday morning of excitement when word was brought that the British, whose vessels were gathering in the Sound, preparatory to the blocade of New London, were about to attack Essex, fifteen miles down the river. General John Brainerd, hearing the news on his way to church, galloped down the turnpike, in his haste forgetting regimentals and arms. A company of Haddam men set bravely forth, but before the militia could gather, the ships on the Essex stocks were burnt, and the English soldiers had returned to their vessel. That was the only fighting in this section and the spot manned at Saybrook now bears the not complimentary name, Fort Nonsense.

For fifteen years before the outbreak of the Civil war, its signs could be seen, mingled intricately in the dissensions over matters of church, school, temperance and local politics. When the final test came, nobly did the little town respond. Many Haddam men joined the army at New Haven or Middletown, but ninety-four enlisted directly from the town, fifteen of these not living to see peace. One Haddam boy, born in the house beside which the Revolutionary troops rested, achieved special distinction in the four years of contest. Alexander Shailer was to lead the First Brigade of the Sixth Corps that saved the day at Marye's Heights; made the famous march to Gettysburg and gave men to every battle of the Army of the Potomac. General Shailer had served eleven years as an officer in the Seventh N. Y. and in '61 he was appointed Major and stationed at Washington. Soon he was made Lieutenant-Colonel of the 65th N. Y., and after the Battle of Marye's Heights was promoted to the rank of Brigadier-General. With the elevation in 1865 to the rank of Major-General came the commendation "for faithful and meritorious service through the war and especially for gallantry in the assualt upon Marye's Heights, Fredericsburg, the battles of Gettysburg and the Wilderness." General Shailer has lived much of the time since, in New York, where he has held two important offices, that of fire commissioner and president of the board of health.

The historical outline of one New England town must needs be very like

GENERAL JOHN BRAINERD.

that of its neighbors. Its personality is shown by its less prominent incidents and by its distinctive features, natural or as moulded by man's occupancy. Starting near where " Deacon Haule and Nathan White found an oak tree by the river side," two hundred years ago, one may drive on the bluff, close above the river, where it spreads like a wide lake after pushing past the narrow bend at East Haddam. By the pleasant homes of Tylerville, known to the railroad on account of the terminus of the East Haddam ferry, as Goodspeeds, one comes into Shailerville street. Across the fields and the water, between the Connecticut and the Salmon, spreads the low "Cove Meadow," set in a frame of gently sloping hills. Above Arnold's Station. the bright faced children of the County Home play in their grove of oak and chestnut or work in their tiny garden spots. Best loved of all the glimpses of river and hill that make Haddam's street a series of pictures, are those that show the Island. It has varied

BRAINERD ACADEMY.

SAMUEL ARNOLD.

climbing to the top of the great rock, the suit was fitted.

Out from Tylerville, by four miles of climbing under interlaced trees by tangled undergrowth, between mossed rails and broken stone walls, one reaches Turkey Hill. The scattered houses seem strangely isolated. Far in the distance Haddam Neck gives now and then, a touch of color to the green landscape. Its little church, facing the unseen street, backs itself against the world with insistent independence. Where one fancies a parting between the lines of hill tops, suddenly appear, faintly showing against the distant background, tips of masts telling that at the instant, five miles away, a vessel is slipping past the village. Back to Haddam one may go down hill all the way, beneath another shelter of saplings and forest veterans. Mr. David Dudley Field used

from a mile in length to its present size, the tides having added to or stolen from either end as suited their pleasure. But its charm never wanes and its fringe of low bending elms and willows does not alter save as the seasons change it from youth to age and back to youth once more. After one glorious view of the river spreading northward till shut in by the Narrows below Middletown, Higganum swings behind a hill, out of sight of the water and tries to make good the loss by showing the prettiest modern places in the town. As the square stone marking the Haddam and Middletown bound is reached, there rises, to the east, across the valley of one of New England's "white brooks" "Shop-board Rock." It earned its name by an incident, which, whether true or legendary is worth believing. One of Connecticut's governors, living in the lower part of the State, being in need of clothes, set forth on horseback in search of the dilatory Hartford tailor. Between Higganum and Middletown, the man of State and the man of cloth met, and

THE ARNOLD HOMESTEAD.

to tell how on the sandy brow of a hill a mile north of Beaver Brook, he, a barefooted boy, driving cows, met another barefooted youngster who called out in excitement, "Boney's licked." The news of Waterloo had come.

Choosing one of many drives, one may follow the woods to Ponset where the meadow land makes a level floor beneath the hills. By the hamlet of Burr District one reaches Johnson's Lane, and, looking

closely ranging hills. Here and there, the white of some building, strikes against the dark foliage assuring that it is not primeval forest stretching on all sides to the sky line. By choosing one of Dame Fortune's good natured days, the height may be gained as the red sun sinks behind Candlewood's round top sending a fiery glow through the grove of small maples that bounds the plateau to the west. Hurrying down the opposite slope of

BIRTHPLACE OF HEZEKIAH SCOVIL.

from the point beyond the last house, gains a grey blue glimpse of the distant Sound. But, better than this, one may turn from the Ponset Meadow to the right up the steep and narrow road that leads over Gunger. Stony fields with now and then a tiny house where a few flowers blossom, make the landscape. The steepest tug of all, lands one on the plateau at the summit. Below, on either hand, lie the vales of Ponset and of Candlewood. Miles to the front, the unseen river parts

Gunger, straight into the flaming sunset, then on through the night of the dark wood road, one comes forth at the valley's entrance into the softened, many tinted lights of the long mid-summer twilight. It will linger lovingly while one loiters by the narrow meadows under Candlewood, till as the street is reached the fading brightness gives reluctant place to the early moonlight.

The "forties" drew many Haddam men to the Pacific. Others later went to try the farming of the western lands that make these meadows seem but pigmy. The cities take the young men to-day. So the old roads, here and elsewhere in New England, show silent houses and tilled ground fast growing wild. The Swedes have taken many of the farms, by thorough, steady labor bringing to mind the simple lives of the earlier owners. These new comers, perhaps are to bring to the township a future of honest, homely toil and plain living like to its past or perhaps the beauty of the country shall crown the hills with summer homes. However this shall prove, the past of the township is honorable and its present, little known though it be, is charming and full of possibility.

Striped Bass
(1883)

STRIPED BASS.

By FRANCIS ENDICOTT.

TO the lover of rod and reel, the striped bass, or rock-fish, as he is called south of Philadelphia, is the most important of all our sea fish. His habitat is so extended and his stay with us so constant; he is so eagerly sought for by anglers of all classes and conditions of life; he affords such sport in the various stages of his growth, from the puny half-pounder found almost everywhere on our Atlantic coast, to the enormous "green-head" who makes his home in the break of the surf; he brings into play such a variety of tackle, from the pin-hook of the urchin fishing from the city docks, to the rods and reels of the crack bass-fisherman,—that he well merits the title which is sometimes bestowed on him of the game fish *par excellence* of the sea.

A bright August morning found the writer, in company with a member of the Cuttyhunk Club, steaming down the bay from New Bedford, bound for a trip to the Elizabeth Islands and Martha's Vineyard, and for a bout with the large bass which frequent the rocky shores of those favored regions.

Arriving at the mouth of the harbor, as our little craft steams around Clark's Point and enters Buzzard's Bay, the whole range of the Elizabeth Islands comes into full view, and we find ourselves trying to repeat the old verse by which our ancestors remembered their uncouth Indian names:

" Naushon, Nonamesset,
Uncatema and Wepecket,
Nashawena, Pasquinese,
Cuttyhunk and Penikese."

339

There is a mysterious influence at work in these regions which seems to gather the sea-fogs and hold them suspended around the islands, shutting them in completely, while all about, the atmosphere is clear. As we approach the land we observe this phenomenon, and are soon lost in its dense vapors. We steam along slowly, our fog-whistle shrieking at intervals, and every eye strained forward for rocks or vessels which may be in the way, until presently we hear a distant fog-horn answering us, and following it we find ourselves among a fleet of sword-fishermen anchored for the night in Cutty-hunk Bay. There is more music by the steam-whistle with an

GOSNOLD'S ISLAND, CUTTYHUNK.

answering shout from the shore, and in a few moments the stroke of oars is heard upon the water. A skiff gropes its way toward us through the fog, we gather our baggage together, and are landed on the shingly beach, where, after a short walk, we find ourselves safe under the comfortable roof of the club-house.

As the tide does not serve until late, we breakfast at the usual hour, and, having tested our line and seen that everything is in order, with a good supply of spare hooks, we start for a brisk walk over the hills, preceded by Perry, our "chummer," bearing a basket full of lobsters and menhaden for bait.

Bleak and uninteresting as these hills appear when seen from the water, every now and then we come unexpectedly on some little gem of picturesque beauty, which is none the less charming from the exceeding plainness of its setting. We hear, too, the abrupt notes

of the upland plover, wildest of all game-birds, as he rises at a safe
distance and speeds his flight to far-off hills. A little later in the
season, large flocks of golden plover will stop on
their way south and make it lively for the grass-
hoppers, which now rise before us in
clouds at every step and scatter away
in uncertain flight be-
fore the wind.

THE CLUB-HOUSE AND
STANDS.

Our brisk walk soon brings us
to the edge of a little fresh-water
lake, separated from the sea by a
narrow shingle beach, where we take a skiff and row
over water as clear as crystal itself to the landing at the
other end. The bottom of this lake is covered with a
growth of aquatic vegetation, which seems as though it might harbor
sufficient insect life to feed millions of fish; while in the shallows
water-lilies grow in profusion, their dark-green leaves crowding each
other on the surface, leaving scant room for the snowy petals to shoot
up and unfold themselves. Some years ago, the club placed several
thousand young trout in the lake, but they did not appear to thrive,
or, rather, they disappeared mysteriously; whether they escaped
through some under-ground outlet to the sea, or whether they furnished food to the enormous eels which inhabit these waters, is a
question difficult of solution. The lake is now stocked with black
bass, and the experiment bids fair to succeed.

Arrived at our destination,—a large granite bowlder, known as Bass Rock, which stands out some distance from the shore and is connected with it by a narrow planking supported on iron rods,—we occupy the seat at the end of the jetty while our chummer, standing behind us, baits the hook with a lobster-tail, and we cast out toward two or three rocks where the waters are swirling with the incoming and receding waves.

The chummer is an important man in his way. He is generally a native of the island, and has done much fishing in his life-time and seen much more. His office is no sinecure; besides keeping four or five baits peeled ready for use, he breaks up the bodies and claws of the lobsters, and chops the head and shoulders of the menhaden into small bits, and throws them out upon the water with an odd-looking wood-and-tin ladle called a "chum-spoon." Without the chum you might catch an occasional straggler, but there is nothing to attract the attention of the fish, and it is only by accident, as it were, that they happen upon the solitary bait with which you are fishing.

But stop! that fellow takes hold as though he meant it, and is laying his course straight for Newport; we must try and stop him short of that. The line whizzes out from the reel, and our thumb would be blistered in a moment were it not for the double worsted thumb-stall which protects it. Perry says he's a twenty-pounder, at least, and he feels like it, for the rod is bent to the curve so beautiful in the eyes of an angler, and the line is strained to the utmost tension. There! he stops and breaks on the surface. How broad his tail looks as he lashes the water in impotent wrath! The worst of his run is over; reel him in carefully, keeping the killing strain on him all the time. He will make two or three more short dashes, and then you may lead him as gentle as a kitten to where Perry stands, with his gaff-hook, ready to reach down and take him in out of the wet. It is a pity to strike the cruel steel into his silvery sides, but it would be dangerous to attempt to land him among the rocks in-shore.

It is true that chumming attracts other less desirable fish. Your blue-fish has an insatiable appetite and a keen nose for a free lunch. We say this ruefully, as we reel in and put on a fresh hook to replace the one just carried away. Egad! that fellow struck like a forty-pound bass, and cut the line as clean as though he had carried a pair of scissors! What a game fish he is! He fights to the very last, and only comes in when he fears that the struggle is becoming monotonous.

What's that—another blue-fish? No, his pull is too steady; it's a bass, surely! This one strikes off in another direction; he lays his course as though he were bound for Pasque Island. There, he has taken the line around that rock; better to give him slack and risk his unhooking himself than have

the line frayed and perhaps parted against the sharp granite edges. Now he's off again; handle him tenderly: there's no knowing what damage that rub may have done

ON THE ISLAND.

to the slender line—phew! how cold the water is! That wave struck flat against the rock which supports the seat, and drenched us.

There is no royal road to this heavy surf-fishing; with all the appliances for comfort which experience can suggest, there is a certain amount of hard work to be done and exposure to be borne as a part of the price of success. Father Neptune is no respecter of persons, and spatters his royal favors so lavishly and so impartially on the just and the unjust that, unless you are a believer in the 'longshore theory that "salt water never hurts nobody," and can take a thorough soaking philosophically and as a matter of course, you had better give up all thought of being a bass-fisherman. It is somewhat trying to the nerves to have a barrel of salt water dashed unexpectedly in your face, sousing you in an instant from head to foot, and at times, when there is a heavy sea running, it is dangerous.

Cases are upon record where anglers have been washed from the rocks, and have narrowly escaped with their lives. Even on these stands it is not always safe, although they are supposed to be above high-water mark. Sometimes, during the spring-tides, when the wind has lashed the sea into a fury, or a distant storm is lending additional force to the breakers, the fisherman will sit securely on his

ON THE WAY TO THE STANDS.

perch and see the white waters breaking angrily among the rocks under his feet. The tide rises higher, but he gives little heed to it, as in such perturbed waters he expects to meet with his greatest success,—perhaps catch the fish which shall make him "high-hook" for the year. The caps of the higher waves sweep over the sag of the narrow plank which connects him with the shore, while the crests of one or two bolder than the rest have lapped his feet with their icy tongues; still he continues to cast, encouraged by the taking of one or two fish, or by the strike of some fish of unknown size, until he is wet to the knees, though the tide cannot be more than three-quarters high. An exclamation from his chummer causes him to look up, and a sight meets his eye which, for a moment, appalls him —an enormous, unbroken roller, stretching the length of the coast, and coming on at race-horse speed, followed by two others equally

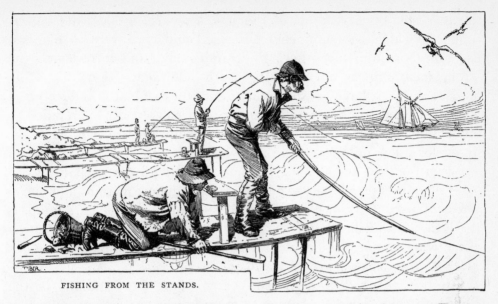

FISHING FROM THE STANDS.

formidable,—for your big fellows generally travel in threes. Escape is impossible, and his only recourse is to hold on tight and take his ducking with what equanimity he can command, when, if he be sensible, he will watch his opportunity and make for the shore, a wetter and a wiser man. Seth Green got caught in this way, on this very rock from which we are now fishing, and retired drenched to the skin, but only for a time; the bass were biting freely, and the "great father of fishes," procuring a rope, lashed himself to the seat, and, in spite of the warnings and remonstrances of his friends, continued his sport, with the waves occasionally making a break clear over his head. Perry tells us this story in the intervals between chopping and chumming, and we notice that the pluck of the old man elicits from him an admiration which no amount of piscicultural skill could have commanded.

Another strike! This fellow betrays himself at the very start, for we see the cloven hoof, or rather the forked tail, which denotes that pirate of the deep, blue sea — the bluefish, and we bring him to gaff as soon as possible, using him rather roughly, for he is seldom alone, and his companions in iniquity are apt to cut him loose by striking at any bit of bait that may have run up on the line, or even at the line itself as it cuts rapidly through the water.

Perry opens this fish and brings us his paunch to examine; in it, besides many pieces of chum, are three hooks—one of them, with the bait still on and a bit of the line attached, we identify as our property, which he feloniously purloined and converted to his own use this morning; the others, of strange make and corroded by the strong gastric juices, are evidently much older acquisitions.

But the bass have ceased biting; our stock of bait is reduced to a few shreds and patches, and the inner man calls loudly for repairs, so our chummer starts on ahead with the heavy load of fish, while we linger for a few minutes at the light-house, built on the rising ground between the lake and the sea, to have a chat with the keeper.

Truly, this is classic ground. Lying almost within a stone's-throw of us, snugly nestled in the bosom of the black-bass pond, is the little island called after Bartholomew Gosnold, that mighty navigator whose name has come down to us in a blaze of posthumous glory as the discoverer of Cape Cod.

In the year 1602, eighteen years before the founding of the Plymouth colony, Gosnold built a store-house and began a fort on this islet and did some trading with the Indians. That he had but little faith in their friendliness is evidenced by his building his stronghold on this island within an island, and in fact history gives the aboriginal natives of Cuttyhunk but a sorry character as neighbors. Dr. Belknap visited the island in 1797, and discovered what he supposed to be the remains of the cellar of Gosnold's store-house, whereupon a later historian breaks forth in this wise: "It is a vestige of the first work performed by Europeans on the New England shores. Here they first penetrated the earth; here the first edifice was erected. Only two centuries have passed away, and from this humble beginning have arisen cities, numerous, large, and fair, in which are enjoyed all the refined delights of civilization."

The first duty of your chummer, on returning from the stand, is to see that the bass are weighed on a pair of scales hanging at the corner of the piazza. This is done in the presence of two members of the club, to avoid—mistakes, the result being entered on a blank slip, which is retained until evening, when the score of each member for the whole day is duly entered opposite his name on the records. Our score for the morning's work shows three bass, weighing eighteen and one-half, sixteen and one-half, and nine pounds. Glancing over the leaves of the record-book, we find some interesting items, which we copy—premising that the season in each year

A GOOD CATCH.

lasts but four months, extending from the middle of June to the middle of October. The honorary title of "high-hook" is conferred on the member taking the largest fish of the season.

On the opening day of the club in June a great deal of sport is sometimes occasioned by the anxiety of the members to wear this coveted honor; and as the member catching the first fish, even if it weigh but four or five pounds, is "high-hook" and entitled to wear the diamond-mounted badge in shape of a bass hook which accompanies the title until a larger fish is taken, it frequently happens that the title and badge will change hands three or four times during the day.

Year.	Weight of bass caught.	High-hook.	Largest fish.
1876	5862	W. R. Renwick	51 lbs.
1877	3311	W. McGrorty	51½ "
1878	5444	T. W. Van Valkenburgh	51 "
1879	4841	H. D. Polhemus	49 "
1880	3619	Andrew Dougherty	50¼ "
1881	1784	W. McGrorty	44 "
1882	2026	W. R. Renwick	64 "

On the following morning we leave our hospitable friends, our destination being Gay Head. We can see its many-colored cliffs from the club-house, across the Vineyard Sound, only eight miles away; but the wind is contrary and the water too rough for the small boat at our disposal, so we conclude to return to New Bedford by the more tranquil waters of Buzzard's Bay, and take the steamer thence

to Martha's Vineyard.   We make an early start, and, as the weather
is fair, get a good view of the island of Pune, or Penikese, and its
elegant buildings (the Anderson School of Natural History, formerly
superintended by Professor Agassiz), which the fog had hidden from
sight when we arrived.   Skirting along the coast of Nashawena,

BACK FROM THE BEACH.

and giving Quick's Hole a wide berth on account of its strong currents, we came to the island of Pasque, or Pesk, as the natives call
it, and, rounding its easterly point into Robinson's Hole, we drop
anchor in front of the Pasque Island club-house.   Some of the members of this club are old friends, and we avail ourselves of a long-
standing invitation to drop in upon them and see what they are
doing with the bass.

Pasque Island does not differ in its general features from Cuttyhunk.   Here there are the same bleak-looking hills, bare of trees, with
the exception of a little clump of locusts, named, after the aboriginal
owner of the island, "Wamsutta's Grove."   Early accounts, which
represent these islands as covered with a growth of beech and
cedars, would be incredible, in view of their present cheerless aspect,
were it not that stumps of those trees are occasionally unearthed at
the present day.   Besides the club-houses, there is but one building
on the island, and this dates so far back in the dim past that the
accounts of its origin are but legendary.   We should like to pin our
faith to the story that it was erected by some straggler from Gosnold's band, which would make it the oldest building in New England; but we fear that this claim rests on the same airy basis, and
must be placed in the same category, as that which carries the
old mill at Newport back to the time of the Norsemen.   The club

owns the whole island, consisting of about one thousand acres, and has in its possession the original deed, dated 1667, from the Indian sachem Tsowoarum, better known as Wamsutta, conveying Pascachanest, and another island whose name is illegible—probably a little one thrown into the bargain as a make-weight—islands were cheap in those days—"to Daniel Wilcocks, of the town of Dartmouth, in the jurisdiction of New Plymouth," for the sum of twelve pounds.

Before bidding our friends adieu and continuing our journey, we gather the following statistics from the club records:

	High-hook.		Largest fish.	
1876	Peter Balen*		50	lbs.
1877	A. F. Higgins		47	"
1878	F. O. Herring		60½	"
1879	J. D. Barrett		51	"
1880	W. Dunning		49	"
1881	W. H. Phillips		44	"
1882	C. P. Cassilly		54	"

In the early accounts of the settlement of New England, the striped bass is frequently mentioned, and it seems at times to have formed the main food-supply of the forefathers when other sources had failed them.†

"Thomas Morton, of Clifford's Inn, gent.," gives a glowing description of their abundance in "New English Canaan, or New Canaan: an abstract of New England, composed in three bookes. The Natural Indowments of the Countrie, and What Staple Commodities it Yeeldeth. Printed by Charles Green, 1632." He writes:

"The Basse is an excellent Fish, both fresh & salt, one hundred whereof, salted at market, have yielded five p. They are so large the head of one will give a good eater, a dinner, and for daintinesse of diet they excell the Marybones of beefe. There are such multitudes that I have seene stopped into the river close adjoining to my howse, with a sand at one tide, so many as will loade a ship of one hundred tonnes."

A pretty good fish story; it reads like the prospectus of a land association—as it probably was. Here is another, antedating it by two years, from "New England's Plantation; or, A Short and True

* Clarum et venerabile nomen.

† In "A Key into the Language of America; or, an Help to the Language of the Natives in that part of America called New England. London: by Roger Williams, 1643," the Indian name of the fish is given thus: "Missuckeke"—bass.

Description of the Commodities and Discommodities of that Countrey. Written by a Reuerend Divine (Mr. Higginson), now there resident. London, 1630":

> "Of these fish (the basse) our fishers take many hundreds together, which I have seen lying on the shore to my admiration; yea, their nets ordinarily take more than they are able to hale to land, and for want of Boats and men they are constrained to let a many goe after they have taken them, and yet sometimes they fill two boates at a time with them."

The famous Captain John Smith, "sometime Governor of Virginia & Admiral of New England," wrote in a little book entitled "Advertisements for the Inexperienced Planters of New England, or Anywhere; or, The Pathway to Experience to Erect a Plantation. London, 1631:"

> "The seven and thirty passengers, miscarrying twice upon the coast of England, came so ill provided they only relyed upon the poore company they found, that had lived two yeares by their naked industry and what the country naturally afforded. It is true, at first there hath beene taken a thousand Bayses at a draught, and more than twelve hogsheads of Herrings in a night."

Sturdy John Josselyn, gent., who never hesitated to use a word because of its strength, writes, in his "Account of Two Voyages to New England in 1675":

> "The Basse is a salt-water fish, too, but most an end *(sic)* taken in Rivers, where they spawn; there hath been three thousand Basse taken at a set. One writes that the fat in the bone of a Basse's head is his brains, which is a lye."

In a curious poetical description of the colony, entitled " Good News from Nevv England, with an exact relation of the First Planting that Countrey," printed in London, 1648, these lines occur:

> "At end of March begins the Spring by Sol's new elivation,
> Stealing away the Earth's white robe dropping with sweat's vexation,
> The Codfish, Holybut, and Basse do sport the rivers in,
> And Allwifes with their crowding sholes in every creek do swim."

Truly, our ancestors must have had glorious opportunities for sport, though it may be considered doubtful whether those stern-visaged men, whose features had grown grim in facing the hard realities of their pioneer life,—sickness, starvation, and an ever-

present and treacherous foe,—found time to "go a-angling," except as a means of warding off famine from their wives and little ones.

There is something very pathetic in the accounts of their fishing

STRIPED BASS OR ROCK FISH. (LABRAX LINEATUS.)

trips as given in Bradford's "History of Plymouth Plantation." It presents the reverse of the rose-colored pictures of Morton and Higginson:

> "They haveing but one boat left, and she not well fitted, they were divided into
> severall small companies, six or seven to a gangg or company, and so wente out with a
> nett they had bought to take bass & such like fish, by course, every company knowing
> their turne. No sooner was ye boate discharged of what she brought, but ye next
> company tooke her and wente out with her. Neither did they returne till they had
> caught something, though it were five or six days before, for they knew there was noth-
> ing at home, and to goe home emptie would be a great discouragemente to ye rest."

At New Bedford, we take the steamer for Oak Bluffs, and sail
down across Buzzard's Bay and through the narrow strait called
Wood's Hole, whose troubled waters bear a close resemblance to
those of Hell Gate. Rare bass-fishing there must be in these cir-
cling eddies, and we half mature a plan to stop on the way home and
have a day at them. Emerging from the Hole into the Vineyard
Sound, we steam away for the headlands of Martha's Vineyard, visible in the distance, and in due time haul up at the wharf of that
marvelous city of cottages, and take the stage to commence a tedious

journey the full length of the
island, some twenty-two miles.

As the stage route does not
extend beyond Chilmark, we
are transferred at Tisbury to a
buggy, with a bright school-boy
of some thirteen summers as a
driver, whom we ply with questions as to the names of localities we pass on the route.

We cross some noble trout-
streams on the way ; on one of
them notices are posted against
trespassers, the fishing privilege
being hired by two or three
gentlemen from Boston. These
streams look enticing, being full
of deep holes overshadowed by

scrubby alders—the lurking-place of many a large trout, if we may believe our young guide. The trout should be full of game and fine-flavored in these streams—pink-fleshed, vigorous fellows, such as we find in the tide-water creeks of Long Island

THE LIGHT-HOUSE AT GAY HEAD.

and Cape Cod, who take the fly with a rush that sends the heart jumping into the throat.

As we approach Menemsha Bight, the roads are heavy with recent rains, and the wheels sink deep in the sandy soil. A queer little popping sound, apparently coming from under the wagon, excites our curiosity; we lean over to ascertain the cause, and find the ground covered with myriads of small toads, any one of which could sit comfortably on a dime with room to spare. Some of these, getting caught in the deep rut of the road, struggle feebly to leap over the barrier, and failing in the attempt, the wheels pass over them, each one exploding under the weight with a faint pop, and flattening out into a grotesque exaggeration of his former self, that reminds us of one of the pantomime tricks of the Ravel family.

It is dark when we reach Gay Head, and as we drive up to the door of the keeper's house, which adjoins the light-house, a voice from some unknown region cheerily invites us to enter. We look around for the owner, but see no one to whom the voice could belong. Overhead, long, slanting bars of white-and-red light flash through the powerful Fresnel lenses in every direction, looking like bands of bright ribbon, cut bias against the darkness of the sky beyond, while millions of insects dance in the broad rays, holding high carnival in the almost midday glare. The mysterious voice repeats the invitation, and without more ado we gather our baggage together and enter a cozy sitting-room, where we proceed to make ourselves very much at home. Here we find Mr. Pease, the keeper of the light, who has descended from his lantern, and a gentleman from New Bedford, who gives but poor encouragement in regard to the fishing. He has been here for a week past, and has not caught a solitary bass in all that time; but he tells us such soul-stirring yarns of fish caught on previous visits, and all told with a modesty which attests their truth, that our spirits are restored at once.

The inhabitants of the town of Gay Head, with the exception of the light-keeper's family, are of somewhat mixed blood. They are called Gay Head Indians, but their features betoken a liberal intercourse with a darker complexioned race ; there is a flatness of the nose and an inclination to curliness in the hair which denote anything but an uninterrupted descent from the warlike tribe that Bartholomew Gosnold found in possession of these islands. The last one among them who could build a wigwam died some years ago, and with him died this invaluable secret.

Here there is room for the moralist to make some wise reflections on the vanity and evanescence of all human greatness, and to draw the parallel between this people's present peaceful occupations of farming and berry-picking (we even saw a young squaw who was engaged in a family as seamstress), and the Puritan-roasting, scalp-raising, and other cheerful and innocent diversions which obtained among their ancestors. But we confess we would rather go fishing than point morals, any day, and our acquaintance with this people is confined to the young brave of some twelve summers whom we engaged in the morning as our henchman, to procure and cut up bait.

The cliffs at Gay Head are interesting alike to the artist and the geologist, and possess still another interest for the angler, who has to carry fifty pounds of striped bass up their steep and slippery incline. They are of clay formation, broken and striated by the washings of centuries, and when lighted up by the sun present a brilliantly variegated appearance, which undoubtedly gave the promontory its name. Black, red, yellow, blue, and white are the colors represented, all strongly defined, and on a clear day, discernible at a great distance. Down their steep sides, our feet sticking and sliding in the clay, moist with the tricklings of hidden springs, we pick our way slowly, bearing our rod and gaff-hook; while our little Indian staggers under a basket load of chicken-lobsters, purchased of the neighboring fishermen at the extravagant rate of one dollar and fifty cents per hundred.

At the bottom of the cliffs we skirt along the beach, stopping now and then to pick up bunches of Irish moss, with which the shore is plentifully lined, until we come to three or four large granite bowlders lying at the edge of the water, and offering such attractions as a resting-place that we stop and survey the field to select our fishing-ground.

ON THE BEACH.

Across the Vineyard Sound, about eight miles away, and stretching out far to the eastward, are Cuttyhunk, Nashawena, and Pasque Islands; and about the same distance to the south-westward, the little island of No Man's Land is plainly visible in the clear atmosphere —even to the fishermen's huts with which it is studded. It is a notable place for large bass, and wonderful stories are told of the catches made there—how, on one occasion, when the fish were in a particularly good humor, three rods caught twelve hundred and seventy-five pounds of striped bass in a day and a half.

Looking out seaward some thirty or forty yards, we see three rocks heavily fringed with sea-weed, which rises and spreads out like tentacles with the swell of the incoming tide, and clings to the parent rocks like a wet bathing-dress as the water recedes and leaves them bare. We like the appearance of this spot—it looks as though it might be the prowling-ground of large fish; and we adjust our tackle rapidly and commence the assault.

Into the triangle formed by these rocks we cast our bait again and again, while our attendant crushes the bodies and claws of the lobsters into a pulp beneath his heel, and throws handfuls of the mess out as far as his strength will allow. He appears to have inherited some of the taciturnity of his red ancestors, for not a superfluous word do we get out of him all day long; all efforts to lead him into conversation are met by monosyllabic answers, so that, after many discouraging attempts, we imitate his reticence and are surprised to find with how few words we can get along. A nod of the head toward the sea brings him into immediate action, and he commences to throw out chum vigorously, like a skillfully made automaton; a nod of another significance, and he brings three or four fresh baits and deposits them silently on the rock at our feet.

Thus we fish faithfully all the morning, buoyed up by the hope which "springs eternal" in the breast of the angler, but without other encouragement of any kind. Many nibblers visit our bait and pick it into shreds, requiring constant attention to keep the hook covered, while rock-crabs cling to it viciously as we reel in, and drop off just as we are about to lay violent hands on them.

The flood-tide, which had commenced to make when we arrived, is now running fast, and has risen so as to cover the rocks on our fishing-ground, leaving visible the dark masses of sea-weed which float to the surface by its air-cells, and wave mysteriously to and

FROM THE DEPTHS (BASKET FISH—ASTROPHYTON).

fro. The surf has risen with the tide, the water is somewhat turbid and filled with small floating particles of kelp or sea-salad, which attach themselves to the line and cause it to look, when straightened out, like a miniature clothes-line. Occasionally, a wave will dash up against the shelving rock on which we stand, and, breaking into fine spray, sprinkle us liberally, and as salt water dries but slowly, we are gradually, but none the less surely, drenched to the skin.

Suddenly, without the slightest indication of the presence of game-fish, our line straightens out, we strike quick and hard to fix the hook well in, the reel revolves with fearful rapidity and the taut line cuts through the waves like a knife, as a large bass dashes away in his first mad run, fear and rage lending him a strength apparently much beyond his weight. Of course, under the circumstances, the strain on the fish is graduated, but the weight of line alone which he has to draw through the water would be enough to exhaust even a fifty-pounder, and he soon tires sufficiently to enable us to turn his head toward land. As we pilot him nearer to the shore, he acts like a wayward child, making for every rock which happens in the way, and as there are many of them, it requires no little care to guide him past the danger. Presently, however, the steady strain tells on him, his struggles grow weaker, his efforts to escape become convulsive and aimless, and we lead him into the undertow, where he rests for a moment until a wave catches him and rolls him up, apparently dead, on the shelving sand. As he lies stranded by the receding water, the hook, which has worked loose in his lip, springs back to our feet. Our little Indian sees the danger and rushes forward to gaff him, with a whoop suggestive of war-paint and feathers; but we push him aside hurriedly—no steel shall mar the round and perfect beauty of the glittering sides—and, rushing down upon him, regardless of the wetting, we thrust a hand into the fish's mouth and thus bear him safely from the returning waves; then we sit down on the rock for a minute, breathless with the exertion, our prize lying gasping at our feet, our nerves still quivering with excitement, but filled with such a glow of exulting pride as we verily believe no one but the successful angler ever experiences, and he only in the first flush of his hard-won victory.

But there is no time to gloat over our prey—bass must be taken while they are in the humor, and our chummer is already in the field, throwing out large handfuls of the uninviting-looking mixture; so we adjust a fresh bait and commence casting again, as though nothing had happened to disturb our serenity, only once in awhile allowing our eyes to wander to the little hillock of sea-weed and moss under which our twenty-five pound beauty lies sheltered from the sun and wind.

Another strike, another game struggle, and we land a mere minnow of fifteen pounds. And this is all that we catch; the succeeding two hours fail to bring us any encouragement, so we reel in, and painfully make our way up the cliffs, bearing our prizes with us.

We are eager for another day at the bass, but a difficulty presents itself; fish are perishable in warm weather, the bass in a less degree than many others, but still perishable, and we have no ice, nor is any to be purchased nearer than Vineyard Haven—which for our purpose might as well be in the Arctic regions. But we bethink us that we have friends at the Squibnocket Club, some five or six miles away, on the south-west corner of the island, and in the afternoon we persuade Mr. Pease to drive us over there.

The comfortable little club-house is built facing and adjacent to the water, and after supper, as we sit chatting over a cigar on the piazza, we look out upon the wildest water we have as yet seen. The shore is exposed to the direct action of the ocean, without any intervening land to break the force of the sea, and the white breakers fol-

ALONG SHORE.

low each other in rapid succession, lashing themselves against the rocks into a foamy suds, which looks as though it might be the chosen home of large bass—as, indeed, they say it is.

The following day is almost a repetition of the first—a long, profitless morning spent in fruitless casting, a sudden strike when we least expect it, and then the catching of three fish within an hour and a half. This capricious habit of the bass is very striking at times. Sometimes, day after day, they will bite at a certain hour, without reference to the height of the tide, and at no other time. Whether it is that they have set times to visit different localities, and only arrive at the fishing-ground at the appointed hour, or, whether they are there all the time and only come to their appetites as the sun indicates lunch-time, we cannot say.

Our trip is over, and we pack our things to return home. Stored in a box, carefully packed with broken ice, are five bass,—we take no account of two blue-fish of eight and ten pounds,—which weigh respectively twenty-five, fifteen, twenty-eight, twenty-one, ten pounds.

MONTAUK LIGHT.

If the reader should wish to enjoy this noble sport, the better plan by far is to purchase a share in one of the great bassing clubs, as at their comfortable quarters you can always be certain of bait, skillful chummers, and ice to preserve the fish when caught; and, moreover,

a good meal and a comfortable bed after a hard day's work, or play, as you choose to call it, are desiderata not always to be obtained at the country tavern where your lines may be cast. But should the intention be to fish only occasionally, then equally good sport may be had in the summer and early autumn months at Montauk Point, Point Judith, Newport, Cohasset Narrows, and many places along shore.

A seventy-two-pounder, caught by a gentleman of New York, is probably the heaviest bass that has yet been landed with rod and reel; and when it is considered that the line used would not sustain much more than one-third that amount of dead weight, and that every ounce of that sev-

enty-two pounds was "fighting weight," some conception may be formed of the skill and patience required in its capture.

Verily there is nothing new under the sun. As I pen these lines regarding the capture of large fish with light tackle, there comes to mind the memory of a screed written in the long, long ago, and I step to the book-shelf, take down the volume, and transcribe for your delectation, O reader, the quaint advice given by that sainted patroness of the angle, Dame Juliana Berners, nearly four hundred years ago. There is a flavor of mold about the fine old English, but it contains the sum and essence of all scientific angling. Here it is, crisp and fresh as when it was first written, though the hand that penned it has long since crumbled into dust, and the generation for whose "dysporte" it was "empryntyd" by Wynkyn de Worde have been casting their flies from the further bank of the Styx this many a long year:

FISHING A. D. 1496. (FROM "WALTON'S COMPLETE ANGLER.")

"And yf it fortune you to smyt a gret fish with a small harnays, thenne ye must lede hym in the water and labour hym there tyll he be drounyd and overcome; thenne take hym as well as ye can or maye, and euer be waar that ye holde not ouer the strengthe of your lyne, and as moche as ye may lete hym not come out of your lyne's ende streyghte from you; but kepe hym euer under the rodde, and euermore holde hym streyghte, so that your lyne may be susteyne and beere his lepys and his plungys wyth the helpe of your cropp and of your honde."

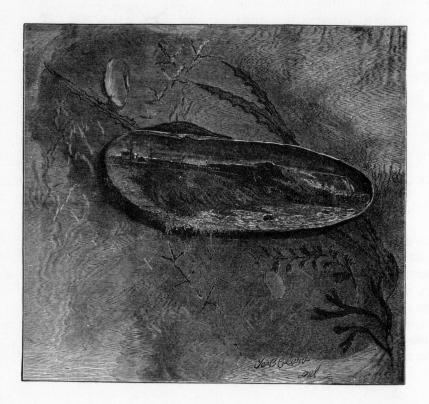

Camps and Tramps
About Ktaadn
(1883)

CAMPS AND TRAMPS ABOUT KTAADN.

By ARBOR ILEX.

THAT noble mountain Ktaadn,* towering grand and peculiar out of the vast and undulating forest of northern Maine, its lofty head a pyramid with ragged apex as of a volcano, its ever luminous face looking serenely southward and mirrored in a hundred lakes, its huge body lying leagues along to the north and plowed into gorges by the glaciers of æons,—Ktaadn and its retinue of magnificent domes, sole representatives of the primal continent,—all these have been sung by the poet and portrayed by the painter.

Imagine that you are fifty miles from any railway, twenty-five from the nearest highway, and thirteen from a practicable footing for any apparatus of transportation other than human legs; that you have come to stay a month; that your party, some of whom are not strong, is to be wholesomely and plentifully fed, and protected against rain, frost, and probably snow; that the forest affords no other habitation or subsistence to you than to the wild animals about you; that game is uncertain, and fish, while large enough, indeed, to delight the sportsman, are not plentiful enough to insure subsistence;—fancy this, and you will indeed have come short of a lumberman's idea of roughing it; but you will have put yourself in a puzzle over two propositions—1st, as the woods provide little, much must be carried in; 2d, as little can be carried in, the woods must furnish much. The resultant of these opposed ideas may be expressed by

---

* The orthography—Ktaadn—is not that of the maps; the Maine State College people, who ought to be allowed to name their own mountains, insist upon "Ktahdin." But those eminent authorities, Thoreau and J. Hammond Trumbull,—the latter our best expert in Indian nomenclature,—prescribe the spelling here adopted.

the following formula:—skill × pork + blankets = success.   Skill, in the form of experienced and strong guides, transports itself and the other necessaries ; pork means heat and tissue in the smallest compass ; warm and water-proof clothing are obviously indispensable. Hard-bread, tea, sugar, and a few lemons (anti-scorbutic) are indispensable ; beans, wheat flour, and baking powders, potatoes, rice, and a few raisins (a little sweet is so sweet in the woods), should be taken where transportation is not too difficult.   Indian meal, canned meats and vegetables, and butter, furnish the means of occasional luxuries.   With regard to spirits, rum is probably the best adapted, and, while a little is necessary in case of exhaustion or chill, and often has a hygienic importance, it is a very serious mistake, as the hardy lumbermen well know, to use it as a stimulant before exertion, or freely at any time.

The natural essentials of a permanent camp are, 1st, convenient proximity to water ; 2d, a forest to shield the works from the sun, and the tents and the fire especially from heavy winds ; 3d, a level bit of ground having as dry a nature as may be, and some natural drainage.   The artificial essentials are, a camp-fire and a tent for the party and another for the guides.   To this may be added a tent to be used for putting supplies out of the rain, and also for putting them out of sight.   The working drawings and the night view so fully illustrate the arrangement and construction of our camp that little other description is required.   Fig. 1 is a cross section through the center of tents and camp-fire.   Fig. 2 is a ground plan and a horizontal section of the surrounding trees.   Permanent tents are "logged" a foot or two high on three sides, and the ends are covered with thin boards split from white cedar logs, or with birch-bark or boughs.   The roof is a piece of heavy cotton cloth soaked in brine to protect it against the sparks of the camp-fire, and

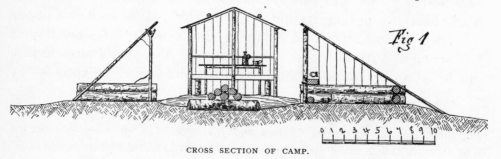

CROSS SECTION OF CAMP.

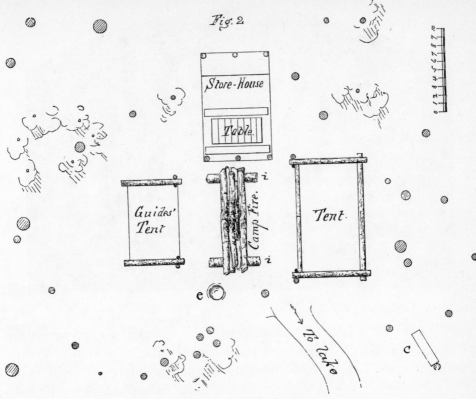

GROUND PLAN OF CAMP.

supported on poles. The front is quite open to the fire, not to speak of the rain. The ground forming the floor is smoothed off and covered thickly with small boughs of evergreen; upon these the rubber and woolen blankets which form the beds are laid. The "Deacon's seat," a, Fig. 1, answers almost every other purpose of domestic furniture. Our store-house and dining-room was constructed of round sticks, roofed and covered at one end with white cedar "splints." The wash-stand was at c; the bean-hole, e, will be further referred to. The camp-fire is laid on two "hand-chucks," i, i, or on two suitable stones, and consists of logs from four to fourteen inches in diameter and eight to fourteen feet long. Three-quarters of a cord of wood are burned per day. Lying in a three-sided tent, wrapped in blankets and water-proofs, with one's feet a length off from such a fire, is protection against any sort of bad weather, and yet it realizes every advantage of being out-of-doors. A temporary tent may consist of a mere cloth or of boughs laid upon inclined

NIGHT VIEW OF THE CAMP.

poles, or it may be logged or otherwise reënforced according to the weather. Smaller parties sometimes prefer the "A" tent. Works like ours may be built from standing trees, in a day or two, by three expert guides. Our camp was placed some thirty rods from Ktaadn Lake, and a good path was cut to it through the underwood.

We are a party of six excursionists and five guides. Four of us are artists, whom we will call Don Cathedra, Don Gifaro, Herr Rubens, and M. De Woods. Two of us are professional men,— M. La Rose and myself, Mr. Arbor Ilex.

At 7 P. M., September 4th, we boarded an Eastern Railroad sleeping-car at Boston. We breakfasted in Bangor and dined in the village of Mattewamkeag, on the European and North American Railway, fifty-eight miles further, where we met our chief guide and bought our heavy supplies. Wedged with our *impedimenta* into two wagons, we jogged twenty-five miles to the northward, and slept in the outlying settlement of Sherman. On the bright morning of the 6th we and our roughing baggage were packed into a four-horse, springless wagon, with the running gear of a gun-carriage and the side-grating of a bear-cage. The significance of this construction soon became obvious. Upon driving some half-dozen miles to the eastward, we suddenly rose upon a crest where Ktaadn and its retinue of lesser mountains burst upon our view,—a revelation of grandeur and beauty all the more impressive because the previous scenery had been so tame. At noon, away out beyond the precincts of permanent habitation, we had our first out-of-door dinner. Our sportsmen cast in Swift Brook for trout without success—it was a bad time of year; but a slice of pork toasted on a forked stick, a piece of hard-tack, and a cup of milkless tea were, thus early in our quest of healthy appetites, more palatable than a *ragoût* at Delmonico's. The excursionists, excepting myself, walked on; two guides and I stuck (with difficulty) to the wagon, upon a road consisting of a slit cut through a dense forest, over a tract of stumps, mud, thinly corduroyed swamps, and granite bowlders. The forest was broken only by "the farm" or "Hunt's," where hay and vegetables were raised in the early lumbering days, now a temporary habitation. Here, on the east branch of the Penobscot, I found our party fishing without success, but canoeing with great satisfaction. This whole territory, except a few tracts, was burned over forty years ago; some of the new growth is already good timber, and here and there a dead monarch stretches his huge form across our path.

A canoe ride two miles up the east branch was to me as delightful as it was novel. Our stalwart guide fairly lifted our larger "birch" with its four passengers over the shallower rapids. A short tramp through the forest brought us before sundown to our first encampment on the "lower crossing" of the Wasatiquoik, twelve miles from Sherman.

Next morning, the 7th, we witnessed the construction, in two hours, of a sled or "jumper," by means of an axe and a two-inch auger. At ten o'clock the baggage was bound to two jumpers and started off by four horses, our party of eleven, on foot, forming advance and rear guards. So we tramped over hill and occasional swamp, up the Wasatiquoik valley, stopping as much time as moving, occasionally holding the craft from capsizing, and prying her over fallen trees, stumps, and rocks. Much of the surface of the country is a mass of granite bowlders of

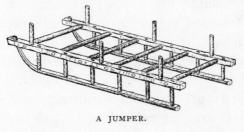

A JUMPER.

THE MISSING LINK.

every size. Where disintegrated stone and vegetable mold have
accumulated for ages, the road is practicable for wagons; but on
slopes, where the filling has washed out, it is amazing to see a horse
get over it at all, especially when he has to drag soft wooden sled-
runners over the serrated edges of big stones.

The rest of the road presented still steeper pitches, deeper bogs,
and more entanglingly strewn rocks. One of our horses, a straggling, raw-boned "missing link," afforded us no little tugging and
plenty of amusement, in our fruitless efforts to keep him right side
up and his various members comparatively collected together.
Along toward evening he quite abandoned the transportation business, flinging himself in wild gymnastics, and finally he slid off the
side of a corduroy and sank up to his middle in the muck. After
we had tugged at him for half an hour, during which time he maintained a strict neutrality, we convinced him, by means of a birch
rod, that he must take a hand in the encounter, whereupon he
roused up and floundered out. We waded the "upper crossing" of
the Wasatiquoik at dusk, having traveled eight miles; the advance
guard had already prepared a camp.

Next morning we got a fair start, and by noon had made the
remaining five miles to Ktaadn Lake, which we should have done
the day before. After we had pried our unfortunate horse out of
several holes in the first mile of road, and the other one had shown

symptoms of collapse, we abandoned the jumper and sent the team back. Meanwhile, one horse of the other jumper having distributed most of his shoes and gone out of service, his companion dragged the vehicle alone up many steep pitches, and was only dismissed, with our blessing, when the jumper had left its starboard runner on a rock. So we had a chance to find out how wonderfully easier it is to walk light over bad roads than to lug twenty pounds of baggage. The guides spent the afternoon in "backing" in our wraps and a day's provisions. We dined by the dam at the foot of the little lake,—one of the many difficult but unremunerative works built a few years ago to "drive" logs,—and got into a temporary camp for the night.

The bean-hole, that principal base in camp topography, is made large enough to take in an iron pot; and when the hole is heated to a cherry-red by a big internal fire, and when the pot is filled with parboiled, yellow-eyed beans and a cube of pork with fat and lean in proper strata, and when the pot is set in the hole for the night and covered with coals, then begins a beneficent tissue-making alchemy which transmutes the humbler food into ambrosia fit for Mount Ktaadn, if not for Mount Olympus.

The fishing along shore now began to abound chiefly in chub, and Don Gifaro, the epicure, was beginning contemptuously to dub this ever-ready-for-breakfast fish as "Ktaadn trout," while at the same time Don Gifaro, the sportsman, was silently determining where the real "fish" lay. All in good time, an ancient and dilapidated raft was discovered, and as soon mounted by the Don, De Woods, and La Rose, who poled and paddled it with no end of work to the previously determined spot. After an hour's fishing, La Rose's bare hands taking the place of a landing-net, they returned laden with trout; seven fish weighed over ten pounds, and one was a three-pounder, twenty inches long. Meanwhile, a guide had shot a brace of partridges, and our style of living was rapidly assuming the Madison Square type. I give all concerned the benefit of two experiences I acquired this day: first, don't lay a trout in a frying-pan of red-hot fat with your fingers; second, when you do, get a distinguished artist to paint them with white lead and turpentine; it prejudices one against a warm tone in art, though the ultimate repose of the composition is charming.

KTAADN, FROM THE SOUTH SHORE OF THE LAKE

The mountain was now growing in our sight, and our artists were already making finished pencil studies and catching the ever-changing tints. Few views of mountains in any country exceed that from the southern shore of Lake Ktaadn, in combined grandeur and beauty,—the great pyramid, ten miles away on the left, ever changing in the varying moisture of air and shadow of cloud, brilliant and rosy in early sunshine while twilight still broods over the valley; each rock-rib, and rift searched out by the full blaze of mid-day, opalescent in the mistier air of afternoon, and then a harmonious mass of blended purple and blue outlined against the sunset and mirrored in the lake; its foreground a densely wooded plain of dark evergreens, broken here and there on the margin by tangled underwood of every hue of green, already richly flecked with autumnal color. In front, on the near opposite shore, abruptly rises Mount Turner.

its flanks dense with primeval hard-woods, the green interspersed with daily deepening red and yellow, and its summit a thicket of evergreens. Twenty miles away on the right, and most beautiful of all, the Traveler,—a flattened dome, rising higher than the loftiest peak of the Catskills, grand and symmetrical indeed, but lovely, as I see it far away in the soft, rosy sunset, when Ktaadn has put on the darker robes of evening. Such appears to be the view from our camp-shore; but as I look over my shoulder at the canvas of my companion, I realize how inadequately it can be described in words.

Our life, pleasant as was its routine by day, was not mere

THE TRAVELER, FROM THE SOUTH SHORE OF THE LAKE.

sketching, fishing, and tramping. The evening meal, with its liberal fare and its rousing appetites, its jokes and its relation of the day's experiences, and then the lying at ease before the glowing camp-fire, with its pipes and punch and stories, and the dropping off of one and another in sweet, healthful sleep, without the formality of "retiring"—these are scenes of which the memories will last like those of Ktaadn itself.

On the bright, clear morning of the 14th, Don Cathedra, Rubens, and De Woods, with two guides bearing supplies, penetrated the trackless wilderness of Mount Turner,—a tangling and difficult progress through primeval forests, to gain what the Don had imagined to be the grandest view of Ktaadn. While the rest of us were consoling ourselves for our loneliness, about dark, with a rice pudding composed of two raisins to one grain of rice, and a ravishing sauce,—a thoughtful study by La Rose,—up rose De Woods in our midst, pale as an apparition. He had preceded and lost his party, ascended a peak of Turner, and being without provisions, descended

KTAADN FROM CREEK AT WEST END OF LAKE.

after four o'clock and waded a mile of lake to escape the entangling thicket of the margin.

The sunrise of the next day was like opening the book of Revelations. While everything was lying asleep in misty twilight, suddenly the lurking leaden clouds in the west blushed as the east flung them its salute across the sea, and wreathed themselves in rosy garlands upon the brow of the monarch. And then the monarch awoke, and rose up in the mirage, and bathed himself in the yellow light, till his crest was transmuted into gold, and his breast into leagues of pink coral, while every glory of the rainbow rolled down his gorgeous flanks as morning broke upon the plain.

The Mount Turner party returned next day, and told their stories over the evening camp-fire,—stories of hard struggles over wind-falls and through tangled underwood, of a few spoonfuls of water apiece on the mountain top, and of compensation for their troubles in the rare beauty of a primeval forest,—singular growths, dead trunks tumbled picturesquely together by the wind, great trees wreathing their roots around big bowlders cushioned all over with mosses, and little rivulets running out below, all variegated with the glistening white birch

WOOD INTERIOR ON MOUNT TURNER.

and the great bronzed and many-tinted leaves of the moose-wood. The Don pronounced the view of Ktaadn "grand, but not pictorial." When rallied about getting lost, De Woods simply told the story of the Indian found wandering to and fro in the wilderness, against whom a similar charge was made. "Lost!" growled he; "Indian no lost, Indian *here;* wigwam lost."

On the morning of the 16th, Don Cathedra and I, with two guides, started toward the Great Basin, lying in the mountain in rear of the pyramid. Two other guides had preceded us, with provisions for the whole party; they were to return the same day, and to go up with the others in the morning. I started earlier, not expecting to be able to make the whole ten difficult miles in one day; but after various halts, we reached the Basin at 5 P. M. and pitched our camp. Being too tired to sleep, I lay for hours in this solemn amphitheater, watching the moon-lit clouds drift over its ragged summit, but not yet appreciating its vastness and its awful grandeur, for the night was singularly mild, and there was no sound but the soft sighing of the wind in the evergreens, as an occasional current circled around the Basin. I was yet to hear the sounds and see the sights of that great gulf.

The first half of our journey was through a comparatively level country, over the remains of an old lumbering road. While there was much good walking, there were occasional swamps over which the footing of stumps and slippery logs was made still more precarious by a low growth of shrubs which quite concealed it. Getting over these places brought a stress upon the temper as well as upon muscle and nerve. The remainder of the way to the Basin was chiefly a line of spotted trees, which gradually led up the lower flanks of the mountain, but wound in detail over steep pitches and through tangled thickets. There were occasional "wind-falls," which were difficult to penetrate or to get around, and where the blazed line was easily lost; and there were rocky stream-beds to be climbed on all fours. A point two miles from the Basin reveals a magnificent view, both of the mountain and of Ktaadn Lake and its surrounding hills. Much of the forest has been harmed by neither fire nor axe, and is full of beautiful pictures.

The body of Ktaadn extends, in bulk, some ten miles to the north of the pyramid. Its east side is gouged out in two enormous chasms —the Great Basin and the North Basin, the depth of which does not appear to the beholder from Ktaadn Lake. The Great Basin is a horse-shoe shaped gorge, some three miles in longest diameter and above a mile deep. Its floor is a plateau, a thousand feet above the general plain, embracing a forest and a little lake. The less precipitous northern lobe is divided from the southern by a "horse-back." The southern lobe of the Great Basin, not visible from Ktaadn Lake, is an amphitheater a mile in diameter. Its formation is not only magnificent, but surprising, in that it occupies the whole interior of the pyramid. The huge head of Ktaadn is hollow, but its hollowness only adds to its pictorial effect. It is the twofold wonder of our eastern scenery,—our grandest mountain inclosing our grandest gorge,—and so associating in one harmonious whole the effects of Sierra peaks with those of Colorado cañons.

At the foot of our camp is the little Basin Lake, a thousand feet long and half that width,—cold, clear, and azoic as the granite cliffs that rise out of its shore. Around it lie drift bowlders of every age, and huge rocks, split from the mountain, like monolithic houses tumbled together by an earthquake. Over the smaller *débris* many-colored foliage creeps up into the rifts, and towering above and beyond is the ragged granite precipice half a mile in sheer altitude. On such a grand scale is everything here that distances are deceptive. What was apparently a mere belt of trees on the opposite shore is a forest more than half a mile deep, through which we followed up a picturesque stream-bed to the foot of the cliffs.

A VIEW IN THE GREAT BASIN.

Don Cathedra was most fortunate in visiting the Great Basin on this seventeenth day of September —one day out of a hundred. It was gloriously bright, and yet there was moisture enough to give the most charming atmospheric effects. The Don made many studies, and worked diligently all day with pencil and brush, catching the effects of golden and rose-tinted rocks at sunrise, the yellow foliage creeping up the dark purple ledges on the shaded side of the ravine, the dim line in the atmosphere between the light and the shadow falling diagonally down the eastern cliff, the wild and ragged slides and stream-beds on the illuminated west slope, the picturesque foreground of autumn-tinted hard-woods and dark evergreens reflected in the lake— that wonderful association of grandeur in mass, with exquisite beauty in detail, such as one can rarely see among all our

Appalachian mountains.   In the midst of our musings, suddenly an avalanche came tearing down the precipice—enormous rocks bounding from ledge to ledge, bursting and scattering as they struck, throwing out white clouds like cannon smoke, and finally lost in the crashing forest below.   The long time occupied in the descent gave evidence of the enormous height of the precipice.

But the afternoon brought a rapid change of scene.   As the party from Lake Ktaadn came straggling in, a storm—which can be so quickly brewed on a mountain-top—had no sooner thrown its shadow upon us than its substance followed in wind and rain, driving us into the little temporary tent while the guides were preparing a better one.   During the intervals in the storm, our united exertions resulted, before dark, in a logged tent, well shielded and floored with boughs.   We supped, and packed our supplies and ourselves into night-quarters during a drizzling rain, choked and blinded every few minutes by clouds of smoke, which the eddying wind flung in every direction, and secretly brooding, every one, over the probability that the equinoctial had caught us in that meteorological whirlpool, Ktaadn Basin.

At midnight, Pomola, the deity of this domain, who had so sweetly beguiled us into his den, gave us a taste of his wrath.   Being at the tempestuous corner of the tent, I was roused from my dreams by a ripping and a snapping of things in general, and awoke to find the roof gone, the protecting boughs blown over, a torrent of rain pouring upon us, and the last embers of the camp-fire nearly extinguished.   The guides' tent had quite disappeared in the gust. But before the general eye had perceived the situation, the ever-ready John had pulled back and fastened down our flapping roof, and given an impetus to the fire.   Then there was a general re-adjustment in the tent ; the edges of underlying rubber cloths were propped up so that water would not run in, and overlying wraps were ridged so that rain would run off.   Always excepting that old campaigner, Don Gifaro—he wasted no time by waking up and fooling around in the dark.   I got hold of the tea, and slept with it the rest of the night under my water-proofs, and somebody else did the same with the sugar.

Ascending the mountain was the prescribed work of the next day, and we made an early start.   It soon became so warm that we

EAST BRANCH OF THE PENOBSCOT.

strapped our coats and waistcoats about our waists (the best way to carry weight, as John Gilpin knew), and scrambled up a dry stream-bed, over every form and size of rocky impediment, till we reached a "slide," which I supposed might conform to the angle of repose; but the unscientific way in which Ktaadn rocks will arrange themselves, overhanging rather than receding, I leave succeeding tramps to account for. It was a hard and exhausting scale, but by no means a harmful one, when there were plenty of rests. We ascended a slide in the north lobe of the Great Basin,—the lowest part of the mountain, and yet so high that lichens were the largest growths,— and there we found what is called the table-land, but which is, in fact, a gradual slope toward the west. Here Don Cathedra and his guide left us to explore the comparatively undiscovered North Basin, and we proceeded up a gradual but rugged incline, now through entangling shrubs, now over patches of huge rocks tumbled together, until we at last reached the summit of Ktaadn.

I have seen many stretches of splendid landscape from many mountain tops, but to my thinking the view from the top of Ktaadn is the most remarkable and the most beautiful I have ever seen. It was, on this peculiarly bright day, a panorama of exceeding splendor. The groundwork of the whole visible landscape is a vast wooded plain, broken in the rear of Ktaadn by a few bold and picturesque hills, bounded on the south-western horizon by the grand group of the White Mountains, and interspersed everywhere with innumerable shining lakes—Moosehead in the far distance, Chesuncook, a river expansion, Millinocket with its hundred islands; and on the other side, our own little Ktaadn Lake, and Mount Turner and the Traveler looking so small from our towering height.

The night of the 20th was a memorable one. Don Gifaro, Rubens, and De Woods were to leave us next morning, and we sat up talking over our adventures, and promising ourselves many happy returns, till the unprecedentedly late hour of ten o'clock.

The remaining days of our camping, although we could not get used to the vacant seats, were full of pleasant incidents. La Rose kept our table loaded with splendid fish, and Don Cathedra and I sketched from morning till night, producing some of our finest studies. The Don manipulated the brush and the palette, to be sure, but as I held the umbrella and generally supervised the work, I feel justified in the foregoing use of the pronoun. The aspects of the mountain were now surprisingly various and beautiful. Our equinoctial storm was chiefly a wind storm. One day it drove the Great Basin all full of clouds, and they poured out of the apex like steam out of a volcano; and when they were luridly lighted by the setting sun, the scene was extremely wild and gorgeous.

And so, day after day, the mountain and the forest grew more beautiful. But the end must come; and on the 25th, with great reluctance, we broke camp and started back to Sherman *en route* for home.

Our supplies for 11 men (6 excursionists and 5 guides) 16 days, and 5 men 5 days, = 1 man, 201 days, were:

Mess pork	115 pounds	Rice	5 pounds.
Hard bread	80 "	Butter	5 "
Crackers	16 "	Raisins	5 "
Sugar (granulated)	80 "	Bread powders	3 "
Wheat flour	70 "	Tea	9 "
Indian meal	25 "	Canned meat	7 "
Beans	65 "	Lemons	8 "
Potatoes	180 "	Sundry preserves, etc	5 "
Ham	15 "	Fish, mostly trout (estimated)	100 "
Onions	10 "	Game	10 "

Total . . . . 813 pounds.

This gives, say, four pounds of raw food per day per man. There was, of course, a large percentage of waste in its preparation and in its transportation from camp to camp. The cost of this raw food (excluding, of course, fish, game, and transportation) was sixty-five dollars, or thirty-two and one-third cents per man per day. Our bill of fare has included the obvious simple and the following compound dishes:

Crackers, dampened and fried in pork fat, with onions *(bisque à la Ilex);* fried cakes, of various mixtures of wheat and corn meal; Indian plum-pudding *(cauchemar);* rice-pudding, with raisins; raisin-pudding, with rice *(ex-cathedra);* baked pork and beans; canned meats warmed up with potatoes and cracker crumbs; eel-pie; partridge-soup and stew; duck-stew, and sauces of sugar, butter, and rum. As the guides were so constantly employed in arranging new camps and transporting supplies, they had no time to seek large game, although we saw both moose and caribou.

The necessary camp utensils (some of which most guides have on hand) for our number and our style of living are: An iron pot with overlapping cover, a tin tea-pot, two frying-pans, four tin pails, two of them having covers and removable wire legs (parboiling vessels), the whole to pack in a nest; a nest of four deep tin dishes or pans, the largest fifteen inches and the smallest ten inches in diameter, to be used as mixing vessels and platters; a tin baker, say 16 x 12 x 7 inches; a dozen of each of the following: tin pint cups, tin dinner plates, and cheap tea-spoons, knives and forks; three larger cooking spoons of different sizes, two butcher-knives, two tin wash-basins, a salt-box, a pepper-box, and a wire grid-iron. We did not have a camp-stove, which would have been a great convenience. The half of a stout barrel is good to keep pork in, and will also hold fish, game, etc., in separate birch-bark vessels. A birch-bark lined hole in the earth is a good store-room for meat. There should be plenty of dish-cloths and towels, and five pounds of bar soap. A can of kerosene and a student-lamp may be readily taken; a dozen candles are convenient, although the camp-fire furnishes the necessary illumination. No work nor amusement requiring a good light is attempted after dark. The matches should be distributed among the party, and each person should carry a few in a corked metal case. Some nails and tacks of assorted sizes prove

KTAADN LAKE FROM THE SLIDE IN THE BASIN.

surprisingly useful. We brought in cheap crockery plates, mugs, cups and saucers, and left them. The guides will, of course, have plenty of axes and guns. A one-and-a-half inch auger and a draw-shave are often very useful. A shovel is convenient, but not indispensable. The provisions and utensils are most conveniently transported in bags.

It is a great mistake to take other than stout clothing. Adaptation of clothing to the great variations of temperature may be readily made by "doubling up." The rubber cloth should be permanently lined with the half of one blanket to lie on, the other half of the blanket and the sides of the rubber cloth forming a cover. The foot of this bed should be made, by means of straps and buckles, into a bag, so that the occupant may roll about, bed and all, without pulling the clothes off or getting them wet when it rains. This bag of bedding, rolled into a bundle forms its own water-proof case. The clothing is transported in a rubber bag, made like a mail-bag, and having an inside flap. To this outfit each person will add the implements of his specialty. A few quires of heavy paper, both for wrapping and for preserving leaves, are of use to all. Pencils, pocket-knives, and such indispensables, should be taken in duplicate. Climbing mountains and tumbling through thickets is pocket-picking business. The party should have a good field-glass, an aneroid barometer for measuring heights, and a pocket-compass.

The cost of the expedition (sixteen days in the woods) to each excursionist was $80.83.

The railway transportation was 47 per cent. of the whole expense. The distance from New York to Ktaadn by our route is exactly 600 miles.

A Model State Capitol
(1885)

THE CAPITOL.

A MODEL STATE CAPITAL.

HARTFORD is a good place to pass through. It is also a good place to stop at. The two great railroads connecting New York and Boston by way of the Connecticut State capital carry across its corporate bounds perhaps two hundred thousand or a quarter of a million travellers every year; but only a small proportion of the persons on that current stop at this point. Still fewer are those who come to stay. It can not be said that many are called, but the few are certainly chosen, the population, which is not much above fifty thousand, being of an unusually high character. Little poverty, large and energetic thrift, ingenious manufactures, ac-

cumulated resources—these are the data one may judge by. The city, in fact, takes its place on statistical tables as proportionally the richest in the United States.*

Set in the black-earthed, fertile Connecticut Valley, encircled by low but picturesque hills over whose violet mass the sunrise and sunset break with peculiar splendor, it is a cheerful and satisfactory place, even to the casual passer, who is struck by

* The assessed valuation is $48,500,000; but counting in establishments situated elsewhere though owned or chiefly represented in Hartford, this would rise to $125,000,000. The city pays one-third of the taxes of Connecticut. The new Capitol, with its land, cost $3,335,000, of which Hartford contributed $1,960,000; that is, nearly two-thirds.

its stately Capitol, near the railroad, and the long line of early French Gothic building farther off that forms one side of the projected quadrangle of Trinity College. The importance of its educational, its benevolent, and protective institutions is at once presented to an observer. In many a village and country by-way had I seen, long before I alighted in Hartford itself, certain unlovely but suggestive tin signs tacked upon the sides of wooden houses indicating by a mystic word or two that those dwellings had been insured with Hartford companies against fire. In like manner the town is a stronghold of life-insurance—a business which, despite its ominous technical phrase describing new policy-holders as "fresh blood," has beneficent results as well as a selfish aim. But I am thinking more particularly of those undertakings meant purely for the relief of the unfortunate. It can not conscientiously be said that it is a cheerful thing, on leaving the station, to find yourself in a thoroughfare which greets you with the name of Asylum Street. A dim suspicion arises that if you follow its lead you will bring up in some place designed for the prompt immurement of strangers; for in old times even temporary residents were not allowed in Hartford except by a vote of town-meeting. This anxiety, however, is dissipated when you learn that the name refers to the American Asylum for the Deaf and Dumb, a most praiseworthy establishment, the first of its kind in the United States. It was founded by a number of gentlemen in 1815, and under the superintendence of the Rev. Mr. Gallaudet it became the inspiration and model of many similar institutions; so that it would hardly be amiss to give the street that devoted teacher's name instead of its present rather doleful one. "Retreat Avenue," painted on the horse-cars, suggests another famous establishment, the Hartford Retreat for the Insane, which likewise antedates all of its class in this country, saving one or two that were publicly endowed. The Retreat was set going by a subscription; and that this was eminently a popular one is manifest in the fact that many of the signers gave but fifty or twenty-five cents, and some only twelve and a half cents. How one charity may aid another I happened to see well exemplified in the case of an insane person who was also a deaf-mute, so that it was necessary for the Retreat to provide an attendant skilled in the manual and sign language—a need which could not easily have been met had it not been for the work of the American Asylum.

But I must hasten to say that the associations called up by street names in Hartford are by no means all of this pensive sort. The horse-cars already mentioned appear to be somewhat browbeaten: they lack the brisk insolence of their species on metropolitan lines; are subject to endless delays at turn-outs and the railroad crossings; are drawn, moreover, by only one horse each, and have not even spirit enough to maintain a conductor; but as they bounce disconsolately along they continue to offer to convey the patient wanderer to Spring Grove and City Garden. There is a fresh rural sound about these names, and others of kindred purport occur, such as Flower Street, Oak Street, Woodland, Laurel, Hawthorn, and Evergreen. The country character reflected in them lingers around Hartford, and enhances its pleasantness. Then we have the historic series, Trumbull, Wolcott, Wadsworth, and the like. Even the early Dutch settlers, so summarily ousted by the English, have returned under the auspices of Colonel Colt (the inventor of the revolver) to haunt Hendricksen and Vredendale avenues; and near Colt's armory likewise are recorded the names of those sachems—Sequassen, Weehassat, and Maseek—who deeded their lands to the colonists. All this reminds us that we are in a city which has an interesting past. The historic impression is deepened if we stray back along Main Street, the single road of the original village, which is wide enough to swallow two or three Broadways without inconvenience, and of about equal proportions with Piccadilly, in London, by St. James's Park. It was where Main Street expands into State-house Square that Washington and Knox met Rochambeau and Admiral Ternay when those leaders of the French allies came from Newport to confer with the commander-in-chief for the first time. A brilliant scene that, and doubtless the most spectacular one in the peaceful annals of the place. On one side were the foreign officers in their royal uniforms adorned with decorations; on the other, Washington and his staff, epauletted with gold, clad in the Continental blue and buff, and attended by Governor Trumbull, with other State worthies, who wore long-skirted

CENTRE CONGREGATIONAL CHURCH.
Photographed by R. S. De Lamater.

drab or crimson coats and embroidered waistcoats. In the American escort was the ancient company known as the Governor's Foot-Guard, resplendent in scarlet and black, which were contrasted with buff breeches and waistcoats, tall bear-skin hats completing what the poets of that period would have called their "horrid front." Then Washington and Rochambeau dismounted, and coming forward into

GEORGE WILLIAMSON SMITH, PRESIDENT OF TRINITY
COLLEGE.
Photographed by R. S. De Lamater.

the open central space, met and shook hands for the two peoples whom they represented.

Once this same square went by the name of "Meeting-house Yard." The church stood on one side of it, and at other points on its boundary were the scene of the weekly market, the stocks and pillory, the jail, and the slave pen. That was before the pen had been raised *against* slavery, and Mrs. Stowe was not then a resident of Hartford. On the site of the old meeting-house stands to-day its lineal descendant, the Centre Congregational Church—a broad-faced edifice painted a cream-custard tint, and displaying a row of slender pillars in front, which feature seems to have pleased the builders, for they repeated it by putting pillars around the spire quite high up. Behind the church,

and protected by a wall with a rusty iron gate, lies the ancient grave-yard, a quaint and melancholy spot containing the tombstones of early inhabitants, adorned with what appear to be owls' heads, but on consideration must be construed as angels. Under two brown-stone slabs raised on little legs like children's dining-tables the first two pastors are buried, those who led their flock from Cambridge, Massachusetts, to the banks of the Connecticut—Thomas Hoolser, whom Cotton Mather in his *Magnalia* called "the light of the Western churches," and the Rev. Samuel Stone. It was at the wish of the latter, who had been born in Hertford, England, that the plantation was called Hartford; and the Saxon name, meaning "hart's ford," was as applicable here as in the mother country, for doubtless the New World river too had been crossed at this spot by many a herd of wild deer. The epitaph cut upon the stone above his resting-place declares that

"Errors corrupt, by sinewous dispute,
  He did oppugne, and clearly them confute.
  Above all things he Christ his Lord preferred.
  Hartford, thy richest jewel's here interred."

Quite forgotten now is all that "sinewous dispute" which so endeared Mr. Stone to our controversial forefathers, unless by professors in the Congregational Theological Institute up on the hill yonder; but his memory has found a surer foothold in its connection with the municipal name.

To this church the Governor of the State used to repair, after the annual election, at the head of a solemn procession, to begin his term of office with divine service. The next evening occurred the great "election ball," followed on the succeeding Monday by another ball more select in character. The whole week, in fact, was kept as a holiday, and it made a useful vacation and festival-time for peo-

TRINITY COLLEGE.

ple who, swayed by their scruples against everything sanctioned by the Anglican Church, refused to observe Christmas. During this little space everybody was hilarious; families made it an occasion pens, is the site of a tavern where another element of former social life used to centre, namely, the Seven-copper Club, which met there in the Revolutionary period to talk news or gossip and drink a

JOSEPH R. HAWLEY.
Photographed by Parkinson.

for exchanging visits, and kept open house, with "election cake" ready for their callers. In our time the cake appears to precede the election, and takes the form of paid tax bills or some other gentle inducement to the free and unprejudiced citizen to vote for the candidate who favors him; but the old-fashioned plan was for the citizen to vote for the candidate *he* favored, and then eat cake impartially. Almost opposite the church, as it hap-

half-mug of flip, the price of which was exactly seven coppers. Prohibitory legislation was hardly needed, for the landlord, Moses Butler, was a law unto the members: he never allowed them more than one half-mug apiece, and sent them home promptly at nine, with the bluff admonition, "It is time, gentlemen, to go back to your families that are waiting for you."

I do not find that the solid household-

STAIRWAY IN THE CAPITOL.
Photographed by R. S. De Lamater.

ing sort of club has ever taken root very widely in Hartford, but there has been in existence for about a dozen years past a very agreeable club of less than a hundred gentlemen, quite unlike the ancient and humble Seven-copper, I imagine. It borrows its appellation from the city itself; its membership is chiefly commercial and professional, under the presidency of General Joseph R. Hawley, formerly Governor of Connecticut, and it occupies a roomy old mansion on Pleasant Street, which is itself a fine relic of the first post-colonial epoch, for the sidewalks are lined with trees, and behind them the houses rise sedate and prosperous of aspect, with gardens that are not above nurturing a little fruit. The crime of arboricide is of recent development, comparatively, and it is to be hoped will be suppressed. Inside the abode of the Hartford Club one encounters the elegance that is inherent in simplicity and reason-

ableness of arrangement. The rooms bear the stamp of a former squirearchy and a commercial gentry, if one may make the phrase, which were intelligent and refined; all is of the past here, except the convenient contrivances and the quiet Morrisian decoration. In summer the members may pass out at the glass doors of the dining-room to a broad veranda overlooking the garden, and there dinners are served under cover of a roof and an awning curtain. A line of low buildings, the "offices" of the old mansion, runs along one side of the grassy inclosure, for it was a house of some grandeur in its day. Mr. David Watkinson, to whom it last belonged, founded a library, the windows of which look across the yard in neighborly fashion at the club; and connected with this library is the granite bulk of the Wadsworth Athenæum, occupying the spot where formerly stood the house of Daniel Wadsworth, a descendant of the

Charter Oak Wadsworth, Colonel Jeremiah. Washington used to come to that house when he visited Hartford, and the exact room in which be reposed would, if it had not disappeared, be still pointed out, for Washington, like other great historic personages, seems to have been an industrious and ubiquitous sleeper.

aspect, on the contrary, is exceedingly modern. "Meeting-house Yard" and Main Street are now hedged in by lofty insurance buildings, hotels, newspaper offices, "New York Stores," "Boston Bazars," and other shops. A little to the north is a well-devised building of brown stone, with good carving about the doors,

BUST OF SAMUEL CLEMENS, BY KARL GERHARDT.
Photographed by Kurtz.

It should not be understood, however, that these reminiscences of antiquity color the aspect of the city perceptibly; the

a fantastic gargoyle or two at the roof, and a pointed red-tiled tower on one corner—an encouraging example of the pic-

SOLDIERS' AND SAILORS' MONUMENT.
From architect's design.

turesque in a structure wholly designed for business purposes. But the square itself is filled up by the Post-office—a Mullett monstrosity of the tasteless order which we may call the Federal; and there also stands the old State-house, now a City-hall, of no special order, but plentifully supplied with little urns placed upon the cornice balustrades, and the obsolete cupola. The State government has now transferred itself to a more fitting habitation in the new Capitol, built within the bounds of Bushnell Park, and—what is more remarkable—within the appropriation. No suspicion of jobbery tarnishes the brilliant effect of this beautiful piece of architecture. The only bad feature about it is the enormously tall, rather spindling, twelve-sided drum that lifts the gilded dome to a height of two hundred and fifty feet above the ground. Out of the harmonious growth of blue and white marble in the main building, with its pointed windows and slated pavilions, suggesting in a modified way the great municipal halls of the Netherlands and France, this addition lifts a giraffe-like neck toward the sky; and even a large broad dome occupying the middle space, though it would have looked better, must have been out of keeping with the rest. The interior, nevertheless, abounds in good qualities. Convenient, spacious, well-lighted, having the air of ease and spontaneity, it gives numerous good vistas, varied by the great central staircases and the airy columned galleries. The battle flags of Connecticut are ranged in

PORTION OF THE FRIEZE OF THE SOLDIERS'

carven oak cases near one of the great entrances; endless offices open upon the corridors and galleried courts; the State library is ensconced in one huge apartment, and the Supreme Court in another. It is, by-the-way, a curious bit of symbolism that the Supreme Court judges' room has its fire-place surrounded with blue tiles illustrating Scripture subjects, while the tiles in the room devoted to counsel depict scenes from fairy tales. The Representatives are accommodated in a rich and sober chamber with stained-glass windows; it is about as large, but much less stuffy, and to my mind much more beautiful, than the English House of Commons. Near the Speaker's dais is an unobtrusive but huge thermometer, by which, I suppose, the heat of debate may be measured. The Senate of twenty-one has another lordly hall to itself, where there is provided for the President of that body a large chair made out of wood from the Charter Oak, richly carved with leaf and acorn. Both these legislative halls are carried out with an excellent appreciation of what is fittest for their purpose in the resources of art as applied to decoration; the natural grain and color of the woods —oak, ash, and walnut—combine with the subdued tones and good ornament of the walls to make a refreshing environment worthy of republican ideals and much above republican practice.

The exterior walls of the Capitol are haunted by birds, and provided with niches for statues of Connecticut worthies, two of which are already occupied by Oliver Wolcott and Roger Sherman; and between these a marble image of the Charter Oak spreads its branches. Have we not all learned the legend of that venerable tree in our histories at school? It seems almost to require setting down as a distinct species in botanical text-books; but in Hartford it becomes like the ash-tree of

Norse mythology, like Ygdrasil, which upheld the whole universe. In spite of historical skeptics, the legend still holds that when Sir Edmund Andros came, in 1687, to reclaim the liberal charter which Charles II. had himself granted, but now wanted to revoke, the lights at the evening council-board were suddenly put out, and that in the darkness Colonel Wadsworth did actually carry off the document and hide it in the hollow oak that stood before Mr. Secretary Wyllys's house. It is not so generally remembered that this tree had been an object of great regard on the part of the Indians before ever the colonists came hither. A deputation of them waited on the white men to ask that no harm be done the oak, since it had long been the guide of their ancestors as to the time for planting corn. "When the leaves," said they, "are of the size of a mouse's ear, then is the time to put the seed in the ground." Time and tempest felled it at last; but it blooms here in marble still; its name is preserved throughout the city as the distinguishing mark of divers stores, shops, and companies; and a pretty marble slab, like a grave-stone, in Charter Oak Place inadequately marks where the original flourished until 1856. In Bushnell Park (named after that eminent theologian, the late Dr. Horace Bushnell, who was the chief promoter of this public pleasure-ground) there is a couple of Charter Oaks junior, sprung from its fruit; and "certified" acorns, possibly taken from these younger trees, but supposed to have grown upon the parent, have been worth their weight in gold at charity fairs. Across the Connecticut, leading to East Hartford, stretches a covered bridge one thousand feet long, and taking up in its construction a corresponding quantity of timber. Mark Twain, showing some friends about, told them that bridge also was built of wood from the Charter Oak.

AND SAILORS' MONUMENT.—From designs by George Keller.

SAMUEL CLEMENS'S HOUSE.
Photographed by R. S. De Lamater.

Not far from the Capitol is the Soldiers' and Sailors' Monument, which takes the unique form of a memorial arch spanning the southern end of an old stone bridge, which leads into the City Park at the foot of Ford Street. The architect, Mr. George Keller, also designed the Buffalo Soldiers' Monument. The arch is thirty feet wide, and springs from two massive round towers, each of which is sixty-seven feet in circumference and sixty feet high, terminating in a conical roof. Above the archway, about forty feet from the ground, a frieze of sculpture 175 feet in length and 6 feet 6 inches in breadth runs around the monument. "The towers," says the Hartford *Courant*, "seem like two huge sentinels guarding the bridge, or mighty standard-bearers holding aloft a noble banner on which is emblazoned the deeds of the men of Hartford who died for their country on land and sea in the war which kept the Union whole." Circular stairs inside the towers lead to the rampart or gallery at the top of the monument, overlooking the park, and protected by a parapet which has the seal of Hartford carved on its face.

It was about ten years ago that Mr. Clemens—or, as we all now prefer to call him, Mark Twain—came to Hartford to live; and he has built for himself there one of the most delightful of houses, in the pleasantest part of the city, just where it ceases to be visible as city at all, and merges into rolling hill and dale. A large structure, irregular in outline, made of red and brown brick in fantastic courses, it stands on Farmington Avenue, upon a knoll well back from the street, with a grove of beeches and oaks and other trees of good deportment clustering around two sides. The shade and flicker of these trees lend their fascination to a spacious *ombra* at the rear, completely hidden from the thoroughfare, and affording good opportunity for open-air suppers in the evenings of early summer. In-doors and out-doors mingle on the friendliest terms, one may say, throughout the interior. There is no room that has not some charming prospect. The library, which appears to be the favorite of the household, is closed at one end by a conservatory, but one deep-recessed bay-window reveals an exquisite glimpse, through the trees close by, of a little winding stream at the foot of a steep bank. This stream is Park River, which wanders from here down to the Capitol circuitously, and in its wanderings has lost the pretty name which the Puritan colo-

SAMUEL CLEMENS'S LIBRARY.
Photographed by R. S. De Lamater.

CHARLES DUDLEY WARNER'S HOUSE.
Photographed by R. S. De Lamater.

nists gave it. They called it the Riveret. The Riveret is bordered by low meadows on one side, and by the sharp acclivity with its fair woodland on the other. Within this woodland, which is not crossed by either fence or hedge, there are several other villas; among them, not far distant, the picturesque, gabled house of Charles Dudley Warner. The plot of cultivated ground which, in *My Summer in a Garden*, the author so generously annexed to the open common of American humor, was attached to his former home, near by. There also was the hearth from the glow of which came the inspiration for *Back-log Studies*. Before its cheerful light Mr. Warner's friends used to gather of snowy nights, enjoying the crackle of the blazing wood, and the flashes of wit that sparkled there; Mark Twain and their pastor, Rev. Joseph Twichell, and Dr. J. Hammond Trumbull—the only man extant who can read Eliot's Indian Bible—with others not less endeared to the circle because they are not public personages; and perhaps a visiting brother author, Howells from Cambridge, or Stedman from New York, or Sanborn from

Concord, all centring about the quiet, thoughtful-looking host, with his rather pallid face, and his hair and beard strewn with snow that will not melt even before his own geniality.

The new house is charming in all its appointments, and especially rich in bric-à-brac, much of it Oriental, collected by the owner during his several tours in Europe, the East, and Africa. The accompanying illustration represents a corner of one end of the music-room. The sideboard is of mahogany, and over it hangs a painting, "The Martyrdom of Santa Barbara," by Vasquez, a contemporary, perhaps pupil, of Velasquez, painted about 1540 for a convent at Bogota, South America, where it has been until two or three years ago. The picture has a curious heavy frame of ebony, inlaid with masses of tortoise-shell. The mantel-piece is unique. It is made of Saracenic tiles framed in California redwood. Most of the tiles are wall tiles from ancient houses in Damascus and Cairo, one from the Mosque of Omar, in Jerusalem, and some small ones at the side from the pavement of the courts in the Alhambra. The tiles are blues and greens, in arabesques and conventionalized flower patterns, one with a legend in Arabic declaring the unity of God. On top of the mantel-piece stands a large Knight of Malta vase, majolica, probably of Abrazzi make. At Malta it was customary to mould such a jar on the a study at home, he nevertheless every week-day when he is at home trudges down into the city to the office, a mile and a half away, of the Hartford *Courant* —to get the true local flavor pronounce "currant"—of which he is an editor and part owner. There he enters another

CHARLES DUDLEY WARNER.
From drawing by F Dielman.

election of a Grand Master of the order. This was made for Adrianolle Vegnian-cort, elected 1690, and has his portrait on one side and coat-of-arms on the other. Its companion was made for Fra Raimon-do Perellos, elected 1697.

Although Mr. Warner of course has apartment consecrated to the pen; cheer-ful, sunny, hung with photographs of Old World architecture, but provided with a large writing-table, on which are the par-aphernalia of practical newspaper labor, and there, too, he remains for several hours, studying the news of the world,

CORNER OF ONE END OF MUSIC-ROOM IN CHARLES DUDLEY WARNER'S HOUSE.

and writing editorials which surprise even his old associates by their wide range and the familiarity they evince with questions of trade, politics, literature, and foreign affairs. Those who know what writing as a profession really means will understand the kind of ability and industry required to sustain this steady journalistic duty, simultaneously with the production of books and frequent contributions to the magazines, and they will not wonder that Mr. Warner should now and then have to travel for health's sake. But he always brings back from his journeys so much of new acquisition that the literary impulse is quickened into fresh activity.

Near by, in a slate-colored cottage of moderate size, lives the famous author of *Uncle Tom's Cabin*. The atmosphere within-doors is that of literary New England twenty-five years ago: the American Renascence has not yet invaded these rooms, so conspicuously neat and com-

fortable, yet with a kind of moral rectitude in their comfort. The library is also a sitting-room; where a glowing coal fire burned on the chilly autumn day when I was admitted there; and in the wall spaces between the windows were placed tall panels painted with flowers, and terminating above in points that gave them a half-ecclesiastical air, as if they were tables of the law.

"Is this your study?" I asked.

"I have no particular study," said the authoress, "and I have not written much lately; but if I were to begin, I should be as likely to write here as anywhere."

Thus easily and informally she treats the genius that has given her a world-wide celebrity; indeed, there is nothing about her manner or in her surroundings to indicate a consciousness of the extraordinary power which endowed her first book with an influence that has never been paralleled. A very quiet little lady, plainly attired, and apt during conversation to become abstracted — a life-long habit of reverie which has enabled her to think out her designs and carry on composition in the midst of those interruptions to most writers unbearable—a lady quiet and undemonstrative, with immense determination and character revealed in her face when seen at certain angles, but with an equally natural gentleness and benignity; this is what one sees to-day on meeting Mrs. Stowe. She gives the impression of one who wielded large weapons because Providence put them into her hands to right a great wrong, and not with any joy in the suffering and harm that must come with the good gained. She appears the

HARRIET BEECHER STOWE.
From a drawing by J. W. Alexander.

wife, the mother, the grandmother, living in her domestic interests, rather than the woman distinguished in national history and literature. We talked on personal topics, and while this was going forward Professor Stowe came in from a walk, with a tall stick in his hand, which he grasped as a support in the middle. It was like a pilgrim's staff, and completed the suggestion of present and militant religion that somehow pervaded the whole spot. The conversation now passed easily to questions of faith, and Mrs. Stowe manifested a strong interest in the old Pilgrim and Puritan qualities of belief. To me it seems regrettable that the physiognomy of a person occupying so remarkable a position should not be carefully recorded in all its stages of development, since a distinctive face increases its sum of meaning with the years; but I learned that Mrs. Stowe had not submitted herself to the arts of the photographer for a long time, and Professor Stowe was firm in the conviction that the portrait painted by Richmond in 1852 was the only one worthy of perpetuation. "That," said he, referring to it, "is the way she will look at the resurrection." I confess that if the resurrection were to preserve the mild womanly maturity of her features as they are at the age of seventy, I should find no fault with its process.

The material aspect of Mrs. Stowe's abode, as perhaps I have hinted, gives little intimation of the part which its occupant has played; but in the small entrance hall stands a plain low cupboard, which, on being opened to the favored visitor, displayed two rows of massive volumes — a dozen on each shelf— containing a petition in favor of the abolition of slavery, signed by half a million women, and offered to Congress as a result of Mrs. Stowe's agitation. In a corner of the parlor, too, there is a closed beaufet well stocked with editions of *Uncle Tom's Cabin*, and others of the authoress's works, in several foreign languages: an impressive collection, certainly, and one which has served a secondary purpose, for it has been duplicated in the British Museum, and is there used as the means of curious studies in comparative philology. Since her husband's withdrawal from his professorship at Andover, Mrs. Stowe has spent her time in these simple surroundings, leading a retired life, and going in winter to Florida, where she finds

WILLIAM B. FRANKLIN.
Photographed by R. S. De Lamater.

refuge among her orange groves, in a town which bears the fragrant name of Mandarin. She was drawn to Hartford partly by its general charm, and in part through associations which her sister had given the place by establishing there the Female Seminary. Speaking of the length of her residence here, she said, "I don't remember when I came; I do not live by years." This being repeated to Mark Twain, "I wish," he instantly observed, "the tax-collector would adopt that principle." One most agreeable memory will long remain with me, of an evening spent in Mrs. Stowe's company at the house of Mr. and Mrs. Clemens. Among other things there was after-dinner talk of the days preceding the war, and of the "un-

der-ground railroad" for escaping slaves, and the strange adventures therewith connected. Mrs. Stowe gave her reminiscences of exciting incidents in her life on the Ohio border at that time, and told of the frightful letters she received from the South after publishing her great novel. These anonymous screeds voiced, no doubt, the worst element there, and teemed with threats and abuse that now, happily, would not be offered by even the most wanton survivor of the fire-eaters. To give an idea of the extremes to which these missives proceeded, Mrs. Stowe mentioned that one of them, duly forwarded to her by United States mail, inclosed a negro's ear! It was inevitable that we who listened should meditate upon the marvellous change that had been effected in the condition of our Union within twenty years, and one gentleman who was present said to another, aside, as emphasizing the extent of that change, "To think that I, who can remember when a Boston mob tried to hang William Lloyd Garrison, should have lived to see twenty respectable free negroes asleep at his funeral!" It was a frivolous remark, no doubt, but it was only the light mask of a sincere respect for the prodigious feat so largely prompted by the pen of the demure lady who had just been speaking with us. Extremely interesting, also, was the eager force with which Mrs. Stowe related one or two stories of later date on other themes that had presented themselves to her as deserving literary treatment. It showed that the narrative instinct was deeply ingrained in her, and had not lost its vigor even after so long an exertion as she has given it. Yet her presence, temperament, and conversation confirmed the theory one is likely to form in reading her books, that her imagination acts inseparably with the moral sense.

It is a convenient thing to have the antipodes anchored just around the corner. A few steps only from Mrs. Stowe's brings you to Mr. Clemens's house, and still fewer, if you take the short-cut through the lawns and shrubbery, by which brief transit you pass from old New England to modern America—from the plain quarters of ethical fiction to the luxurious abode of the most Western of humorists. It is not difficult to trace, however, the essential kinship between Sam Lawson of *Oldtown Folks* and the equally quaint and shrewd but more expansive drollery of Mark Twain; and, on the other hand, those who see much of this author in private discover in him a fund of serious reflection and of keen observation upon many subjects that gives him another element in common with his neighbor. The literary group in this neighborhood do not seem to fancy giving names to their houses: they are content with the arithmetical designation. "No, my house has not got any name," said Mr. Clemens, in answer to a question. "It has a number, but I have never been able to remember what it is." No number, in fact, appears on gate or door; but the chances are that if a stranger were to step into any shop on the business streets he could at once obtain an accurate direction to the spot.

And a charming haunt it is, with its wide hall, finished in dark wood under a panelled ceiling, and full of easy-chairs, rugs, cushions, and carved furniture that instantly invite the guest to lounge in front of the big fire-place. But it is a house made for hospitality, and one can not stop at that point. Over the fire-place, through a large plate-glass suggesting Alice's Adventures, a glimpse is had of the drawing-room, luminous with white and silver and pale blue; and on another side, between a broad flight of stairs and a chiselled Ginevra chest drawn against the wall, the always open library door attracts one's steps. There is more dark wood-work in the library, including a very elaborate panel rising above the mantel to the ceiling. This was brought from abroad, and in other portions of the house are other pieces representing the spoils of European tours; one in particular I recall, covered with garlands and with plump cherubs that spring forth in plastic rotundity, and clamber along the edges. But it adds to the pleasurableness of the home that all the cherubs in it are not carved. A genial atmosphere, too, pervades the house, which is warmed by wood fires, a furnace, and the author's immense circulation. One would naturally in such a place expect to find some perfection of a study, a literary work-room, and that has indeed been provided, but the unconventional genius of the author could not reconcile itself to a surrounding the charms of which distracted his attention. The study remains, its deep window giving a seductive outlook above the library, but Mr. Clemens goes elsewhere. Pointing to a large divan extending along the two sides of a right-angled corner, "That was a good idea," he said, "which I got from something I saw in a Syrian monastery; but I found it was much more comfortable to lie there and smoke than to stay at my desk. And then these windows—I was constantly getting up to look at the view; and when one of our beautiful heavy snow-falls came in winter, I couldn't do anything at all except gaze at it." So he has moved still higher upstairs into the billiard-room, and there writes at a table placed in such wise that he can see nothing but the wall in front of him and a couple of shelves of books. Before adopting this expedient he had tried a room which he caused to be fitted up with plain pine sheathing on the upper floor of his stable; but that had serious disadvantages, and even the billiard-room failing to meet the requirements in some emergencies, he has latterly resorted to hiring an office in a commercial building in the heart of the city.

"About four months in the year," said he, "is the time when I expect to do my work, during the summer vacation, when I am off on the farm at Elmira. Yes," he continued, when I expressed surprise, "I can write better in hot weather. And, besides, I must be free from all other interests and occupations. I find it necessary, when I have begun anything, to keep steadily at it, without changing my surroundings. To take up the train of ideas after each day's writing I must be in the same place that I began it in, or else it becomes very difficult."

But nothing, apparently, interrupts the spontaneous flow of his humor in daily life. It is the same in kind with that of his books, though incidental and less elaborate. It is unpremeditated, and always unexpected. He never takes what may be termed the obvious and conventional witty view, yet neither is there any straining for a new form of jest: the novelty comes of itself. Moreover, unlike certain wits whose quality is genuine, but whose reputation becomes a burden to them, he appears to be indifferent whether he ever cracks another joke, and thus lulls his companions into a delusive security, only to take them unawares with some new and telling shot. There is less exaggeration in what he says than in what he writes; but the essence of his fun lies in that same grave assumption of absurdities as solid and reasonable facts with which we are familiar in his works. By a reverse process, when talking to a serious point, or narrating some experience not especially ludicrous in itself, there is a lingering suspicion of humorous possibilities in his manner, which, assisted by the slow, emphatic, natural drawl of his speech, leads one to accept actual facts of a prosaic kind as delicious absurdities. In fine, it is a sort of wizardry that he exercises in conversation, stimulating the hearer by its quick mutations of drolling and earnest.

The life that this Nook Farm literary group have shaped for themselves and their friends is a quiet and retired one. The world does not see much of it, though they see a good deal of the world. The part of Hartford where they live is on the

rolling hill to the west of the railroad, laid out in broad streets, with brick houses embowered in the trees of their lavishly spacious grounds; it is the main district apportioned to residences, in fact, and a very attractive district too. Many of these houses are of the old type—square and bare, with small rectangular cupolas on top, one the counterpart of the other, like boxes containing some mysterious piece of machinery for running the family affairs; but they look eminently comfortable, and at night you see their private gas lamps in porch or veranda, at the end of the driveway, throwing out a cheerful glow. But the new architecture asserts its power over the more recent buildings, and one begins to discern how picturesque even a practical New England city may become in the future. Like Boston, Hartford is accused of having a frigid social atmosphere, but others say that it is very warm and encouraging: a thing like this is as difficult to define as the New England climate. At all events, the inhabitants are, I believe, fond of the usual gayeties of society; and although there is so much accumulated wealth among them, it is said that money has very little to do with the standing of persons in any of the various circles of the local world. A commendable sentiment of democracy seems to prevail, and there is little tendency to ostentation. That particular circle which takes the Nook Farm group within its compass has a fondness for amusement clubs—the Surprise Party and the As You Like It, two of these organizations have been named—consisting of about twenty members, that meet fortnightly at each other's houses, and bring guests to about twice their own number. There is also a large theatre in the city, where most of the notable actors playing in New York and Boston give performances in passing.

On the evening of my arrival, as it chanced, I was taken to the Monday Club, to which Warner and Mark Twain both belong; so, too, does their friend General Hawley, who, after being a lawyer, a journalist, a military leader, a Governor, is now a Senator of the United States, and continues his editorial connection. Of him it is related that, when the war broke out and the first call was issued for volunteers, he made several attempts to write an adequate editorial sustaining the call; then suddenly throwing down his pen, he exclaimed to his associates, "Boys, I'm going to do the fighting for this office; you must run the paper." Forthwith he went out and enlisted, and now enjoys the honor of having been the first volunteer from Connecticut. At the Monday Club was present another distinguished officer, General William B. Franklin, who commanded a corps in the Army of the Potomac. We had, besides, an ex-mayor of Hartford, a professor of Trinity College, two Congregational ministers, a second journalist, the State Attorney, and two other members. I am particular in this enumeration because the whole thing was so significant. Here were these gentlemen, busy citizens of a small city, representatives of what Matthew Arnold calls "the great middle-class public of America," coming together quite informally to exchange views—on what subject? Of all things the least likely to occur to an uninformed observer like Mr. Arnold, the subject was England in Egypt. There was no regular debate, but each person spoke in order, setting forth his opinions in few words or many, with occasional breaks of dialogue as the mood prompted. Two or three had been in Egypt, and had made observation for themselves. The rest had read and thought. What was interesting was the amount of careful knowledge and reflection developed in the course of an hour and a half; the Eastern question and possible policies affecting it were treated as comprehensively as if they had been matter of home politics, instead of something as remote from our own affairs as could well be chosen. To an American this is not a startling phenomenon. Why should it be? But it is a good illustration of what goes on in those smaller cities and towns concerning which there has of late been discussion with foreigners who insist upon knowing all about them by intuition.

Alert intelligence and varied activity have always characterized Hartford, and a local vein of literature is traceable from the close of the Revolution down. Here that group of writers assembled who made a reputation under the name of the Hartford Wits: John Trumbull, author of "McFingal," the ponderous mock-heroic poem of the war of Independence; Timothy Dwight, who produced an epic on "The Conquest of Canaan"; and Joel Barlow, whose "Columbiad" has successfully resisted the author's attempt to install it among the world's classics. Lesser lights, who co-operated with these in satirical effusions that had a political value, were Lemuel Hopkins, David Humphreys, and Richard Alsop. The house of Mrs. Sigourney is still standing, and her bust may be seen in the rooms of the Historical Society; it has a serene expression, as if the original had never suffered from that infliction which her poems imposed on the rest of the world. Here, too, Noah Webster lived, thought out his impossible etymologies, and compiled his dictionary. S. G. Goodrich, who employed Hawthorne in his early days to write the "Peter Parley" geography, and then published it as his own, was a resident of Hartford; so was the disappointed poet James Percival. Edmund Clarence Stedman, who so immortally sang John Brown, and has given us the best book of criticism upon the Victorian poets, came from Hartford; and one of its later representatives in current literature is Mr. Bishop, the new novelist. The town is plentifully supplied with arsenals for future authors in its several libraries, which have made a sort of treaty with one another to follow out special lines, in order not to conflict. The Hartford is a popular subscription concern, which supplies the reading immediately in demand; the State library at the Capitol is chiefly devoted to law, in which its collections are peculiarly complete, including many rarities. At Trinity College the library is especially strong in classics; the Theological Institute embraces religious and archæological works; and the Watkinson gives its attention more to general literature of a standard sort. The Historical Society, too, has a special accumulation of its own. Together, they contain something over a hundred thousand volumes. In artistic development the city has not been so forward. The Wadsworth Athenæum (in the same building with which are the Hartford, the Watkinson, and the Historical libraries) contains a few old pictures; among them some interesting landscapes by Thomas Cole, and a portrait of Benjamin West by Sir Joshua; but the institution appears to be lifeless. A branch of the Decorative Art Society, however, has lately been established; and Hartford has produced several painters who have gained a good standing: Gedney Bunce, the colorist, who treats Venetian fishing-boats with strong poetic feeling; Gordon Trumbull, who is called one of the best American fish painters; and the great landscape painter, F. E. Church.

When one reflects upon the literary associations of Hartford, and the number of things in which it has shown excellence or commendable energy—on one side its humane establishments, including that where the deaf-mute children lead with so much good cheer their life of silent imagery, and on the other its hum of factories, producing all manner of things, from paper, pins, paper barrels, to machinery, revolvers, and Gatling guns (the invention of a Hartford citizen) — one is led to ask what is the cause of it all. Perhaps the character of the place is in part explained by the fact that of Rev. Mr. Hooker's company "many were persons of figure, who had lived in England in honor, affluence, and delicacy," but likewise did not shrink from the hardship of their journey hither on foot through the wilderness. They knew how to build up the centre of a commonwealth with force and enterprise, as well as with refinement; and their spirit has survived. But be the causes what they may, Hartford offers perhaps our best example of what an American city may become, when it is not too large for good government, when it avoids stagnation, preserves the true sentiment of a democracy, cares well for education and literature, and has had two centuries and a half of free and favorable growth.

Lobsters and Lobster Pots
(1889)

LOBSTERS AND LOBSTER POTS.

BY JOHN L. ROGERS.

 T' was one evening in the latter part of November, and Joe and myself had dropped into the store for an hour's smoke, where we always found entertainment which we enjoyed much more than any the city could furnish.

"Whose store," do you ask? Why "the store," to be sure. In a country town or large village one speaks of "Smith's" or "Brown's;" but in a very small village boasting only of one or two mercantile establishments the term "the store" is sufficiently lucid, and such was the case in the little Maine fishing hamlet which we had visited in August, intending to stay two weeks; but we were so pleased with the place and found so much that was novel, original and quaint to interest us that we had decided to remain till the holidays.

Among the constant attendants at the store in the evening was Bill Gardner, in checked jumper and number eleven boots, who talked continuously, even in his sleep, they said. He used to make us extremely weary, but we made allowances for him as he was unable to read; and besides his talk was harmless, for no one ever listened to him if he could help it. "Ole Cap'n Maker" was always on hand, but it was a mystery to us why he walked the half mile from his house down on "Bug P'int" only to drop off into a nap immediately after saying "Evenin'" or "Howday." But he did, and his snoring could be heard like bugle blasts above the conversation, no matter how loud.

Bije Tuttle had missed but three nights from the store in two years, and that was when he had a "risin'" in his ear. Bije was full of reminiscences and (usually) rum. No one could spin a yarn or state a startling fact but Bije would start up, always commencing with "That remin's me of ther time ——." Bije could always tell a bigger yarn than anyone else, but as Pete Brush frequently affirmed, "He'd

orter, fur he allers waits till the others as hed ther say."

On this particular evening, after politics had been carefully discussed and the question whether the person the stage had left that afternoon at Captain Buck's was his wife's sister-in-law who lived "up to ther west'ard" had been argued but not settled, conversation drifted around to lobsters.

On hearing lobsters mentioned Captain Maker, who had recently come in and was only partly asleep, roused himself, for he was, to a certain extent, authority on that kind of fish.

"What's ther biggest lobster you ever see, cap'n?" asked Jones' boy.

"Well, my boy, I'll have ter think," and the old man straightened up, shifted his quid and tried to look wise. Then, continuing, "I guess ther biggest one I ever see was one we ketched 'bout eleven years back—lobsters was lobsters in them days. Me an' Tish Gardner was goin' pardners. It was early in ther Fall, an' we sot our pots putty clost in shore. We had one string to ther east'ard er Duck Island, an' one day we'd hauled about half on it when we pulled up a pot with the biggest lobster in it ever was. He'd got nigh onto half way inter ther pot, an' seein' he couldn't get no further he'd tried ter get out, but got stuck and ther he was wedged in tight. I biled him, an' Abel Wyman's woman she said he was ther sweetest lobster she ever eat. How much did he weigh? Well, we put him onter ther scales, but I most forget now what he did weigh, an' if I told ye I'm afeared yer'd think I was a-lyin'; but anyway I remember that we cut his tail in slices crossways, like as we would a steak cod, an' ther meat in his claws was thicker'n through than my thumb. We had ter saw his shell afore we could git inter him, an' Bill Holt he took a half of one of his big claws an' made a cod line fast to it in three places an' used ter draw water from ther well in it. 'Twould hold nigh onter two gallon."

This remarkable narrative made such an impression on those present that at its close there were several minutes' oppressive silence, broken only by the noise made by Jones' boy. Finally, all eyes turned instinctively toward Bije Tuttle.

"Well," said Bije, "I never see no sech big lobster as that. But that remin's me of the time last summer when I see a pretty knowin' one. It was down near Rockland, to Ed Ackley's ; you remember he married my sister Mary, cap'n. Well, I was ther a visitin' last summer fer a spell, an Ed he had a tame lobster, ther only one I ever see or hear'n tell on either. He'd had him then 'long about four months. He was a bilin' some one day, and this one seemed so kind er knowin' like that he saved him and took him up ter ther house. Ed lived close to ther water, and 'twan't long afore Jim— they called him Jim—got acquainted with all ther family, and seemed ter enjoy his-self fust rate. He used ter crawl down ter ther water onct or twict er day fer er swim, and then he'd go back to ther house and lay on ther piazzer and sleep with one eye open. Why, Jim got that way so he liked ter chaw terbacker.

"But Jim was fond er music, an' when Ed sung or whistled ther ' Juba' or ' Shoo Fly,' he'd lay on his back and keep time flappin' his tail on ther floor. But ther pore feller died while I was there. It happened this way : Jim got to be quite a—not a watch dog but a watch lobster— an' one day a young dude from ther ho-tel—one of those fellers with short pants an' long stockin's an' his hair cut steve-dore — ain't it ?—no, pompeydour — well, this feller he come down ter ther house one arternoon with er big black-an'-white haound with long hair, an' went up on ther piazzer an' knocked on ther door. He didn't get no answer, so he made bold an' went in. Well, Jim was there kinder dozin', an' he didn't say nothin' when ther dude went in, but when ther haound started ter foller, Jim he up an' grabbed him by ther tail with his right claw—no, 'twar his left one, warn't it ? No, I was right afore, it was his right one.

"Well, ther haound give a yell an' started straight 'cross lots, an' jest as he wos a jumpin' ther stone wall what di-vided the skule lot from Lize Brown's place—Jim hangin' on ter his tail all ther time, mind ye—he slatted Jim up agin' a rock, an' he cracked his shell an' hurt his-self so he let go his grip on ther tail. Well, Ed come an' tuk Jim home an' laid him on ther piazzer in his old place. But, bless ye, they couldn't do nothin' for him. Pretty soon he kinder groaned, rolled

over onter his back an' looked up ter Ed in a knowin' way. Ed he knew what Jim wanted, an' whistled ther ' Juba,' an' pore Jim he flopped his tail, keepin' time all ther way through, an' then keeled over onter his side and tucked up his toes."

When Bige had finished the above anec-dote he settled down in his seat and acted as if he wished someone would intimate doubts as to the truthfulness of his story, or try to tell a more startling one. If such was the case he was disappointed, for no one seemed anxious to dispute with him for the title of the chief Ana-nias of Kennecope.

As for Joe and myself—well, we felt fatigued, and thought we would go out and seek the fresh air, take a walk up the main street, and then return to our lodg-ings.

We had bidden the little company good night and Joe was just opening the door when Captain Maker called after us :

"Don't you two gents want to go out lobsterin' with us in ther *Jane* to-morrer ? I can't agree to catch a lobster like the one Bije tells about, but like's not ye'll have a right good time. Ain't seasick, be ye ?"

We promptly accepted his invitation and assured him that, although we were not proof against *mal de mer*, it would take a pretty rough sea to cause us to pay Neptune tribute.

"Then you be on Job's Wharf at a quarter before 6 and we'll call and take ye off."

We turned in that night anticipating not only an enjoyable but an instructive outing next day, for we were not familiar with the details of lobster fishing. We were a little better informed than the Hibernian who, so says tradition, on being asked if there were any lobsters in Ire-land, replied, "Sure the say is rid with them," for we had seen the fishermen about the harbor at low tide in their dories spearing flounders and sculpins for bait ; we had seen them leave the harbor in the morning with empty tubs and return with them in the afternoon filled with lobsters, which they transferred to the cars anchored in the channel. In these they were kept till a shipment to New York was made, when they were taken out and sent away alive in barrels.

We arose unwillingly at 5 the next morning, dressing more warmly than usual, and after a hearty breakfast of baked beans, brown bread, mince pie and coffee, lighted our pipes and started down the road for Job Butler's fish wharf, a quarter of a mile distant. The air was cold but pleasant, and although half an hour before sunrise it was quite light, and over toward the "east'ard" the sky was tinted a bright red, indicating that the sun would soon be up. We had waited on the wharf about five minutes when we were startled by a yell, which for suddenness, vigor and volume would have compared favorably with a blast from a steam calliope, and soon from around the end of the wharf came a dory, manned by Sile Giddon and Enoch Parkins, Captain Maker sitting comfortably in the stern. Upon inquiry we found that the yell emanated from the vigorous Sile. "It's a way he has," explained the captain ; " an' if he didn't yell he'd bust. He can't help it ; he's built that way." Realizing the seriousness of the result if Sile did not yell, we assured him that we enjoyed it and not on any account during the day to restrain himself, and he did not.

The little schooner *Jane* was near the end of the long line of vessels in the channel, ranging from a twenty-foot catboat up to a one-hundred ton banker. In passing the boats, one after another, one could not help wondering at the paradoxical names they bore. One might expect to see on their sterns *Yankee Girl, Vixen, Tom and Jerry*, and similar names ; but if so he would be disappointed, for nearly all bore a feminine proper name of a sentimental order. There was old Jim Paterson, who, the villagers said, killed his wife by hard work and abuse in three years, and who rarely drew a sober breath, He had named his sloop the *Gertrude*. Bill Moody, who was past fifty and always went to bed at 8 o'clock, and who was so bashful that he dared not look at a woman, much less speak to one, had painted on the stern of his catboat, in large letters, *Estelle*. Thus there were the *Maud, Alice, Clarissa, Belle* and *Mabel*, and many others bearing similar names.

The *Jane* was a stiff little schooner of about twelve tons, with a roomy forecastle comfortably fitted up. In a few minutes we had got under way and were nearly out of the harbor, abreast of the lighthouse. Enoch commenced to build a fire and Joe and I helped him, as we were cold and anxious to get warmed up ; but we beat a hasty retreat to the stern when Enoch started to hurry up the fire already burning by pouring in kerosene out of a two-gallon jug which was nearly full. Upon our return we remonstrated with him on his carelessness, but desisted when he presented the powerful argument that there was no danger, for he had used kerosene that way "for mor'n ten year, an' never had no trouble." The stove looked like a relic of mediæval times, and, of course, was a stranger to blacking and was covered with a thick coating of dirt ; but if the captain's statements could be relied on it was the most remarkable stove in existence, inasmuch that he occasionally used rocks for fuel instead of coal, and the only reason why he did not burn them altogether was that they made too hot a fire, except when the mercury was down below zero.

After the fire was well started Enoch filled up the tea kettle and put it on the stove, and then put in the tea with reckless prodigality, throwing it in by the handful from a quantity he had in a large paper bag. The tea kettle baffled description. To quote from the prospectus of a new invention, "it should be seen in order to be appreciated."

After getting warmed we stood on the forecastle steps, where we could see all that was going on and be comfortable at the same time. There was a stiff easterly breeze and the *Jane* made good time toward the grounds, which were about eight miles from the harbor.

After an hour's sail, devoid of special incident, Enoch, who was up forward, cried out, "Thar 'tis, right ter larb'rd ! " and looking in the direction he pointed we saw a large buoy painted blue and white, which marked one end of the first string of pots. The captain brought the *Jane* up into the wind, while Sile and Enoch pulled the dory which had been in tow alongside, and putting a tub into it they steered off to haul the pots, the captain commencing to "jog" first on one tack and then on the other, always keeping within a few hundred yards of the dory, in order to render assistance, should any be needed.

We were near enough to the dory the greater part of the time to observe the movements of the men, and by watching them closely, coupled with what information we already had and what we obtained from the captain, we were soon in possession of the following facts :

The pots were about four feet in length

and made of laths nailed to a frame of withes bent in such a manner that the top and sides were rounding, forming a little more than half a circle, while the bottom was flat. Each end was unlathed, but in it there was a knitted arrangement of fish line fastened to the outside edges and drawn in toward the centre of the pot, forming a sort of cone-shaped tunnel, which ended in a round entrance hole about six inches in diameter.

In the centre of the pot and about a foot from each entrance hole there was suspended from a cord a piece of wire called the "needle," on which was strung the bait, which was cod or haddock heads, small flounders or the festive sculpin. The pots were fastened to a strong line at a distance of about fifteen fathoms, or ninety feet, apart, each line usually having forty and sometimes fifty pots attached, and was called a "string." The strings were anchored fast at each end by a killeck, which is a home-made anchor, consisting of a rock held in place by stout withes, a couple of buoys or "bys" marking the spot. The lobster catchers visited their pots two or three times a week when the weather permitted, but not infrequently in winter would ten days or two weeks elapse before the weather would allow of a small boat venturing in safety outside the harbor. Frequently, after a storm, the lobsterman would find not only a great number of his pots broken almost beyond repair, from having been smashed against the rocks at the bottom of the sea, but oftentimes a whole string would be lost, involving not only a loss of about $50, but the time necessary to make new gear, for the pots were not an article of commerce but were made by the fishermen as they needed them.

Upon coming in the harbor with his lobsters the fisherman would put them in his car, which lay in the channel, where they would remain till they were sent by express alive to some New York commission merchant. The cars are usually made of plank, although old dories are often utilized by boarding over and leaving their sides and bottom full of holes. Sometimes the lobsters remain in the cars several weeks, perhaps a thousand in a space containing not more than two hundred cubic feet, and they are well fed. The local authorities seem to differ in regard to the effect keeping them in the car any length of time has on lobsters. Some think that they lose in weight and

become flabby, while others maintain that they come out of their confinement in better condition than they were when put in. It would seem natural, however, that to deprive a lobster of his stamping ground, the bottom of the ocean, and to put him in a box in shoal water already full of his brethren and sisters, could not fail to have a bad effect on him—not morally, but from a gastronomical point of view.

All the lobsters in Kennecope that were sent away were shipped to New York, as prices were much better in that market than in those nearer home. Indeed, the fishermen often received much more per pound from the commission men than the retail price in Boston, although, of course, it would be difficult to decide whether or not it was a "bait."

There were no official lists or bulletins published or otherwise obtainable on the lobster market, and as prices went up and down in an inscrutable manner, apparently regardless of the supply and demand and the weather, it was difficult to a person of only ordinary intelligence to know when to ship to the best advantage, and as the majority of the fishermen belonged to this class they shipped haphazard whenever the fancy took them, sometimes sending off six or seven barrels at once and then allowing the lobsters to accumulate in the cars for a month or more.

Occasionally a man would receive a large sum when he got returns from a shipment, and then that particular commission man would get about all the consignments for the next week; but, strange to say, the price would almost invariably drop about the time the lobsters reached New York. It was at least singular that when Jim and John shipped lobsters on the same train, consigned to men in business under the same roof, and received their returns by the same mail, Jim's check would be double the amount of John's, especially in view of the facts that there was no superiority in one man's lobsters over another's and that there was no skill necessary in packing.

The amounts received for a barrel of lobsters weighing 140 pounds varied from $5 to $17 net, and averaged about $10; but in years gone by the returns often were as high as $28 per barrel.

When Sile and Enoch left the schooner in the dory they rowed a short distance till they reached the buoy, and then taking their positions, Sile in the bow and

Enoch just back of him, commenced hauling. Well forward in the bow of the dory there was fastened a strong wooden wheel or roller about six inches in diameter, with a deep groove in its edge. Sile hauled up the line to which the lines attached to the pots were fastened, and putting it into the groove of the roller both pulled hand over hand till the first pot was reached, Sile pulling it into the boat and removing the old bait and stringing fresh on the needle, while Enoch took out the lobsters, throwing the very small ones overboard and putting the others into the tub. Then they put the pot overboard and hauled along up to the next one. It was hard, tedious work. The water was so rough that frequently the dory would not be seen from the schooner, and it was so cold that the spray froze on the men's clothing almost as soon as it struck. There were fifty pots on the string, necessitating a haul of nearly a mile ; but in about an hour and a half they had finished the string and returned to the *Jane*, when they put the tub nearly full of lobsters on deck and went below to get warm internally and externally through the medium of the hot tea and still hotter fire. In a quarter of an hour they started off again, and reversing their positions in the dory commenced hauling the second string, and becoming tired of watching their somewhat monotonous movements we turned our attention to the captain.

Captain Maker had been lobstering "off an' on" for nearly fifteen years, usually turning his attention to lobsters in the fall, as soon as the cold weather commenced and prices started upward, and continuing until spring, when he would go fresh fishing in the *Jane*, taking with him a crew of three or four men. In former years he went mackereling and halibutting, but as these fish became scarce he alternated between swordfishing and haddocking for a few seasons. For the past five years, however, owing to the uncertainty of swordfishing, he had fished for cod and haddock exclusively. He was an interesting old man ; a typical fisherman, in his big boots, patched clothes and sou'-wester ; bluff and rough, but giving ample evidence of the possession of a warm heart. He was the most original, versatile and artistic user of profanity I ever met ; so much so that if a strongly religious person, and one who was at the same time a lover of the unique and original, had

heard some of his choicest expressions, it would have been an open question whether he would have been pleased or shocked. The captain had a history which would put to shame many of the heroes of juvenile story books. He ran away from home at the age of fifteen, not because he had a yearning for the sea and his parents intended him to enter the ministry, but because his parents were both dead, and the distant relative — in name only — who housed him abused and underfed him and made his life unbearable. He shipped from Portland as cabin boy on a ship bound to Japan, but the vessel was wrecked in the Indian Ocean, and after drifting for two weeks in one of the ship's boats he and his six companions were picked up by a bark bound for San Francisco. On arriving in that port he gave up the sea, and after a year of knocking about he found himself on a Texas ranch. ; but tiring of a landsman's life he worked his way down to Galveston and shipped on a coaster bound to Philadelphia.

After working in a coal yard for six months in Philadelphia, he went as cook on a coal schooner to Portsmouth, N. H. Although then only thirty miles from his home he did not visit his friends at all, but shipped on a vessel bound to Mediterranean ports, and afterward cruised around the world till the war broke out, when he made a number of trips as pilot on a blockade runner, where he made "bar'ls of money, but blowed it all in." But he saved up a few hundred dollars, and before the war was over went back to his native place, bought a little cottage near the water and a fishing sloop, and settled down for the rest of his days as a fisherman.

The captain was well off financially for those parts ; he always had a vessel that would sail to a market as quickly as any other along that part of the coast ; he was strong and well, and took chances in venturing out fishing when his neighbors were loafing at the store ; he was very well posted on market prices, and consequently he made two dollars while the other fishermen made one. No one could truthfully say that the captain did his own housework, yet no one else did it, and he had no housekeeper to pay. He did not drink anything intoxicating, and tobacco, of which he used a vast quantity, must have been his principal item of expense.

It seemed, according to the captain's

statement, that during the war a great many vessels had trouble in getting sailors, and used decidedly questionable methods in making up their crew. He said :

"Ye see, a chap would come down to ther city from back in the country for er day, an' he'd take er walk down on ther wharves, mouth and eyes wide open. Wen he'd be er standin' gawpin at er vessel, liker not jest wishin' ter go aboord of her, then the cap'n or mate would come ter ther rail an' say, reel plessant like, 'How dy ! Come aboord an' look roun's much as ye like an' welcome.' Well, the greeney, he'd go right aboord most tickeld ter death, an' then ther caᴅ'n he'd ask him ter go below an' take er little suthin, an' of course he'd go. But he'd no sooner git down ther companion way than scat ! er blanket would be thrown over his head with some chloryform on't an' when he'd come to ther vessel would be out of sight of land."

The captain had caused the time to pass so quickly that before we were aware of it Sile and Enoch had hauled their second string and had returned to the *Jane* and renewed their attack on the tea kettle. The number of cups of hot tea they seemed capable of drinking would equal the record of a beer-drinking German student.

When they started out again for their third and last string it was nearly noon, and the wind having worked 'round to "no'th," made the water much rougher and choppier than before. The *Jane* tossed and pitched, and Joe, who had been looking a little off color for some time, edged apparently carelessly toward the bowsprit. There he was shielded from observation, but did not remain long at his post. He soon sought the seclusion of one of the bunks, and was very quiet for the rest of the trip.

A little before 2 o'clock the last string had been hauled, the lobsters were in the tubs on deck, the dory fast astern and the *Jane* with wind abeam was making good time for home. Sile and Enoch went below to eat the lunch they had brought with them and to empty the tea kettle for the third time, after which they enjoyed a well-earned smoke, and then went on deck to sort and count their lobsters. Each man had a short stick with a deep notch cut in the side, two and one-

half inches long, which is the length of a marketable lobster. They sorted the lobsters out, putting the large ones into one tub and those under the legal size into another, keeping the small ones only till they reached their car, giving anyone a mess who was on hand to take them away and then throwing the remainder overboard. The small ones would not average an inch under size and they seldom had recourse to the measuring stick, as they had culled out the very small ones thoroughly when taking them from the pots. On completing their work they announced that they had one hundred and eighty-seven "counters" or lobsters over legal size. As that made each man's share about $8 it was not a bad day's work, although it really represented the labor of two or three days. The men had no sooner finished sorting than a sloop came alongside and the owner, Peter Wildes, sang out, "How many did ye git, boys?" and the truthful Sile promptly answered, "Forty-three, Uncle Pete."

Lobsters are more or less migratory, and consequently each man guards a good locality when he finds one as zealously as an urchin a favorite shiner hole, and he is also anxious to know how his neighbors are doing.

When we were about half way home we passed a number of dories, and upon learning that their owners rowed to and from their strings our sympathy was transferred from Sile and Enoch to the men who were obliged to row eight or ten miles and haul their pots without the comparative luxury of a warm forecastle and hot tea.

The *Jane* was made fast to her moorings, and the captain and Enoch started for the car with the lobsters, while Sile rowed us ashore in a dory which he borrowed from the next vessel. He left us where we had embarked with a cordial invitation to take another trip some time, and with a parting yell moved up the "crick" toward his home.

We would have known it was 3 o'clock as we started up the road even if our watches had not apprised us of the fact, for on the top of Spun Hill was Rhueben Gill, driving down into the village with the daily mail, and Rhueben had carried the mails for fifteen years, and had never, except when the roads were blocked with snow, been five minutes late.

The New North-East
(1895)

THE NEW NORTH-EAST.

by

Winfield M. Thompson.

THE man who goes into the New Northeast for even a short stay comes back an enthusiast though he goes a cynic. His blood quickens the moment he leaves Bangor, and by the time Katahdin looms into his vision across South Twin Lake he forgets himself in his contemplation of the incomparable picture of lake, forest and mountain. He begins to chat with the conductor and the porter, and even goes into the vestibule for a few moments' talk with the brakeman about the best places for fishing and shooting. He is informed that from the little station at which the train is slowing up as he talks — Norcross, near the famous North Twin Dam — four hundred deer, six moose and seven caribou were shipped for sportsmen in the shooting season of 1894. He revolves these figures in his mind as the train plunges on through the woods in the gloaming, and smokes in ecstatic reverie until the train arrives at Houlton and he finds himself in the famous farming section of the Aroostook. If he cares to go further, he may ride sixty miles north to Caribou, but he can proceed at leisure if he desires, and he probably decides to stop off and see the country.

Beginning at Houlton one may journey north one hundred and fifteen miles by rail and road, through an almost unbroken belt of splendid farms to Fort Kent, the most northern town in New England. The way lies for the most part through border town-ships in the fruitful valley of the St. John River. Practically all of Aroostook County's famous farms lie within twenty-five miles of the New Brunswick border, and the fences of many mark the line. The streams all run northeast, and give their waters to the tributaries of the St. John, which join that river a few miles east of the border.

The first impressions of the traveller are most pleasing. There is an open-handed cordiality on the part of the people which wins the stranger at once. They are warm-hearted, hard-working Yankees, without axes to grind, and their greeting is free from guile. They are not " promoting " town sites or starting mortgage loan companies. Chances for investment are to be found in the county in abundance, splendid opportunities for making fortunes in manufacturing, and if capitalists are inclined to come and secure them, the thrifty Aroostook people are certainly ready to meet them half way. The spirit of the pioneer still lives, for the region is yet new, and it is safe to say there are more workers and fewer financiers in Aroostook than in any other newly settled section in the United States.

Most people locate Aroostook vaguely as "down in the Maine woods." To be exact, Aroostook County lies between the forty-fifth and forty-eighth parallels of latitude, not so far north as Belgium and Holland. It is as large as the state of Massachusetts, leaving out Cape Cod, its area being six thousand eight hundred square miles, and that of Massachusetts seven thousand two hundred miles. It is larger than Connecticut and Rhode Island combined. It is one hundred and twenty miles in extreme length and one hundred and five miles wide in its widest part. It contains four million three hundred and fifty-two thou-

ered with a heavy growth of spruce, pine, hemlock, cedar and various hard woods, yellow birch, which is a beautiful wood, being especially abundant. The streams of the county afford unlimited water power, which is as yet practically undeveloped, the public attention being absorbed by agriculture.

In Aroostook one instinctively falls into the habit of figuring on the size of crops until he almost finds himself computing the yield of potatoes per acre in his sleep. The potato is the sign and symbol of Aroostook's life and prosperity. It is the staple product of the county, has made the farmers rich, and promises to make

A TYPICAL AROOSTOOK POTATO FIELD.

sand acres of land, of which three hundred and twenty-five thousand acres, or only about one thirteenth, have been improved. This leaves more than four million acres of unsettled land in the county, or enough to give a homestead plot of about six acres to every person in the state of Maine. The most of this wild land is as well adapted to cultivation as that already settled, and the yielding capacity of the poorest of it, susceptible of cultivation at all, is equal in value of crops to that of the best prairie land in the West. In addition to its vast agricultural resources, Aroostook is immensely rich in lumber, the most of its four million acres of wild land being cov-

the six thousand eight hundred square miles of northern Maine one of the most notable agricultural sections in the United States.

It has been urged against this far northeastern territory that the winters are so long and cold that the soil is capable of raising nothing but potatoes. Statistics show, however, that from thirty to thirty-five bushels of wheat or sixty bushels of oats to the acre can be raised in Aroostook on the same land now given over to potatoes. Kansas raises but 13.1 bushels of wheat to the acre, as shown by agricultural reports. In sixteen years the yield has decreased from 17.2 bushels to the figure quoted. Aroostook

THE GRAIN HARVEST.

land will yield two hundred and fifty bushels of potatoes to the acre. With wheat at forty cents a bushel and potatoes at the same figure, the Kansas farmer gets $5.24 an acre for his crop, while the Aroostook farmer gets $100 an acre for his. The Aroostook farmer raises potatoes instead of wheat, because he cannot afford to waste his time on grain when his land will produce potatoes in such enormous quantities. In Aroostook at least two hundred bushels of potatoes can be looked for to the acre, and often crops run more than three hundred bushels. In some instances more than

raised seven hundred and thirty-eight bushels of potatoes on one acre, taking two prizes, one of $500 and one of $600. Fred S. Wiggin and Delano Moore of Presque Isle raised five hundred and thirty-seven and five hundred and twenty-three bushels per acre respectively in the same year. In 1890 Philo Reed in Fort Fairfield raised seven hundred and forty-three bushels and twenty-five pounds on a single acre. The crop of the county last year was about eight million bushels, worth to the farmers about $3,500,000. If the farmer does not want to till his land, he raises hay, two tons to the acre,

THE VALLEY OF THE AROOSTOOK, NEAR NEW BRUNSWICK.

seven hundred bushels have been raised on a single acre, and a yield of five hundred bushels is by no means rare. In 1889 Charles B. Coy of Presque Isle

of a quality that brings $2 a ton more in the market than other hay, and in this way he realizes at least $30 an acre from his land. With industry and mod-

HON. LLEWELLYN POWERS.

furrow, drops fertilizer and a certain amount of seed at given intervals, and covers them all, as a pair of horses walk along, or a machine that hoes a whole row of potatoes in five minutes, or another that digs them at harvest time with equal facility. In his household the farmer is also liberal; his home is always comfortably and often luxuriously furnished; the piano is there, and everything necessary to give his children comfort and education. The bicycle flourishes; and the head of the house indulges his love for horseflesh by the ownership of well-bred driving and work horses. He pays cash for what he buys, he belongs to a grange, he takes the papers, and is up to date.

So much for the farmer. What does the county offer the settler? It offers him quicker and greater returns for his labor, I think, than any other section in the country. Unfortunately for the settler and for the northern section as well, the public lands of Maine have all been given away or sold. Wild land may be had at low figures, however. In Aroostook County land may be bought near the towns from three to five miles out, and in some places along the railroad for from $3 to $5 an acre. It lies just as the woodsman who stripped it of its heavy timber left it when he shouldered his axe and walked out. A good name

erate sagacity he can lay aside money even in the poorest years, and that is the reason why the visitor finds him contented.

In keeping with his prosperity, the Aroostook farmer stints himself in nothing that will facilitate his work. He buys the most modern machinery for planting and harvesting, and all the tools used about the place are the best. The stranger from many another section of New England finds pleasure in watching the operation of a machine that makes a

A NORTH AROOSTOOK SCENE.
POTATO FARM, SAW MILL AND STARCH FACTORY ON ONE ESTATE.

and an axe are about all a smart man needs to make his way on this wild land. A few hundred dollars will certainly help him, but he need not give up so long as he has simply health and backbone. Land-owners are willing to sell to settlers with twenty-five per cent of the price paid down, and wait for the crops to pay the balance. It costs $10 an acre to clear the land, and ten acres may be cleared and planted with potatoes the first year. The wood on the land, sold for lumber, spools and last blocks, will often pay the purchase price. In four years the settler, by industry and thrift,

do not fail. Drought does not affect them owing to the nature of the soil. The chief cause of diminution in the yield is rust, caused by hot, moist weather in August, but this is seldom serious enough to destroy a crop. The soil of Aroostook County is a rich vegetable loam, free from stones, which lies from two to three feet deep over a stratum of calcareous limestone and slate. This formation lies on edge, so to speak, and is full of fissures which absorb the moisture in wet weather, and give it up again when the ground becomes dry and heated by the sun. As the rock formation contains

WATER WORKS AND ELECTRIC LIGHT PLANT, CARIBOU.

can pay for a good farm and buildings, and become comfortably established. Aroostook is still such a new country that the poor settler may live in a log house within five miles of a village, and nobody will think it strange. The most of his more prosperous neighbors started that way.

We dwell on these particulars because we believe many in New England will be interested to know that right here among us is a new, rich, undeveloped country as promising as any in the great West.

Suppose the crops were to fail the first year! some anxious intending settler might exclaim. The crops in Aroostook

a great quantity of lime, the land of Aroostook never " runs out." Fertilizers are freely used, however. In its general characteristics the soil is the same as that in the famous Genesee and Shenandoah valleys.

The surface of Aroostook County rolls gently in beautiful dome-shaped hills, which give a pleasing diversity to the scenery, and afford warm, productive slopes. The highest elevation is Mars Hill, eighteen hundred feet high, about midway up the border range of townships.

All the farms of Aroostook are marked at intervals with elm trees standing alone or in groups, which add much to the

ON THE CARIBOU TOWN FARM.

beauty of the scenery. The elm is the distinctive tree of the settled portions of Aroostook, and seems to attain a greater height there than in other parts of the state. Its beautiful slim trunk and graceful branches are seen in chaste and exquisite outlines all the way from Wytopitlock to Madawaska. It is with a sense of delight that one looks out on a bright summer morning over a stretch of undulating Aroostook farm land, marked off in great squares by straight fences, the neat farm buildings telling of peace and plenty, the hardy green of the potato fields giving a softer color to the grass, the slim branches of the elms waving gently in the breeze, and soft clouds floating lazily out of the north, casting shadows over the country as they sail along.

One observes in the New Northeast three modes of life, distinct yet blending naturally, and without sharply drawn social lines. There is the life of the woods and streams, that of the farms, and that of the towns. Aroostook County has a quartet of large towns, Houlton, Presque Isle, Caribou and Fort Fairfield, which are as progressive as any in the East, and most attractive places to live in. Since the opening of the Bangor and Aroostook Railroad the growth of the towns has taken on new impetus, and the time is not far away when one, and perhaps two of them, will secure a city charter. Before the building of the

new railroad these towns, with the country back of them, were obliged to look to the Canadian Pacific Railroad for transportation. The road operated from its New Brunswick division a branch to Houlton and another to Fort Fairfield, Presque Isle and Caribou. A roundabout route through New Brunswick was the best offered the Aroostook people who desired to go down the state; and all their potatoes, general produce and manufactured lumber had to be shipped in bond under manifest over this foreign road. Rates were high, owing to the absence of competition. It was therefore with manifestations of delight that the building of the new railroad was hailed.

Houlton, which is the county seat, is the sixth town in the border range, and is one hundred and forty miles from Bangor by the Bangor and Aroostook Railroad. The population of the town in 1890 was four thousand and fifteen. At the present time it is probably five thousand. Houlton was the principal military station in the " bloodless Aroostook war " over the boundary question, and the parade ground constructed there during the trouble is still to be seen. By the treaty of 1783 our northeast border was not satisfactorily defined. New Brunswick laid claim to territory that lay in Maine, and for many years the few residents there were much disturbed by the indignities put upon them by marauders who cut off the timber, and the petty officials in the provincial towns. The lower half of what is now the town of Houlton was granted by the legislature of Massachusetts in 1799 to the trustees of New Salem Academy, Massachusetts, for the use of the academy. The north half of the present town was in a tract granted to

called Hancock Barracks, and was under the immediate command of Major N. S. Clarke. All marauding and pilfering from New Brunswick ceased on the appearance of the troops. Houlton was a military post until 1845. A military road from Mattawamkeag to Houlton was begun in 1829 and completed in 1832. It was afterward extended to Presque Isle and Fort Fairfield. The view from the old Houlton parade ground is locally unequalled in extent and beauty. The state has established here a meridian line, and all surveys of the state lands in Aroostook are based on this line.

SALMON JUMPING AT CARIBOU DAM.

Williams College. A number of persons gave up their farms in Massachusetts to New Salem Academy about 1804, and took in exchange wild lands in the wilderness grant. Among them was Joseph Houlton, for whom the town was named. The troubles concerning the boundary line between Maine and New Brunswick began about 1825, and broke out in an intensified manner in 1827. In 1828 Company C of the Second Regiment of United States Infantry was encamped on what is now known as Garrison Hill, Houlton. Three other companies afterward joined Company C. The camp was

The trade centre for a great lumber region, Houlton is the home of a number of timber-land owners. One at least, Hon. Llewellyn Powers, may be entitled to the latter-day title of "lumber king." Mr. Powers owns more good timber than any other man in Houlton, if not in the state. He can count his possessions by the township, and they aggregate no less than one hundred and ninety thousand acres. The holdings of himself and his brother, Hon. Frederick A. Powers, attorney-general of Maine, amount to a quarter of a million acres. Mr. Powers was born in a log house, is a self-made

A NORTH AROOSTOOK GUIDE.

A BATTEAU PARTY.

man, and his varied experience as collector of customs, county attorney, speaker of the Maine House of Representatives, and member of Congress, has given him a thorough political training, fitting him for any office which his countrymen may call upon him to accept.

Houlton was incorporated March 8, 1831. It is a handsome town, lying on the east bank of the Meduxnekeag stream, a tributary of the St. John River. Its streets are broad, lined with handsome elms, and bordered with well-kept lawns surrounding neat and in some instances pretentious residences. There are several small streams and lakes within the border of the town. Nickerson Lake, four miles from the village, is Houlton's summer resort, and several cottages are built there. The town has a fine system of water works, electric light plant, sewers, and ample telegraph and telephone facilities. It has two national banks, a savings bank and a loan and building association, handsome business blocks and a $75,000 government building containing custom-house and post office. There are several excellent school buildings, and the church-goers are well supplied with comfortable houses of wor-

ship, the Congregational, Methodist, Baptist, Presbyterian, Free Baptist, Episcopal, Unitarian and Catholic denominations having each erected a fine church. The leading educational institution in the county, the Ricker Classical Institute, is in Houlton. It was established in 1848 as Houlton Academy. In 1877 it was made a fitting-school for Colby University. In 1886 Mrs. Catherine Wording of Grand Forks, Dakota, donated $30,000 toward the erection of a new building in memory of her husband, William E. Wording. The new school was named in honor of Rev. Joseph Ricker, D. D., who raised the endowment fund to the sum of $40,000. The new building is of brick with freestone trimmings, and is a handsome structure. There is a dormitory four stories high, which has twenty rooms for students. Houlton has always been a trading centre. There are more than a hundred mercantile establishments in the town. There are a number of manufacturing industries, including a foundry and machine shop, lumber and shingle mills, planing and wood-working mills, a woollen mill, starch factories, corn and flour mills, brickyards, etc. The town has two good hotels, and a third one is being built.

ON THE AROOSTOOK.

Presque Isle is pleasantly situated on Presque Isle stream, a mile and a half from the Aroostook River, which flows through the northern part of the township. The country around the village is a little more rolling than further south. The fertile farms and diversity of scenery delight the eye, while the Aroostook climate,

THE CHURCH AT NEW SWEDEN.

rare and invigorating, seems here at its best. Fogs and protracted periods of dampness are not known in Aroostook; the air is surprisingly clear and fresh, and summer or winter there is a uniformity of temperature not noticeable in other parts of New England. This steadiness in the temperature makes the winters delightful, though they

are long and cold. Snow comes before the ground is frozen and stays until spring, affording good sleighing and a trackless highway through the woods and over the lakes and streams. As soon as the snow disappears in the spring, the farmers put in their seeds, and summer activity at once begins.

Presque Isle has been twice destroyed by fire since 1860, the last time in 1884. It has made headway in spite of adversity, however, and is now a prosperous and inviting village, with a population of four thousand. The town was settled in 1828. In 1860 its population was about seven hundred. In 1883 it was united with the town of Maysville, and in 1890 its population was about three thousand. The part of the town which retains the name of Maysville contains some of the finest farms in Aroostook. A few years ago, seven hundred and twenty-eight bushels of potatoes were raised on a single acre in this town. St. John's English and Classical School is located here, and the town has a fine high school in a new $21,000 building. It

BUILDINGS OF A SWEDISH IMMIGRANT WHO MADE HIS START IN 1870.

has six churches, a national bank, a trust company, admirable stores for an interior town, a good hotel, an electric light system, water works, and excellent water power, from which are operated saw and grist mills and starch factories. The town is a shipping point for thousands of barrels of potatoes and tons of starch. Mr. T. H. Phair, who is said to be the leading starch manufacturer in the world, resides in Presque Isle. He owns six starch factories in different parts of the county, as well as four lumber mills and several farms. He is also one of the leading shippers of potatoes in the county. Mr. Phair came to Aroostook when a lad, from the state of New York,

unmarketable potatoes, which are hauled directly from the fields. For these the farmer gets from fifteen to twenty-five cents a bushel, which is clear gain, for without the starch factories he could do nothing with the small potatoes in his crop. A bushel of small potatoes will yield about eight pounds of starch.

The process of making starch is very simple, the chief essential being plenty of clean water. The potatoes are washed and grated by machinery, and the waste taken away on an endless sieve. The starch filters down through the sieve and is washed along to vats, where it is allowed to settle. When it is settled, the water is drawn off and the starch

FORT KENT, THE MOST NORTHERLY TOWN IN NEW ENGLAND.

and he worked himself upward from the humble place of boy in a general store.

Aroostook supplies fully two thirds of the potato starch manufactured in the United States, its annual output being from five ·thousand to eight thousand tons. Last year Mr. Phair manufactured fifteen hundred tons in his six factories. The starch is sold principally in cotton-manufacturing centres, being used for sizing cotton goods. It is the best made, being much stronger than that made elsewhere. There are between forty and fifty starch factories in Aroostook County, and they grind up from a million to two million bushels of potatoes a year. The factories run six weeks in the fall, and use the small and otherwise

shovelled out and put into a dry-house, where, after the drying has been done by steam heat, it is finally shovelled into casks for shipment. It then contains about fifteen per cent of moisture, is of a silver-white color, and is in kernels about the size of sago. The casks in which it is shipped hold from six hundred and fifty to seven hundred pounds each. The largest starch factory in the United States is situated at Monticello, the second town north of Houlton on the Bangor and Aroostook Railroad.

Fort Fairfield, reached by a thirteen-mile branch from the main line of the Bangor and Aroostook road below Presque Isle, is charmingly situated on the Aroostook River, where the stream slips over

FISH RIVER, NEAR FORT KENT.

country. Between Caribou and Houlton there exists a friendly rivalry, the business men of one seeking to outstrip in enterprise their brethren in the other. As Houlton is the distributing point for the south part of the county, Caribou is for the north, and the same causes have contributed to the growth of both towns.

the border and into the St. John. The town is full of reminiscences of the border difficulties, for during the trouble it was a garrison post. In the winter of 1838–39, the state troops, striking the Aroostook River at Masardis, after marching through the wilderness from Bangor, came down on the ice, and built here the fort which was named Fort Fairfield in honor of John Fairfield, governor of Maine at that time. From this fort the town derived its name. The town was incorporated in 1858. In 1850 its population was four hundred. In 1890 it was over thirty-five hundred. Now it is about four thousand. The town has a fine system of water works, and is lighted by electricity generated at Caribou, twelve miles away. The falls of the Aroostook are only three miles from the village, and a splendid water power is idle there. Fort Fairfield has six churches, a high school, two hotels, a national bank, and commodious stores. It was in this town that the biggest crop of potatoes ever raised on a single acre in Maine was harvested.

From Fort Fairfield the trip to Caribou may be made either by the Bangor and Aroostook or Canadian Pacific Railroad. Caribou is the present terminus of the Bangor and Aroostook road, and the end of the most northern feeder which the Canadian Pacific operates in Maine. An extension of the Bangor and Aroostook road to Van Buren on the St. John, twenty-two miles, is projected, the preliminary survey having been made. This will open up a fine farming and lumber

The stranger finds it hard to decide which is the more attractive town. The scenery at Caribou is perhaps a little bolder than further south, the surface of the region swelling into splendid ridges or stretching away into beautiful valleys. The Aroostook River, the only highway of the early settlers, courses through the town to the north, then makes a sharp curve to the southeast, making the triangle at the points of which the three large northern Aroostook towns are situ-

RESIDENCE OF HON. WILLIAM DICKEY, FORT KENT.

ated. A big dam was built across the river in 1889, and enough power is generated there to run a score of mills. The only power now used from the dam is that which operates the Caribou water works pumping station and electric light plant. At the foot of the dam there is a fine salmon pool, which is attracting the attention of sportsmen far and wide.

The settlement of Caribou, which until 1877 was known as Lyndon, was due to the border trouble. Ivory Hardiston of

China, Maine, came up from the Kennebec valley in the winter of 1838–39 with a wagon load of soldiers for the Fort Fairfield garrison. He remained a year in the wilderness of township H, and was so pleased with it that he returned home and got his family to settle there. In 1842 he built a house of hewn timber and harvested his first crop. The house is still standing in the bustling town of Caribou. The town has all the "go" of a western place, and its residents claim for it the largest population in the county. It has a high school and excellent lower grade schools. It has fifty stores, excellent hotels, six prosperous churches, a library association, a banking institution, starch factories, and mills of various sorts. A large seed warehouse, from which seed potatoes are shipped all over the country, is located here. The first starch factory established in Aroostook was built here about 1874 by Albe Holmes, who came from New Hampshire. In Caribou may be found a model country newspaper office, the home of the *Aroostook Republican*. Aroostook has a number of good weekly newspapers, led by the *Republican* and the *Aroostook Pioneer*, the latter published at Houlton. Both papers recently issued handsome souvenir editions, descriptive of the region and its resources, to which the writer is much indebted.

There is a cosmopolitan flavor about Caribou not noticed in the towns further south. Here one comes in contact with the French, descendants of the Acadians who were expelled from their homes "on the shores of the basin of Minas" by the English about 1763. Their story, moulded into a classic by Longfellow, will always stir the sympathetic heart, while their descendants thrive and multiply in the fertile valleys of the far northeast. About twenty miles north of Caribou are a number of settlements of the Acadian French, which ex-

ONE DAY'S CATCH.
LARGEST TROUT, TWENTY-TWO INCHES LONG.

tend along the St. John River from Van Buren fifty miles to the northwest border, and are collectively known as the Madawaska settlements. A corresponding strip of country on the New Brunswick side of the river is also taken up by these children of the Acadians. They sprang from about two hundred refugees who made their way into the country after 1783, when they were driven from near Woodstock, further down the St. John, whither they had fled twenty years before when first turned out of their homes. The present representatives of the race preserve the tongue and

BLOCK-HOUSE AT FORT KENT.

NEAR CHESUNCOOK.

consul to Gothenburg in 1863, and twice since has been our minister to Sweden. In 1869 he was appointed one of the commissioners to settle the public lands of the state, the other commissioners being Hon. Parker P. Burleigh and Hon. William Small. Mr. Thomas went to Gothenburg, got together fifty-one persons, — twenty-two men, eleven women and eighteen children, — came to Halifax and up the St. John, and July 23, 1870, arrived with them at the spot in the forest six miles from Caribou where they were to settle. The state had cut a road through the woods, had made a clearing of one hundred and twenty-five acres, and had built six log houses for the settlers. Each house had a good cooking-stove in it. To each man the state gave one hundred acres of forest land, and in the centre of the town fifty acres were reserved, where the state constructed a building for public use. It was two stories high, and thirty by forty feet. The basement was frost proof for storing crops. The upper part was a hall, to be used as a schoolhouse and church. The settlers were so pleased with their reception that they sent for their friends, and before winter thirty-two others came. The cost of getting the colonists here and establishing them was $4,000. This was all repaid by the settlers in labor on the roads and in other ways. Not a colonist abandoned his farm. Others followed, and the colony prospered. The state erected in all twenty-six houses for the immigrants. The Swedes erected one hundred and fourteen houses up to 1876, and an equal number of barns. There are at present about one hundred and forty voters in the town. The children are all taught English, and there are no illiterate children in the town. The population of New Sweden is now more than one thousand. There are not less than sixteen hundred Swedes in the state. They have all paid their own passage, and have brought with

many of the customs of their fathers, and live in peaceful ease. They are a prolific race, families of twenty children not being unusual among them. On one occasion recently a visitor stopped at a small cabin in which there was but one room, where the happy head of the family could call around him twenty-three children. He counted fifteen houses near each other occupied by families which averaged twelve children each. The number of these people on the American side is about five thousand, and on the British side about two thousand. Those on the southern and western banks of the St. John became American citizens in 1843 by virtue of the Ashburton treaty, which settled the border trouble, and the title to their lands was confirmed to them by the same instrument.

Adjoining Caribou on the northwest is a town which is in many ways the most interesting in Aroostook County. It is called New Sweden, and is settled entirely by immigrants from Sweden who were brought here in 1870 by the state, under the direction of Hon. W. W. Thomas of Portland, who first went to Sweden as

them $100,000 in coin. New Sweden is now one of the handsomest farming towns in the state. The former immigrants live in fine houses, where they entertain all comers with open-handed hospitality, no visitor being allowed to depart without partaking of cake and coffee. They are a very religious people, Protestants, and have three neat and commodious churches, the denominations being Baptist and Lutheran. No better example is to be found of what a state may do in settling its wild lands, or what the poor

music of the lumberman's axe. The logging camps are silent in summer, and the sinewy and fleet-footed guide, who on snow-shoes in winter tends his traps in the woods, is not now to be seen. He is doubtless plying the paddle on some lake or stream, finding the haunts of the biggest and gamiest trout. Everywhere the influence of the north is felt, — in the air, the cool blue of the sky, and even in the sturdy build and bronzed skin of occasional batteau men whom one sees in the streams and lakes on the way. The

BIG GAME — NORTH TWIN DAM.

man may do for himself in Aroostook, than in the prosperous farming town of New Sweden.

A good carriage road has been recently built through New Sweden from Caribou to Fort Kent, the most northern town in Maine and in New England. The drive over this road, about fifty miles, is one of the finest in the state, taking one past beautiful lakes, over purling streams alive with trout, and through sweet and silent stretches of hardwood and evergreen forest, which in winter resounds with the

batteau is itself a boat of the north, designed to shoot any rapid that a log will float through, a strange toothpick of a craft, like a dory stretched to twice its proper length, yet buoyant and of great carrying capacity. You find them everywhere north of Bangor where lumbering operations are carried on, and the more you learn of their qualities the better you like them. They are to the lumberman what the canoe is to the guide and fisherman, — his home, vehicle and best friend.

A LUMBER CAMP AT HEAD WATERS OF THE AROOSTOOK.

In Fort Kent one finds himself in the heart of the Acadian region. The town was founded by a handful of French refugees; but though the atmosphere around it is strange and a bit foreign, the true Yankee patriotism is found there as strong and undefiled as if the town were not tucked off in the farthest northern corner of the land. Here one finds a unique personage in Hon. William Dickey, jocosely known as " The Duke of Fort Kent," who has represented the district in the state legislature for more than thirty years, and — what is more, perhaps, than any other representative in the United States can say — for fifteen years by a unanimous vote. When he went into the Madawaska region it was a wilderness without a road or bridge within fifty miles, and he has done more toward obtaining for the section the common conveniences of civilization, such as roads, bridges and general public works, than any other man. He is now eighty-five years old. The house in which he resides is in a way as interesting as himself; it was the headquarters of officers stationed on the frontier during the boundary troubles, and sheltered men who afterward became famous, including McClellan, Ricketts, McDowell and Fighting Joe Hooker. The block-house erected as part of the town's defences in 1841 still stands. The fort was named in honor of Governor Kent, and from it the town took its name. The town has communication with the outside world by way of the Temiscouta Railroad of Canada, which has its terminus at Edmundston, in New Brunswick, opposite Fort Kent, and connects with the Canadian Pacific seventy-five miles down the border. When the projected Ashland division of the Bangor and Aroostook road is extended north to its terminus, Fort Kent will have direct communication with the lower part of the state in a direct line and over American soil.

Riding down from Caribou, in a comfortable railway car of the latest pattern, the enthusiast finds himself wondering why a railroad was not built into the northeast country years ago. He looks out at the beautiful Aroostook River, which the track skirts for ten miles below Caribou, and over the smiling country on either side, and sees in the charming prospect a promise of rich reward for the corporation which has at last given easy access to this fruitful land. Others saw this promise long ago, but it took men of eloquence and energy to make people go down into their pockets to render the fulfilment possible. Those men were Hon. A. A. Burleigh and Mr. Franklin W. Cram, who are now the president and the vice-president of the railroad company. Mr. Cram is general manager of the road, and his achievement in getting the system into successful operation in a time so unpropitious as the period of depression in 1893 has drawn to him and his road the attention of railway men, and hoisted him several rounds on the ladder of fame and fortune. He worked his way up from the position of newsboy in the old Bangor station, and has lived in an atmosphere of steam and cinders all his life. He resigned as manager of the New Brunswick railway to take his present position. Aroostook County issued its own bonds to the extent of $500,000 to help start the road, and with the mortgage bonds placed in New York and money derived from stock subscriptions the money required to build and equip the road was secured. There were about one hundred and seventy miles of track laid in 1893–94, the road being completed to Caribou in December, 1894. The new road had leased the old Bangor and Piscataquis road to Moosehead Lake and Katahdin Iron Works, and it was at Brownville, on the Iron Works branch of the old road, that track-laying through the wilderness was begun. The distance from Bangor to Caribou is two hundred and seven miles, and to Houlton one hundred and forty miles. In the Fort Fairfield branch there are thirteen miles. The Ashland division will leave the main line about twenty miles west of Houlton and extend north through an unbroken wilderness to Masardis and Ashland, about forty miles, opening a new and rich country for settlement.

The Bangor and Aroostook road is the longest railroad ever chartered in Maine at one time. It is built for the heaviest traffic, with seventy-pound steel rails, and its roadbed is as good as that of any trunk line in the country. Its equipment is in every respect first-class, with cars of latest pattern and one-hundred-ton engines to draw them.

Crossing the lower part of Aroostook County, the upper part of Penobscot, and a strip of Piscataquis, the new railroad skirts some of the most beautiful lakes in the Maine wilderness, including Mattawamkeag Lake in Aroostook, South Twin Lake in Penobscot, and Seboeis and Schoodic Lakes in Piscataquis. It also crosses the east and west branches of the Penobscot River, the former at Grindstone and the latter below North Twin Dam. It is a rare sight to see the pent-up waters of the mighty West Branch come tearing over the dam and roaring down the gorge below it, as the train runs slowly over the bridge across the torrent, and one feels an irresistible desire to make a stand here and become acquainted with the region of which sportsmen have told so much. There is a famous camp near North Twin Dam, kept by Luther Gerrish, and in front of it the accommodating conductor will bring the train to a stop for passengers to alight. A low log structure is the camp, but roomy and comfortable, standing on an elevation overlooking South Twin Lake, with Katahdin looming up in the northwest. Its guide-proprietor will greet you with a friendly shake of the hand and a twinkling eye. He has bidden many people welcome to his forest home; and now that the railroad passes his door he begins to feel the need of enlarging his quarters. Often in the fall, passengers on the trains see the front of the camp fairly covered with deer hung up around the piazza awaiting shipment. The camp is in the centre of the most famous region for big game in New England. What luck sportsmen had here in the shooting season of last year — October, November and December — is indicated by the shipment of carcasses from Norcross, the shipping point for the region. From all the stations on the Bangor and Aroostook road there were shipped in the three months named one

thousand and one deer, fifty caribou and forty-five moose, and these did not represent fifty per cent of the number killed or one hundredth part of one per cent of the number running wild in the district. In fact, big game seems to be increasing there, in spite of sportsmen. Deer are so plenty and so tame, that a number have been killed on the tracks this year by the engines; and hardly a day passes but passengers on the trains catch glimpses of them in the woods. Not long ago a buck brought a train to a standstill by rushing under a car platform and setting the brakes by getting entangled in the air-hose. His carcass was hoisted into the baggage car, and the train proceeded.

The fisherman finds no less delight than the hunter in this region of the woods. Trout fill the streams and lakes, and seem waiting to be caught. There is no end to the devious waterways one may enter in quest of fish or in pursuit of the exhilarating sport of canoeing in that wonderful land of lakes and streams. The famous Bangor canoes, light, buoyant, tight craft, made of canvas and light wood and finished with some sort of enamel that makes them snag-proof, are found everywhere here. The sportsman is indebted to E. H. Gerrish, a brother of Luther Gerrish, and no less skilled than he as a guide, for these remarkable boats. In twenty years' experience as hunter, trapper and guide in the Maine woods, Mr. Gerrish formed the ideas which resulted in the production of the canoe which is now found in all the lakes and streams of northern Maine, and is becoming known all over the country.

One may enter a canoe at North Twin Dam, or at Grindstone, on the East Branch, and paddle a month in this land of lakes and streams without going out of sight of Katahdin or turning on his course. The whole northern part of Maine may be traversed by canoe with short carries. The head waters of the St. John, the Penobscot and the Kennebec almost touch each other in the region north of Moosehead Lake; and the skilled canoeist may make a summer trip from Kineo to the Bay of Fundy if so inclined.

The dominant influence of Maine's mighty mountain, Katahdin, in this northern region, is thus described by a canoeist who took a trip down the West Branch, starting at Northeast Carry, Moosehead Lake: "Old Katahdin, first seen from Moosehead Lake, then from Lobster Lake, loomed up before us continually as we came down Chesuncook. When the moon came up that evening we stood on the beach, awed by the view — the old mountain towering grandly in the night, with the sheen of the bright moon on his sides and his brow capped by clouds. There was no day on the trip that the mountain was not in sight, sometimes nearer, at others more remote; sometimes bright, then gloomy and threatening; sometimes clearly outlined, and at other times thrusting his head out of sight in the clouds. In one aspect or another old Katahdin is the presiding genius and ever-present guardian of the West Branch region."

And so, with Katahdin looming darkly over his shoulder, mysterious, immutable, grand, one swings his grip aboard the cars at Norcross, shakes hands with his hospitable guide, casts a look up the track in the direction of that wonderful valley of the north which he has traversed and marvelled at, and with a sigh of regret at leaving, drops into his cushioned seat and is whisked out of the New Northeast.

Some American Prepatory Schools (1910)

The Phillips Inn at Andover.

Formerly the home of Harriet Beecher Stowe, and now used as an inn principally by guests of the school and parents of the boys.

SOME AMERICAN PREPARATORY SCHOOLS

By Arthur Ruhl

THE Phillips Academy at Andover, the oldest of our preparatory schools, was opened in 1778 for the purpose, as Mr. Samuel Phillips, its founder, stated in its constitution, of "instructing Youth, not only in English and Latin Grammar, Writing, Arithmetic and those Sciences wherein they are commonly taught, but more especially to learn them the Great End and Real Business of Living."

These latter words are written, I suppose, above the gateway of every preparatory school to-day—over high-schools in kindly little Western towns, over fashionable Groton, St. Mark's, and St. Paul's. One can not see them perhaps, but founders and teachers and fond parents, at least, honestly believe they are there. The words are doubtless the same but their meanings must be as varied as American life to-day is varied.

When Andover was founded Washington's army was still at Valley Forge. When Exeter was founded by Mr. Samuel Phillips's brother, John, Cornwallis had not yet surrendered. And young Americans who would be playing foot-ball to-day were fighting for their lives in this world, and their souls in the next, and sitting down by

their candles each night to reproach themselves in neatly written diaries for the moments of eternity they had wasted that day.

If the real business of living was not a simple matter for a generation that had few alternatives and many necessities, it must be complicated indeed for a generation which has the time and money to live comparatively at its ease. Except for the poor, making the acquaintance of the three R's is no longer romantic. The three R's are everywhere. Boys no longer need tramp hundreds of miles to find ordinary instruction as they used sometimes to come tramping up to the New England schools clear from the Mississippi Valley. The little red school-house has followed the railroad and even the "Fresno" scraper. A boom town scarcely springs up in the Western sage-brush which hasn't a high-school almost as soon as it has a hotel and a bank. As a place for final instruction, the need for the old-fashioned "academy" has long since passed away.

Going to college, meanwhile, has become with an astonishingly varied class of boys, almost a matter of course. A vast and heterogeneous army, freed from the immediate necessity of earning a living which worried their fathers, flings itself more or less blindly each autumn into the unknown

It is in the preparatory schools, perhaps, that foot-ball is at its best. The proportion of boys who play is much larger than in

and fascinating possibilities of "college life." And you have but to glance casually at this multitude—all American citizens of to-morrow—to see that it stretches between widely separated extremes.

On the one hand is the high-school in the typical American town—the comfortable little Middle-Western city, for instance, where none is very rich nor very poor. A boy lives with his father and mother and brothers and sisters at home. He learns Gaul's three parts, and the square of a+b, and also, probably, how to take care of a furnace and shovel snow. All the varied human relationships of a home and a town still fairly homogeneous, and scarcely aware of such words as "tradesman" or "serving class," gradually shape and color his mind and character.

The Swedish carpenter's son beats him in geometry; the washer-woman's daughter knows more than he of Byron and Shakespeare. His own wit is leaden beside the repartee of the expressman, and he knows the grocery-man very well because the groceryman, who used to go to school with his father, regards him affectionately as a sort of nephew, and always asks him if he won't have a

ride when he happens to drive by. All the kindly humanity of the place steeps into him—far more, probably, than he realizes at the time. He can't quite escape observing that there is illness and failure in the world as well as foot-ball heroes and banjo clubs, and his own enthusiasms are set against a saving background of men with lines in their faces who have to hustle to pay rent and coal bills. He is part, in short, of a commonwealth instead of a cult; a school-boy instead of a college "man" in miniature.

The Commons at Andover.

This building, originally planned by the famous architect Bulfinch, later partially destroyed by fire and restored, was the old brick academy building referred to by Dr. Holmes in his poem "The School Boy."

and little—at Andover.

the colleges. There is not so much at stake and the whole atmosphere surrounding the game is more sensible and natural.

Also, probably, he is indifferently taught, crude in manners and clothes, and although he may go down to college with a general knowledge of human nature, and an instinctive democracy which his more specially prepared classmates may not acquire until years after they have left college, he goes awkwardly, like a tourist suddenly stepping into Paris or Timbuctoo.

At the other extreme is the fashionable preparatory school, cloistered away in some peculiarly agreeable and beautiful corner of the country. The little boy of twelve is taken here before he has begun, so to speak, to wake up. He may even have begun earlier and "prepared" for the preparatory. Surrounded by other little boys exactly like himself, he is shut away from the rest of the world for six impressionable years. He is taught charming manners, kept from the hurly-burly of the public school, and from temptation in so far as temptation resides in outside things.

He is trained almost as rigorously for a special rôle as if he were the son of an acrobat following his father's trade, or some rich little city girl preparing to "come out." If he isn't in the class room, he is hard at it on the foot-ball or base-ball field, or track or river. There are no loose ends or waste. Every moment is filled with carefully planned work or play, and watched over by older men—men who have travelled, alumni of the college for which he is preparing, perhaps, who have played on the teams and belonged to the clubs he hopes to play on and belong to.

Naturally he develops rapidly, and as this development is all along the line of making him a "gentleman" and a success in college, his comparative progress is astonishing. He learns loyalty to an ideal—his school, and what it stands for—when the public school-boy still considers teachers his natural enemies. He makes many delightful and valuable friends. He puts on a black coat and pumps each evening, perhaps, learns to play cricket or fives, always uses the "Sir" when addressing a master—acquires as a matter of course a thousand little agreeable graces. There is nothing "fresh" about these little gentlemen when they enter college. They come down to Cambridge or New Haven—you can tell them at a glance—as serenely almost as they might go to visit an uncle or a grown-up brother.

How far this preparation for college life is a preparation for ordinary life is, of course, another and more difficult story. If the mould into which they are run sometimes hardens around them, it is not surprising, for that was a charming place, there in the country, where all were light-hearted and polite and healthy and nice, and our ordinary world doubtless often seems badly arranged and rather tiresomely difficult.

Were these two alternatives equally practicable much might be said for either—the

The Clement House at Andover.
This old colonial house is one of those used by boys who are working their way through the school.

"loose" home and high-school training; the special preparation of the "tighter" boarding-school life. But of course there is rarely so simple an alternative. The mere cost of board and tuition—nearly a thousand dollars a year in the more exclusive schools—practically eliminates, for them at

The Gilman House at Exeter.
Typical of the fine old New England houses characteristic of both Exeter and Andover.

least, all but the sons of the fairly well-to-do. And the rich little boy rarely has the choice between a fashionable school and the broad humanizing experience in a small town. His parents may have three houses and no home, or prefer to travel, or get divorced. And the choice is more likely to be between being really trained in a boarding-school or spoiled at home by private tutors. And even the robustious democracy of a Walt Whitman might balk, for reasons of health alone, at forcing a boy to grow up in a city like New York.

Moreover, "going to college" is coming to mean at least two rather different things. In the West the co-educational State university, aiming at "results," is the last stage of a system of education which has much in it to appeal to a democracy—a

Looking across the Exeter campus.

system, that is, which is an organic part of the State, which keeps as close as possible to what seem practical needs, and through which the future citizens, boys and girls alike, march together side by side until they emerge prepared to establish homes and serve the State which trained them.

Those who prefer the older universities, however—and it isn't apparent that the success of Wisconsin, for instance, has lessened the desire for Harvard, Princeton, or Yale—find it increasingly difficult to enter there without special preparation. In the West, if not everywhere, the high-schools tend to become more and more vocational, to prepare their pupils for self-support rather than for a more extended quaffing of the Pierian spring. And excepting those who hold to the public school experience for such reasons as I have suggested, there are enough

who prefer the old-fashioned training of the Eastern universities, apparently, to demand private preparatory schools, and more of them, for some time to come.

The venerable academies at Andover, in Massachusetts, and at Exeter, just across the line in New Hampshire, come nearer,

Dunbar Hall, one of the new dormitories at Exeter intended for younger boys.

Two masters and their wives live in this hall. There is a matron as house-keeper and the manner of life is very much like that led by the younger boys in the smaller schools.

Within the quadrangle at the Hill School.
Except for a few detached buildings, all the work and living rooms at Hill are gathered under one roof.

perhaps, than any other of our prepara-
tories to bridging the gap between the
average high-school and such American
developments of English models as are
represented by Groton, St. Mark's, or St.
Paul's. They were started in the heart of
Puritan New England, in the midst of the
War for Independence, and for over a century they have kept alive the sacred fire with
which the young nation was burning at
their birth. No other schools have helped
in the making of so many distinguished
men, nor are any, perhaps, so saturated
with traditions so peculiarly American.

In their early days, when most of the boys
were working their way as they went, raising vegetables to help pay their board,
bundling up as if for a sleigh ride on Sundays to listen to three sermons in an un-
heated church, and on Monday reciting
what they could remember of the discourses
of the day before; in the day of Master
Eliphalet Pearson—

". . . Great Eliphalet (I can see him now)—
Big name, big frame, big voice and beetling
    brow. . . ."

the boys boarded with the towns-people, and
looked out for themselves very much as if
they were at home. Of late years, as the
type of boys has changed with the changing
times, it has been found advisable more and
more to gather them—especially the younger ones—in dormitories controlled by the
schools.

Eventually, I suppose, they will be all
lodged in school buildings. The newer
dormitories, like Dunbar Hall at Exeter
and Bancroft Cottage at Andover, are quite
as fine as any buildings at the more fashionable schools, and discipline in them is
much the same, but many of the sedate
old colonial houses, with their broad white
faces and green blinds, are still used as
boarding-places, and the practice of encouraging a strong sense of personal responsibility still survives. As the Andover
catalogue says: "The Academy aims to
attract students with a definite educational purpose and a high moral standard. The Academy is not a suitable school
for boys who are idle, insubordinate, or
lacking in self-control; or for such as require the constant supervision of a teacher
and the routine of the school-room in order to enforce industry and fidelity. Students who are found to be unable or un-
willing to meet the school requirements

The out-door gymnasium at the Hill School.

The running track, roofed to keep off rain and snow but open to the air, encircles the floor space. The boys are exercised here instead of in-doors, and during sunshine hours whenever possible.

and those whose influence is injurious must be withdrawn from the school."

And nearly a fifth of those who register are sometimes dropped before the end of the year. This does not mean dismissal necessarily; it may mean merely that for one reason or another they can not keep the pace. A boy is asked, so to speak, not how long he has studied, but does he know his lesson: "Make good or get out," as one might paraphrase the motto of one of England's famous schools. It is a wasteful method, from the point of view of the more paternal schools, but those who survive are likely to be pretty fit.

As boys may enter any of the four classes, both Andover and Exeter are much used by those who can take only a year or two of special preparation. And as there is no age limit—a few years ago a bricklayer employed on one of the Andover buildings, and recently supervising mechanical engineer of one of the tallest buildings in New York, laid down his trowel and joined the school —the boys are likely to be older than in the more restricted schools. Their age, their numbers—there are nearly five hundred—

and their comparative absence of restriction give to both Andover and Exeter much of the atmosphere of small college towns— an atmosphere robust and bracing; perhaps, for tenderly nurtured boys, too little restricted, too much as freshman year at college might be without the steadying influence of upper classmen.

There are sons of millionaires at Andover and Exeter, and side by side with them mill boys from the near-by towns and big-fisted youths from the Pennsylvania mines. Sixty or seventy at each school are helped by scholarships, and it is no disgrace whatever to pay for one's board by waiting on table. Many people are opposed to such supposedly menial tasks, but I think that if they could see these boys rush in to the Commons together from their noon recitations, and see those who are working throw off coats, shoot into duck jackets and begin to "rustle" food, sometimes picking up the talk where they left it, and with no more self-consciousness than you would pass the sandwiches at a summer picnic, they might feel differently. There is something in the air of those two old New England towns which makes such things possible, and it is a fine and impressive thing in this day and age that it should be so.

This atmosphere of old-fashioned Americanism—that all the schools considered here have a more or less similar scholastic and athletic equipment is assumed as a matter of course—is an especially important influence of Andover and Exeter. I do not refer to mere democratic rawness, but to that air of earnestness, sincerity, and

Society when there was none, an Education Society when there was none. She invented the first religious newspaper, and has sown her Greek fire and her Hebrew fire on this Continent all the way to the Pacific seas."

The theological seminary is no more, but the boys live in its dormitories and use its chapel each morning and on Sundays. And it was on one of their frosty November Sunday mornings that I went to church

Commencement day exercises at the Hill School.

independence, dignity without pose or affectation, which fairly seems to radiate from these fine old white houses and ancient elms.

One feels this especially, I think, at Andover, the Andover of which that fiery old divine, the Rev. Joseph Cook of Boston, once said after Dr. Holmes had smiled at the rectilinear nature of New Englanders. "She may have lacked imagination, but she lifted up her thoughts to the Chinese junks, to the pagans of Burmah, to the isles of the South Seas, to the Indian Empire, and when there was no missionary society she invented one. Andover may have lacked imagination, but she imagined a Tract Society when there was none, a Temperance

there with them. Outside the air was crystal clear, the elms stood gray and bare in its clearness, and Broadway seemed very far away. Across the street was the home of Harriet Beecher Stowe, and a few doors away the house in which "America" was written. And for a boy born in New York or the West it must have meant a good deal to stand up in that place and sing as those five hundred husky young Americans sang to the tune of "Elton," Whittier's hymn:

Dear Lord and Father of Mankind forgive our
    feverish ways
Reclothe us in our rightful mind
In purer lives our service find
In deeper reverence, praise.

Lawrenceville boys on their way to practise cheers and songs before the annual game with Mercersburg.

Drop still thy dews of quietness till all our striv-
ing cease
Take from our souls the strain and stress
And let our ordered lives confess
The beauty of thy peace.

Life isn't polished at either of these
schools, but one can not help feeling that
there is something very valuable here for
young Americans destined to spend their
lives afterward amongst automobiles and
stock exchanges and the rush and glitter
of our day. Something is preserved here
which still lives in the Harvard Yard and
which to-day's undergraduates will scarcely
find in the weathered oak and swimming
pools of Harvard's "Gold Coast."

Although Andover and Exeter are substantially alike, there are various little differences apparent enough to those familiar
with the schools. Goings and comings are
a trifle more carefully watched at Andover
and the boys incline to go to Yale. Exeter
men incline to go to Harvard, and they like
to think that they are even more democratic
than Andover.

Carelessness in clothes—not an important symptom of democracy to be sure—is
almost a fad at Exeter. Flannel shirts are
common, and sweaters, although not permitted by most instructors, are worn to

class sometimes. The typical Exeter costume seemed to include, when I was there,
a negligee shirt with the collar turned up so
as somewhat to resemble the collars Mr.
Gladstone used to wear.

Exeter has more scholarships—about
fifteen thousand dollars a year is available
—and the scholarship boys are, in a way,
the backbone of the school. They are compelled to stand well in their studies and,
as they are often the school's best athletes,
they almost succeed in making hard study
and high marks fashionable. They seemed
amused at Exeter at a recent visitor who, in
addressing the boys, had good-naturedly assumed that they preferred C marks to A's
or B's. And there were many stories here,
as at Andover, of boys who had worked
their way through and made a great success
afterward in college or business. Recently
the rich father of a boy had suddenly lost
his money. A wealthy uncle offered to pay
the boy's expenses, but he would have none
of it. He opened a clothes-pressing shop in
his room, the other boys loyally sent him
their clothes, and he was able to carry himself through without help.

Stories of this sort are characteristic
of Exeter. It is part of the school's tradition, stoutly preserved no matter how

Lawrenceville boys marching onto the field just before a game.

many rich boys may come. Mr. Tufts, whose kindly scholarship has been initiating barbarous young Exonians into the beauties of the English classics for more than a quarter of a century, conducted chapel exercises the morning I was there, and he asked one of the boys to see him after the service was over. The boy had a library book long overdue, and I happened to be standing near enough to hear him mumble, with a grin, that he hadn't had any money to pay the fine.

"There's a wood-pile in my back-yard," said the old gentleman dryly. It was the sort of reply which would be cherished at Exeter whether or not there was any likelihood of the boy sawing wood.

These morning exercises, which are held in an assembly room instead of a separate chapel, begin at a quarter to eight, an engagement somewhat difficult for an uninitiated city man to meet in the cold dawn of a New England winter. I hurried in with the boys, unnoticed, just as the room was quieting down. The opening hymn had scarcely been given out when the room suddenly broke into loud applause. I asked the boy nearest me what they were clapping about. "You, I guess," he smiled. And the same embarrassing salute, given with the same matter-of-fact air, followed us from the doorway each time we marched to our table in Alumni Hall.

A custom similarly quaint is the finger-snapping in class. There is more or less of this in every high-school, of course, but these athletic youths have attained an astonishing proficiency. Unless the victim answers the question immediately—and it must take rare presence of mind to keep one's head—the room is alive with arms, hurled at the instructor and quickly snapped back, and a racket like so many fire-crackers.

At St. Mark's this has been refined into an excited "Oh, sir! Oh, sir! Oh, sir!" and at most schools it would make the master's blood run cold, but it was from just such boys as these doubtless that Exeter helped to make during the first century of her existence "nine college presidents, including three of

Harvard, fifty-two college professors, two hundred and forty-five teachers, thirty-six authors, five ambassadors, seven cabinet ministers, twenty-eight members of Congress, twelve governors of States, a long list of Federal and State judges, and such men as Daniel Webster, Lewis Cass, Edward Everett, Jared Sparks, John G. Palfrey, Richard Hildreth, George Bancroft, James Walker, and Francis Bowen."

others might have been picked out—Hotchkiss in Connecticut, Belmont in California, and so on—quite as well as these two. They are intended for the sons of well-to-do parents—although Lawrenceville has scholarships, the boys themselves are not supposed to know who gets them—and it costs just as much to send a boy to Hill or Lawrenceville as to Groton. The boys may come, too, from just as charming families, but the

From a photograph, copyright by Kimball and Son.

The new Upper School at St. Paul's.

In this beautiful building the boys of the sixth form live. The dining-hall is in the wing beneath the cupola.

It has been under Dr. Amen, formerly of Harvard, that Exeter has regained the standing which a period of executive laxness caused her somewhat to lose a generation ago. The principal of Andover is Mr. Alfred E. Stearns, who combines in an uncommon way the old New England traditions with a sense of humor and an enthusiasm for out-door sports more typical of our day.

The Hill School, at Pottstown, Pennsylvania, and the Lawrenceville School, in the pleasant country near Princeton, differ from each other in many ways, and yet they may be grouped here as schools more exclusive than Andover or Exeter, and yet not quite as "tight" as the fashionable "church" schools of New England. Many

names of the parents are rather less likely to be familiar to the newspaper readers of Boston or New York. Walking on eggs is an absurdly simple pastime compared to making generalizations in such matters as these, but I shall perhaps not hazard too much by repeating the remark of a well-informed Lawrenceville alumnus that the boys in his school might be said to represent the "second generation." It is rather hard to say what that is, but I suppose it might mean that their parents had arrived at the Oriental rug period, although their grandparents were not accustomed to mahogany and plate.

Lawrenceville was founded in its present form by the legatees of the estate of Mr.

In addition to the spacious pond beside the school, St. Paul's boys are fortunate to have the use of a larger lake about two miles away.

John Cleve Green, a New York merchant who had grown rich in the Chinese trade. Started in 1810 and continued as a small boarding-school, it was acquired in 1878 by these legatees and opened in 1884. Several buildings have been added since then, but it was the school's good fortune to start with a liberal endowment and a definite architectural plan. It has room for nearly four hundred boys—more than twice the number at either Groton or St. Mark's—and its equipment includes a golf course, a lavish supply of out-door fields, and the finest school gymnasium in the country.

Lawrenceville's most characteristic feature is its house system. The boys below the upper form occupy separate houses, looked over by a master and his wife, assisted sometimes by an unmarried master. Each of these houses or dormitories is a home unit. The boys eat, sleep, and study there, and there are inter-house contests in athletics. The boys of the upper form live with two masters in the Upper House, a spacious dormitory presided over by two unmarried masters. They have no pre-

scribed study hours, provided they keep up a certain grade in their marks; they can smoke during certain hours in a room arranged for that purpose if they have their parents' permission, and the seven directors chosen by themselves attend to a considerable extent to discipline.

"To combine the great world with the little world by the house system," as Professor William M. Sloane put it in his Founder's Day address two years ago, "to fit any graduate of Lawrenceville for the larger liberty of the university by his year under the self-government of the Upper House"—such was the purpose of the plan. Lawrenceville grew rapidly under its first master, Dr. Mackenzie, and its popularity —particularly among those who prefer to have their sons go to school in the Middle Atlantic States rather than in New England —continues under its present master, Dr. McPherson. Closely affiliated by proximity, its Presbyterian leanings and the sympathies of its founders with Princeton, it is generally thought of as the latter's natural preparatory.

lake near St. Paul's.

Here the crews of the two clubs, the Shattuck and Halcyon, train and race. Many college oarsmen have learned to row at St. Paul's.

Among Lawrenceville's historical exhibits is the Jigger Shop, a semi-scholastic refreshment parlor kept by a Jersey philosopher who has learned the tastes of boys. His place is a sort of museum in which everything from macaroons to golf clubs or writing-paper to ginger-snaps can be obtained. One of the masters, as a mark of special courtesy, treated me to a "jigger," the proprietor being left to choose the one at the moment most in vogue.

He filled a tall soda-water glass half full of marshmallows. Over this he poured a thick chocolate syrup. He put ice-cream on top of this, and an inch or two of whipped cream on top of the ice-cream, gave a stir, and the "jigger" was ready. The counter was lined with glass bowls filled with chopped nuts and syrup, breakfast foods, chopped bananas and syrup, chopped oranges, pineapples, etc., which, mixed in various combinations, are daily devoured by the young Laurentians.

Although the Jigger Shop is not included in the gymnastic equipment of the school, it strikes one as a fairly adequate test of physical prowess, and one might say of it as James G. Blaine once said of Andover after seeing the old "commons," that a school which could stand that must have some hidden strength that did not meet the eye. The lighter side of Lawrenceville, as at least one group of school-boys saw it, may be found in Mr. Owen Johnson's book of short stories, "The Eternal Boy." The school's more serious purpose has not, perhaps, been better defined than by Professor Sloane: "Here men are disciplined; made to work, not for immediate fruition but for training; not for earning, but for learning; not to be snobs, but to be aristocrats; not to be tail-enders in the scrimmage, but to head the wedge and win the victory for peace and righteousness."

The Hill School is a family school, like Groton and St. Mark's, and, in a rather special sense, a private school. It has neither endowments nor scholarships, and in its present form, with its two hundred and fifty boys, it is a continuation of the school started in 1851 by the Rev. Matthew Meigs, reorganized in 1876 by Mr. John Meigs, his son, and conducted by him ever since. "Neither the fad of any social set, nor the pet of any religious denomination," as one of its friends rather bluntly described it to me, as we stood in its sunny quadrangle on the day of the annual game with Hotchkiss, it is conducted along the same lines of compactness and efficiency as any other modern business enterprise, with the differ-

uct to turn out—boys prepared thoroughly for college—and he has gone about his task with the same executive energy and eye to results that would be used by a capable organizer in other fields. The Hill School masters good-humoredly sigh now and then at the pace they have to keep, and it is a matter of record that Hill boys rarely fail to pass their entrance examinations.

The hockey rinks at St. Paul's School.

The old mill-pond beside which the school is built makes hockey the most popular winter sport, and the St. Paul's boys hold their own even with the college teams.

ence that its primary object is preparing boys for college instead of merely making money.

There are the usual out-door athletic fields at Hill, and unusually careful training is given to the athletic teams, but the in-door gymnasium is small. Instead of an expensive gymnasium there is a large out-of-door floored space, with a roofed dirt track, open to the air, around it. Here the boys are exercised, in sunlight whenever possible; and it is believed that they get more practical good than they would from an expensive gymnasium. I should say that this was rather typical of Mr. Meigs's keen interest in results. He has a certain prod-

Set on the outskirts of a small Pennsylvania manufacturing town, the Hill School is not noticeable for scenic or architectural beauty—although the immediate surroundings are spacious and restful—and its charm is found rather in the busy family atmosphere enclosed by its compact walls and spread over its playgrounds. Except for the chapel—a gift of the alumni—the gymnasium, masters' club, and a few detached cottages near by, nearly all the school's life—as at St. Mark's—is carried on under one roof. And in this family atmosphere the head-master's wife—a lady of strong religious feeling—has had an important part. Mrs. Meigs came to the

A general view of St. Mark's School.

The gymnasium and a few masters' cottages are behind this building—otherwise the boys eat, sleep, study, and go to chapel under the one roof.

school as a bride, and she has grown up a part of that little court-yard life. At eleven each morning when the boys are nibbling crackers—just as they do at Groton—the masters drift into her cheerful drawing-room for tea or coffee, and some of her famous cinnamon buns. Here, too, after the game with Hotchkiss, I watched the foot-ball team, looking absurdly small and boyish in their every-day clothes, learning manners and being fed with tea and cakes and tactful praise. And the discussions about their future which these young men have with the head-master's wife in the "sky parlor" are matters of school history.

A master's wife in such a school has a wide field for the exercise of her influence. For several very important years she and her husband are switchmen, so to speak, turning all these little human ventures from one track to another. She may not be able to follow Dr. Holmes's advice and begin the education of children with their grand-parents, but she often can, as I heard Mrs. Meigs herself say, turn the advice about and begin the education of grandchildren.

Scarcely less potent is the influence of the athletic instructor, Mr. Sweeney, who was brought to the school from a lithographer's office and, breaking records in a high jump,

to become an unusual power not only over the boys' bodies but also their minds. I suppose there is not a better trained eleven in any of the preparatory schools, and it is said that the plays worked out by Mr. Sweeney and the boys at Hill are sometimes used by next season's Yale team. They looked, indeed, like little Yale men in the bud when they came swinging on to the field the day of the Hotchkiss game, in sailor hats and blue and white sweaters, and one wasn't surprised to hear that a majority of them go to Yale.

The St. Paul's School lies about two miles from Concord, New Hampshire, in a rolling, rather hilly country, covered with white birches and pines. Its size—it has room for nearly four hundred boys—and the arrangement of its many buildings make it differ from such small parental schools as St. Mark's and Groton, and yet it falls rather more naturally into a class with them than with Lawrenceville or Hill. All three are New England "church" schools, all suggest American adaptations of English forms, and the social flavor of the three—although St. Paul's is more differentiated—is much the same.

I asked a St. Paul's man, a keen observer, whose grown-up stories have given real

The school-house at Groton where the morning recitations are held.

pleasure to a great many Americans, if it were true that at St. Paul's, as some one had told me, "they went in for the handsome animal or Yale type of man." "It didn't make handsome animals of all of us," he wrote back, "and thank God it didn't make us all Elis; but it helped what little we had in the way of physique, and it gave us a mighty good time. The

The chapel at Groton.

The finest school chapel in the country and one of the best American specimens of Gothic architecture.

The Hundred House at Groton School.

The head-master and his family live in the wing on the right and the rest of the building is occupied by one hundred boys and their masters. The rest of the boys, about fifty, live across the campus in Brooks House.

memory of the place which seems to linger most pleasantly in my mind is of the out-door life—of the playground and of the country roundabout, with its ponds and woods."

And I think—of course assuming those things which it has in common with other good schools—that the casual visitor, too, carries away some such impression as most characteristic of St. Paul's. It is, indeed, a beautiful country, a school-boy's paradise. The school was built on the banks of an old mill-pond, where the boys canoe in summer and play hockey in winter, and there is a larger pond two miles away to which the crews are carried in big stages every spring afternoon. Something like a thousand acres of woodland are under the school's control, and the boys can even go trapping and chop down trees.

Dr. George C. Shattuck, who founded the school in 1856, expressed in his deed of gift his desire for physical and æsthetic educa-tion in the school's constitution—a rather startling innovation in those days—and Dr. Coit, for many years head-master, had the boys play cricket for the excellent reason that cricket is so uninteresting to watch that any normal boy would be more likely to play it than to loaf on the side lines. Row-ing and foot-ball have taken the place of cricket now, and the whole school, you might say, plays.

For foot-ball, the boys are divided among three clubs, the Isthmian, Delphic, and Old Hundred, and each club has six teams, graded as fairly as possible according to weight and age. The big boys of one club play the big boys of another, and so on down to the midgets of the first form. Eighteen elevens are therefore hard at it during the autumn. A percentage is kept and there are mugs for the winners, and big permanent cups in the library to record the victories of the clubs.

Track athletics and hockey are arranged in the same way. The oarsmen are di-vided between the Shattuck and Halcyon clubs, and during the spring there are four eights, two sixes, and three fours. All their contests, except for occasional hock-ey games, are with each other. Under these conditions the overwrought atmos-phere of interscholastic games is escaped, athletics become fun, and sport what it should be.

St. Paul's grew very fast during Dr. Coit's administration, and the school is rather more cosmopolitan than either Gro-ton or St. Mark's. Many boys come from the West. In a sixth form Latin class of eleven boys, I found five from Pittsburg, and the eleven were to be scattered to Harvard, Yale, Princeton, Trinity, and the University of Pennsylvania.

The founder of Andover would have been peculiarly interested, I imagine, if he could have returned and dined with us in the spacious old English hall of the Upper School at St. Paul's. I do not suppose that he would have noticed how agreeably these young sixth formers were dressed; doubtless all our clothes—so tragically im-portant to a school-boy sometimes—would seem outlandish to him. But he could not have failed to observe the physical beauty, the general alertness, and winsome charm of these finished little gentlemen. Picked boys they are certainly. If you wanted to fill an eight-oared shell, or start a fashion-able club, or lead a forlorn hope, or show Mr. Phillips the best type of modern young American, I don't suppose you could do better than to pick them here.

"It always gives me an emotion," a lady confided to me as we rode back toward New York. She had been to visit her son, and she referred to the sight of the boys marching into the stately English chapel in the morning, two by two, bareheaded, and glowing with health and good spirits. Well, I think it would have given the Hon. Samuel Phillips an emotion too. But he would have been most impressed, I imagine, to see these boys pore over their papers—dinner hour is mail hour in the Upper School—from the colleges for which they were preparing.

The *Crimson, News, Princetonian*—these they ripped open and ran over with exact-ly the business-like air of stockbrokers running ticker-tape through their fingers. Who was picked for the 'varsity boat, how many were trying for the college daily, who would manage the base-ball team?—all the gossip of the college world was their gossip too. Ahead of them was last year's class and the classes before that, pioneers paving the way. To take up the pleasant burden, meet the right people, make the right teams and clubs, "make good," in short—and it called for ability and hard work, too—was their "great end and real business of living."

And one could not help thinking, as one watched them, of boys in far-away high-schools who must next fall meet and compete in this curious business with these finished little men of the world. Obviously, the former stood no chance, no more than a Cook's tourist on his first visit to London would have of dining with the King. And being for the most part well-mannered, sensible American boys, afraid, above all things, of "butting in" and being "fresh," they would flock by themselves, criticising the others for snobbishness, or sorrowing silently at their own unexplained lack of social success.

St. Mark's and Groton, in spite of various differences—the St. Mark's boys are gathered under one roof, for instance, the Groton boys in two houses at opposite sides of a broad lawn—may be classed together very much as were Andover and Exeter. They lie near each other in the pleasant rolling country of Eastern Central Massachusetts, St. Mark's at Southboro, and Groton about two miles from the village of the same name. St. Mark's was founded in 1865 by Mr. Joseph Burnett, and Groton was organized nineteen years later by the Rev. Endicott Peabody, its head-master still. The present head-master of St. Mark's, the Rev. William Greenough Thayer, is a graduate of Amherst, and a former master at Groton. Both schools are of the small parental type—there are about one hundred and twenty-five boys at St. Mark's and about one hundred and fifty at Groton—and both are intimately associated with the Episcopal Church.

Both of these schools are "fashionable" in the sense that socially ambitious parents will move mountains to get their sons admitted, and that a list of the boys' names reads like a rather carefully expurgated Social Register of Boston and New York. Both schools have waiting lists more than filling up their future classes until 1923—boys enter between the ages of twelve and fourteen generally—and, roughly speaking, it might be said that a child isn't likely to get into either unless he is registered as soon as he is born. "Of course," as I was gravely informed at Groton, "a Groton man wires to Dr. Peabody as soon as his son is born. Others generally think that a letter is quick enough."

When one uses the word "fashionable,"
on the other hand, one doesn't imply superficiality or lack of earnestness. Many of these boys come from families whose names are familiar to the readers of the newspaper society columns, but the majority of them, also, come from families which are "best" in a truer meaning of the word—families which stand for broad culture and solid attainment. Merely as a preparatory school, for instance, Groton has perhaps no superior in America. When President Hadley of Yale and Mr. Roosevelt send their sons thither, something besides mere social glamor is doubtless in their minds.

Groton's special quality is due to the personality of its head-master, and the fact that it started with, and because of its small numbers and careful selection has been able to keep, an unusually picked lot of boys. Mr. Peabody is an American with an English school and university training, and an American meeting him for the first time would doubtless take him for an Englishman. He is an all around athlete—he used to play with the boys on the school teams until he became too heavy for them—and yet a churchman; a scholar and yet a very graceful and sophisticated man of the world. Altogether his is a personality peculiarly fitted to win the confidence and lead the type of boy for whom the Groton school was started.

The English feel that our college athletes think too much of winning, train and specialize too seriously. To make a business of sport seems scarcely gentlemanly, according to their tradition that a gentleman does a great many things rather well in an off-hand way, but doesn't do any one thing so painfully that you might mistake him for a professional.

Such an athlete is the head-master himself, and something of his attitude is absorbed doubtless by the boys. Mr. Peabody once discovered two of his boys dragging a third about in the mud in order to give his new foot-ball clothes the proper veteran atmosphere. "Come, come!" he said, "that's like a soldier taking off his tunic and shooting it full of holes to get a reputation for bravery."

The night before the game with Hotchkiss at the Hill School, I heard a master telling of a Hill captain who had once stayed out of the big game because he thought he hadn't been playing as well as the school had the right to expect. It was an act which required real moral heroism. "It was more than that," said the master solemnly, groping for the proper word; "it was a—a sort of consecration." The story was told to illustrate the do-or-die spirit of the Hill boys, and it did so excellently, and it also illustrated what the head-master of Groton, I imagine, would consider the rather morbid seriousness with which alumni, coaches, and grown-ups generally contrive to invest the sports of school and college boys. Mr. Peabody once came across a big sixth form foot-ball player weeping in the locker room because his team had been beaten by St. Mark's. There are fashions in these matters, you know, as Mr. Peabody would say, with his whimsical smile, and it was the fashion to weep that year. "It isn't as bad as that," he suggested. "I can't help it," blubbered the young giant. "Oh, yes; you can," said the head-master, "and you will at once." "Yes, sir," said the boy, and ceased forthwith.

In his classes, too, the head-master preserves, in the most engaging fashion, a similar attitude of tolerant superiority to, and polite detachment from, over-seriousness and mere strenuosity. I never listened to a more lively and vigorous recitation than that of his little first formers in Latin. They piped out their answers and shifted up and down the benches as the answers happened to be right or wrong, as if they were playing some delightful game. They were as trim and well-disciplined as so many little soldiers, and yet, between the head-master and these neat little fellows in their broad turnover collars, there was always a certain half-whimsical, unpedagogical air as of "one gentleman to another." It was "Right you are!" when little Mr. Delancey Beekman III gave the proper ablative, or "Bless my soul—shocking—shocking!" when he was wrong; "Good shot!" when the boy at the foot of the class guessed right, "but only a shot, wasn't it?" lest he be too complacent; and "Steam ahead—steam ahead!" when any one hesitated too long.

I recall a rather Anglicized young master at one of the other schools who was trying, I fancy, to hit a similar note, and who did it very badly. The class was reading "Sir Roger de Coverley," and the instructor

wished to point out that the office of justice of the peace was a less exalted position in America than its equivalent in England. "Of course over *they-ah*," he said, "he's a —a—a gentleman and—and all that kind of thing. Whereas *he-ah* he might be—I mean to *say*—our little friend of the country—the cobbler, you know, who dispenses justice as he makes his shoes!" And with a pleased air he tucked his handkerchief into his cuff.

The point he was trying to make was a perfectly good one, and he might also have explained that the English "public schools" can draw their masters from a class of men of force and a broad culture, which, for such work, has scarcely more than begun to exist here.

Every night the hundred boys in the Hundred House (the other sixty boys live in the Brooks House across the lawn), file past Mr. Peabody, shake hands, and say "Good night, sir," before they go upstairs to bed. Every morning, in the robes of an Episcopal clergyman, he strides into the beautiful Gothic chapel—which represents, to quote the careful description of Mr. Oscar Fay Adams, the "Curvilinear half of the Middle Pointed style, often called the Late Decorated, but so far along in the style that its transition to the Third Pointed or Perpendicular is already manifesting itself"—a moment later in a plaid cap he strides out the side door and across to the recitation hall. The prefects, as the monitors chosen from the fifth form are called, sit at the head-master's table and talk over with him all the school problems, exactly like the big brothers of a large family, and every evening, after the younger boys are tucked away, the other instructors gather in the head-master's study or dining-room for a talk and a bite of supper before they go to bed.

A difficulty in a school of this type is that it will become too much like a family, and it was with the hope of getting more differentiation that the plan has recently been tried of going outside the waiting list and admitting each year, after an examination, a few boys from the West and South. Even with this break in the walls, however, there is a series of questions framed so ingeniously to reflect the applicants' general culture and previous environment, that there is little danger of the admission of any very startling alien influence. As it was explained to me at Groton with obvious truth: "Of course *we* should like to have the blacksmith's son here, only—it wouldn't be kind to the blacksmith."

A school of this type is a very interesting and significant thing, and it must be taken pretty seriously. The high-schools and even such schools as Andover and Exeter decline to admit, so to speak, that our democracy is any less simple than it was a hundred years ago. Such a school as Groton implies that we have an aristocratic, if not a leisure class, and that there is a place in America for schools performing a function similar to that performed by the famous old "public" schools of England. That there is a demand for such schools their tremendous vogue is sufficient proof, and whatever one may think about them— as about automobiles or steam engines—it seems apparent that they are here to stay.

There is no question that the English public schools send out year after year an unusually fine and virile type of young men to take up the burden of a ruling class and hold up the pillars of the empire. We have no such traditional ruling class. Our best men generally go into business. They rule, to be sure, through the power of their money, but it is an unconscious, generally, rather than a conscious responsibility. And it may be the mission of such schools as Groton is to teach to our chosen few some proper traditions of responsibility.

It is not for this, however, that ambitious parents and boys generally struggle to get into such schools. They are not thinking of duties but of privileges. And the real danger is not that the school is a poor school but that it is such a good one. It is not vulgar snobbishness that weakens democracy, but a refined and intelligent scepticism. And it is not every son of well-meaning but thoughtless parents who can break through the stamp which such a school sets upon him and get the best afterward out of our boisterous and disarranged world.

The little Groton boy in his pumps, black coat, and broad white collar is very charming saying "Good night!" to Mr. Peabody.

He is not quite so charming five or six years later in college as he lets a good part of that vigorous, mixed-up stimulating world sweep by unheeded—those who are big enough to break through their environment are perhaps the finest type of young Americans—outside the doors of his particular fashionable society. And he is sometimes not charming at all ten years later when you see him of a late afternoon gloomily lapping up highballs in his New York club —a good deal fatter now, a good deal lazier, and a good deal less interested in everything not included in his little circle.

It is not fair of course to blame any school for the dangers of wealth and the common weaknesses of humanity, any more than it is fair to allow another school the credit for giving to the nation the distinguished men whose school-days there were merely part of a long life work. But it is fair and it is important to consider the slant which a boy's surroundings are likely to give his natural tendencies.

"Of course," a master said, referring to the almost military régime of work and play, "we don't make poets here—but I fancy the poets would be poets anyway." The important thing isn't the poets they don't make, but the poetry they may help to destroy—the poetry of common things, the kindly beauty of our varied American life; the stirring fret and urge, different temperaments and different breeds living and working and playing together. This is the real tragedy of these societies for the prevention of knowing what other Americans are like.

It isn't that the boys aren't carefully chosen, but that they are too carefully chosen. It is precisely because these boys are all so nice and good-looking and polite, and "the kind they are likely to know afterward," that half the bracing charm and romance of American life, school-boy or grown-up, is lost. It isn't that so few of us can get inside to know them; it is that so few of them ever get outside to know us. It isn't that America particularly needs this or that one hundred and fifty boys, but that these one hundred and fifty boys rather particularly need America.

Nashua,
New Hampshire
(1897)

By Henry B. Atherton.

A PICTURESQUE manufacturing town of twenty-five thousand inhabitants, in the heart of New England, Nashua never fails to attract and interest all who become acquainted with its scenery, its history or its people. For sixty years the frontier settlement of the Massachusetts Bay Colony on the north, it is now the "Gate City" of New Hampshire, the second in population in that state, and second to none in its public spirit, industrial activity and educational facilities.

Nashua is the youngest and lustiest child of ancient Dunstable, which was the nursing mother of seventeen thriving communities in two states, all of which, either in whole or in part, have been carved out of her broad territory. The compact part of the city lies within the radius of a mile from the intersection of Hollis and Main Streets, just south of the City Hall. Beyond that limit are still to be found the "ffarmes," mentioned in the early records, with many pleasant dwellings and comfortable homes, but no shop, store or outlying village. The surface is undulating and varied, comprising broad plains, gentle hills, beautiful sheets of water, cultivated fields and tracts of wild woodland.

Pennichuck Brook, with its succession of lovely ponds, forms the north-

ern boundary. Salmon Brook, with its picturesque surroundings, the placid Nashua, moving quietly along between its wooded banks—except where it rushes headlong and turbulent over the rapids at Mine Falls— and the majestic Merrimack, with its mighty current, add charm and variety to the scenery. Shade trees are numerous, and nowhere does the American elm attain to greater symmetry and beauty than on the banks of the Nashua.

The first settlers in the vicinity of Boston had been on this side of the Atlantic less than thirty years, and had just begun to be concerned about the character of some of the newcomers —especially the Quakers—and to enact immigration laws forbidding their introduction under a penalty of £100 for each offence, when, in the year 1656, as along the coast they began to flog and exile those unoffending people, three Puritan worthies, Maj. Simon Willard, Capt. Edward Johnson, the author of "The Wonder Working Providence of Zion's Savior," and Jonathan Danforth, the surveyor, made an excursion inland. Their object was to select and survey a tract of eight thousand acres granted to the town of Billerica. Striking the Merrimack near where that river changes its course from south to northeast, and passing north-

INDIAN HEAD COFFEE HOUSE.
Photograph by P. F. Porter.

was accustomed in buying peltry to reckon his foot as weighing a pound, or that in consequence his customers, on finding out the iniquity of it, burnt down his "howse," is a doubtful tradition. It might have been true, but the same story is frequently told of other early Indian traders. Cromwell abandoned the locality, leaving only his name, by which the beautiful falls on the Souhegan are still called, and the last we know of him he was a dweller in "Lubberland" on Great Bay. The true reason why he retired from business at Naticook was because in the following year a number of others, including the doughty Major Willard himself, William Brenton, Thomas Wheeler and Thomas Henchman, procured from the General Court the exclusive monopoly of this traffic with the Indians. Their successors in business from Boston still furnish necessaries

ward along its right bank, they were soon beyond the last log house of the sparse settlement, and leaving the clearing they entered the confines of that immense forest which then extended, unbroken by the white man's ax, northward for three hundred miles to the banks of the St. Lawrence. Following an Indian trail through the dusky glades of the "forest primeval," they bivouacked at night beneath the stars, and still wending their way northward under giant oaks and lofty pines, they crossed Salmon Brook and the corn lands of the Indians, passed near their favorite fishing place at the falls on the Merrimack, and, fording the river of the Nashaways near its mouth, passed the Pennichuck and, on the afternoon of their second day, came to Naticook and the Souheganock. Here, on the northern verge of the territory subsequently to become the township of Dunstable, they found the "trucking howse" of a white man, one John Cromwell. What relation, if any, he bore to the Lord Protector, who also it is said once designed to emigrate to New England, history does not inform us. But true to the instincts of his race, self-reliant, surrounded by the wilderness and its dusky denizens, and fifty miles from his base of supplies, he was exchanging commodities with the aborigines at a profit. That he

ON FAIRMOUNT.

to the residents of Naticook and vicinity, but have long since ceased to take their pay in furs.

In 1673 the Artillery Company of Boston received a grant of a thousand acres north of the Nashua and west of the Merrimack, which embraced the site of all the compact part of the present city lying north of the first mentioned river, including Artillery Pond and the North Common. The same year (October 15, 1673, O. S.),

Charlestown School farm and was on the Souhegan at Dram Cup Hill, a name ominous and suggestive both as to shape and size.

About the mouth of Salmon Brook the first settlers came and occupied the lands formerly cultivated by the Indians. Their farms were laid out in narrow strips reaching from the Merrimack on the east to the brook and, farther south, to Long Hill, on the west, and extended in succession

THE NASHUA NEAR FAIRMOUNT.

Dunstable was chartered by the Massachusetts Bay Colony, and in May of the following year it was surveyed and its boundaries were described. It covered about two hundred square miles. At this time Edward Colburn, Henry Kimball and Capt. Samuel Scarlett had already located farms, which are mentioned in the record. The northwest corner of Dunstable was the northwest corner of Middlesex County and of the

southerly toward Chelmsford. The infant settlement was protected by a ditch and block house or garrison erected about a mile northwest of the mouth of Salmon Brook and about the same distance southwest from the mouth of the Nashua and from the falls on the Merrimack, much frequented by the Indians for fishing. It commanded the trail, afterwards the "country road" which ran northward parallel to the Merrimack across

COLONEL GEORGE BOWERS.

GENERAL AARON F. STEVENS.

the ford of the Nashua. The neighborhood which was protected by this log fort is still known as the "Harbor," meaning, I presume, shelter or place of refuge. Here came John Blanchard, Jonathan Tyng, John Lovewell, Thomas and John Cummings, John and Henry Farwell, Thomas Lund, Joseph Hassell, Robert Usher, Robert Proctor, John Sollendine and Christopher Temple. Capt. Thomas Brattle of Boston headed the petition for a charter. He was son-in-law of William Tyng, and at a town meeting holden at a safe distance, in Woburn, in 1677, was chosen one of the selectmen of Dunstable.

This little settlement in the great woods, the advance guard toward the north for more than half a century of Anglo-Saxon civilization on this continent, underwent the ordinary vicissitudes and trials of nearly all the early New England com-

GENERAL JOHN G. FOSTER.

munities. During King Philip's War, with the exception of Jonathan Tyng, all the settlers prudently withdrew toward the coast, and later, in 1692, when the epidemic for hanging witches broke out along the coast, they prudently remained in the wilderness a long day's journey from the centre of contagion.

In 1686 the Indians who had claimed any rights in the territory of Naticook and Dunstable sold out their interest to Mr. Tyng and for the most part moved away. A few remained, however, among whom was Joe English, the grandson of Masconnomet, sagamore of Agawam. Many are the wonderful exploits related of this friend of the white man. In the end he was killed by hostile Indians, his loyalty to the settlers having cost him his life. A precipitous rocky hill in New Boston, lying west of the Unconoonucs and

HON. CHARLES G. ATHERTON.

HON. JOHN M. HUNT.

visible from Nashua, still bears his name. The last friendly Indian was Philip Anthony, who lived here late into the last century.

Mine Islands at the foot of Mine Falls, laid out to Hezekiah Usher in 1682, were said to be the source whence the Indians obtained their supply of lead for bullets, and traces of both lead and silver have been found there,—but Mr. Usher was disappointed in his quest there for valuable deposits of either metal.

The first meetinghouse was built in 1678, and the next year Rev. Thomas Weld became the settled minister. Six years later it became necessary to build a larger meetinghouse, "about the size of the one at Groton," as described in the records. The first recorded birth is that of William, son of Jonathan and Mary Tyng, April 22, 1679; the first marriage, that of John Sollendine, August

2, 1680; and the first death, that of Hon. Edward Tyng, December 22, 1681, aged 81.

Sollendine, who was probably a carpenter, was the architect of the first meetinghouse, which structure was built with Puritan simplicity, we may be certain. The conduct of religious services within that edifice, however, seemed to require some offices, the necessity for which is not now generally recognized. For example, it is recorded that on May 21, 1688, "Samuel Goold was chosen Dog Whipper for the Meeting House." The necessary inference is, that dogs, being useful for protection against both wild beasts and wild men, were numerous, and that, partaking of the spirit of that age, even the dogs had the habit of going to meeting.

Sollendine was also *pontifex primus;* he built the first bridge. On June 29, 1699, the town voted that "John

HON. ORREN C. MOORE.

Sollendine build a sufficient bridge over Salmon Brook near Thomas Clark's ffarm house;" but with rare thrift and prudence, which the modern municipality might well imitate, the proviso was added "that the cost do not exceed the sum of forty shillings," and it was on condition also

THE OLD OLIVE STREET CHURCH.
Photograph by P. F. Porter.

that the builder should pay one half the expense in the first instance himself, and if the bridge was carried away by the water within a twelve month, he was to be at the whole expense of rebuilding.

Near this bridge, on Allds' road, John Lovewell, who had served as an ensign under Cromwell, and also with Captain Church in the great Narraganset swamp fight, had his house. Here, just two hundred years ago, on the last day of March, at dusk, he had an unexpected call from three visitors from the north, who desired to

put up for the night. They were Hannah Dustin, a woman of forty, the mother of twelve children, her nurse, widow Mary Neff, who had been captured with her by the Indians a fortnight before at Haverhill, and Samuel Leonardson, a lad of fourteen, who had been carried away from Worcester a year and a half before. They had drifted down the Merrimack forty miles in an Indian canoe from the mouth of the Contoocook. John Lovewell might well have been surprised at the unusual character of the luggage carried by these two women and the boy; for besides a tomahawk and other plunder, they brought to his little dwelling at nightfall the fresh scalps, taken by themselves the morning before starting, of two Indian men, two squaws and their six children, ten in all. They had at first merely cut off the Indians' heads with their own tomahawks and started away, and their grim booty, which they turned back to obtain, was the result of an afterthought. They received a bounty of £50, one-half of which was paid to Mrs. Dustin and the remainder in equal shares to her companions. The savages, a few days before, with a hearty contempt for child life, had dashed out the brains of her baby before the mother's eyes, and had burned the roof-tree that sheltered them. One learns to do cruel things by the force of exam-

UNITARIAN CHURCH.

METHODIST CHURCH.   FIRST CHURCH.   PILGRIM CHURCH.

ple, and poor Mrs. Dustin proved an apt scholar.

This exposed settlement did not wholly escape the perils of savage warfare. On the north bank of the limpid little stream which runs from "Silver Spring" to Salmon Brook, Joseph Hassell, Sr., had his house. The place where the cellar was can yet be seen and is appropriately marked. Here, on the night of September 2, 1691, the enemy appeared, and Hassell, his wife Anna, and their son Benjamin were slain. At the same time Mary, the daughter of Patrick Marks, was killed, as tradition has it, about a mile north of the house near the south bank of the Nashua, probably while trying to make her escape from her pursuers. On the morning of the 28th of the same month, Obadiah Perry, Hassell's son-in-law, and Christopher Temple were slain. A rock in the river, about thirty rods above the upper mill, was called Temple Rock, and is said to mark the place of his death. They were all buried on a little knoll near the Lovewell house.

Capt. William Tyng was the first to embrace the offer of £40 a scalp made by the general assembly, and in the winter of 1703-4 returned from Pequawkett with five scalps. Six years later he perished by the tomahawk. Robert Parris, who had a garrison near Mr. Weld's in the southern part of the town, and his wife and daughter were slain. Two younger girls who hid under a hogshead in the cellar escaped; one of them lived to become the mother of Col. John Goffe. July 3, 1706, a large party of Mohawks came from New York and attacked the Weld and Galusha garrisons. Goody Cummings, wife of John Cummings, Nathaniel Blanchard, his wife Lydia, and daughter Su-

WINTER ON THE NASHUA.

sannah, and Rachel Galusha were slain.

This little advance guard on the frontier had become almost a forlorn hope. September 4, 1724, a party of French Mohawks fell upon Dunstable and carried away Nathan Cross and Thomas Blanchard whom they found upon the north side of the Nashua engaged in making turpentine. A rescue party of ten was ambushed and all but one killed. Penhallow relates that a second engagement took place, the Indians, elated with their success, having m o v e d down to the ancient ford of the Nashua, where their further advance was re-

also to one of the national banks of the city, and to that renowned hostelry, the Indian Head Coffee House, which for many years occupied the site of the present elegant First Church. The cotton mills of the Jackson Company are known as the Indian Head mills, and thousands of bales of their product have been sent to far Cathay, bearing the trademark of an Indian's head, defying all the

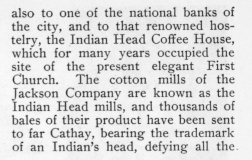

JACKSON COMPANY'S MILLS.

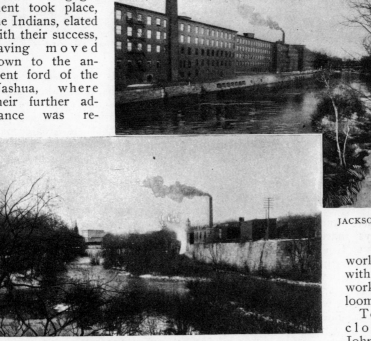

BELOW THE DAM.

world to compete with the honest work of t h e i r looms.

T o w a r d the c l o s e of 1724, John Lovewell, the son of the first

sisted by the English settlers on the south side of the stream. The deefense of the little settlement was so successful that the Indians finally withdrew; but tradition has it that, in defiance, they left the rude outlines of an Indian's head carved on a large tree by the river's side near the ford. That rough carv-ng gave the name of Indian Head to the little cluster of houses which years later was to be found in that locality,

settler of that name, together with Josiah Farwell, Jonathan Robbins and forty or fifty others, offered themselves to the General Assembly to serve as rangers and to "employ themselves in Indian hunting one whole year," if they could have suitable encouragement, which in their memorial they put at five shillings a day provided they killed any Indians; "and if within that time they do not kill any they are content to be allowed nothing for

ON THE NASHUA.

their wages, time and trouble." The Bay Colony, having apparently become of the opinion that "the best Indian is a dead Indian," accepted their services and offered them £100 for each scalp and two shillings sixpence a day. Their first scalp was taken north of the White Mountains, December 10, 1724. They next took ten more, February 10, 1725, and killed a whole party of hostile Indians armed with new Canadian guns and within two days' march of our frontier. This was at Lovewell's Pond in Wakefield. Their third expedition, in May following, was disastrous. Captain Lovewell and eight more were killed outright, while others died of their wounds. The chief, Paugus, was killed by John Chamberlain, and henceforth Dunstable was free from the attacks of the savages.

For thirty years after Lovewell's fight, or until the beginning of the French and Indian War, in 1755, this region rapidly increased in population, and settlements were begun as far north as Concord. During this period the old township was rapidly being dismembered. Brenton's farm became Litchfield. Nottingham West, now Hudson, was set off east of the Merrimack. North of Pennichuck Brook, Rumford, now Merrimack,

was incorporated. The West Parish, later called Hollis, was taken away, and the town itself was severed in twain by the location of the province line in 1741, so that the greater part of the original township was brought under the jurisdiction of New Hampshire.

At the beginning of the French war the command of a regiment of five hundred men was given to Col. Joseph Blanchard of this town. Later he was succeeded by Col. Zaccheus Lovewell, the brother of the hero of Pequawket. In this command was the famous company of rangers led by Robert Rogers, with John Stark for lieutenant. The forest, says Fox the historian, was their home, and they excelled even the Indians in cunning and hardihood. Everywhere they wandered in search of adventures, fearless, and cautious, until their very name became a terror to the enemy. At midnight they traversed the camp of the enemy or carried off a sentinel from his post as if in mockery. Their blow fell like lightning, and before the echo had died away or the alarm subsided another blow was struck at some far-distant point. They frequently imitated the strategy as well as the dress and war paint of their savage enemies; and it is no wonder that, after three generations of almost continual contact with them, they should have taken on some of the actual characteristics of their foes. Many of the descendants of the first settlers of Dunstable took an active part in the contest which resulted in the overthrow of France on this continent.

The list of the men who were in the Revolutionary War comprises nearly all the adult male population; and in the War of 1812, the Mexican War and the war for the suppression of the rebellion the town has fully sustained her reputation for patriotism. Gen. John G. Foster, who was with Anderson at Sumter, an officer in the regular army, was a native and resident of Nashua. The large Grand Army Post of the city bears his name. In the war for the Union, company after company was raised without

the 13th New Hampshire regiment on its organization; and Col. George Bowers, a descendant of John and Col. Zaccheus Lovewell, who had commanded with distinction a company in the Mexican War, was the lieutenant colonel of the same regiment.

On the Fourth of July, 1803, there was a celebration on the occasion of the launching of a canal boat on the Merrimack near the mouth of the Nashua. The oration was by Daniel Abbot, an eminent lawyer and the friend of Webster. The new boat was christened *The Nashua;* and the village which had hitherto borne the name Indian Head became Nashua Village. Nearly thirty-four years later, January 1, 1837, that part of the

RUNNELL'S BRIDGE.

MINE FALLS.

ancient township lying in New Hampshire laid aside its historical and time-honored name and became Nashua. In 1853 the town became a city. The orthography of the name varies in the ancient records, being given as Nashaway, Nashuway, Nashua, Nashoway and Nashawake. Those familiar with the origin of the name generally give the long sound to the vowel in the last syllable.

effort in this city; and on many a well-contested field the descendants of the early settlers showed by their superb valor that they were worthy of their virile and sturdy ancestors. Gen. Aaron F. Stevens, a distinguished lawyer and subsequently member of Congress from Nashua, commanded

The first dam was built by the Lovewells at Salmon Brook about one hundred and eighty years ago; and that stream has ever since furnished water power for

POLICE STATION.

first named company was chartered in 1823, and sold the lower privilege in 1825 to the Indian Head Company which began to manufacture woolens the following year. The Jackson Company was incorporated in 1830 and converted the establishment into a cotton manufactory. These two concerns are both under the efficient management of William D. Cadwell, Esq., employ twenty-five hundred hands and have a monthly pay roll of $66,000.

CENTRAL FIRE STATION.

The next important manufacturing interest in the city to-day is the shoe industry, Established only twenty-three years ago, one shop, that of the Estabrook-Anderson Shoe Company employs a thousand hands, and its daily output of shoes is ten thousand pairs. Bracket and Company employ 250 hands, with a pay roll of $12,500. Both these companies are well housed in spacious and substantial brick buildings. The Nashua Boot and Shoe Shop employ

manufacturing purposes. The Underhill Edge Tool Works were located near its mouth, and the Vale Mills utilize its power at the present day. The dam on the Merrimack fourteen miles below at Lowell, setting the water back, has prevented Nashua from obtaining its water power from that river. So it has come about that the Nashua has been the main reliance for power for manufacturing purposes, largely supplemented by the use of steam. Both of the large cotton manufacturing concerns, the Nashua Manufacturing Company and the Jackson Company, are located on this river, the first bringing the water about three miles from Mine Falls, and the other taking its power at the dam below the Main Street bridge. This dam was built originally to supply the canal connecting the village with the Merrimack. The

HIGH SCHOOL

225 hands, with a monthly pay roll of $7,000.

The card and glazed paper business, which has been a considerable and profitable industry in Nashua for many years, having been started in 1849, is now carried on in a very extensive brick building on Franklin Street erected for the purpose six or seven years ago.

Nashua is proud of her workmen and their work. The engine lathes of Flather and Company are of such un-

ary engines made by Rollins, the iron castings of the Coöperative Company, the planers made by Mark Flather, the sash, blinds and doors of Gregg and Son, the registers made by Enoch Shenton, the kits, tubs and barrels made in Proctor Brothers' extensive shops, and the White Mountain freezers, all serve to sustain the enviable reputation which the city has acquired. Hall's Hair Renewer, not unknown to fame, Dunlap's seeds and Londonderry Lithia water are all

CONCORD STREET.

rivaled excellence that they find a ready market, not only in this country, but in nearly every country in Europe as well. "Made in Nashua" has come to mean honest work done with superior skill, so that many of the companies have prefixed the name of the city to their corporate names,— as the Iron and Steel Company, the Saddlery Hardware Company, the Textile Machine Company of William White, the Iron and Brass Foundry Company, and others. The station-

put up in Nashua. The power shearer, an interesting and useful machine made by the American Shearer Company, was invented in Nashua by R. T. Smith and J. K. Priest.

The American system of manufacturing watches, as pursued in Waltham and Elgin, originated with the Nashua Watch Company, which went to Waltham. Among the famous industries of a former day were the Underhill Edge Tool Company and the Nashua Bobbin, Spool and Shut-

MASONIC TEMPLE.   ODD FELLOWS BUILDING.

tle Company, each taken away and absorbed by a trust.

The change from a system of manufacturing on a small scale by hand in each household to the use of power, the division of labor and employment of aggregated capital in large establishments has been coincident with the rapid growth of Nashua and most of the large towns of New England as well as elsewhere, and suggests many interesting problems. In the forthcoming voluminous history of Nashua, now in press, a detailed history of the various industries of the city is given in a valuable article written by Mr. R. T. Smith, an expert in mechanical matters and a well-known inventor.

As we have seen, Dunstable was originally a settlement of English Puritans within the limits of the Bay Colony. The settlement of the Scotch-Irish fifty years later, in close proximity, at Londonderry, was destined to change somewhat the character of the people in the neighborhood. Mr. Cochrane and Mr. Morrison, both authors of histories of towns within their sphere of influence, insist that Scotch-Irish is the proper appellation of these people, while our genial friend Colonel Linehan, with equal insistency claims they were Irish and not Scotch at all, and never called themselves Scotch or Scotch-Irish,—though some like the emigrant ancestor of General Stark were not born in Ireland but in Scotland,—and that, Ireland being the original Scotia whence all the inhabitants of Scotland came a thousand years ago, all the inhabitants of Ireland were necessarily Scotch. I hope I do not misstate his argument.

Be that as it may, these Presbyterians from the north of Ireland were inclined originally to be clannish, they were capable of entertaining strong prejudices, and, perhaps from a lack of cordiality in their reception, conceived a hearty hatred of the Puritans and their descendants within the Bay Colony. This strong race soon spread through the adjoining towns, sending out many swarms from the parent hive, and not a few settled in Nashua. Of this sturdy stock were Gen. George Stark, Col. A. H. Dunlap, Hon. Albert McKean, Hon. Orren C. Moore, editor and proprietor of the *Telegraph* and member of Congress, all now deceased, and the Whittemores, the McQuestens, Allds, Wilsons and many others prominent in the history of the town.

The date of the advent of the undisputedly Irish in Nashua is the year of the last great famine in Ireland. Shortly after that they began to come

proving condition is a significant commentary upon such adverse criticism. In the third generation the peculiarities of speech and physiognomy regarded as Irish, entirely disappear, and they are Americans.

The influx of Canadian French into Nashua began in earnest a generation ago. The absence of the native born producers in the ranks of the Union army, the great waste of all the products of human industry entailed by the war and the consequent demand for labor and increase of wages brought them here. At first they came a few at a time to work through the summer and return; then they began to stay a little longer; and finally from their earnings they established homes for themselves, and then their priests came also and built churches and parochial schools, and now they have prosperous parishes. At first they were inclined to believe there was no God across the border and that they would be threatened with all possible dangers both temporal and spiritual; but they have found their fears were groundless. Their pastors keep up the French language in their

MAIN STREET.

in considerable numbers, and the movement though now diminished has not wholly ceased. Accused by their English neighbors at home of being lazy and thriftless, here they have shown the opposite characteristics. No labor has been too arduous for them, and their constantly improving

churches and schools, in order that they may be in less danger of losing the faith; but the children all learn English. They have drifted from their provincial isolation into the current of American progress, which cannot be resisted. They still continue to come whenever there is

THE ARMORY.

stout hearts and strong and willing hands.

In 1760, when they surrendered to the British, there were sixty thousand French in Canada. Of their two and one-half millions of descendants who are alive to-day, Mr. Mercier, the ex-premier of the Dominion, shortly before his death assured the writer that one-half had already crossed into the United States. They are the most fecund race in Christendom, while the home stock in France are probably the reverse. Pierre Lessard of Nashua is one of twenty-seven children, the mother of all of whom was living a short time ago, at an advanced age, at St. Hyacinthe. She also was one of twenty-seven children, all having the same mother.

an increase in the local demand for labor; but they no longer come as their fathers did with their Indian allies armed with the tomahawk and scalping knife, traversing the frozen wastes of the wilderness in the dead of winter and leaving caches of food at intervals to insure a safe return with their captives. Now they glide swiftly along the Grand Trunk or Canadian Pacific clad in the garb of peace and ready to do any honest work. And they are welcome; there is work for them to do, and they do it well. They are engaged in the annexation of Canada to the United States piecemeal. They leave behind them the barren lands where for more than two centuries they have hibernated, and bring with them all that is of any value,

EDGEWOOD CEMETERY.

There are two French Catholic churches in Nashua. The parish of Father Milette is the larger of the two and comprises all of Nashua south of the river. His church is on Hollis Street. On the north side, on Chandler Street, the parish of Father Lessard is erecting a spacious and lofty church of gray marble. On Kinsley Street a pretty little chapel has been built for the use of the Protestant French.

The Irish Catholics have their place of worship on Temple Street, in a church built under the auspices of Rev. John O'Donnel, the first Catholic priest settled in Nashua. Father Buckle is the present pastor. Their parochial school is on Spring Street opposite the High School.

Nashua has a system of well-graded public schools unsurpassed by any in the state. There are nineteen school buildings with over twenty-five hundred pupils. The system is complete from the kindergarten to the high school and training school for teachers. Most of the school buildings are a credit to the city and are pleasantly located. Two handsome new schoolhouses have just been completed.

The city has a free public library of 15,000 volumes, now located in Odd Fellows Block. A new library building is in contemplation, for which a conspicuous site fronting the whole length of Main Street has been secured. For the erection of this building, Mrs. Mary A. Hunt and Miss Mary B. Hunt, the widow and daughter of the late Hon. John M. Hunt, a native of Nashua and a successful banker and business man, gave in 1892 the sum of $50,000. The gift was in memory of the husband and father and was but the beginning of other and still more important benefactions by the same donors. The initiative for the establishment of the library was taken thirty years ago by the "Young Ladies Soldiers' Aid Society," an association of about fifty patriotic young ladies of Nashua

formed for the purpose indicated by its name. A fair was held and $1,200 raised, the books of "The Union Athenaeum" and of the library kept at the Nashua Manufacturing Company's office were donated and the support of the city obtained, and the library finally opened to the public. The schools make free use of the volumes upon the shelves, and the work done by the library fairly supplements the work of the public schools. The library has a reading room in which are kept many of the leading periodicals and newspapers. This room is open from 9 A. M. to 9 P. M. on week days and on Sundays from 2 to 5 P. M. Miss Harriet Crombie is the librarian. Two daily newspapers, both republican, the *Telegraph* and the *Press*, are published in Nashua. The latter succeeds the *Gazette* which was for many years the organ of the democracy of the city under the management of Gen. Israel Hunt, B. B. Whittemore and others, and is now edited by William O. Clough. The *Telegraph* was founded by Albin Beard and his brother Alfred about 1833, and was first issued as a weekly under the name of the *New Hampshire Telegraph*. Alfred Beard died soon after the beginning of its publication and the paper continued under the ownership of Albin Beard, who was also its editor until his death in 1862. Mr. Beard, who was a great favorite, was one of the first mayors of Nashua, and his paper had a wide circulation and influence in this section of the state. Mr. Beard's funny stories and quaint witticisms will long be remembered by the residents of Nashua of the last generation. For a year and a half after the death of Mr. Beard, the present writer had the editorial management of the paper. Some time subsequently the paper came into the possession of Hon. Orren C. Moore, a man of rare natural ability and energy. He began the issue of a daily edition and kept up its publication until his death, in 1893. The paper under his management was always a wholesome family paper. No improper advertisement could find a place within its columns, and its editorial opinions were never for sale. He was never afraid single handed and alone to attack any form of injustice. If a public corporation sought to put a blanket mortgage upon the resources of the community by means of watered stock, he was quick to see the iniquity and take up arms against it; and the people soon came to know him and have confidence in his motives even when they differed from him in his conclusions. The publishing company is now under the management of his widow, Mrs. Nancy W. Moore. Mr. James M. Adams is the editor.

Nashua is well supplied with churches. Besides those mentioned there is a large Baptist Society which continues to worship in the brick church it has long occupied. This society has two offshoots. A chapel on Crown Hill and the French chapel in Kinsley Street already mentioned. The original society was the largest in the state, with the largest congregation of any in that denomination. The present pastor is the Rev. Charles L. White.

The Unitarian Society occupy the picturesque old church adjoining the Nashua Cemetery, where rest so many of the former residents of the town. Here beneath the shelter of the ancient oaks repose the remains of the brothers Beard, Col. L. W. Noyes, Hon. Charles Williams, Gen. George Stark, Hon. Charles G. Atherton, who forty years ago was a member of the United States Senate from New Hampshire, Gen. John G. Foster and many others of the professional and business men of Nashua. The church seems to harmonize with its surroundings. The pastor is Rev. Enoch Powell.

The handsome new edifice of the First Congregational Church is of granite. Here worship one of the largest societies in the city, under the ministry of Rev. Cyrus Richardson.

The building on Main Street next to the Post Office, formerly occupied by this society is now owned by the Free Baptist Society, Rev. C. S. Perkins, pastor. Pilgrim Church stands on the site formerly occupied by the Olive Street Church, for many years one of the interesting landmarks of the city. This society was formed by the union of the Pearl Street Congregational Society with the Olive Street Society. Rev. Reuben A. Beard is now the minister of the church.

The Methodists of the city are united in one society, and worship in their handsome brick church on Main Street under the ministry of Rev. J. M. Durell. The Church of the Good Shepherd is a handsome stone church on Main Street. Rev. James Goodwin is the rector.

The water of Pennichuck Brook is pumped into a reservoir on Winter Hill in the north part of the city and furnishes an unfailing supply of good water. The waterworks are owned by a private company, which has recently made many improvements and is well managed. A private corporation also lights the streets. With the agitation of municipal reform the question of ownership by the city of its water and electric-light plants is under discussion.

Nashua is one of the most favored centres in New England. Six railroads converge here from all quarters of the compass, so that this city cannot be excelled as a shipping point. All these different lines are now leased to the Boston and Maine Company, and the handling and transfer of freight and passengers are all done under a single management. That railroad has recently constructed large freight sheds and storehouses. The surface of the ground is such that the city can be extended in nearly every direction, and the several lines of railroad are laid out so that there are many good chances for the location of large plants using steam or electricity as a motive power along the different lines. Many of the most successful manufacturing concerns in the city have already taken advantage of such locations and thereby effected a great saving in the cost of manufacture. Coupled with this advantage for the location of such large plants handling heavy freights and requiring large space, is to be considered the generous policy of the city, which invariably gives any worthy industry desiring to locate here, exemption from taxation for a term of ten years.

While the locations for large industrial plants by the railroads are by no means exhausted, there are also eligible building sites in healthful situations for large houses with spacious grounds and wholesome and desirable surroundings to be obtained within three quarters of a mile of the city hall. This is notably the case on Fairmount Heights, a broad level terrace half a mile long in the northwest part of the city, at an altitude of fifty feet above the level of Main Street, with beautiful views in all directions. Many handsome houses have been recently built on the Lowell road and on Concord Street, somewhat farther away and beyond the compact part of the city. The Nashua street railway with its commodious cars furnishes an easy means of reaching any part of the city. This electric railroad plant is planned to accommodate a city of twice the present population of Nashua. The industrial growth of the city has been steady and sure without a break for the past quarter of a century. Without haste and without rest, moving steadily forward, Nashua seems destined to continue indefinitely on her career of prosperity.
